THE
METAPHYSICS
OF
SEX

Julius Evola

THE
METAPHYSICS
OF
SEX

INNER TRADITIONS INTERNATIONAL
New York

Inner Traditions
377 Park Avenue South
New York, New York 10016

First U.S. edition 1983

Library of Congress Cataloging in Publication Data

Evola, Julius, 1898-1974.
    The metaphysics of sex.

    Translation of: Metafisica del sesso.
    Includes bibliographical references.
    1. Sex.   2. Sexual ethics.   3. Love.
I. Title.
HQ21.E9613   1983   306.7   82-11909
ISBN   0-89281-025-4

Edited by Deborah Forman and Claudine Fischer

Printed in the United States of America

Cover illustration: Leda and the Swan (Flemish artist c. 1540. The
John G. Johnson Collection, Philadelphia Museum of Art.
Reprinted by permission.)

Introduction

The term "metaphysics" in the title of this book needs to be defined, for it will be used here with two distinct meanings. The first is commonly employed in philosophy, where metaphysics is understood as the search for first principles and fundamental meanings. The metaphysics of sex will therefore be the study of what from an absolute point of view is signified by the sexes and their interaction. There has been little precedence for this kind of research. After mentioning Plato and leaving aside certain hints found in mystical writings of the Renaissance—and also ignoring the theories of Boehme and some heterodox mystics influenced by him, up to and including Franz von Baader—only with Schopenhauer do we find a precursor. After him, we can only cite Weininger and, to a certain extent, Berdyaev and Klages. In the modern era and above all in our own day, studies of the problem of the sexes from anthropological, biological, sociological, eugenic, and psycho-analytic points of view have multiplied endemically; in fact, a neologism, "sexology," has been created to label research of this kind. But none of this has any relation to the metaphysics of sex. In this field, as in every other, our contemporaries have shown no interest in the search for ultimate meanings, or if they have, the search has appeared inconclusive and uninteresting; rather, they have thought to attain more important and serious knowledge by keeping to an empirical and more strictly human level, whenever their attention has not been focused on the pathological by-products of sex.

The same is mainly true of the writers, past and present, who have dealt with love rather than specifically with sex itself. For the most part, they have kept to the field of psychology and, within that, to a general analysis of feelings. Even the writings of such authors as Stendhal, Bourget, Balzac, Solovieff, and D. H. Lawrence have little to do with the deepest meanings of sex. Moreover, references to love—in view of the general meaning of that word nowadays, and given the sentimental and romantic disintegration in the experiences of the majority of people—were bound to create ambiguities and to limit research to a narrow and rather commonplace field. Only here and there and, one might say, almost by chance have such writers approached the true depth or the metaphysical dimension of love in its relationship with sex.

But in this study, metaphysics will also have a second meaning, one that is not unrelated to the word's origin since "metaphysics" literally means the science of that which goes beyond the physical. In our research, this "beyond the physical" will not cover abstract concepts or philosophical ideas, but rather that which may evolve from an experience that is not merely physical, but transpsychological and transphysiological. We shall achieve this through the doctrine of the manifold states of being and through an anthropology that is not restricted to the simple soul-body dichotomy, but is aware of "subtle" and even transcendental modalities of human consciousness. Although foreign to contemporary thought, knowledge of this kind formed an integral part of ancient learning and of the traditions of varied peoples.

From this context we shall take our reference points for a metaphysics of sex, and we shall verify the possibility of erotic experience leading to a displacement of the boundaries of the ego and to the emergence of profound modes of consciousness. It has been observed that a different rhythm is established in every intense experience of eros, which invests and transports or suspends the normal faculties of an individual and may open vistas onto a different world. But those who are the subjects of such an experience almost always lack the discernment and sensibility to comprehend anything beyond the emotions and feelings that affect them; they have no basis for self-orientation.

Scientists who try to investigate sexuality by studying others rather than themselves are in error, for they cannot approach the depth of the metaphysics of sex. Only the lost sacred science is able to provide the necessary references for investigating the potential dimensions of the experience of eros. Thus we lack the indispensable knowledge needed to identify in terms of reality the possible content of that which is generally assumed to be unreal. Without this knowledge, man can only take eros to the exalted borders of the human, of his passion and his feeling. Only poetry, lyrics, and idealized romanticism are created, while everything else is eradicated.

With these observations, we have in view the profane erotic field which is roughly the only sexual experience known to men and women of the West today and which alone is taken into account by psychologists and sexologists. It may be that the majority of people will not recognize the deepest meanings that we shall ascribe to love in general and even to the crude act that expresses and ends it. Barbusse has described the fact as one in which "a manifold and monstrous being is formed" and man and woman "seek to humiliate and sacrifice everything that is beautiful within them." It may be that the majority will think us capricious and arbitrary, and consider our interpretations abstruse and hermetic. This will only seem so to one who assumes his own limited experience as absolute. But the world of eros did not begin today, and a glance at history, ethnology, the history of religions, mysticism, folklore, and mythology will reveal the existence of erotic forms and sexual experiences in which deeper possibilities were recognized.

References of this kind, well documented in the traditions of diverse civilizations, will suffice to refute the idea that the metaphysics of sex is merely a concept. The conclusion must be quite different. We would say rather that, as if through atrophy, certain aspects of eros have become inactive almost to the point where they are no longer discernible and only their traces and symptoms remain in the sexual love of the present time. Thus, in order to make them evident, an integration is needed, a procedure like the passage from the differential to the integral in mathematics. Indeed it is not likely that in the ancient forms of eros, which often belonged to sacred rites or initiation ceremonies, something was invented and added that did not correspond to human experience; nor is it likely that a use was made of such experience for which it was completely unfit either essentially or in principle. It is much more likely that with the passing of time this experience deteriorated, being impoverished, obscured, or hidden in the vast majority of men and women belonging to a phase of civilization oriented toward materialism. It has rightly been said that "the fact that humanity makes love foolishly and unconsciously, as it does almost everything, does not prevent love's mysterious nature from upholding the dignity that belongs to it."[1] Moreover, it is useless to object that certain possibilities and meanings of eros can only be witnessed, if at all, in exceptional cases. It is precisely these exceptions of today which give us the key to understanding the deep, potential, unconscious content of the unexceptional and the profane. Although Mauclair only considered the profane and natural character of passion, yet he said with reason: "In love, acts are carried out without thinking, and its mystery is evident only to a tiny minority of human beings . . . In the numberless crowd of beings having a human countenance there are very few men; and in this select company there are very few who can understand the meaning of love."[2] In this, as in all other spheres, statistics are worthless. Such a criterion can be left to the trivial methods of a Kinsey. In our research, it is the exceptional that provides the norm at an ideal level. We can now mark out the fields that our investigation will cover. The first will be that of erotic-sexual experience in general: namely, the profane love that any ordinary man or woman may know. We shall look in this field for "intervening signs" that will take us beyond the simple physical, sentimental fact. We can start with a number of constant expressions, the universal language of lovers, and recurring behavioral patterns. The stereotypical and trivial, considered in a new light, will provide some interesting clues.

As for the phenomenology of profane love, further material can be gleaned from novelists and playwrights. Their works nowadays deal almost exclusively with love and sex. We do not deny that such productions may have a certain worth as evidence and as "human documentation," for usually a personal experience that has actually been lived constitutes the raw material of artistic creation. And what such artistic creation presents in the feelings, dialogues, and actions of its characters should not be dismissed as mere fiction or imagination. It may highlight through integration, amplification, and intensification the personal experience of the author, however incomplete. By this standard, art and the novel can provide further material that in itself may be considered objective and that often concerns already differentiated forms of eros.

Our research meets with special difficulties in a sphere important for our investigation: the states that develop at the height of erotic-sexual experience. Literature offers little help here. Until recently there were the taboos of puritanism, and now in the most daring modern novels, the banal and vulgar predominate over any useful material. Pornographic literature is also a scanty source. Produced to titillate the reader, it is dreadfully squalid not only in the facts and scenes described, but in its essence.

In the direct collection of material, we encounter a twofold problem, both subjective and objective. The problem is subjective because people are reluctant to speak even to their partners, let alone to strangers, about their experience in the most thrilling moments of sexual intimacy. It is objective because these moments often coincide with such reduced states of consciousness that people sometimes forget what they felt, said, or did. We have indeed been able to ascertain that the ecstatic or maenadic moments of the heights of sexuality often provoke interruptions of consciousness and are phases from which lovers return to themselves as if stunned or confused by paroxysmal feeling and emotion.

In principle, neurologists and gynecologists would be very well placed to gather useful material, if only they were trained or interested. But unfortunately this is not the case. The positivist school of the last century went so far as to publish photographs of female genitalia in order to establish likenesses between delinquent women, prostitutes, and women belonging to savage races. But apparently no one has shown any interest in presenting introspective evidence about the innermost experience of sex. Furthermore, papers on sexological research with scientific pretension are in general ludicrously incompetent; for here firsthand understanding of the experience is the *sine qua non*. Havelock Ellis rightly remarked that "the women who write books about these problems in all seriousness and sincerity are often the very last persons to whom one should turn as representatives of their sex; those who know most are those who write least."[3] We should say furthermore that they are those who have not written anything at all, and the same applies, of course, to a great extent in the case of men.

Lastly, as far as the field of profane eros is concerned, our investigation is affected very little by contemporary psychoanalysis, which has created a sort of fixed concept of sex and "libido." Psychoanalysis can provide us with only a few useful indications here and there; its research in general is in disarray from the outset because its prejudices distort the concept of the human being. Furthermore, since psychoanalysis has emphasized the subpersonal primordialism of sex by applying a degrading inversion, it is necessary to oppose it with a metaphysical perspective. The basic purpose of this book is to provide that opposition.

The above concerns the sphere of ordinary sexuality whether differentiated or not. A second and much more important sphere embraces the traditions that have recognized a sacred nature in sex, a magical ritual or mystic use of the sexual union and of sexual orgies, sometimes performed in collective and institutional forms as in seasonal festivals, holy prostitution, sacred marriages, and the like. In this respect sufficient material is available, and its retrospective nature does not in any way lessen its worth. Here, too, the validity of our research depends on having or not having adequate knowledge to arrive at a correct interpretation. We must not treat this evidence with the neutral interest that a historian of religion or an ethnologist would show toward museum pieces.

This second dimension, with its phenomenology relating to a no longer profane sexuality, also contains a division corresponding to the split between the exoteric and the esoteric, between general customs and secret doctrines. Various erotic cults, including the well-known popular worship of Bacchus and Tantrism, not only recognized the most profound dimension of sex but even formulated techniques whose purposes were often openly and consciously initiatory; a particular method of sexual union was enacted to induce special forms of ecstasy and to obtain an anticipation of the absolute, free from restrictions. Documentation for this special sphere also exists, and the obvious agreement between the doctrines and methods of the various traditions is highly significant.

Both the reality and the meaning of the metaphysics of sex will become evident if we regard these different spheres as parts of one whole, integrated and mutually illuminating. The special knowledge only revealed to those united in love will be restored to the vaster whole, of which everything in principle is a part. Owing to special circumstances, this present work will form little more than an outline. I have already had the occasion to write about the esoteric doctrine of androgyny and about the sexual practices of which that doctrine is the basis. I would have liked to obtain additional material on profane love, but apart from the above-mentioned difficulties, a fortuitous personal situation prevented me from gathering more information. However, there will be enough here to develop our theme.

Sex in the World Today

Before we embark on our subject, some remarks about the age in which this book has been written are in order. Everyone knows the part played by sex in our present civilization, and indeed there is a kind of obsession with it. In no other era have woman and sex taken the front of the stage in such a manner. They are dominant in a thousand forms in literature, theater, cinema, advertising, and the whole of contemporary practical life. Woman is presented in a thousand forms to attract man and stupefy him sexually. The striptease, wherein a woman undresses little by little, shedding ever more intimate garments until the bare minimum is reached, keeps the onlookers in a state of tension suited to that "complex of expectation" or state of suspense which a full, immediate, and shameless display of nakedness would destroy. Thus the striptease epitomizes the most recent decades of Western civilization under the sign of sex. The most fascinating and exciting female types are no longer known, as they were in the past, only in the restricted areas of the countries in which they live. Actresses, celebrities, and models, carefully selected and made to catch the eye in every possible way through an incessant barrage of media, become the burning focus of a sensualism worldwide in scope. Their zone of influence is collective and does not exclude that social strata which in other times used to be restricted within the bounds of a normal and soothing sexuality.

The cerebral nature of this modern universal worship of sex should be emphasized. We are not dealing here, as was the case in other eras, with more violent impulses that are shown only on the physical plane and give way to an exuberant, uninhibited sexual life or even to licentiousness. Nowadays sex has, to quite an extent, permeated the psychic field and caused a constant, insistent gravitation toward woman and love. Thus we have sensualism as a basic influence on this mental level with two outstanding characteristics: First is a widespread and chronic excitement, almost independent of every concrete, physical satisfaction because it persists as psychic excitement; and second, partly as an outcome of the first characteristic, this sensualism can even coexist with apparent chastity. As to the first of these points, it is true that people think much more about sex today than they did in the past. When a free expression of physical love was more strictly limited by custom, we might expect to find precisely that mental stupefaction which instead is typical of our own times. As to the second point, certain female forms of sexual anesthesia and depraved chastity related to what psychoanalysis calls the autistic varieties of libido are highly significant. An example is the type of modern woman whose main interests are exhibitionism, the accentuation of everything that may make her alluring to man, and the worship of her own body. Such women derive from this a vicarious pleasure which they prefer to the specific pleasure obtained from real sexual experience. The outcome for them is lack of sensitivity and in certain cases even neurotic denial.[4] These types fan the flames of chronic wantonness that is so widespread today.

Tolstoy once had occasion to say to Gorki: "For the French a woman comes before anything else. They are a weak, degraded people. Doctors say that all consumptives are sensual." If we leave the French aside, it remains true that a universal and feverish interest in sex and woman is the mark of every twilight period and that this phenomenon today is among the many signs that this epoch is the terminal phase of a regressive process. Classical antiquity formulated an analogy with the human organism: In man, the head, the breast, and the lower parts of the body correspond respectively to the seats of intellectual life, of spiritual and heroic courage, and finally of nourishment and sex. Corresponding to this are three human types and, we may add, three types of civilization. It is clear that today by regression we are living in a civilization whose predominant interest is neither intellectual, spiritual, nor heroic, nor even directed to the higher forms of emotion. Rather the subpersonal—sex and the belly—are idolized; and therefore the unfortunate saying of a poet may become a reality: Hunger and love will shape history. Hunger is the chief cause of social disaster and economic strife. The emphasis given to woman, love, and sex is its counterpart.

Further evidence is provided by the ancient Hindu tradition of the four ages of the world in its Tantric formulation. A fundamental characteristic of the last or so-called Dark Age (Kali Yuga) is the awakening and ultimate dominance of Kali, who stamps the epoch with her sign. We shall have reason to speak of Kali later on; in one of her main aspects she is the goddess not only of destruction but also of desire and sex. In this respect the Tantric doctrine formulates an ethic and indicates a way that in preceding epochs would have been censured and kept secret: the transmutation of poison into medicine. In considering the problem of our civilization, we hold no illusions for such a prospect. The reader will see later on to what levels these possibilities relate. For the present it is enough to establish the universal feverishness of sex as one of the signs of the regressive nature of the present era. The natural counterpart of this universal feverishness is gynocracy, that tacit preeminence of everything conditioned directly or indirectly by the female element; in another book, too, I have indicated the varieties of recourse to the female element in our civilization.[5]

This study will highlight the opposition of the metaphysics of sex to established, conventional viewpoints, and this contrast will make even more apparent the inner fall of modern man.

1

Eros and Sexual Love

The Evolutionary Prejudice

The meaning given to sex will depend on how one views human nature in general, on the particular system of anthropology adopted. An anthropology that recognizes in man the dignity of a being who is more than merely natural will necessarily oppose a system that considers man to be just one among many species of animals and which, as H. L. Philp has said, writes "Natural Selection" with capital letters, just as we do the name of God.

Since its inception, sexology, in monographs having scientific pretensions, has been influenced by the legacy of nineteenth-century materialism, which took as its premises the theories of Darwin and biology—theories that in our opinion promulgate a distorted and mutilated concept of man. They tell us that man sprang in the beginning from the animal by "natural evolution," and they have described man's sexual and erotic life in terms of an extension of animal instincts. They explain the ultimate, positive basis of human eroticism by the merely biological purpose of the species.

The modern tendency to explain the higher by the lower, the human by the physiological and animal, exists even in the field of psychology. Psychoanalysis has contributed its own sophisticated viewpoint but still confirms the same tendency. Indeed, psychoanthropology insists on a prepersonal and subpersonal element (the world of the unconscious, of instinct, of the Freudian id and the archaic archetypes that take us back to our primitive ancestry) as the basis of man. Psychoanalysts assume they can explain everything in man that has previously been deemed to form an independent psychic life, especially love and sex, within this framework.

Our premises are totally different. Our starting point will be not the modern theory of evolution but the traditional doctrine of involution. We do not believe that man is derived from the ape by evolution. We believe that ape is derived from the man by involution. We agree with De Maistre that savage peoples are not primitive peoples, in the sense of original peoples, but rather the degenerating remains of more ancient races that have disappeared. We concur with the various researchers (Kohlbrugge, Marconi, Dacqué,

Westenhöfer, and Adloff) who have rebelled against the evolutionary dogma, asserting that animal species evince the degeneration of primordial man's potential. These unfulfilled or deviant potentials manifest as by-products of the true evolutionary process that man has led since the beginning. For this reason, ontogenesis, the biological history of the individual, does not repeat in any way the process of phylogenesis, the presumed evolutionary history of the species, but passes again through some eliminated possibilities. It stops to roughly outline them and then moves beyond, subordinating these possibilities to the superior and specifically human principle, which is defined and fulfilled little by little in the development of the individual.

Therefore, we shall not consider human sexuality as an extension of animal sexuality; we shall rather explain animal sexuality—in beasts and as it may sometimes appear in man as well—as the fall and regression of an impulse that does not belong to biology. From a metaphysical point of view, the instinct for reproduction and the very "survival of the species" do not in any way represent the primary fact; they are mere derivatives.

Love and Sex

The object of our investigation is not sex in its raw and physical aspects. Since we are concerned essentially with man, the wider and more complex phenomenon of love enters somewhat into the question. But a natural restriction arises. It is possible to speak of love in a generic sense: love of parents, love of beauty, love of country, maternal love, and so on. An ideal or sentimental concept of love exists when love is felt softly as simple affection in the normal interaction of the sexes or in intellectual affinity. Therefore we shall confine our subject to the narrower concept of *sexual* love. The human experience of this love, which may include mental, emotional, moral, and even intellectual factors, supersedes the biological but nevertheless centers in the actual union of two beings of opposite sex in coitus.

Various forms of human love have been distinguished. Stendhal's famous distinction identifies passion-love, aesthetic love, physical love, and love based on vanity. A distinction of this kind is not very useful, for it is based on peripheral elements, which, if predominant, would eliminate the possibility of deep experience. Actually, it is only a partial distinction between differing aspects of the erotic phenomenon taken as a whole. The love with which our research is concerned is essentially passion-love, the only type that deserves the name of love. Bourget's definition may be satisfactory: "There exists a mental and physical state during which everything is annulled in us, in our thoughts, in our hearts, and in our senses. . . . I call that state love."[1] Physical love in Stendhal's sense may appear as a separate variety of love only if we assume a process of dissociation and a change to a primitive state. It is normally an integrating part of passion-love. Taken on its own, it forms the lower limit of passion-love, but it always retains that intrinsic quality.

In general it is important here to establish the fundamental difference between our concept and that of the positivists. The difference lies not in the physical or biological interpretation, but in the root meaning of sexual union; for otherwise we both see in that union the essential end and conclusion of every experience based on mutual attraction between the sexes, the center of gravity of all love.

Love can also include ideal affinities, devotion and affection, the spirit of sacrifice, deep manifestations of feeling; but all of these represent, from an existential point of view, something else or something incomplete wherever there is not present, as a counterpart, that "physical" attraction resulting in the union of bodies and the trauma of coitus. At this point we have the *precipitate*, the movement to the act, and the consummation (the natural *terminus ad quem* or end purpose) which is the point and purpose of the erotic experience. When the sexual impulse is aroused by "physical" attraction, the deepest layers of our being, layers existentially elementary by comparison to simple sentiment, are moved. The highest form of love between man and woman is, in a sense, unreal without that short circuit, the coarsest form of which is the climax of the sexual orgasm; and it is precisely this which encompasses the transcendental and nonindividual dimension of sex. It is true that Platonic love can also take us beyond the individual through continuous and absolute self-denial, but only as a spiritual disposition. It can bear fruit in a different way, but not in the actual experience, in a true fission of the being. Let us say it once more: The depths of a being, in the sphere were are discussing, are reached and moved only by the actual union of the sexes.

On the other hand, the fact that sympathy, tenderness, and other forms of immaterial love are often connected to sexuality and often represent only sublimations, transpositions, or regressive, infantile deviations, can be favorably ascribed to psychoanalytical research and must not be overlooked.

We therefore oppose the concept that represents as progress and enrichment the passage from sexual love to domestic love consisting mainly of affection and social feeling, based on family life, offspring, and all the rest. For this represents existentially not a plus but a minus and a sharp drop in level. In such forms, the contact with primordial forces, however dim to begin with, is lost or kept only by reflex action. As we shall see, a love conducted at this level, at the Nietzschean "too human" level, is only a substitute. From a metaphysical point of view, man creates with it an illusory solution for that need for confirmation and ontological completeness which constitutes the essential and unconscious basis of the sexual impulse. Schiller wrote: "Passion disappears; love must remain." In that we can only see a last resource to one of the dramas of the human condition; for only passion can lead to that "dazzling moment of unity."

Eros and the Instinct for Reproduction

The considerations set forth in the preceding section are intended to show the intensive level of the erotic experience, excluding broken or incomplete forms of that experience. Apart from that, just as we have taken up a position opposed to the sexuality propounded by the biologists, in order to avoid any ambiguity, we shall now oppose those who, as if renewing the attacks of Rousseau against "culture" on behalf of "nature," took the trouble to proclaim a new naturalistic religion of sex and the flesh. The best-known exponent of this school was D. H. Lawrence. His point of view was summarized in the words of Campion in Aldous Huxley's *Point Counter Point*. Campion states that the natural appetites and desires of men are not what make them so bestial: "No, bestial is not the right word because it implies an offense to animals—let us say: too humanly wicked and vicious. . . . It is the imagination, the intellect, the principles, the education, the tradition. Leave the instincts to themselves and they will do very little evil." And so the majority of men are considered to be like perverts, far from the central norm of humanity both when they excite the "flesh" and deny it for the soul. Lawrence added the following: "My religion is belief in the blood and the flesh, which are wiser than the intellect."[2] It is strange that Lawrence also wrote words that are not trivial, such as these: "God the Father, the inscrutable, the unknowable, we bear Him in our flesh, we find Him in woman. She is the door by which we come in and go forth. In her we return to the Father, just like those who, blind and unconscious, were present at the transfiguration." Moreover, he had certain correct intuitions regarding the union that is fulfilled through the blood. However, in spite of this view, he fell into an avoidable ambiguity and made an ideal of salvation out of a mutilation. Péladan was right when he said: "Realism is worth no more in love than in art. On an erotic level imitation of nature becomes imitation of the beast."[3] When taken in this sense, every "naturalism" can, in fact, only signify degradation, for what is called natural for man as man is not at all the same as what the term "natural" signifies in the case of animals; instead, conformity is natural when it is conformity to *one's own* type, to the place that belongs to man as such in the overall hierarchy of beings. Thus, to define love and sex in man requires a group of complex factors, which in certain cases may even include what may seem to be perversion when compared with an animal criterion. To be natural in the sense of Campion's words means only distortion for man. In man, sex has its own specific physiognomy. It is already free to a very large extent—the more the individual is differentiated, the freer it is—from the bonds and seasonal periods of sexual excitement that are maintained in animal sexuality (and more so in the case of females than males). Man can desire and make love at any time, and that is a *natural* extent of *his* love. It is in no way an artificial fact of "corruption" derived from his "separation from nature."

Let us go a step further and say that the notion of sexual love as one of the *physical* needs of man is also the outcome of a misunderstanding. Basically, physical sexual desire never exists in man; the desire of man is substantially always psychic, and his physical desire is only a translation and transposition of a psychic desire. Only in the most primitive individuals does the circuit close so fast that only the terminal fact of the process is present in their consciousness as a sharp, driving carnal lust unmistakably linked to physiological conditional qualities which take the foremost place in animal sexuality.

As this stage, it is best also to criticize the myth created by contemporary sexology when it speaks of an "instinct for reproduction" and defines it as the primary fact of all sensualism. The instincts of reproduction and for preservation are denominated the fundamental forces, linked to the species, which operate in man as much as in beasts. The boundaries of this dull and wretched theory are marked out by those positivist biologists and psychologists who, like Morselli,[4] go so far as to subordinate one instinct to another and believe that the individual feeds himself and struggles to survive only in order to reproduce himself, the supreme purpose being "the continuity of universal life."

The relativity of the "instinct for preservation" can be shown by indicating how many impulses exist in man that can neutralize or fight that instinct to such an extent that they lead to its destruction or else to behavior that is absolutely separate from it and in no way related to "the final purposes of the species." And in certain cases this part may be played by the "instinct for reproduction," when it does not make us consider our own health or self-preservation.

This "instinct for reproduction" represents a wholly abstract explanation of the sexual impulse, as it lacks any psychological basis and finds no support in conscious individual experience. Instinct in man is a conscious fact. But as content of consciousness, the instinct for reproduction does not exist in man; the "genesic" moment has no place in sexual desire as experience nor in developments of desire. The knowledge that the union of man and woman, moved by sexual desire and sensualism, can result in the begetting of a new being is *a posteriori* or empirical knowledge. We find this confirmed in the fact that some primitive peoples attributed births to causes bearing no relation to coitus. Therefore, what Klages wrote is completely right: "It is a willful falsification to call the sexual instinct an instinct for reproduction. Reproduction is a possible outcome of sexual activity but is not in any way included in the actual experience of sexual excitement. The animal does not *know* of it; only man knows"[5] and has it in mind, not when he *lives* the instinct, but when he subordinates the instinct to some end. However, it is useless to recall how many cases have occurred wherein the beloved's pregnancy was not only not sought but was even resisted. It is unthinkable to associate the most exalted models of *human* love in history and art, such as Tristan and Isolde, Romeo and Juliet, Paolo and Francesca, with a happy ending and a baby, or rather a whole brood as a crowning feature! A character of d'Aurevilly says of a pair of lovers who have never had any babies: "They love each other too much. The fire burns, consumes, and does not produce." When asked if she was sad because she had no babies, the woman answered: "I don't want any. Children are only useful to unhappy women."

The truth has been expressed in these humorous words: "When Adam awoke next to Eve, he did not cry out, as a contemporary makes him say, 'Behold the mother of my children, the priestess of my hearth!' " And even when the desire to have offspring plays a fundamental part in establishing the relations between a man and a woman, considerations based on deliberation and social life are involved, and that desire has nothing to do with instinct except in the special metaphysical sense which we shall discuss later. When a man and woman copulate only to bring children into the world, they certainly do not have this idea in mind at the moment of their union, nor is it this idea which arouses and transports them during coitus.[6] It may be that the future will be different and that, in deference to social or even Catholic ethics and guided by advances in artificial insemination, efforts will be made to diminish or even eliminate the irrational, disturbing factor consisting of the pure erotic act; but even in this case it would not be right to speak of instinct. Indeed, the primary fact is the attraction that arises between two beings of opposite sex, together with all the mystery and metaphysics which that attraction implies; it is the desire of one for the other, the

invincible impulse toward union and possession in which their acts
obscure a still deeper impulse. In this, "reproduction" is wholly
excluded as a conscious motive.

Some comments made by Solovieff are also relevant in this
context. He showed the error in thinking that the reason for sexual
love is the multiplication of the species. Many organisms in both the
vegetable and the animal realms reproduce asexually; the sexual fact
occurs in the reproduction not of the organisms in general but of the
higher organisms. Therefore "the meaning of sexual differentiation
(and of sexual love) is to be sought not at all in the idea of the survival
of the species and its multiplication, but only in the idea of the higher
organism." Furthermore, "The higher we climb up the ladder of
organisms, the more the power of multiplication decreases, whereas
the force of mutual attraction increases. . . . Although sexual love
reaches its greatest importance and strength in man, he reproduces at
a lower rate than the animal species." It seems, therefore, that sexual
love and multiplication of the species are in an inverted ratio to each
other: The stronger the one, the weaker the other. When we consider
the two extremes of animal life, if multiplication without sexual love
is at the lower end, then at the upper end, the summit, there will be
sexual love that can exist with an almost complete lack of
reproduction, but with the fullest expression of passion.[7] It has only
recently been affirmed that "sexual passion almost always involves a
deviation of instinct . . . in other words, reproduction of the species
is almost always avoided in the presence of sexual passion."[8] This
indicates that we are dealing here with two different facts, the first of
which cannot be presented as the means or tool of the other.[9] In its
higher forms, eros has an independent and not deducible character,
which is not impaired by anything that may be materially required
for its arousal in the sphere of physical love.

The Myth of the Genius of the Species

It is strange that one of the few attempts to delineate the metaphysics
of sexual love undertaken in modern times was based on the error
that we have just exposed. To maintain the concept that the essential
purpose of love is procreation, "the formation of the next
generation," Schopenhauer had to introduce a mythical "genius of
the species," which apparently arouses the attraction between the
sexes and is the determining factor in sexual choice. It is unknown to
the persons involved, whom indeed it deceives and uses as mere
tools. "The birth of a given baby," said Schopenhauer, "is the true
objective of all the romance of love, even though the protagonists are
not aware of that objective; the way in which this objective is reached
is purely secondary."[10] To be more correct, the objective would be

then the procreation of a new being as close as possible to the pure, perfect type of the species, able to survive. Thus the "species" should induce every man to choose the woman best fitted for such biological purposes and make her seem ideal, clothing her in such an aura of beauty and seduction that the possession of her and the pleasure she can give seem the essence of all happiness and the real meaning of life. "The best for the species lies where the individual believes he will find the greatest pleasure." And so feminine beauty and pleasure are made out to be illusions, mere baits with which the "genius of the species" cheats and makes a fool of the individual. Schopenhauer adds, "This is the reason why every lover feels disappointed after he has finally attained his purpose, sexual satisfaction, for the illusion with which the species has deceived and aroused him has vanished by then."[11] Essentially, these are mere speculations on the borders of Darwinism, and their one-sided and abstract nature is obvious. First, this mechanism of biological end purpose should belong to the unconscious (to which it was assigned most decidedly by E. von Hartmann when he took up once more the theories of Schopenhauer and developed them coherently). It would have to be a fully unconscious instinct that steers an individual toward the particular man or woman who shows the most suitable qualities for re-production since there is nothing of this kind present in the cons-ciousness of the one who loves and desires. The elementary attraction of the sexes and the fluid-intoxication that arises between them is innocent of such an instinct or its hidden knowledge. As we shall see later, even when looked at from the outside and stripped of subjective evidence, the problem of sexual choice is much more complex than the theory of natural selection implies. If we shift our attention to a mundane activity, nourishment, and compare it to sexual choice, we find that no man but the most primitive will choose or prefer only those foods best suited for the survival of his organism. This is the case not because he is "corrupt" but because he is man.

Furthermore, many instances can be cited wherein a strong or even "fatal" attraction arises between beings who in no way represent an *optimum* choice for the purposes of procreation; therefore, even if it is referred to the realm of the unconscious, Schopenhauer's impulse is at best relative or indeed nonexistent. Moreover, we should expect to find a reduced sexuality among the less noble examples of the human species; yet it is in fact the most primitive people who are the most prolific. Indeed we might say that the "genius of the species" is in need of an education since through its agency the average world population falls so far below man's potential or true norm. The mental and physical characteristics of an individual depend on the specific combination of his parents' chromosomes, which bear complex and remote heredities that may not appear at all in the phenotype of visible qualities of the parents. Generally, therefore, according to Schopenhauer, it should follow that visible qualities such as beauty, shapeliness, strength, and health should not be the governing factors in sexual choice, if solely oriented toward procreation, but the "genius of the species" should arouse a man's desire for the particular woman who has the most fitting chromosomes. Such an absurd conjecture is not very profitable since it would be necessary, whenever insemination takes place, to see *which* female and *which* male chromosomes will prevail, joining together to give form to the new being. Even biological science has not mastered this knowledge.

That question aside, in cases of strong passion and sensual pleasure among the most evolved individuals (to whom we should look for the true norm in its highest sense), we seldom find evidence of the "biological end purpose," even retrospectively. Often, and not by pure chance, such unions are childless. Man can indeed fall if he allows himself to be unnaturally overwhelmed by the daemon of *bios*, and it is at this level that procreation takes place. In man there is a nonbiological element that activates the sexual process even at the moment when sex invests and moves the physical element, bursting out in insemination. The procreative instinct, especially in the selective function imagined by Schopenhauer and the followers of Darwin, is a myth. Between love and procreation there is no direct, living connection.

Last, though banal, it is valid to refute "biological finalism" by pointing out that physical love has many aspects that this theory does not include. They are so integral a part of human erotic experience that when lacking, the purely physical union may lose a great part of its interest and, in certain cases, be thwarted and rendered primitive. Kissing, for instance, is not required for procreation, and if kissing on the mouth is not universal, equivalent customs such as rubbing noses or touching with the forehead have an erotic purpose. As for the mingling of breath or inhaling the breath of a woman while kissing her, such acts have as their real purpose a "fluidic" contact that enhances the elementary state governed in lovers by the polarity of the sexes. In fact a similar consideration holds true in the passionate desire of lovers to extend and increase during coitus the surface contact of their bodies or to cleave to each other fully ("just like two parts of a living animal which seek to be joined together again," to make use of Colette's image). A biological end purpose would be content with a simple and strictly localized act, whereas these and other aspects of the same profane, physical love include a special symbolic content, as we shall now see.

Eros and the Tendency toward Pleasure

In the elementary impulse that drives man toward woman, we must recognize a priority and an individual reality; but this must not give rise to ambiguities.

Let us take the theory that sets the tendency toward pleasure at the very base of sexual instinct. It is certainly evident that in most cases, when a man feels attracted by a woman and desires her, he seeks to imagine the "pleasure" she may give him and to foresee the expression on her face and her behavior in general during the crisis of coitus, rather than to determine whether she can ensure the birth of offspring best fitted to the end purposes of the species. In natural erotic development, every experience of deep passion and strong inclination doubtless follows the path of that which is called "pleasure," but it does not have pleasure as a principal and preset objective; if it does, we may well speak of lust and debauchery, which are trends corresponding to dissociations, degradations, and "rationalizations" of physical love. The idea of "pleasure" as a ruling motive does not exist in the "normal state of eros," but the impulse aroused by sexual polarity causes a state of intoxication reaching its apogee in the "pleasure" of physical union and orgasm. Any man who is truly in love, in possessing a woman, entertains the *idea* of "pleasure" as little as that of children. The teachings of Freud, therefore, were mistaken in his earliest phase when he established the pleasure principle, the *Lustprinzip*, as the basis not only of eros but of the whole human psychic life. In this the theories of Freud were just the products of his time. In periods of decadence such as the present one, sensuality develops in the dissociated form of simple pleasure. As a result, sex becomes a kind of drug, and the addiction to it is no less profane than actual drug addiction.[12] Freudianism soon abandoned its initial position, however, and in fact *Beyond the Pleasure Principle* was the title of a successive work of Freud's.[13]

But this train of thought must not lead us to consider every *ars amandi* to be corrupt and decadent. The art of love once existed as a discipline that was not reduced to an assemblage of devices and techniques depending on mere lust. This art was known in ancient times and is still practiced among Eastern peoples. Both then and now, women skilled in this art have been esteemed and respected no less than virtuosi of any other art. In classical times the courtesans were publicly held in high regard by men such as Pericles, Pheidias, and Alcibiades; Solon had a temple built in honor of the goddess of "prostitution," and such temples existed in Rome for the worship of certain forms of the goddess Venus. In the days of Polybius, statues of courtesans stood in temples and public buildings near those of soldiers and statesmen. Such women in Japan have also been honored with monuments. And, as with every art in the traditional world, there is associated with this art a secret knowledge. Priestess prostitutes of the *ars amandi* were linked to certain initiatic cults.

The higher capabilities of the experience of eros will not manifest when this experience takes place in its coarsest and blindest forms. We shall see whether the most profound dimension of eros holds its ground or can predominate in conscious developments of sensation or whether those developments degenerate into a licentious, extrinsic search for "pleasure." Two possible and distinct sides of the *ars amandi* must be defined. We are often deceived in the second of the two cases; there is no technique of love that, in the realm of "pleasure," can lead to an intense or differentiated quality without assuming an innermost psychic nature. If this is present, the touch of a hand can sometimes provoke a greater intoxication than any skillful activation of erogenous zones.

Later, the reader will see why the word "pleasure" has been put between quotations marks in discussing what generally takes place at the peak of physical love. In the meantime it will be useful to debunk certain sexological views that have been formulated regarding this question, since our intention is to free this field of every materialistic explanation of eros.

Sensual Pleasure

Piobb wrote: "The sexual spasm is one of those phenomena that elude physiology proper. The latter has to be content with stating the fact and showing only its nervous mechanism."[14] That is true, and every effort to give a "scientific" or profane explanation of this pleasure is condemned to failure. In this field, as in so many others, ambiguities have multiplied owing to the failure to distinguish the *content* of the experience itself from the *conditions* that are needed for it to occur, even more so when such conditions are studied by physiology rather than by psychology.

The prize for vulgarity was won by eighteenth century positivism when it gave weight to the following theory: "The genetic need can be considered as a need to evacuate; the choice is governed by stimuli which make the evacuation more pleasurable."[15] In this view, pleasure would apparently be caused by evacuation, by the process of discharging the sexual products. We should ask ourselves why analogous processes, beginning with the emptying of the bladder during urination, do not bring as much pleasure. Next, it is obvious that this theory can be right, if at all, in the case of man only, since the sexual climax in woman is not linked to an ejaculation. In her the appearance of vaginal secretions runs parallel to her general state of erotic excitement and may even be lacking; if vaginal fluids are secreted by a woman, they are linked to the reduction of swelling, to the lessening of congestion of the blood in the sexual organs, which in some cases may coincide with the moment when she is bathed with semen but in other cases is independent thereof and, in any event, is only the effect of a psychic and nervous fact.

Sexologists have mistakenly paid little attention to the fact that orgasm can be felt in a dream without ejaculation by both men and women. Some say that this pleasure can have a more ecstatic and all-pervasive nature than that of the actual sexual act, and we shall see the reason for this.[16] It often happens in both men and women that pleasure is interrupted at a given point of intensity and the person awakens at that moment. Correctly interpreted, it is the normal association of pleasure with the physiological that automatically brings the dreaming person back to the physically conditioned plane by interrupting the process. In principle, however, the pleasure in the dream can be adopted as one of the arguments for demonstrating the possibility of an erotic process separated from habitual, physiologically conditioned circumstances. Men can even experience pleasure in sleep when generative capacity has become exhausted through old age or when the ability to ejaculate has been destroyed by traumatic conditions in the nervous ducts.

For that matter, the impulse to coitus cannot be understood by a materialistic explanation in the animal world either and is, in a certain way, endogenous. Some experiments, conducted first by Tarchanoff, showed that in certain cases the seminal vessels of an animal were empty before copulation and filled up gradually during copulation, thus inverting the relationship between cause and effect; far from being governed by the state of fullness and swelling of the organs, the sexual impulse itself brought about that state.[17] If analogous research were to be carried out on man, this fact would be confirmed. Eunuchs whose seminal glands have been removed usually suffer from sexual anesthesia; yet there have been cases where their sexual desire persists and even becomes sharpened. In some instances, desire is so intense that, far from needing depletion, it drives the genital organs to the extremes of their capability, doing violence to nature so that man emits blood rather than semen. Also, a very high intensity of desire can inhibit rather than provoke ejaculation (we shall return to this point).[18] Finally, in passion-love, when all the resources of the physical have been exhausted in coitus, the feeling often remains that it has not been enough, that more is wanted, yet the physiological conditions and the capabilities of the flesh in general do not permit it. This becomes a torment.

Thus, Havelock Ellis, after various attempts to explain sensual pleasure, again concluded that the impulse which leads to pleasure is, in a certain way, independent of the seminal glands and their condition.[19] From a physio-anatomical point of view, the existence of sexual centers in the brain (already presumed by Gall) as well as in the spine and in the sympathetic nervous system is now generally accepted; this is the counterpart of the essential role played by the imagination not only in love generally but in sexuality itself, for the imagination accompanies and sometimes even starts and activates the whole process of copulation, whereas at other times it can stop it irreversibly.

Other modern research has attempted to explain sexual excitement as an effect of hormone intoxication; indeed some have cited this cause as the very basis of falling in love. In order not to be caught in a vicious circle, we must completely clarify the cause of hormonal intoxication since it could be a psychically conditioned fact; but even where it is not, we must not confuse something that *favors* an experience (like "hormonic saturation" or "hormonic threshold") with something that *determines* an experience and constitutes its real content. In regard to providing favorable conditions, the part attributed to hormones may even be played by certain substances, such as alcohol. But it is known that one's reaction to these depends on a "personal equation," and the causal reasoning in this respect is as naive as that of the person who says that the lifting of the barriers of a dam is the cause that produces the water that bursts through the opening.

We must credit the psychoanalytic theory of libido for its recognition of the autonomous *psychic* and elementary nature of the impulse for sexual union. However, psychoanalysis also believes that libido is not necessarily connected with physiological processes; the possibility of displacing "charges" of libido is, for example, attested in many typical cases when its realization causes morbid symptoms to disappear. Nor does this connection exist in pregenital stages of libido and its forms of satisfaction. The material gathered in this research constitutes a further argument against every physiological theory regarding the sexual impulse. In its assessment of pleasure, the psychoanalytic theory is equivalent to that of Fere, which we have already criticized.[20] Both theories are mistaken in conceiving pleasure as a solely negative phenomenon, like relief of a painful or unpleasant state. The same misconception is applied to sexual pleasure deemed as a mere relief from the physiological discomfort caused by the swelling of the organs. Psychoanalysis only sees mechanical and interchangeable processes wherein pleasure is apparently derived from the termination of any state of tension, from the discharge of a concurrent "charge" (*Besetzungsenergie*) of the libido. Indeed the term in German that signifies sexual satisfaction or pleasure—*Befriedigung*—connotes a sense of perturbation because it also means the pacification, almost the cessation, of a disagreeable state of tension, agitation, or excitement. We should ponder whether this theory is not merely symptomatic of our times, for to perceive sexuality and "pleasure" in these simple terms proceeds from an eros that has become primitive and physical.[21]

We can therefore conclude that sexual desire is a complex fact of which the physiological is only a part; sexual excitement, which is substantially psychic, forms the primary element that under various conditions causes physical excitement and sets in motion all the physiological phenomena that accompany the excitement but are often absent prior to it. Only the metaphysics of sex, not psychology or physiology, can shed light on this subject. We can already foresee that physical union, taken on its own, is only the mechanism through which is conveyed a process of a higher order, transcending that union and showing it to be part of a whole. When this transcendental aspect is recognized, "pleasure" as a coarse and carnal satisfaction depending strictly on the physiological conditioning or Schopenhauer's "bait for procreation" is a problematical solution.

The Magnetic Theory of Love

Further on we shall attempt to investigate the ultimate meaning of sex; for the moment we shall attend to an intermediate domain in order to shed light on the elementary substratum of every eros, and we shall now employ the term "metaphysics" in its other sense, meaning knowledge of the supraphysical, invisible side of the human being.

As we have seen, eros cannot be explained by biological finalism, by the genetic impulse, or by the detached idea of pleasure as the end purpose. Apart from all these theories, eros must be considered as a state governed directly by the polarity of the sexes in the same way that the presence of positive and negative poles governs the phenomenon of magnetism and everything connected to a magnetic field. Any empirical and material references we may cite to explain this elementary "magnetic" phenomenon contributes only to the presupposition of the phenomenon and has in turn to be explained by it.[22]

This point of view is no mere fantasy on the author's part; it corresponds to the knowledge of ancient traditions. For example, in the traditional teachings of the Far East, when a man and woman meet, even without any physical contact, a special energy or immaterial "fluid" called *tsing* is aroused in the deepest layers of their beings. This energy springs from the polarity of the *yin* and the *yang*, which we provisionally define as the pure principles of female and male sexuality. This energy, *tsing*, is a specification of the radical, vital force *tsri* and grows in proportion to the degree of *yang* and *yin* present in man and woman. This special magnetically induced force has as its psychological counterpart the state of diffused intoxication, vibration, and desire proper to human eros. The occurrence of this state causes the first displacement of the ordinary level of waking consciousness, which can be followed by other stages. The mere presence of the woman in front of the man arouses the elementary degree of *tsing* and its corresponding state. In societies where a sense of this elementary force of sex has been retained, strict conventions are formulated from this deep existential basis rather than a moralistic one. This applies to the rule "that no woman can visit a man except in the presence of another man, particularly if the first man is married. The rule applies to all women, for sex has no age, and to break the rule even in the most innocent of ways is to have sinned." If a man and woman are alone before each other, even if no contact takes place, it is just the same as if it had. This is because the first level of *tsing*, the elementary magnetism, has been awakened. The second level, already more intense, happens with bodily contact (ranging from holding hands and touching each other to kissing). The third degree is reached when the man penetrates the woman and is embraced by her. This is the limit of the magnetic development for most modern lovers. However, it is not the true limit, for yet other stages are reached in the practice of sex in sacred and evocatory forms or in sexual magic in a specific sense. "Subtle" changes, particularly in the breathing and the blood, accompany and are proper to these various degrees. The psychic correlative is essentially like a state of vibration and heightening, of exaltation in the true sense of the word.

Therefore, we may speak of a "natural magic of love" as a fully real, hyperphysical fact that occurs in the life of the most commonplace, materialistic, and primitive of humans. Even if the views we have just expressed are incompatible with modern psychology, they are confirmed by popular knowledge. Even without having a clear idea of the content of the word, it is generally recognized that an attraction between a man and a woman is born only when something "like a fluid"—a certain chemistry—is established between them. We ought to consider cases of a brutal and immediate lust for a woman as instances of a short circuit and "drop in potential" of this immaterial fluid. When this fluidic relationship is lacking, any exchange of feeling from the coarsest to the most spiritual is impossible. It is still customary to speak of the "fascination" of a woman, a term that brings us back to the magical definition of love; *fascinum* was, in fact, the technical term used in earlier times for a kind of enchantment or witchcraft.

This concept was part of the theory of love held in the West even into the Renaissance, and it was known in other civilizations as well, notably in Islam. For instance, we find it set forth in Lucretius and Avicenna and later in Marsilio Ficino and Della Porta. Ficino said that the basis of love-fever consists of a *perturbatio* (disturbance) and of a kind of infection of the "blood" provoked under the same conditions as the so-called evil eye, for it was actuated by means of the eye and the glance. If this is understood as happening on a subtle rather than on a material plane, then it is strictly correct. The fluidic state, the *tsing* force of Chinese teaching, is aroused in the beginning by a look and then goes on to spread thoughout the blood. From that moment on, the lover bears his beloved in a certain way in his blood, no matter what distance may separate them.[23] Theories aside, this knowledge is present in the universal language of lovers: "I've got you in my blood," "I feel you in my blood," "I've got you under my skin." These widespread and stereotyped expressions describe a fact that is much more essential and real than those focused on by contemporary sexology.[24] But we should bear in mind that when ancient traditions spoke of blood, they almost always referred to a transphysiological doctrine. The traditional concept is well enough expressed in the following terms, which may perhaps seem rather sybilline to the ordinary reader: "Blood is the great sympathetic agent of life; it is the motor of the imagination; it is the animated foundation of the magnetic or astral light polarized in living beings; it is the first incarnation of the universal fluid; it is vital light materialized."[25]

In our own times a "magnetic" theory of love was roughly sketched by Mauclair, ignoring the foregoing antecedents. He saw that this theory helped to overcome the dichotomy between body and spirit, flesh and soul, a contrast that is really nonexistent in erotic experience. Everything takes place on an intermediate plane on which the two elements are fused and aroused by each other (whether the senses arouse the soul or the soul arouses the senses is a matter that depends on the particular constitution of the individuals, but in both cases the end state contains within itself both elements fused together and transcends them at the same time). In this intermediate condition we can speak legitimately of a "magnetic" state observed directly. Mauclair's magnetic hypothesis explains best the unusual state of hyperesthesia of a couple transported with love and confirms "our daily experience that the state of love is neither spiritual nor carnal and escapes all categories of current moral philosophy." He adds: "The magnetic reasons are the only true ones and remain secret from and sometimes ignored by those who are themselves in love; for they cannot give precise motives for their love and, if they are questioned, bring forth a set of allegations . . . which are nothing other than reasons close to the essential reason, which cannot be articulated. A man does not love a woman because she is beautiful, pleasing, intelligent, or charming, nor because she is likely to produce an exceptionally strong sensual feeling. All these explanations are only given to satisfy ordinary logic. . . . He loves because he loves, quite apart from all logic, and it is precisely this enigma that reveals the magnetism of love."[26] Lolli had already distinguished three kinds of love—"platonic" love, sensual and physical love, and magnetic love—when he said that magnetic love is a mixture of the other two and is tremendously strong, spreading throughout every single part of man but having its main seat in the breath.[27] But in reality, it is not a particular kind of love but is the ultimate basis of all love.

These ideas can be readily integrated with the traditional teachings mentioned just now. They give prominence to a fact that is elementary or primary (though it will no longer continue to be so, only because of a properly metaphysical consideration of the matter), namely the "magnetic" structure of eros. And just as there is no attraction between man and woman when a special "fluid" has not been established between them either actually or potentially, so in the same way sexual love dies away when the magnetism wanes. In such a case all efforts to keep alive an amorous relationship will be doomed to failure, just like trying to keep a machine running when energy is lacking or (to use an image that is better fitted to magnetic symbolism) like trying to keep a metal joined to an electromagnet when there is no longer any current to create a magnetic field. External conditions may even remain unchanged: youth, handsome bodies, liking, intellectual affinity, and so on; but when the state of magnetism comes to an end, eros and desire also fade away inevitably. And if everything does not end, if every interest of the one in the other does not die away, yet there will be a change from love in its full and proper meaning to a relationship based on affection, custom, social factors, and so forth. This represents not a sublimation but a substitute, a last resource and basically *another* thing as compared with that which is conditioned by the elementary polarity of the sexes.

It is important to observe that although the magnetic or magic fact or fascination—whatever we wish to call it—takes place spontaneously between lovers, they also find it useful to nourish and develop this magic intentionally. Stendhal's concept of

crystallization in love is very well known:[28] Just as the naked boughs
of a tree are sometimes clad with crystals in the salty atmosphere of
Salzburg, so the desire of a lover, when concentrated on the image of
his beloved, crystallizes, as it were, an aura composed of every kind
of psychic content. That which is called magnetic fascination from an
objective viewpoint can be rendered in psychological terms with the
word "crystallization," "monoideism," or "forced image"
(*Zwangsvorstellung*). This last is a very essential element in every
amorous relationship; the thoughts of the one are held more or less
obsessively by the other in a form of partial schizophrenia (expressed
in such phrases as "to be madly in love" and "I'm crazy about you").
This phenomenon of mental concentration, as Pin said quite rightly,
"is an almost automatic fact, completely independent of the
personality and will. Anyone who, whether lacking in will power or
energetic, lazy or busy, knowledgeable or ignorant, poor or rich, falls
in love, feels that at a certain moment his thoughts are literally
chained to a given person without any possibility of escape.
Concentration, therefore, is a phenomenon that is in a certain way
hermetic,[29] massive, uniform, not subject to argument, reason, or
modification, extremely tenacious."[30] For lovers, this concentration
is a kind of barometer of love, and they take constant readings
through such questions as "Do you think about me?" and "Will you
always think of me?" They consciously nourish and strengthen this
concentration as it gives the measure of their love, making use of all
sorts of expedients to make it as continuous as possible. The phrase
"You are always in my thoughts" is the correlative of "You are in my
blood." Thus, unconsciously, lovers activate an authentic magical
technique, which is grafted onto the primary magical magnetic fact
and causes a further development of Stendhal's crystallization as an
outcome. In his *Liber de arte amandi*, Andrea Cappellano defined love
as a kind of agony due to extreme meditation about a person of the
opposite sex.

Eliphas Lévi, a writer who, unlike those already mentioned,
professes with some foundation to be a believer in magic sciences and
in the Kabbala, says that the meeting of the magnetic atmospheres of
a man and woman leads to a complete intoxication of "astral light,"
the signs of which are love and passion. The special elation caused by
the congestion of "astral light" should constitute the basis of amorous
fascination.[31] These ideas, drawn from traditions that we mentioned
earlier, may illuminate another aspect of the phenomenon
considered here. However, the terminology used by Lévi will remain
obscure for the ordinary reader unless we add some clarification.

The congestion of astral light is the objective correlative of what we
called "exaltation." "Astral light" is synonymous with *lux naturae* (a

term used in particular by Paracelsus), with the *akasha* of Hindu tradition, the *or* of Kabbalism, and the *ch'i* of Chinese philosophy. Many other expressions of esoteric teachings have the same meaning and refer to the hyperphysical foundation of life and of nature itself, to a "vital ether" understood as the "life of life." In the Orphic hymns, the ether is the "soul of the world," from which every vital force springs. Regarding the term *lux naturae*, it can be noted that the association between light and life recurs in the traditional teachings of widely varying cultures and is echoed in the first words of the Gospel of John. The point of interest here is that this light can, to a certain degree, become an object of experience, but only in a state of consciousness different from the normal waking state, in one corresponding more to the dream state in ordinary man. And just as in the dream, the imagination acts freely, so any displacement of consciousness provoked by a congestion or intoxication of "astral light" involves a form of imagination that in its way is magical.

However obsolete this concept may seem in the context of modern science, the fundamental facts mentioned above relate to this astral realm. As we shall see, operative sexual magic is also based on this, among other things. It is this magnetized imagination or "exaltation," rather than the intellect, which acts in lovers. And just as the British expression for being in love, "to fancy one another," is very significant, so Chamfort touches on something essential when he defines love as "the contact between two skins and the exchange of two fantasies." Again we find that the common language of lovers, usually taken as sentimental, romantic, or flaccid, meaningfully relates to this point. A. Husson certainly did not realize how close to the truth he came when he said that lovers live between dreams and death. "Dream of love," "dream of you," and "like a dream" are familiar phrases. The "dreaming" aspects among lovers is typical. The stereotyped repetition of such expressions in pulp romances does not count. The positive and objective content is the obscure feeling, the foreboding, of a shift in the plane of consciousness linked in varying degrees to eros. Such expressions, therefore, are so many "intervening indices," as are the continued use, rationalism notwithstanding, of words such as "fascination," "fluid," "charms," and "enchantment" when talking of the relations between the sexes. How odd all these facts would seem if love had a mere biological end purpose!

The Degrees of Sexual Development

In speaking of the teachings of the Far East, we said that the state of eros springs potentially from the relationship between the *yang* and *yin* qualities of two human beings. Eliphas Lévi was referring to the same phenomenon when he identified the cause of that state as the coming into contact of the magnetic atmospheres of two individuals of the opposite sex. It is best to go into this point more deeply, and that will lead us to the problem of sexual choice as well.

The current concepts of man and woman are little better than approximations. Indeed, the process of sexual development consists of multiple degrees, for we are not all men or women to the same degree. From a biological point of view it is known that during the earliest embryonic phases, hermaphroditism or bisexuality is encountered. Orchansky showed earlier that the primitive genital gland, extracted from the body of Wolff, is hermaphroditic. In the formation of a new being, the action of the force that causes the sexual differentiation of organic matter becomes increasingly precise. By means of this force, the capabilities relating to one sex are developed, whereas those of the opposite sex are eliminated or stay in the embryonic or latent state, or are present only in varying quantities, depending on the predominant capabilities that define the actual male and female type. There is thus an analogy with what happens in ontogenesis. Just as the process of individuation of a human being leaves behind it, in its rudimentary state, the capabilities corresponding to various animal species, so also, in man and woman, the process of sexual development leaves behind it, in the rudimentary state, the capabilities of the opposite sex which were present in the original state. (One aspect of this is the existence of hormone complexes of the two sexes and, herewith, a latent bisexuality in every individual.)

When sexual development takes place, sexual characteristics of various types are usually classified separately, as follows: primary characteristics linked to the genital glands and reproductive organs; secondary characteristics regarding typical male and female traits of the body along with the corresponding anatomical and humoral differences; tertiary characteristics, which mainly concern the psychological sphere of behavior, of mental, moral, and emotional dispositions. All of this lies within the field of *effects*, whereas the cause is sex as a molding and differentiating force.

In biology, the vitalism of Driesch and other authors has by now won acceptance, and so it is no longer heretical to look into forces of that kind. The Aristotelian concept of entelechy has been revived, and indeed had to be revived, as a heuristic biological principle. And entelechy is precisely the force that molds from within, being biological and physical in its manifestations alone; it is the "life of life." In ancient times it was deemed to be the soul or "form" of the body; considered in this way, it has a hyperphysical, immaterial character.

It seems clear, however, that at the base of the process of sexual development there is a differentiated entelechy which constitutes the true root of sex. The various primary, secondary, or tertiary sexual characteristics of man or woman come later and are its outward expressions.

Weininger, in seeming to go deeper into the problem of sexual differentiation, asked whether it would not be right to revive a theory defended earlier by Steenstrup, who had presumed the existence of a differentiated plasma in individuals of the two sexes. For this plasma Weininger proposed the names "arrenoplasma" and "taliplasma," and he said that it would make sex present in every cell of the organism.[32] New and deeper biological research will be able to confirm or refute this hypothesis. However, by means of it, an undeniably accurate intuition had been applied at the wrong level. Since the basis of sex is supraphysical, it lies in what we and the ancients have called the soul of the body, that "subtle body," intermediate between the material and the immaterial, which appears under various names in the traditional teachings (for instance, the *sukshma-sharira* of the Hindus and the sidereal body of Paracelsus). Moreover, we must think of something comparable to a "fluid" that surrounds, saturates, and qualifies the bodies of man and woman—not only in their physical aspects, by giving each organ, each function, each tissue, and each humor a sexual imprint, but also in their inner nature, as a direct outward expression of a different entelechy.

If there truly were a difference between the plasma of man and woman, then it would be due to such an entelechy. Thus, when Weininger said that sex is present in every part of the body, he was right so long as he was not referring only to the biological plane. In effect he had already gone beyond that plane when, to prove his thesis, he declared that *every* part of the body of one sex produces erotic excitement in the body of the other sex; for to explain this, it is necessary to bring in a supraphysical factor.

By means of all this we have already come close to the concept of that "magnetic differentiated atmosphere proper to individuals of different sexes" of which we spoke before. In Far Eastern terms this is a question of the *yang* and *yin* principles, which penetrate both the inner being and the material body of man and woman under the form of a fluid and an elementary molding energy.

One of the names given to this subtle body is "aromal body." The relationship with smell is not without sexological importance. The special part played by sweat in certain popular enchantments is well known.[33] Smell plays an important part in the magnetism of physical love and in the "fluidic intoxication" of lovers. It was believed in olden times and is still believed among certain primitive peoples today that the fluid of a being penetrates to such an extent that it impregnates not only the body but also the clothing (with this are associated some cases of fetishism). Hence arise practices that are often continued in the customs of both lovers and primitive peoples. To breathe in the smell and to always carry a piece of the lover's clothing is believed to enforce the relationship and mutual faithfulness (a custom followed in the Philippines). These practices would seem to be merely superstitious if one overlooked the "psychic" element. The extreme case is that of an erotic intoxication that is liable to be aroused not only by a glance but even by a smell ("He looked at her and inhaled her, she looked at him and inhaled him"—W. Somerset Maugham).[34] Furthermore, it should be noted that the Latin term *fascinum* has, in origin and literal meaning, an essential connection with the sense of smell. Anyone whose sensitivity is sufficiently refined will recognize that in amorous relations there is a kind of mutual psychic vampirism that is partly rooted in the sense of smell. The smell of man or woman in purely material terms concerns us here only in a secondary way; the possibility of a corresponding psychic effect in the case of human beings can only be explained in terms of an equally psychic, subtle counterpart. This fact clearly demonstrates characteristics that are instinctive and rather coarse and that are often more highly accentuated in various animal species; for here, as elsewhere, that which in man belongs in principle to a higher plane is made visible and specific in animal life in terms of a kind of daemonism of the *bios*. It is also possible to see the basis of the ancient Mexican belief that reproduction is the outcome of the mingling of the breath of man and woman.

Having completed this not unuseful digression, let us return to the problem of sexual development. We have said that there are various degrees of sexual development. The physical-anatomical fact that in every individual of one sex there are also rudiments of the other sex corresponds more generally to the possibility of an incomplete sexual development and therefore of beings who are exclusively men or women but who have characteristics of intermediate grades. That is the same as saying that in every person both male and female qualities are present in different degrees, even if the vital force or "fluid" of the person is fundamentally *yang* or *yin*. Weininger deserves special praise for having emphasized this point and also for having formulated a corresponding methodological criterion: It is necessary to start by defining absolute man and absolute woman, male and female in their pure state as Platonic ideas or archetypes, so that we may discern the degree of actual sexual development in given individuals.[35] In the same way, the study of the abstract triangle as a pure geometric figure can provide us with knowledge applicable to the numerous triangular forms of reality, which are only approximations of the perfect triangle, in order to characterize and distinguish those forms in real life. Our sole reservation lies in the fact that, as opposed to the case of geometry, the absolute man and absolute woman are conceived not only from a heuristic point of view as being abstract measurements for masculinity and femininity, but also ontologically and metaphysically as being real primordial powers that are always and inseparably present and active in men and women, even though actual men and women show such powers to a greater or lesser degree.

However, except in extreme cases (or, it is very important to add, in very unusual experiences), the picture we get of every normal man and woman is one in which the content of pure male or female quality varies, whence springs the first law of sexual attractions. In origin this law was first expounded by Plato when he set as the basis of attraction the need for a complement; for this he employed the image of the *símbolon*,[36]a word that described an object broken into two parts, as used in ancient times by two persons to identify each other: The part shown by one person had to match perfectly the part kept by the other person. In the same way, said Plato, every human being bears within himself a distinctive sign and seeks instinctively and unendingly "the corresponding half of himself which bears the same distinctive sign," the complementary signs that make the two parts mate together.[37] The same idea, more closely specified, was developed by Schopenhauer,[38] who said that the right conditions for a strong passion arise when two persons neutralize each other in turn, just as an acid and a base do when forming a salt. Thus, as there are various degrees of sexual development, such a situation arises when a given degree of virility finds its counterpart in a corresponding degree of femininity in the other being. Lastly, Weininger put forward a real formula for the first basis of sexual attraction.[39] When the absolute man and the absolute woman are taken as criteria, there is generally something of man in a woman and of woman in a man. He believed that the greatest attraction is aroused between a man and a woman when the masculine and feminine parts in both are added together and the totals obtained are the absolute man and the absolute woman. For instance, a man who is three-quarters man (*yang*) and one-quarter woman (*yin*) will be irresistibly attracted and develop the strongest magnetism with his female complement, a woman who is one-quarter man and three-quarters woman; this will be so because the sums of the fractions will reestablish the whole absolute man and absolute woman.[40] In fact, it is the absolute man and absolute woman who form the true basis of the primordial polarity of the sexes and therefore provoke the first spark of eros. We can affirm that they are the ones who love each other and seek to be united with each other through the persons of every man and every woman; and so the saying is true that all women love only one man and all men love only one woman.[41] The formula put forward by Weininger, therefore, establishes one of the essential conditions of sexual choice when it calls into play the deepest layers of a person's being.

Physical Sex and Inner Sex

At this point we have to consider the following principle: Except in cases of complete transcendence of the human condition, sex must be conceived as a "destiny," a basic fact of human nature. There is no existence except as men and women. This point of view is held steadfastly against the belief that being a man or a woman is something accidental or secondary as compared with being human in general; sex is seen as a difference that concerns only the physical and biological part of human nature, to the degree that sex has meaning and implications only with respect to the naturalistic side of human life. Such a point of view is abstract and inorganic and in reality can only be held by a human race disintegrating through regression and degeneracy. This view only considers the final, most coarse and tangible aspects of sex. But the truth is that, before and besides existing in the body, sex exists in the soul and, to a certain extent, in the spirit itself. We are man or woman inwardly before being so externally; the primordial male or female quality penetrates and saturates the whole of our being visibly and invisibly, in the terms used here earlier, just as color permeates a liquid. Moreover, if intermediate degrees of sexual development exist, as we saw earlier, that can only mean that the basic quality mentioned shows an intensity that is sometimes higher, sometimes lower, depending on the individual. This does not explain the conditional nature of sex.

Apart from those exceptional cases in which sex is transcended because the human condition in general has been transcended, we often mistake as "beyond sex" a condition that, in effect, concerns a realm detached from life and from every deep formative force. This is a realm of superstructures and of intellectualized and social forms whose excessive growth characterizes the degenerating and bourgeois phases of a civilization. Later on we shall emphasize the fact that every human being consists of two parts; one the essential part and the other the outer, artificial, acquired part that is formed in the life of relationships and creates the persona of the individual. The word "persona" is used in the original sense of an actor's mask (as opposed to the "face," which can be said to correspond to the essential part). Either of the two parts can be more developed than the other, depending not only on the individual but also on the kind of civilization. This can degenerate to an almost exclusive, teratological development of the outer and artificial mask of the social, intellectual, practical, and spiritualized individual, which maintains few organic relations with the essential being. It is only in such cases that sex can be considered secondary and negligible; an anesthetization or a primitivistic coarsening of sexual life is its usual resulting counterpart. Only then will it seem of little importance whether one is man or woman, and such a fact will have less and less value in the determination of vocations, self-development, conduct of life, model of occupations—a value that has always been honored by civilizations. This very assumption implies that the difference between male and female psychology has been considerably reduced.

Modern civilization, being expedient, intellectualist, and socialized, has given an increasing emphasis to things totally unconnected with the essential side of human beings. It is inorganic and potentially standardized; its values are partly derived from a regression of types and partly foster and increase that regression. Thus modern woman is penetrating into every sector of life and making herself the equal of man; for the merits, capabilities, behavior, and the most typical activities of modern civilization have only very scanty links with the deeper plane where the law of sex is in force in ontological terms rather than physical, biological, or even psychological terms. The mistake that underlies feminist competition and has made it possible is the overvaluation natural to modern civilization of logical and practical intelligence, which is actually a mere accessory of life and the soul; for these latter two are both equally differentiated, whereas the intelligence is formless and "neutral" and can be developed to an almost equal extent in man and woman.[42]

Here we shall make only a passing reference to the vexed question of the inferiority, equality, or superiority of woman as compared with man. A question of this kind is lacking in sense because it assumes that the two can be measured against each other. If we set aside everything artificial, external, and acquired, we find that there is a difference of Platonic ideas between man and woman that makes impossible any common measurement. Even faculties or gifts that appear to be common to both and to be "neutral" have a different functional character and imprint, depending on whether they are present in a man or a woman. We cannot ask ourselves whether "woman" is superior or inferior to "man" any more than we can ask ourselves whether water is superior or inferior to fire. Thus the standard of measurement for either of the sexes can be provided not by the opposite sex but only by the "idea" of the same sex. In other words, the only thing we can do is establish the superiority or inferiority of a given woman on the basis of her being more or less close to the female type, to the pure and absolute woman, and the same thing applies to man as well. The claims of modern woman, therefore, spring from mistaken ambitions as well as from an inferiority complex, from the mistaken idea that a woman as such is inferior to man. It has been said rightly that feminism has really fought not for "woman's right" but, without knowing it, for the right of woman to make herself equal to man. Even if this could be achieved on a level beyond the outer expedient and intellectual level mentioned earlier, it would amount to a woman's having the right to pervert herself and to degenerate.[43] Let us say it once more: The only qualitative standard is the degree of more or less perfect realization of the nature *proper* to a person. There can be no doubt that a woman who is perfectly woman is superior to a man who is imperfectly man, just as a farmer who is faithful to his land and performs his work perfectly is superior to a king who cannot do his own work.

In the range of ideas we are dealing with, we should take it as being settled that manhood and womanhood are, above all, facts of an inner nature. It is possible to be a man as far as the body is concerned without being equally so in the soul (*anima mulieris in corpore inclusa virili*—the soul of a woman enclosed in a manly body), and the same is of course true of a woman. Such cases of asymmetry are due to various factors and are similar to cases encountered in the realm of race (individuals of a given race who have the psychic and spiritual characteristics of another race). This, however, does not prejudice the basic quality of the fluid that a being has, depending on whether that being is physically a man or woman; nor does it prejudice the unity of the process of sexual development. The phenomenon mentioned can be explained by the fact that in given cases this process is centered principally on a given domain, creating asymmetry because the remaining areas have not been developed to the same degree. From a typological point of view, however, the inner fact, the inner sex, is always decisive; a sexual development appearing only in physical terms, however advanced it may be, is in a certain sense truncated and empty. He who is not a man in spirit and soul is not truly a man, and the same applies to a woman. It is best to emphasize this point because we must bear it in mind in the law of sexual attraction mentioned earlier. The "proportions" of masculinity and femininity being integrated in turn, as cited in that law, should be understood in a complete sense in all their possible complexity.

In effect it is spiritual manliness that, even though only obscurely, excites and awakens the absolute woman; in the extreme case this manliness, beyond that of a warrior or ruler, leads even to the supernatural. We shall deal later on with the metaphysical as well as the existential side of such a case. An example created by art, Oscar Wilde's *Salome*, is illustrative. Salome does not see the centurion struck with love for her, who offers her everything and in the end kills himself for her. She is fascinated by Jokanan, the prophet and ascetic. She, the virgin, says to him, "I was chaste and you have defiled me; I was pure and you have filled my veins with fire. . . . What shall I do without you? Neither the rivers nor the great lakes will ever again extinguish the fire of my passion."[44]

One other point should be added to the possible differing degrees of sexual development in the physical and spiritual fields: namely, the varying conditions prevailing in inner sex as compared to bodily sex. The respective conditions are rigidly maintained only in the case of primitive individuals who are degraded compared with the pure type in question. If, on the other hand, the inner sex is sufficiently differentiated, it may assert itself with a certain independence from the physical conditions. In this way all the hormonic manipulations to which modern biologists are devoted actually have a necromantic character, being based on the idea that sex depends only on a different "hormonic formula." They can produce important effects in altering the true characteristics of sex only in animals and in little-differentiated humans, but no effects in complete, "typical" men and women. This independence from physical conditioning is also confirmed in some cases of eunuchs, whose physical impairment may not only fail to destroy their sexual impulse, but may also not harm their inner manhood. Examples of this have often been cited, including Narses, who was one of the best generals of later ancient times, Aristonicus, the ministers Fotinus and Eutropus, Solomon (a lieutenant of Belisarius), Haly (grand vizier of Suleiman II), the philosopher Favorinus, and even Abelard, among many others.

Conditional Nature and Forms of Erotic Attraction

For a complete definition of the factors involved in sexual choice, we must consider in greater detail the structure of the human being with reference less to modern studies than to traditional teachings.

We have distinguished two main parts or layers of the human being, the essence and the persona; now we must take the more profound part, the essence, and divide it in two parts. Thus there will be three levels in all. The first is the level of the outer individual, which is a social construct, an entity whose form is fairly arbitrary, "free," and unsteady because of its artificial nature. The second level belongs to the profound being, to the depth dimension, and is the site of what in philosophy has been called the *principium individuationis*. It is here that those forces act by which a being is what it is, both physically and psychically, and is distinguished from every other being of the same species; thus it is also the site of the inborn nature of each person. These formative forces are called *samskara* or *vasana* in the Hindu tradition; They not only are related to hereditary or racial factors, but are conceived as comprising heredity, as causes, preformations, and influences whose origin may lie beyond a single human life.[45] Psychologically, this level may be related to everything in man that is his inborn character and nature, which we have called his "face," as opposed to his "mask." Contrary to everything belonging to the first and outermost of the three levels, that which refers to the second level has a marked degree of determination and stability. Thus Kant and Schopenhauer were led to talk of a "transcendental nature" of every individual as of a "noumenal" fact, that is, relative to the realm that lies behind the whole order of phenomena perceived in space and time.

The third and deepest level concerns elementary forces superior and prior to individuation but acting as the ultimate seat of the individual. In this realm, where the first root of sex is found, the original force of eros is aroused. In itself, this level is prior to form and determination. Each process assumes a form and determination in the same measure that the energy of this level invests the two other levels and to the degree that the process is continued in them.

With this background it is possible to apprehend every aspect of what happens in sexual attraction. At the deepest level, that attraction is something that goes beyond the individual, and erotic experience reaches this level in the final and traumatic form of coitus. In this regard, we see the validity of the saying that all women love only one man and all men love only one woman. Here there is a principle of indifference and interchangeability. By virtue of the analogical correspondences between upper and lower limits, this principle is in force in the blind impulse that drives a person toward someone of the opposite sex because of the sexual polarity, an impulse proper to animal and brute forms of eros (the "animal lack of choice"). The same principle is in force in the positively disindividualized forms of eros, which can be seen in a Dionysiac experience, for example. Therefore, it is not always true to say that the most vulgar and animalistic form of love is that in which one loves not *a* woman, but *the* woman. Exactly the opposite may be true.[46] The same can be said concerning the fact that during the crisis of coitus, the man almost loses his individuality; he can lose it in two opposite ways, since there are two opposed possibilities of disindividualization, two intoxications: the anagogical ascent above individuality and the catalogical descent below. The "replacement of the individual by the species" at such moments is pure myth. Lastly, when it is said that love is born at the first instant or not at all, when we speak of a *coup de foudre*, this refers mainly to cases where, owing to special circumstances, it is the force of the deepest layer that acts in a direct, unhindered, predominant way.

The first law that governs the process of sex at its third and deepest level is the one governing the desire for a complement, for the reintegration of the pure male quality and the pure female quality by the union of man and woman. At the boundary between the second and third layers, the intermediate and the deepest levels, the conditional qualities of bonds belonging to the individuation or inborn nature of a given being start to act almost at once. At this new stage, as regards erotic passion and inclination, it is no longer a matter of indifference what a given woman is besides being a woman and constituting the elementary, ontological complement of which we spoke. Here, above all, choice is influenced, for example, by the conditions of race, physical type, and character, and the whole may be accentuated and fixed in the mind until it creates the illusion of irreplaceability;[47] it is the belief in "one love only," the idea that a person can love only one given individual, one specific man or woman. And whenever *all* the elementary force belonging to the deepest layer and to the primary process fixes itself at this intermediate level—the level of individuation and of the "transcendental character"—the "fatal passion" will occur. This passion, as we shall see, is almost never happy if it stays in the human, profane field, inasmuch as a force and a charge are activated here which go beyond the individual; wherefore there often take place some real short circuits and situations such as illustrated by Wagner's *Tristan and Isolde*.

The intermediate level is generally also the level at which the woman loved is idealized; in it there arises the illusion that a woman is loved for one or another of her qualities, whereas that which is truly loved and which binds the lover is her naked being. When the profound force of eros does not permeate the intermediate level directly or fix itself there completely (as happens in the great majority of cases), there remains a certain margin of indetermination; instead of the "sole, irreplaceable woman" there will be a given approximate type or genre, represented by more than one woman (or man) and constituting the condition for a strong enough attraction. But this freedom of movement or ability for displacement of the eros can also have another cause, namely the imperfect individuation of a given being. If the inner face of a person is not very definite, so equally will the object of his desire be less definite and, within given limits, more changeable. The repetition of experience too, can undermine the stability proper to the first period of the erotic life. Thus Balzac found that in the first woman one loves, one loves everything, as if she were the only woman; afterward, one loves the woman in every woman.

Let us now pass on to the level of the outer individual. When a person's center of gravity falls within this level, the changeability we mentioned and the indetermination of its proper sexual complement in his choices become excessive. As we said before, everything at this level is inorganic and lacks deep roots. Thus in some cases we may find the type of libertine who seeks "pleasure" alone and values a woman by the amount of pleasure he thinks she can give him; in every other respect one woman is for him more or less the same as another. In other cases the deciding factors may become social and environmental ones, such as class, fashion, tradition, and vanity. When this is the case, eros constellates itself on this level, and it is mainly by such qualities that normal, "civilized," bourgeois love is defined. However, should eros suddenly recover its fundamental character and follow the conditional qualities belonging to its deepest layers, it will then act in a catastrophic manner on everything that has formed in the outer realm of the social individual and therefore in the sexual relations. In a case where a person finds his true complement, all the affinities determined by the level of his individual nature and *samskara* can upset or undermine everything that the social individual has won for himself in the framework of institutions of the civilization and society of a "divine right of love": "They [the lovers] have a share of divine right, notwithstanding human laws and conventions."[48] Such cases are numerous nowadays and have provided material for certain kinds of drama and literature, precisely because in modern times there exists the illusion that the relations between the sexes can be centered and systematized on the outer, social, inorganic, artificial level.[49]

We can similarly explain the case of the libertine who becomes a victim of his own game and ends up falling in love with a particular woman, thus terminating the ability to change the object of his eros, or who undergoes maniacal sexual transformations as a result of playing with fire and provoking the activation of a "voltage" fitted to the deeper level.

These events can in turn act in a catastrophic manner even on the plane of the "one true love," just as the law of affinities in force on that plane (at the intermediate level) can act catastrophically in the realm of the social individual and his arrangements whenever the right complementary partner is encountered. Then the true love fails once more, even the uniqueness of the "fatal passion." But these cases are very rare in the field of profane love, and when they do happen, they are never evaluated according to their true nature.

Another case that can be analyzed in this context is an elementary sexual passion and attraction that can be accompanied by disdain and even hatred between two lovers; it is the energy of the deeper plane that is acting to undermine all the determining affinities of character and all the values that would normally be focused on the intermediate plane. This case is symmetrical with that in which the affinities proper to the intermediate plane can, in their turn, negate everything which belongs to the outer realm of social morals and institutions.

Finally, we can mention the fact that there are artificial means of arousing in a more or less free state the elementary force of eros by neutralizing those more superficial layers. Here we can note the action of alcohol and some drugs; these were sometimes employed in sexual rites, such as Dionysiac ceremonies and Tantrism. Love potions, whose true nature is lost to the modern world, have played a similar role. By this, as we shall see, eros can lead to some forms of daemonic worship as well as to sexual magic proper.

In everything we have said so far we should never confuse the role of that which *conditions* with the role of that which *determines*. For a machine to function properly, it must consist of given parts that interact correctly; this is the condition. But when motor energy is lacking, even the most perfect machine will stay still. The same is true of all the conditional qualities in man which, on the two more superficial levels of his being, can theoretically correspond to the *optimum* as regards sexual attraction; but the primary force of eros must be roused with "voltage" in order to establish that magnetic or magic state which is the true foundation of all sexual love.

In an ordinary individual, and especially in a civilized individual of the Western world, erotic experience often has a passive nature. It is as if the corresponding processes begin and proceed on their own without the action of man's will. He cannot even focus these processes accurately on any of the three levels. This situation is considered so natural and normal that a person thinks his desire must be compulsive, beyond his control, or else he doubts the sincerity and depth of his feeling or desire. In languages of Latin origin, the word for "passion" expresses precisely the idea of submitting or suffering. The same is true of the German word *Leidenschaft*, from the verb *leiden*, which also means to "endure" or "suffer."

The degree of passivity depends on the individuals and their inner differentiation. Furthermore, one must take into account differential psychology based on varying social institutions. For instance, the institution of polygamy naturally fosters a male type in which the ego has a greater degree of freedom as regards eros (with greater mutability and hence less stability). In this male type the erotic experience per se has more importance than the relationship with a specific woman as a person (an Arab proverb says: "One fruit, then another fruit"). Polygamy does not always correspond to the outer and inorganic situation proper to a libertine. The change from polygamy (or from marriages that allowed concubines as an integral part of the family) to monogamy, notwithstanding the conformist views prevailing today, is in no way a replacement of a lower type by a higher type of manhood, but is exactly the opposite; it is rather a symptom of a potential and much greater enslavement of man by eros and woman, and that is not a thing which marks a higher civilization.[50]

In the ancient world or among primitive peoples, we encounter the elements of a technique disposed to act on various existential conditional qualities of eros. For the present we shall give only one example: the fact that among such peoples, wedding ceremonies are identified with love spells that arouse the force of attraction between the two sexes as an irresistible power.[51] According to our scheme, these spells arouse and activate the eros on the elementary plane and involve the risk of feeding a kind of devilry or possession.

Before going any further, let us cast a glance over the ground we have covered. We have rejected every finalistic, biological interpretation of eros, and we have dismissed the Freudian pleasure principle as no better than the theory that posits an imagined "instinct for reproduction" as the primary fact in the erotic impulse. The magnetic theory, in our view, corresponds more closely to reality. We have gone deeper into this theory by means of data taken from traditional teachings, which talk of a state or fluid that determines itself "catalytically" in lovers through the presence of the basic forces (yin and yang) that define sexual polarity and sexual development in general. The correlative thereof is a displacement of the plane of consciousness, which in turn becomes the cause of a magical activation of the power of the imagination and of a more or less strong obsession of the mind with one dominant idea. The ancient doctrine of an invisible change, produced in the blood when a person is seized by eros, has been restored to its true value. Finally, we have examined the conditional qualities linked to the existential desire for a complement within the framework of the doctrine of the manifold layers of a person. However, we have emphasized that the primary force and basis of everything shall always be deemed to be that which proceeds directly from the ratio of absolute manhood to absolute womanhood; and in this regard the more intense the process, with all its attendant effects of elementary attraction, the more decided the differentiation of the sexes or, in other words, their sexual development.

But here it may be said we have taken a circuitous route and evaded the essence. No matter how much we try to explain eros, we always come back to eros itself and inevitably meet the fundamental question: Why are man and woman attracted by each other? Having succeeded in recognizing this elementary and uncompromising fact, we must seek its *meaning*. This is precisely the same as asking what is the meaning of sex itself, and we now find ourselves led to the center of the metaphysics of sex proper.

yin
yang → displacement
of consciousness → release of
imagination
a obsession

↑

think of other uses of this creative energy (Jane)

2

The Metaphysics of Sex

The Myth of the Hermaphrodite

Myth is the means by which the traditional world expressed the ultimate significance of being. The traditional myth has the value of a key, but it has been neglected as such in past attempts to explain myth within the framework of natural history, biology, and psychology. Our intent is to reinstate myth as a resource in order to explore the metaphysics of sex.

Several myths lend themselves to this investigation, but let us choose one that is most familiar to Western man, while bearing in mind that the same meanings are contained in myths of other cultures. As a basis, then, let us look at the discussion of love in Plato's *Symposium*. Here, two theories of love, intermingled with the myth, are expounded by Aristophanes and Diotima respectively. We shall see that in a certain respect the two theories are complementary and illustrate the contradictions and problems of eros.

The first theory concerns the myth of the hermaphrodite. As with almost all the myths introduced by Plato into his philosophy, we must suppose its origin to stem from the initiatic cermonies of the ancient Greek mysteries. Indeed the same theme winds its way below the surface of the most varied literature, ranging from the gnostics and ancient circles learned in the mystery cults down to authors of the Middle Ages and the early centuries of the modern era. Corresponding themes can also be found outside Europe.

According to Plato[1] a primordial race existed "whose essence is now extinct," a race of beings who contained in themselves both principles, male and female. This hermaphroditic race "was extraordinarily strong and brave, and they nourished in their hearts very arrogant designs, even unto an attack upon the gods themselves. The traditions recounted by Homer regarding Otho and Ephialtes and their attempt to scale the sky so as to assault the gods is also attributed to this race." This is the same theme of the *hubris* of the Titans and Giants and of Prometheus. It can be found in many other myths as well—even, to a certain degree, in the biblical myth of Adam in the Garden of Eden, in which we find the promise "Ye shall be as gods."

According to Plato, the gods did not strike the hermaphrodites with lightning, as they had the Giants, but paralyzed their power and broke them in two. Thenceforth there arose beings of one sex or the other, male or female; they were, however, beings who retained the memory of their earlier state and in whom the impulse to reconstitute the primordial unity was kindled. According to Plato, in that impulse should be sought the ultimate metaphysical and everlasting meaning of eros: "From such an ancient time has love goaded human beings, one toward the other; it is inborn and seeks to renew our ancient nature in an endeavor to unite in one single being two distinct beings and, therefore, to restore human nature to good health."[2] Quite apart from the joint participation of lovers in sexual pleasure, the soul of each of them "tends toward something *different*, which it cannot express but which it feels and *reveals mysteriously*."[3] Almost by way of *a posteriori* counterevidence, Plato makes Hephaestus ask the lovers:

> Is it not perhaps this for which you long, a perfect, mutual fusion so that you will never be sundered from each other by day or night? If this is what you wish, I am ready to melt you and weld you together with fire into one and the same individual so as to reduce you to one single being instead of the two which you were beforehand; in this way you may live united to each other for the whole of your lives and, when you are dead and down in Hades, you may be only one instead of two and may share together one single fate. Well, then, ask yourselves if this is what you want and whether you think you can be happy if you obtain it.

"We know very well," said Plato, "that no one would refuse such a proposal or show himself desirous of something else, but each person without any hesitation would deem that he had finally heard expressed that which had certainly been his desire for a long time, namely to be united and fused with his beloved so as to form one single nature from two distinct beings. Now, the cause of this desire is to be sought in the fact that this was indeed our primitive nature when we constituted one unit which was still whole; it is really the burning longing for this unity which bears the name of love."[4] Almost like a symbol is "the clinging of the two parts to each other, as if in a desire to pervade each other wholly."[5]

Within this context, the accessory elements that are metaphorical and "mythical" in a negative sense should be separated from the fundamental concept. For example, the primordial beings whom Plato has described, even recounting their physical features, ought not, of course, to be conceived as actual members of some prehistoric race whose remains or fossils we would expect to find. Instead, we should conceive of a *state*, a spiritual condition of origins, not so much in the historical sense as in the framework of an ontology, of a doctrine of the manifold states of being. By stripping away the overlying myth, we can understand the state as one of *absolute being* (neither divided nor dual), of a complete entity or pure unity which, in itself, is the state of immortality. This last point is confirmed in the doctrine expounded by Diotima later on in the *Symposium* and also set forth in the *Phaedrus*, where, in reference to so-called Platonic love and to the theory of beauty, the connection between the ultimate goal of eros and immortality is explicit.

A second aspect of Plato's myth is a variation of the traditional theme of the Fall. The differentiation of the sexes corresponds to the condition of a divided being, finite and mortal, partaking in the dual condition of one who has life, not in himself, but in another being; this is not the original state of being. In this respect a parallel could be made with the biblical myth, inasmuch as the Fall of Adam has as its outcome his exclusion from the Tree of Life. The Book of Genesis also speaks of the hermaphroditic nature of the primordial being made in the image of God ("Male and female created He them"). Some have attributed to the name of Eve, symbol of the complement of man, the meaning of "life," or "living." As we shall see, in the interpretation of the Kabbala, the sundering of the woman-life from the hermaphrodite is related to the Fall and ends with the equivalent of the exclusion of Adam from the Tree of Life lest he should "become as one of us" and "live forever" (Gen. 3: 22).

As a whole, the myth of Plato alludes to the change from unity to duality, from being to the loss of being and of absolute life. Its distinctive character and importance, however, lie precisely in its application to the duality of the sexes and direct us to the hidden meaning and ultimate object of eros. The purpose set forth in the Upanishads is the same when it speaks of what is really sought in the course of ordinary life: "It is not for love of woman that woman is desired by man, but rather for love of the *atman*" (for the principle "all is light, all is immortality").[6] In its most profound aspect, eros embodies an impulse to overcome the consequences of the Fall, to leave the restrictive world of duality, to restore the primordial state, to surmount the condition of dual existentiality broken and conditioned by the "other." This is the absolute meaning of eros; this is the mystery hidden behind man's drive toward woman in an elementary state. It precedes all the conditional qualities that human love shows in its infinite varieties in beings who are not even absolute men or absolute women but merely by-products of one or the other. Here is the key to all the metaphysics of sex: "Through the Dyad toward the Unity." Sexual love is the most universal form of man's obscure search to eliminate duality for a short while, to existentially overcome the boundary between ego and not-ego, between self and not-self. Flesh and sex are the tools for an ecstatic approximation of the achievement of unity. The etymology of the word *amore*, as given by a medieval "Worshipper of Love," although unfounded, is nonetheless meaningful: "The particle *a* means 'without'; *mor* [*mors*] means 'death': If we join them together, we get 'without death' or life everlasting."[7]

Fundamentally, therefore, by loving and desiring, a man seeks the confirmation of self, participation in absolute being, the destruction of *stérēsis*, and the loss and existential anguish associated with it. When looked at in this light, many aspects of profane love and of sexuality are clarified. At the same time, we can already foresee the path leading to the sphere of mystic eroticism and of the sacred or magical use of sex belonging to so many ancient traditions. For already at the beginning of our inquiry, we have revealed the elementary basis of the erotic impulse to be metaphysical and not physical. Therefore our way is now open to the series of investigations that will be the subjects of the subsequent chapters.

In the meantime we must not overlook a particular point. As we have seen, Plato formulated the doctrine of the hermaphrodite in such a way that he gave it a "Promethean" appearance. If the mythical beings of earliest times were such that they could strike terror in the gods and vie with them, then we can hypothesize that eros—the ultimate search for integration—is not so much a nebulous mystic state as a condition of being that is also potency. This factor will have a bearing in our study of the initiatic forms of sexual magic, but this motive must be stripped of pathos. In a wider context, Prometheanism can shed its negative character of breach of trust. The tradition that gave form to the myth of Prometheus and the Giants is also that of the Heraclean ideal. This ideal is an equivalent to the aim pursued by the Titans; it belongs in general to those who, despite everything, pursue access to the Tree of Life. When Heracles attains enjoyment of the apples that confer immortality (according to one version of the legend, it is Prometheus who shows him the way), he attains Hebe, everlasting youth, on Olympus, not as a violator of a trust but rather as an ally of the Olympians.

Related to this, we can allude to the fact that the Promethean moment latent in eros is effectively attested to in scattered accounts belonging to various traditions. We shall limit ourselves here to recalling that in the cycle of the Holy Grail (a cycle replete with initiatory content under the guise of chivalric adventures), the temptation that woman represents for an elected knight is sometimes attributed to Lucifer,[8] thus taking on a very different meaning from the moralistic notion of the mere seduction of the flesh. Moreover, Wolfram von Eschenbach relates the fall of Amfortas to his having chosen "Love" for his device—a device, says the poet, that is not in keeping with humility.[9] This is tantamount to saying that in love is hidden the opposite of humility, namely the *hubris* or overweening pride of the "unified" beings of the origin of mankind. Moreover, it should be noted that Wolfram speaks of the "opening of the path to the Grail with arms in hand," that is, in a violent manner, and that the main hero of the poem, Parzifal, in fact reaches that situation with a sort of rebellion against God.[10] Now, the opening of the path to the Holy Grail is more or less the same as the opening of the way to the Tree of Life or everlasting life, for the rather flaccid framework of Wagner's *Parsifal* in no way corresponds to the original predominant themes and should not be taken into account at all. Last, it should be noted that the circles in which sexual magic and mystic eroticism have been practiced have openly professed the doctrine of "unity," thus denying any true ontological distance between creator and creature, with a contempt for both human and divine laws as well. These circles range from the Hindu Siddha and Kaula of the "Way of the Left Hand" down to the Brothers of the Free Spirit of the Christian Middle Ages, to the Sabbatism of Jakob Franck, and to Aleister Crowley in our own century.[11]

But we must emphasize that these references are to be purged of their problematic "Promethean" aspect and are exclusively concerned with "guided" experiences of eros outside the realm of common love between men and women. In conclusion, we should add that in the work of Plato himself,[12] the recovery, the return to the ancient condition and the "supreme happiness," understood as being the "highest good" to which eros can lead, are associated with the overcoming of godlessness, the prime cause of the existential separation of man from the divine in general. It is only a different orientation that, alongside some morphological likenesses, differentiates Prometheus from Heracles, or the experience mentioned from Satanism; but this is not the time to dwell on that subject.

Eros and the Various Degrees of Intoxication with It

We must next consider the theory of love that Plato made Diotima expound; but first it is best to mention Plato's statement concerning the higher form of eros as a state, regarded simply as a content of the conscious self. Eros is called a "mighty daemon" in the *Symposium*; "being an intermediate between the nature of a god and the nature of a mortal," he fills the gap between the one and the other.[13] In the *Phaedrus*, a great deal is said about *manía*. It is hard to translate this word correctly since today it connotes something unpleasant and mad; the same can be said of *furore* (frenzy), which was the translation adopted by the humanists of the Renaissance (the "heroic frenzies" in Giordano Bruno). We should rather speak of a state of rapture, of "divine inspiration," of exaltation or lucid intoxication, and thereby we are brought back precisely to what we said before regarding the raw material of every erotic state. At this stage Plato emphasized an essential point by distinguishing between two kinds of "mania," one of which "arises from human illness and the other from divine exaltation, whereby we feel ourselves to be extraneous to normal laws and customs."[14] The second of them, said Plato, "is far from frightening," for great benefits may arise from it; and in a specific reference to eros, he said, "Very good luck lies in the mania which the gods lavish on us by causing love to be born in the soul of him who loves and of him who is loved."[15]

What is more important here is that eros as "mania" is introduced into a wider context, which makes its possible metaphysical context very noticeable. In fact, Plato distinguishes four kinds of favorable manias, which are not pathological or subhuman, and refers them to four divinities respectively: the mania of love, linked to Aphrodite and Eros; the prophetic mania of Apollo; the mania of the initiates of Dionysus; and the prophetic mania of the Muses.[16] Marsilio Ficino[17] would say that these are "the kinds of exaltation which God inspires in us by raising man above man, and this exaltation changes man into God." Apart from "poetic mania," which was only capable of having a character that was not profane in ages when art was not a subjective matter and when a poet was also a minstrel and poetry a song, the common basis of all such forms of mania is a state of exaltation able to bring about a self-provoked condition of transcendence and also varieties of a supersensual experience. This is the case with a lover as much as with a Dionysiac initiate or with anyone whose vision surpasses the limits of time or with a person undergoing a magical experience.[18] It is only odd that neither Plato nor his commentators have mentioned a further variety of the same lucid and mystical kind of exaltation (which leads men upward): the heroic kind, which could be allotted to the sign of Mars, is singular inasmuch as the ancients considered some cases in which heroic experience, too, could offer initiatory possibilities.[19] Last, we may recall the kind of holy intoxication proper to the Corybantes and Curetes with their corresponding techniques, which bear an unmistakable relationship to dance.

In any case, the references are precise. Thus Plato recognizes one tree trunk, of which sexual eros is a branch, a specialized type. Its raw material is an animation and liberating exaltation (that almost grafts a higher life onto human life in mythological terms; a fertilizing and integrating possession by a daemon or god), which, if it obeyed only its own metaphysics, as defined by the myth of the hermaphrodite, would have as its highest possibility a *teletē* or initiation (as Plato said), an equivalent of the initiatic ceremony of the Greek mysteries. Moreover, it is noteworthy that the word "orgy," now associated only with the unleashing of the senses and sexuality, was linked in the beginning to the attribute "holy," the "holy" orgies. In fact, *órgia* meant the state of inspired exaltation that began the initiatory process in the ancient Greek mysteries. But when this exaltation of eros, itself akin to other experiences of a supersensual nature, becomes individualized as a longing that is only carnal—when it becomes conditioned instead of itself conditioning, because it is wholly linked to the biological determinisms and muddy sensations of the lower nature—then it deteriorates and ends finally in the form constituted by mere "pleasure," or venereal lust.

Here we must distinguish various degrees. Pleasure has a widespread and still ecstatic nature when the "magnetic" moment of love with its consequent fluidic amalgamation of two beings is quite intense. As this intensity lessens or as a lover becomes used to performing the physical act with the same person, the pleasure tends more and more to be localized bodily in given zones and essentially in the sexual organs. Man is notoriously more predisposed than woman to this further deterioration. In the end, we are left with a dissociated pleasure, detached from every profound experience. In general, "pleasure" is the effective breakdown of the state of mania, of pure, exalted, and lucid intoxication induced by a supersensual element. This condition represents the counterpart of a miscarriage of the impulse of eros, as an impulse directed toward the absolute being and the immortal, within the circle of physical generation; to this will correspond the other theory of love, as expounded by Diotima, which we shall consider below.

In the present context, it may be worthwhile to refer again for an instant to the Platonic difference between two kinds of mania so as to develop their respective natures. In general, when this state occurs, the faculties of a normal individual are suspended and his "thought power" (*manas* in Hindu terminology) is shut off or transported, being subject to a different force. This force may be ontologically higher or lower than the principle of the human personality. Hence there arise the possibility and concept of an ecstatic intoxication that also has a decidedly regressive character. Sexual magic in particular rests on this very thin dividing line.

To use a theoretical example, we may mention the divergent interpretation given by Ludwig Klages. Klages took up in part the viewpoint of Plato and emphasized the elementary nature of the intoxication or mania that constitutes eros, and he recognized its nonphysical dimension and ecstatic capability; but the critical difference in his interpretation was that "it is not man's spirit but his soul which is set free [in ecstasy], and his soul is freed not from his body but from his spirit."[20] However, in Klages's work, "spirit" is not the spirit but basically a synonym for "thought power"; yet it is true that for him the "soul" corresponds to the almost unconscious, lower layers in a human being that border on the *bios*. It corresponds to the *yin* (or female, dark, nighttime) part and not to the *yang* (male, light, daytime) part of a human being. Thus the ecstasy that he speaks of could well be called an earthly or perhaps even a daemonic ecstasy. Its emotive content had already been described in Hindu tradition with the word *rasavadana*.

A well-differentiated phenomenology of mania and of eros exists, therefore, and from a practical viewpoint, its importance can never be sufficiently emphasized. However, it is certain that both the foregoing negative possibility and a positive possibility of a divine exaltation are equally far from one based on pathological origin and from the brutish and blind impulse of eros on an animal level. Neither the ethnologists nor the historians of religions nor the psychologists have taken any notice of such important distinctions.

The Biological Treatment and Fall of Eros

In Plato's *Symposium*, Diotima seems at first to argue against Aristophanes. She says that all men in love tend toward the good and that "the everlasting essence of love consists in possessing the good," not the half that is lacking, but the whole.[21] But in reality the two are the same thing expressed in different words, for according to the Hellenistic concept, the "good" had a meaning that was ontological but not moral, to the degree that it was identified with the state of being in a lofty sense, with that which is perfect and whole; and the myth of the hermaphrodite alludes to that and to nothing else under the cloak of the fable. Diotima then says that "the ardent concern and tension" of anyone tending toward that higher state take on a specific figure of love in relation to "the creative force inborn in all men according to the body and to the soul," the force that aims at the "act of procreation in beauty." And this is the case "also in the union of man with woman." She then states, "In the living, which is also mortal, this union is the root of immortality."[22]

The meaning already given for the metaphysics of sex receives here, on the one hand, a confirmation. As a wish for the everlasting possession of good, love is also the wish for immortality.[23] On the other hand, we pass with Diotima's doctrine to a "physics" of sex that almost strangely anticipates the views of Schopenhauer and the school of Darwin. Mortal nature, overworked and subdued by the onslaught of love, seeks to reach immortality in the form of the continuation of the species by *generating*. "Only in this way," says Diotima, "can [everlasting life] be achieved by the act of procreation

cf p 55 beauty

inasmuch as the act always leaves a different being alive to take the place of the aged being." Thus she speaks of man as almost a superindividual who continues through the unbroken chain of generations owing to "eros, the procreator." It can be stated that no living being ever retains within himself the same qualities; yet he is always considered as having one identical personality while he goes on renewing himself forever, even though such parts as his hair or flesh, bones or blood, are continually changing. This is also the process through which no human being perishes: not that he remains himself, as happens with a god, but through ensuring that when he grows old, deteriorates, and dies, he will be replaced with another individual. It is indeed immortality in the sense of the perpetuity of the species.[24] And Diotima speaks exactly like a follower of Darwin when she explains in these terms the deep, natural urge to ensure that one's own stock does not die out but also the urge that, blindly, without being guided by any reasoning, drives animals not merely to copulation but to sacrifices of all kinds so as to feed, protect, and defend their offspring.[25]

It was not by chance that this theory was put into the mouth, first, of a woman and, second, of Diotima of Mantineia, an initiate of those mysteries which may well be called the "mysteries of the Mother" and which take us back to the pre-Hellenic, pre-Indo-European substratum of a civilization oriented toward the earth and the rule of woman. Let us reserve the right to return to this subject later and say here only that in the eyes of such a civilization, which set the maternal mystery of physical generation at the summit of its religious concept, the individual has no existence on its own; it is a fleeting thing that lasts for a day. Only the maternal cosmic womb is everlasting, for the individual beings return and are dissolved in it but also swarm forth forever from it, just as new leaves sprout on a tree in the place of those which have fallen. This is the opposite of true Olympian immortality, which implies instead the abrogation of the naturalistic and earthly-motherly bond, the departure from the everlasting circle of generation, and the ascent toward the region of immutability and pure being.[26] Beyond these aspects of a disconcerting Darwinian modernism, therefore, the spirit of the old Pelasgian and chthonic religion of the Mother shows itself in the theory of eros expounded by Diotima. We shall see later on what are "the higher, revealing mysteries" to which she alludes.[27] Here it is essential to note that in the theory of the hermaphrodite and in that of the survival of the species, we have two opposing concepts: The first has a metaphysical, Uranian, virile, and perhaps Promethean spirit, whereas the other has an earthly-maternal and "physical" spirit.

Leaving aside this antithesis, it is even more important to consider the point of the ideal transition of one view into the other and its meaning. It is clear that "earthly immortality" or "temporal immortality" is a pure illusion. At such a level absolute being escapes into the individual endlessly; and, by generating, the individual will endlessly give life anew to another being affected by the same impotent impulse.[28] Moreover, a bloodline may meet its end, for a stock can be wiped out and disaster can bring an end to the existence not only of a family but indeed of a whole race; therefore, the mirage of that immortality is highly misleading. At this rate, we may well introduce the mythical, Schopenhauerian daemon of the species and say that lovers are deceived by him: Pleasure is the bait of generation, and that bait is also the charm and beauty of woman; although lovers deem they are living a higher life during the exaltation of their coitus and are grasping at unity, they are actually serving the purpose of generation. Kierkegaard perceived that during their union lovers form one ego only but are nonetheless deceived, because at the same point the species triumphs over the individual. This contradiction, as he said, is even more ridiculous than everything for which Aristophanes found love to be a laughingstock. He noted rightly that a higher prospect should not be excluded: One could believe that if lovers did not attain an immortal and unified nature, yet by agreeing to act as tools for generation and sacrificing themselves, they could see that goal attained in a being they generated. But this does not happen; the son is not born as an everlasting being that ends the series and goes upward, but is born as a being exactly the same as they are.[29] This is the everlasting vain filling of the barrel of the Danaides or the eternal weaving of the rope of Oknos, which the donkey of the underworld continually gnaws away.[30]

But this vain and hopeless vicissitude in the "circle of generation" also hides its own metaphysic: the obscure impulsion toward absolute being, while deteriorating and deviating, passes into that which is hidden behind animal copulation and procreation. Its purpose is the search for a substitute for the real need of a metaphysical confirmation of oneself; and the phenomenology of eros follows this descent, this degradation. From exaltation, eros becomes an ever more extroverted desire, thirst, and carnal lust, which ends in pure animal sexual instinct. Eros then has a syncope in the moment and spasm which results in the collapse into physical, sensual pleasure, a state more conditioned, particularly in males, by the physiological process essentially directed toward insemination. The wave swells, comes to its peak, reaches the dazzling instant of coitus and of the destruction of the dyad, only to be overturned by the experience. It is drowned and dissolved in what is in fact called "pleasure." *Liquida voluptas* or liquid pleasure, a phenomenon of dissolution, is the Latin expression rightly mentioned by Michelstaedter.[31] Yet it is as if the force has escaped the hand of him who sets it in motion: It passes into the realm of the *bios*; it becomes "instinct," almost an impersonal and automatic process. Nonexistent as a fact of the erotic consciousness, the generative instinct becomes real in terms of the id (to use the psychoanalytic term), of an obscure gravitation, of a vital compulsion that conceals itself from consciousness and undermines and overthrows it. This happens not because of an instinct for species survival but because the will of the individual to overcome his own finite nature can never be wholly uprooted, silenced, or repressed. That will survives desperately in this obscure and demoniac form, which provides the power (*dýnamis*), the primordial impulse toward the everlasting circle of generation. In the same relationship as that existing between temporality and eternity, in the succession and repetition of individuals according to the "immortality in the Mother," it is still possible to have a last, misleading reflection of the immortal. But on such a level the very boundary between human world and animal world fades away little by little.

As we said at the beginning, the normal explanatory process is to be reversed: The lower is to be deduced from the higher, not the other way around. Physical instinct starts from a metaphysical instinct, and the primordial impulse is directed toward "being." It is in fact a metaphysical impulse: Both the biological impulse toward self-conservation and that toward reproduction are "precipitates," materializations that are created at their own level by their physical determinisms. Having exhausted human phenomenology, which starts from a hyperphysical exaltation and a transfiguring, mystical intoxication and finds its lower limit in the truly carnal orgasm of a generative function, we pass on to the forms of sexuality proper to animals. We can see in various animal species some degenerate hyperdevelopments of certain potentials latent in human beings, some ending in culs-de-sac and corresponding to human types that embody a dissociated, grotesque, obsessive development of those potentialities. It is therefore necessary to consider every possible likeness between the sex and love life of man and that of the animal world. Obscure and extreme distortions in one or another aspect of human eros are often to be found in the animal world as natural developments.

Thus we can see the magnetism of sex driving and guiding—sometimes by telepathy—some species in nuptial migrations that cover extraordinary distances and involve extreme privations and conditions that kill a large part of the migrants on the way. No sacrifice is spared, provided that the place is reached where the seeds can be fecundated or the eggs laid. We can see the manifold tragedies of

sexual choice among wild beasts, the blind and often destructive urge
toward the sexual contest, which is fought, not for ownership of the
female, but for possession of "being." The farther away the level at
which that "being" can be found, the more savage the search for it.
We can see the metaphysical cruelty of the absolute woman minia-
turized in the female mantis, which kills her mate during coitus as
soon as she has used him. We can see the same phenomena in the life
of the *Hymenoptera* and other species: deadly marriages, with males
who die after the procreative act or are slain and eaten during its very
occurrence, and females who die after having laid their fertilized
eggs. We can see in the *Batrachia* the absolute coitus, not interrupted
by death-dealing wounds or mutilations, and in the love play of snails
we can note the ultimate limit of the need for full prolonged contact
and of the sadism of multiform penetration. We can see human
"proletarian" fertility become pandemic and swarming endlessly in
the lowest species until the level is reached where, with the
hermaphroditism of the mollusks and tunicates and the
parthenogenesis of the one-cell organisms, of the protozoans and
some of the latest metazoans, the same principle is encountered,
although inverted and lost in the blind and nondifferentiated *bios*, as
we find at the beginning of the whole descending series. All these
forms are described by Rémy de Gourmont in his *Physique de
l'amour*.[32] But this whole world of correspondences now appears in a
different light; those found here are no longer the antecedents of
human eros, the evolutionary stages lower than it, but are the liminal
forms of its involution and degeneration under automated,
demonized impulses, cast into the limitless and insensate. But how
can we fail to see that the metaphysical root is more apparent in
certain features of this animal eros (where we normally only
recognize the imperative of the "survival of the species") than in
many disintegrating and "spiritual" forms of human love? For,
according to an inverted reflex, we can read there that which, beyond
the fleeting life of the individual, is brought about by the will to
absolute being.

These meanings also provide the right points of reference for understanding the more profound factor acting behind daily human existence itself. At the level of the life of relationships, man needs love
and woman to rid himself of existential sorrow and to invent for himself a meaning for his existence; he seeks unconsciously a substitute
of some kind or another and accepts and nourishes every illusion.
Jack London was right to talk of the "subtle atmosphere spread
abroad by the female sex, an atmosphere which we do not notice
while we are immersed in it; but when it is missing, we feel a growing
void in our existence and are tormented by a vague wish for some-

thing which is so indefinite that we cannot explain it." This feeling acts as a substratum for the sociology of sex, for sex itself is a factor in the life of companionship, ranging from marriage to the desire to have a family, offspring, and lineage. This desire becomes ever more alive the further we fall from the magical plane of sex and the more we become dimly aware of the delusion of the most profound impulse of our being, behind the gleaming mirage of the moments of first contacts and the summits of passion. This realm, within which domesticated man normally encloses sex, especially in our times, may well be called the realm of the second-degree by-products of the metaphysics of sex and, according to the meaning given by Michelstaedter to such expressions, a world of "rhetoric" that replaces the world of "persuasion" and truth.[33] Still further toward the edge and as if going in a direction of its own, we find the abstract and vicious hunt for venereal pleasure as a drug and liminal soothing agent for the lack of meaning in finite existence; but that is a subject to which we shall return.

Aphrodite Urania; Eros and Beauty

We said earlier that in the *Symposium*, after having spoken about temporal immortality in the species, Diotima alluded to "higher revealing mysteries." Then Diotima took up a theory that had been attributed to Pausanias, namely that two kinds of love exist because there are two Aphrodites, Aphrodite Urania and Aphrodite Pandemia.[34] The first embodies love of a divine nature; the second, profane love.

This leads to a problematical issue. It is a question of humanism, not of higher mysteries, when Diotima contrasts those who give life to immortal children such as artists, lawgivers, moralists, and the like with those who procreate carnally. "Many forms of worship have already been directed toward the former," says Diotima, "because of such unusual children, whereas no one has yet attained such honor in children produced according to human nature." Immortality, reduced to mere survival in fame and in the memory of mankind, is of course even more short-lived than that proper to survival of the species; here we are in a wholly profane realm, almost in the sphere where the highly mortal members of the Académie Française have been called ironically *Les Immortels*. But it was already a teaching of the Hellenic mysteries that men with good cause to aspire to such immortality, such as Epaminondas or Agesilaus, could not expect to obtain in life after death the privileged destiny that even evildoers, if initiated, would enjoy.[36] Diotima, in her belief that such immortalizing human works had been inspired by the love for beauty, passes on to deal with love as dependent on beauty and expounds a kind of mystic and ecstatic aesthetic.

Such a theory offers little that can be used in solving the problem as we have stated it. It sets out with a dualism that basically desexualizes the whole. In fact, it now speaks of an eros that is no longer one aroused by woman or by a magnetic relationship with woman, but that is aroused by beauty as an idea: a beauty that has become little by little no longer the beauty of bodies or of a particular being or object but an abstract or absolute beauty.[37] Even the myth that plays the key part has changed; eros under the sign of Aphrodite Urania is identified with that which in the *Phaedrus* is based on anamnesis, on "memory" not of the hermaphroditic state but of the state before birth when the soul was contemplating the divine world and thus "there was fulfilled that which it is legitimate to call the most blessed of initiations, celebrated as perfect beings."[38] The love that is properly linked to sex is, instead, presented as the effect of the black steed prevailing over the white one and pulling upward the symbolic chariot of the soul,[39] or almost as a fall due to a defect in transcendental memory: "He who has not the blessed visions of above fresh in his memory or has forgotten them wholly, cannot recall at once the essence of beauty when he sees its image down here on earth; he does not, therefore, worship it when he sees it but instead gives himself over to pleasure and proposes only to lie with beauty and beget offspring in the manner of the beasts."[40] Hence arises the following rather problematical definition of the love of that day: "Passion, which is not coupled with reason, but which overpowers contemplation of all that is beautiful and lets itself be carried away by the pleasure aroused by beauty, being made ever stronger by kindred passions to covet the beautiful as expressed in the physical, this is that which is called love."[41] Having defined true love as the "desire for beauty," Marsilio Ficino[42] goes so far as to say that "the venereal fury," "the appetite for coitus and love are not only not the same emotions but show themselves to be the opposite of each other."[43]

In conclusion, we can only use the idea of an eros that through transposition and exaltation is prevented from animalistic and generative degradation, provided that eros continues to be related to woman and sexual polarity; we shall return to this question when dealing, for instance, with the inner side of the courtly love of medieval times. Instead, the theory of love as the desire for pure, abstract beauty may even remain within the field of metaphysics but is certainly outside the field of the metaphysics of sex. There are also reasons to doubt whether that theory is linked to some teaching in the mysteries, as Diotima claimed. For whereas we can see the theme of the hermaphrodite recurring in the study of the mysteries and in the secret lore of most traditions, the same cannot be said of "platonic love."[44] Even in subsequent developments, in the Renaissance, platonic love is almost exclusively presented as a simple philosophic theory; we know of no mystery schools nor mystical teachings in which such a theory led to a technique of ecstasy that was actually followed. Plotinus' mysticism of beauty has quite a different character. The beautiful in Plotinus refers rather to the "idea that binds and dominates hostile nature, lacking forms." From this context there arises also a relationship, outside the sphere of erotic tension and sex, of beauty proper to a form and to an inner domain manifested "in the greatness of mind, justice, pure wisdom, manly energy with a stern countenance, in the dignity and modesty shown in a fearless, steadfast, and impassive demeanour and, even higher still, in an understanding worthy of a god, shining over everything outside itself."[45] Finally, we cannot say to what extent the validity of Kant, Schopenhauer, and recent aesthetics depends on modern man's having a different constitution. According to them, the special nature of aesthetic feeling—that is, of the emotion aroused by the "beautiful"—is its "Apollinism," its lack of relationship to the faculty of desire or to eros. If one wants to take sex into account, it is a banal enough observation to say that a woman considered solely from the point of view of pure beauty is not the most suitable woman to arouse sexual magnetism and desire; she will be like a nude marble statue with a perfect form which, when contemplated, may indeed arouse an aesthetic emotion but which provides nothing in terms of eros. The *yin* quality is lacking, the daemonic, the unfathomable, the fascinating.[46] Very often the women who have the greatest success cannot be rightly called beautiful.

Thus the Platonic theory of beauty constitutes something in itself that is hard to understand in existential terms. As a whole, platonic love can be compared to a very special intoxication, half magical and half intellectual (the intoxication of pure forms). As such, it is distinct from the "humid way" of the love of the mystics and inseparable from the spirit of a civilization such as the Hellenic one, that saw the chrism of the divine in everything having a perfect limit and form.[47] When applied to the realm of the relations between the sexes, however, concepts of this kind lead to a paralyzing dualism. We see that Giordano Bruno, in treating "heroic fury" with reference to the Platonic theory, begins with a violent onslaught against anyone who obeys love and desire for woman, whom he ruthlessly describes: "That final insult and ill-deed of nature, which under the guise of beauty tricks us with a surface, a shadow, a ghost, a dream, a Circean incantation directed toward the service of procreation; a beauty which comes and goes, is born and dies, blossoms and festers; and woman is a little beautiful outside, for her true inward self contains permanently a potpourri, a warehouse, a grab bag, a market of all the filth, poisons, and harmful substances our stepmother Nature has been able to produce; which, after having collected that seed which served her, comes often to pay with a stench, a repentance, sadness, weariness . . . and with other ills which can be seen throughout the whole world."[48] Therefore, Giordano Bruno thinks it right that women should be loved and honored only "as much as is owed to them for the little they give at that time and on that occasion, unless they have some virtue other than a natural one, namely the virtue of that beauty and splendor and service without which they must be deemed to have been born more uselessly into the world than any diseased fungus which occupies the ground to the detriment of better plants."[49] This clarifies how the concept of the double eros leads to a degradation of sexual love, to its fall into savage conditions and to a failure to recognize its most profound possibilities. The same Giordano Bruno, in the epilogue of the work we have quoted, makes Julia, the symbol of real womanhood, say to her lovers, whom she refuses, that "it is precisely because of [her] so reluctant and yet simple and innocent cruelty" that she has shown them incomparably greater favors "than [they] could have obtained otherwise, however great [her] kindness"; for, diverting them from human love, she had directed their eros toward divine beauty.[50] Here the separation is complete; the direction differs from one that has any connection with sex whatsoever, no matter how exalted its form.[51]

Plotinus knew well how to keep this Platonic order of ideas within its proper limits by considering not only him who "loves beauty alone" but also "him who carries love as far as union and also has a wish for immortality through mortals and who seeks for the beautiful in a procreation and form of beauty which continues. Thus those who love beauty in bodies, although theirs is a mixed love, still love beauty, and, in loving women to perpetuate life, they love that which is everlasting."[52]

Lust and the Myth of Poros and Penia

We must consider one final myth found in the *Symposium*, one that contains profound significance in cryptic form. This is a special version of the origin of the god Eros. When Aphrodite was born, the gods held a banquet in the garden of Zeus. Poros, who participated, became drunk and sleepy. Penia, who had come to beg and was kept at the threshold of the garden, took advantage of his condition and made Poros copulate with her, plotting to have a son by him. The son was Eros.[53] Various interpretations of this myth have been put forward. The most weighty view, which is strengthened by the context of the whole passage, is that Poros expresses fullness and therefore, from a metaphysical standpoint, being, whereas Penia represents poverty, privation (of being), the *stérēsis* that plays so great a part in Greek philosophy and is linked essentially to the concept of "matter," *úlē* (cf. chapter 4). In an atmosphere similar to that of Aphrodite's birth—that is, under the sign of that goddess—being is united to nonbeing in a moment of blind intoxication; and this irrational union (Poros, drunk, has here fallen below his real nature as a son of Metis, who represents wisdom) characterizes its own product, the love and desire personified by Eros.

From this point of view, Eros has in other respects, too, that intermediate, ambivalent nature of which we spoke. He is at once both rich and poor because of his double (maternal and paternal) heritage. Besides being a "fearful enchanter" and a "troublesome hunter," he bears in his bosom the poverty, the nonbeing proper to Penia, and never attains possession (his gain "from time to time, imperceptibly, escapes him").

Although mortal on one side, he is immortal because of his paternal heritage; therefore, he dies and is extinguished only to awaken again, endlessly. In other words, he is a thirst for which every satisfaction is momentary and illusory. Such is the nature of love, of Eros as the "faithful minister of Aphrodite."[54]

When explained in these terms, and after certain intellectual references in Plato's account have been eliminated, such a myth of the origin of Eros is profound. It sheds light on the metaphysical meaning of the extroverted desire of sex as a substratum of the "circle of generation" and shows its fundamental, incurable contradiction.

This myth can be linked to many others that refer to the Fall. The drunken union of being (Poros) with privation (Penia) is basically the same as the mortal love of Narcissus for the reflection of his image in the water. Oriental traditions in particular, based on the idea of finite existence governed by illusion (Maya), contain the mysterious and irrational fact of transcendental imperfection or darkness (equal to the drunkenness or swooning of Poros) and of desire or emotion that led being to identify itself with the "other" (the state other than being). Therefore, being is subjected to the law of duality and of becoming; or rather it generates that law, and desire or thirst becomes the root of its existence in time.[55]

Here we may turn once more to the interpretation of Plotinus regarding the twofold birth of Eros. The first of these births is related to Aphrodite Urania, who is presented by Plotinus as embodying the female counterpart of the pure male intellectual principle, nous or the mind. Fecundated by the mind and everlastingly joined to it, she produces eros. This is the original love that is born between two persons from their own beauty; it is the mutual desire of man and woman in love with each other, each of whom sees himself or herself reflected in the other, for the generation of spiritual beings.[56] As for the second birth of Eros, Plotinus in fact refers to the myth of Poros and Penia. The eros produced by that couple is the desire aroused in the lower region, being affected by lack of reason and everlasting want, and having sprung here below in this world from the union of itself with a simple reflection or phantom of the true "good" (as in the myth of Narcissus). Plotinus wrote:

> Thus reason joined to the irrational has produced, by a mistaken desire and an unfit substance, something imperfect and impotent, something needy born of an illusory desire and an intellect conforming to it. . . . And it [eros] remains suspended from Psyche [here equivalent to Penia] from whom it is born, as her principle, apart from the mixture with this logos, which has not stayed within itself but has mixed with this indefinite substance [ûlê or matter]. . . . And so this love is like a gad-fly tortured by its own unsatisfied desire: Even after it has obtained satisfaction, its want persists; for fullness cannot be brought about by a mixture but can only exist in that which has wholeness in itself by virtue of its own nature. That desire arising from a privation of nature, even when unexpectedly it finds a satisfaction, will always desire again, because that satisfaction is only an expedient of its own insufficiency, whereas a suitable satisfaction would lie only in the nature of logos.[57]

The Greek philosophers saw, as the substance and sense of the *génesis* (creation) of existence enclosed in the everlasting circle of generation, the state of "that which is and is not," a "life mingled with non-life"; and nonlife is the nature of love and desire as revealed to us by the myth of Poros and Penia. Lovers, inheriting the intoxication that overcame Poros when Aphrodite was born, are actually giving themselves to death when they believe they are continuing life by desiring and procreating. They think they are overcoming duality, when in fact they are reconfirming it.[58] This is precisely so because desire, when it is extroverted craving dependent on "another," as indeed it is in most cases, implies want, an inborn and elementary want; and precisely when desire deems itself to be satisfied, it confirms that want and strengthens the law of dependence, of insufficiency, of impotence toward "being" in an absolute sense. It renounces absolute life when it seeks it outside, spilling and losing itself in woman. This is the paradox of thirst when considered from a metaphysical point of view; satisfaction does not quench thirst but confirms it by implying that a "yes" has been said to it. It is the everlasting privation of Eros, whom possession always escapes. Through his many rebirths, Eros retains the same privation and the same need. Thus it is an extroverted and universal eros that thrusts men into unions in which the dyad is not overcome; the duality man and woman presupposed by the situation of craving fatally stamps the result: The act is one that brings "another," the offspring, to life. The "other," which in the form of a woman has conditioned a moment of intoxicated, spasmodic ecstasy and union, will in general be represented as the "other" represented by the child, to whom is transmitted, together with life, the recurring destiny of death (the mortal immortality of Eros). With the child, there will be indeed an enduring, a continuity, but only a continuity of the species, of so many separate existences, each pursuing "being" in vain, it will not be the continuity of a transcendentally integrated consciousness, which halts the flow. Thus it could be said that the son kills the father and the god of the earth cheats those who believe that in woman they have found their fulfillment and the end of anguish. Animal birth abbreviates and cut short eternal birth or rebirth. Heterogeneration (the procreation of the other, or the child) takes the place of self-generation—of the androgynous integration.[59]

This can serve us as a further contribution toward the metaphysics of what we called the direction of eros toward its fall. It is also with reference to this context that often in the world of tradition, both in the Orient and in the ancient West, the divinities of love and fertility were at the same time divinities of death. For instance, this inscription to Priapus at a burial place is well known: "I am the god Priapus, guardian of the grave with penis gripped tight. This is a place of death and life."

We can indicate here one of the possible interpretations of another well-known Hellenic myth, that of Pandora. The chaining of Prometheus (from whom Zeus had once again taken away fire) has as its counterpart the gift of Pandora, the woman of desire, the "object of a hope that will be disappointed," given by the gods to Epimetheus, the brother of Prometheus. Epimetheus (meaning "he who finds out too late") is actually deemed to be not a separate being but another aspect of the Titan, also made of Titanic substance but more slow-witted. Here it is as if the gods had found a way to ward off the Promethean attempt undertaken in the form that is proper to eros. Notwithstanding the warnings of Prometheus, Epimetheus accepts the gift of Pandora, allows himself to be bewitched, and enjoys her without becoming aware of the deception practiced on him by his desire, at which the Olympians laugh. In the box of Pandora (she has been given this name because she seemed to gather the gifts of all the gods) there remains only misleading hope. The myth says that with Pandora an epoch is ended; for by means of the woman of desire, death reaches the world.[60]

At this level, we can also understood the condemnation of woman and sexuality by those who seek to attain everlasting life and the over-coming of the human state along the straight road of asceticism. It is against such a background and not against that of Platonism that one Eros can be opposed to another Eros. At the beginning of chapter 6, we shall discuss the "upward flow" and the practice of transmutations, but our horizon here is the one sketched out earlier; opposed to eros as a positive intoxication, in a magnetic circuit in which the "other" being serves only as food and the dyad has already from the onset been resolved, stands the carnal afflicted eros, or thirst and craving, a blind impulse for confirmation by means of an illusory possession, which miscarries in procreation and animal generation.

In this respect the decisive point has perhaps been expressed best in certain sayings in the apocryphal Gospels having an occult and gnostic inspiration. In the Gospel of the Egyptians we read: "Because they say that the Savior declared, 'Come to make an end to the work of women, that is, of craving [*cupiditas, ĕpidýmis*], the work of generation and of death.' " This, therefore, is the first possibility; and "When our Lord had spoken fittingly of the final conclusion, Salome asked, 'Until when shall men die?' and our Lord answered, 'So long as ye women shall give birth'; and when she said 'Should I do well, then, not to give birth?' our Lord answered and said, 'Eat of every plant, but eat not of that which has the bitterness of death.' And when Salome asked when the things she wanted to know would be made clear to her, our Lord said, 'When the cloak of shame shall be trodden under foot and *the two shall become one* and man with woman shall become neither man nor woman.' "[61]

Plotinus, therefore, spoke of a love that is an illness of the soul, "just as when desire of good brings an ill with it."[62] With this he indicated exactly the ambivalence of the phenomenon he was dealing with.

The essential reference points for the metaphysics of sex have thus been established. To sum up, by referring to the myth of the hermaphrodite, we have first shown the metaphysical significance of eros as a primordial fact, the state or experience of eros that submits to a tendency toward reintegration and being, toward the nondual state from which we have fallen. We have next introduced it into a wider context and placed it beside other forms of transport and active, disindividualizing exaltation (*manía*) that the ancient world deemed capable of suspending the human condition in one form or another and leading it to contacts with the supersensual. Developing the Platonic distinction, however, we have indicated the difference between a mania determined from below and one determined from above and the resulting bivalency of the ecstatic fact. Next, we have seen in the metaphysics of "survival of the species" and of the "instinct for reproduction" an involutive displacement of the primary meaning inherent in eros—namely, the wish to be absolute and immortal. At this same level, in relation to more excessive involutive phases, we have looked briefly at the sexuality of the animal world; here, too, metaphysics provided us with the key to biology but also to compensations that the common man has created for himself in his socialized sexual life. Finally, an adequate interpretation of the myth of Poros and Penia has enabled us to foreshadow the structure of the force that, with its incurable, everlasting want, feeds the unending circle of procreation.

These data should suffice to orient us in the analysis of various aspects and mingled forms of the phenomenology of eros, both sacred and profane; this analysis, integrated by an examination of the mythology of man and woman and by reference to the techniques of sexual magic, will form the subject of the following chapters.

Appendix

Homosexuality

Homosexuality is so widespread a practice that it cannot be overlooked in a doctrine of sex. Goethe wrote that "it is as old as mankind and therefore can be said to be a part of nature although it is contrary to nature." If it is "an enigma which appears more mysterious the more we attempt to analyze it scientifically" (Ivan Bloch), it also forms a complex problem from the point of view of the metaphysics of sex as formulated in the foregoing pages.

We have already mentioned that in his theory of eros Plato often referred not only to heterosexual love but also to love for epheboi and male paramours.[63] Now let us consider "eros" in those of its exalted forms that are linked to the aesthetic factor, according to the Platonic sequence already mentioned. We should pass gradually from beauty as seen by a given being to rapture that can be aroused by incorporeal beauty not linked to any particular person: divine beauty in an abstract sense. There is no real problem if the accidental starting point is a being of the same sex. The word "uranism," which some use to mean homosexuality, springs from Plato's distinction between Aphrodite Urania and Aphrodite Pandemia; Aphrodite Urania is the goddess of a noble love which is not carnal and unconcerned with procreation, as is the love which has woman as its object. It may be that pederasty (*paidon eros*, or love of boys) had in the beginning and to a certain degree a noble character when it was honored by ancient writers and poets and practiced by important personages. But it is now enough to read the last pages of the *Symposium* and the speech of Alcibiades in order to realize how little this eros remained "Platonic" in Hellas and how it also led increasingly to carnal developments as the ancient customs in Greece and Rome declined.

If, therefore, we assume homosexuality to conform to these carnal conditions or to correspond to ordinary sexual relations between man and woman, then we may well describe it as a deviation, not from a conventional or ethical point of view, but precisely from the stand-point of the metaphysics of sex.

It is inappropriate to apply, as Plato does, the metaphysical mean-ing made evident by the myth of the hermaphrodite to homosexual love or to love as practiced between pederasts or lesbians. In fact, in the case of such love, it is no longer allowable to speak of the impulse of the male or female principle, as present in the primordial being, to be reunited. The mythical being of our origin would, in such a case, have to be not hermaphroditic but homogeneous and of one sex only, either all man (in the case of pederasts) or all woman (in the case of lesbians), and the two lovers would seek to unite themselves as simple parts of one and the same substance. Thus the essential, which gives each myth its whole value, loses its meaning, namely, the idea of the polarity and the complementary nature of the two sexes as the basis of the magnetism of love and of a "transcendency" in eros, and of the blinding and destructive revelation of the One.

To find an explanation it is necessary to descend to a lower level and examine various empirical possibilities. Normally two forms of homosexuality are distinguished in sexology: One has an inborn, natural character, whereas the other has an acquired character and is conditioned by psychological and sociological factors influenced by a person's environment. But in the second of these forms it is necessary to give a proper value to the distinction between forms having a vicious nature and forms that presuppose a latent predisposition which is aroused under given circumstances. It is necessary to set forth this condition because, given the same situation, different types behave in different ways and may not become homosexual. It is important, however, not to consider the inborn form of homosexuality in a rigid way but to allow a certain possibility of variation.

In natural homosexuality or in the predisposition to it, the most straightforward explanation is provided by what we said earlier about the differing levels of sexual development and about the fact that the process of sexual development in its physical and, even more so, in its psychic aspects can be incomplete. In that way, the original bisexual nature is surpassed to a lesser extent than in a "normal" human being, the characteristics of one sex not being predominant over those of the other sex to the same extent (see chapter 1). Next we must deal with what M. Hirschfeld called the "intermediate sexual forms." In cases of this kind (for instance, when a person who is nominally a man is only 60 percent male), it is impossible that the erotic attraction based on the polarity of the sexes in heterosexuality—which is much stronger the more the man is male and the woman is female—can also be born between individuals who, according to the birth registry and as regards only the so-called primary sexual characteristics, belong to the same sex, because in actual fact they are "intermediate forms." In the case of pederasts, Ulrichs said rightly that it is possible to find "the soul of a woman born in the body of a man."

But it is necessary to take into account the possibility of constitutional mutations, a possibility that has been given little consideration by sexologists; that is, we must also bear in mind cases of regression. It may be that the governing power on which the sexual nature of a given individual depends (a nature that is truly male or truly female) may grow weak through neutralization, atrophy, or reduction of the latent state of the characteristics of the other sex, and this may lead to the activation and emergence of these recessive characteristics.[64] And here the surroundings and the general atmosphere of society can play a not unimportant part. In a civilization where equality is the standard, where differences are not linked, where promiscuity is in favor, where the ancient idea of "being true to oneself" means nothing anymore—in such a splintered and materialistic society, it is clear that this phenomenon of regression and homosexuality should be particularly welcome, and therefore it is in no way a surprise to see the alarming increase in homosexuality and the "third sex" in the latest "democratic" period, or an increase in sex changes to an extent unparalleled in other eras.[65]

But the reference to "intermediate sexual forms," to an incomplete process of the development of sex or to a regression, does not explain all the varieties of homosexuality. In fact, there have been male homosexuals who have not been effeminate or "intermediate forms" but even men of war, individuals decidely manly in their appearance and behavior, powerful men who have had or could have had the most beautiful women at their disposal. Such homosexuality is hard to explain, and we have the right here to speak of deviation and perversion, of "vice" linked, perhaps, to a fashion. Indeed, it is hard to understand what can drive a man who is truly a man sexually toward an individual of the same sex. If appropriate material for the realization of the zenith of the orgasm of heterosexual love is almost nonexistent, this is even more the case in the embraces of homosexual love. However, there is reason to suppose that it is merely a matter of "mutual masturbation" and that the conditioned reflexes are exploited for "pleasure" since not only the metaphysical but also the physical premises for a whole and destructive union are lacking.

On the other hand, classical antiquity bears witness not so much to a homosexuality having sole rights and being the foe of women and wedlock, but rather to a bisexual attitude in which both women and young men were used (as a counterpart, there are generally many cases of very highly sexed and also very feminine women who are at the same time lesbians, with bisexual practices). Here it seems that the governing motivation was simply the desire to try everything. However, not even this point is very clear because, apart from the fact that there was femininity in the epheboi and youths who were the favourite object of those pederasts, we may also refer to the crude saying, taken by Goethe from a Greek writer, that if one has had enough from a girl as a girl, she can always play the part of a boy ("*Habe ich als Mädchen sie satt, dient es als Knabe noch*").

As to the claim for an ideal nature of hermaphroditic wholeness in the pederast who acts both as man and as woman sexually, that is obvious fallacious beyond the level of straightforward sensations; hermaphroditic wholeness can only be "sufficiency," for it has no need of another being and is to be sought at the level of a spiritual realization that excludes the nuances that the "magic of the two" can offer in heterosexual unions.

Even the rationale sometimes found in countries such as Turkey and Japan, that homosexual possession gives a feeling of power, is not convincing. The pleasure of domination can also be felt with women and with other beings in situations free of sexual intercourse. Besides, such a pleasure could be involved only in a completely pathological context where it would develop into a true orgasm.

Thus overall, when homosexuality is not "natural" or else cannot be explained in terms of incomplete inborn forms of sexual development, it must have the character of a deviation, a vice, or a perversion. And if some instances of extreme erotic intensity in relations between homosexuals should be adduced, the explanation is to be sought in the possibility of the displacement of eros. Indeed, it is enough to go through any treatise on sexual psychopathology to see in how many unthinkable situations the erotic potential of a human being can be aroused, sometimes to the level of orgiastic frenzy (from fetishism even to animal sodomy and necrophilia). The same anomalous background could include the case of homosexuality, although the latter is much more frequent: a displaced eros for which a being of the same sex can serve as a simple, occasional cause or support, as in so many cases of psychopathy, although it must wholly lack every profound dimension and every meaning higher than experience because of the absence of the necessary ontological and metaphysical premises. As we shall see in certain aspects of sadism and masochism, it is possible to find elements that can be included in the deepest structures of heterosexual erotics and that become perversions only when freed from limitations. No similar recognition can be given in respect to homosexuality.

3

Phenomena of Transcendency in Profane Love

Sex and Human Values

The characteristic of truly intense love in its hidden metaphysical basis is its "transcendency": transcendency in respect of the individual being; in respect of his values, his standards, his ordinary interests, his most intimate ties, and, in an extreme case, his well-being, his peace, his happiness, and his actual physical life.

The absolute unconditional can only lie beyond the life of an ego enclosed within the limits of the empirical, physical, practical, moral, or intellectual person. Thus, as a principle, only that which goes beyond such a life and such an ego, which creates a crisis, induces a stronger force, and displaces the center outside of itself (this, too, may happen, if necessary, in a problematical, catastrophic, or destructive way)—only that can, perhaps, open the way to a higher region.

Now, it is a fact that in ordinary life, in few situations other than those conditioned by love and sex, this condition of transcendency is rarely attained. It would indeed be a waste of time to emphasize what love, the everlasting and inexhaustible subject of art and literature, has been able to do in the history of mankind and in individual and collective life. It has propitiated eminence and heroism as well as baseness, unworthiness, misconduct, and betrayal. If one were truly to see in sexual love an impulse linked genetically to animal nature, then one could draw the conclusion that man stands at a level much lower than any other species, for he has allowed love, sex, and woman to intoxicate and govern not only his physical being but, even more so, the realm of his highest faculties to such a degree that they have extended the area of their encroachment far beyond trivial instinct. If, instead, we follow the metaphysical interpretation of sex, all these facts can be seen and evaluated differently. The tyranny of love and sex that in eros is able to overthrow, undermine, or subordinate everything else, becomes, instead of an extreme degradation and ineradicable devilry in human existence, the sign of man's irrepressible nature and of his urge to move beyond the limits of his finite individuality.

Biology has put the functions of feeding and reproduction on the same level (sometimes considering the first as primary, since people cannot live without food), yet the absolute difference in status between the two functions seems obvious. Only in extreme cases of absolute hunger can the nutritive function overthrow the individual. But that function is destitute of any psychic counterpart; throughout history under normal social conditions, nothing in regard to food corresponds to the part that the sexual function plays in individual or collective life, or to the profound and manifold influence exerted by that function at the emotional, moral, intellectual, and, not seldom, even the spiritual level. Man has no other need that reaches the depths of being in the same measure as the erotic-sexual need; none attains the status of a "complex" that develops its influence before, after, and even outside of that satisfaction.

It would be banal to dwell on the social aspects of the "transcendental" power of love. It can violate the boundaries of caste and tradition, make persons of the same blood or persuasion enemies, separate sons from fathers, and break the links established by the most holy institutions. History has shown us this in the house of the Hapsburgs and in that of England. The story of Shakespeare's Ferdinand, who, through his love of Miranda, declared himself ready to give up his rank of king and be content to be the slave of Prospero, is a theme restricted to literature or to the romantic princes of operettas. The incentive for the creation of the Anglican church against Rome lay in the sexual problem of Henry VIII. A part that cannot be overlooked was played in the genesis of the Reformation by the sexuality of Luther, who could not bear monastic discipline. Confucius remarked that there was never done as much for justice as there was for a woman's smile; Leopardi in his *Il Primo Amore* (First Love) acknowledged in eros the power to arouse a sense of the vanity of every design or study, the very love of glory and every other pleasure. The classical myth makes Paris, under the sign of Aphrodite, prefer the most beautiful woman to the highest learning promised by Athena-Minerva and to the empire of Asia and the riches promised by Hera-Juno. "I have greater joy in one look or word from you, young lady," says Goethe's Faust, "than in universal knowledge." From ancient times there resounds the disconcerting questions of Mimnermus—whether in general there is life or enjoyment of life without "golden Aphrodite" and whether life without her is still life.[1] Sexology agrees in acknowledging that love, "as unleashed passion, is like a volcano that burns and consumes everything; it is an abyss that swallows down honor, fortune and health."[2]

In a properly psychological field, some favorable effects of love can be noted. Plato remarked that in the case of unworthy behavior or base action, no man would ever be so ashamed of himself as when his lover was present; "No one is so base that love itself cannot inspire him with divine bravery and make him the equal of a man who is very bold by nature. . . . Precisely that hardihood which is inspired in some heroes by the god is bestowed by Love on lovers because of her own nature."[3] To all of this can be linked the part, which is even exaggerated by romantic literature, that love and woman have played in driving men to high deeds and sublime actions. If "There is nothing I would not do for you" is a trivial commonplace in the language of lovers, it echoes the ideals of medieval chivalry according to which a man would willingly risk his life for a woman in fighting or in dangerous undertakings and would make her the inspiration for all his glory and honor. Here we must distinguish between that which is done simply to obtain possession of the woman one loves and all that which, in regard to favorable disposition, self-conquest, and creative enthusiasm, has had woman and erotic experience as mere propitiatory means; of these two cases, only the second should really be taken into account.[4]

But as signs of the power that shatters the individual, the negative effects of passion are more interesting: the aspects of a transcendency that does not spare the moral personality and undermines its most essential values. Once more we can refer to Plato, who notes how lovers "agree to a servitude that not even a slave would undergo" and do not deem themselves worthless because of a flattery such that not even the most degraded tyrant would wish for it. "If someone, to enrich himself or make his way in the world, should wish to behave as he does for love . . . a friend, even an enemy, would prevent him from sinking so low."[5] In the ethics of the Aryan people, no other virtue was honored so much as the truth and nothing inspired so much horror as a lie. In Indo-Aryan morals, a lie was allowed only for the purpose of saving a human life or in love. Along with self-respect, we can include the criterion of fairness—"All is fair in love and war." A very oath ceases to be sacred—"He who loves is the only person who can swear and be forsworn without incurring the wrath of the gods," says Plato;[6] and Ovid, to support him, says: "Jove in the highest heavens makes a game of lovers who are forsworn, and he desires the breeze and the wind to carry them away without any effect." "Virtue . . . which has become deception and breaks its faith with them [women] does not deserve the name of dishonor."[7]

The moral to be drawn is that because something absolute is to be expected from love, it preempts even virtue itself. Its ultimate goal is beyond good and evil. If the ultimate meaning of man's drive toward woman is what we said earlier, namely the need to "be" in the transcendent sense, what we have just revealed and what is confirmed by everyday life appears perfectly comprehensible. And it also seems to make sense that in extreme cases of the elementary force of eros, the

individual may be driven to suicide, homicide, or madness if he cannot satisfy his desire. The illusion that profane love offers in reflect-
ing what eros can give where it passes to a higher plane (the total
happiness of union) is such that, if it is denied or interrupted, life itself loses every attraction and becomes empty and void of sense, so
that it can lead to suicide. For this very reason, the loss of a loved one
owing to death or treachery can be an agony that surpasses all other
agonies. Schopenhauer expresses this better than anyone else.[8] But
though his observation of a motive and value that go absolutely
beyond the individual in love is accurate, his references to the omni-
potence of the species and his failure to see anything except the tragic
effect of an illusion are absurd. The positive contribution of
Schopenhauer was his indication that the sufferings of a betrayed
love surpass all other sufferings, not because of an empirical and
psychological element but because of the transcendental element, the
fact that not the finite but the essential and eternal individual is
struck. This, however, is a question not of the species in man but of
his deepest nucleus in the absolute need to "be," to be confirmed,
this need being aroused through eros and the magic of woman.

In this same order of ideas, we find interesting cases where sexual
love persists despite disparity of character and intellectual inclinations and is reaffirmed even when scorn and hate are felt by the individual. Situations actually exist that fit the strange definition of love
given by one of Bourget's characters: "This is love, a deady hatred
between two copulations."[9] The hate element in love requires a
separate study because it may have a deeper meaning, not existential
but metaphysical, as we shall see in the next chapter. On the other
hand, it may be considered and integrated in the wholeness of
transcendency, in relation to the three possible levels of the occurrence of eros in a human being. It takes place mainly when the
force of the elementary layer is reaffirmed as stronger than the conditional characteristics of both the individual's values and the
individual considered at the level of his preformation, his own
nature, and his character. The desire is absolute, against which even
hatred and contempt toward the loved one have no power. It is
precisely these examples that count as a "litmus test" since they tell
us what is truly fundamental in eros even in cases where there are no
contrasts or appreciable human heterogeneity between the lovers
and, therefore, the elementary magnetism may be awakened in a
climate free from tensions.

"Everlasting Love," Jealousy, and Sexual Pride

The positive counterpart that is present even in problematic cases is
the feeling that in woman there is life, that she is life itself, life in a

higher sense. The banal language of lovers contains the recurring theme "You are my life," "I cannot live without you," and so on in unending, manifold varieties. Trivial, no doubt; but the plane on which we shall see this theme reappear and be integrated in a cycle of myths and sagas that encompasses traditions far distant in time and space is far from trivial. Thus, the feeling of a higher life is foretasted and reflected if only for a moment through woman in confused, emotional states and is also echoed in the stereotypical expressions of the universal language of lovers.

It is therefore natural that love should be linked both to anguish and to a need to make oneself eternal. It is anguish lest one should fall from such heights. And so in every love there is always fear, even in the most intense moments. Indeed, more than ever is a lover afraid that everything may end; for this reason, he expresses his wish to die and ask continuously, anxiously, and untiringly through fear of change, "Will you love me forever?" "Will you ever tire of me?" "Will you always want me?" There is no love so secure that it does not need an "always," an endless duration. The sentiment governs us for a moment even though reason is perfectly aware of its absurd and illusory nature, and even though the same sentiment is rekindled again and again, in subsequent erotic relationships. A typical case is the passions of Shelley. The sentiment represents an essential moment in the gathering of experience.[10] When this feeling is present, there is also a correlative in transcending the temporary element and going beyond the limit of the present; there is a feeling of familiarity frequent among lovers, of having known each other for a very long time: "You are the image that I always carried hidden within me," or "It seems to me that I knew you before I knew myself. You seem to me to have been before everything that I am" (Melandro, in Maeterlinck). These are all real facts of erotic experience. They would be completely absurd if love's sole reason for existing was procreative coitus; for it would have no need for possession beyond the stage linked to the momentary act of simple union; but such facts show a precise logic of their own in light of the metaphysics of sex.

The same can be said for faithfulness and jealousy. Neither is required by nature or by the species. Indeed, the opposite would be natural, for attachment to one being could only have a restricting effect on freedom of procreativity when other partners would offer the same, or better, biological capabilities for reproduction. Instead, we should understand that, when a beloved woman sets at rest the need for self-confirmation and for "being," the existential privation of the creature is removed and he feels he possesses Life in himself. The notion that his beloved may betray him or pass on to others makes him feel utterly broken and harms the deepest existential nucleus within him; and the stronger the erotic magnetism, the more weight such an idea will have. It can be understood, then, how love changes into hate, how the feeling of his own destruction could drive man savagely to destroy and even kill the person who has betrayed him; this would be nonsense in the context of mere survival of the species or the field of psychology. With a love-hate that slays, neither the individual nor the species gains anything.

There are cases in which love's need to possess another being wholly, physically and morally, in the flesh and in the soul, can be explained in its most superficial aspect by the pride of the ego and the impulse toward power. We say "its most superficial aspect" because these impulses are not primary but rather complex ones formed at the level of the social individual, whose root is more deep and hidden. The *Geltungstrieb*, the need to have worth, the need to enhance one's value in one's own eyes even more than in the eyes of other people, the "manly protest" that Adler set as a central theme in his analytical psychology, are not so much the causes of neurotic overcompensation as the effects of an inferiority complex. This complex is transcendental in nature, stemming from an understanding of man's inborn privation as a finite being, shattered and problematical, a mixture of being and nonbeing. Eros is one of the natural forms with which man seeks to reduce and suspend this feeling of privation. It is logical that some people strive for self-confirmation and a sense of self-worth through erotic and sexual possession; it gives them the illusion of "being"—and the phenomenology of both jealousy and sexual tyranny arises from it. But, let us repeat, none of this has a primary character; it only concerns transpositions belonging to the sphere of the most peripheral consciousness. A man who limits himself to this level does not understand the ultimate sense and the depth dimension of the impulses that he obeys in these cases; thus, he often nourishes the deflected and distorted compensatory manifestations we have just mentioned. That quite ridiculous thing called the "pride of the male" is of this sphere. Even more external is that which, in the occurrence of jealousy, may be governed by simple love of oneself and by the social idea of love. We speak of deflected transpositions because, when the ego seeks in the feeling of possession and in sexual egoism a compensation or anesthetic for its own dim feeling of inferiority, and when the feeling of possession provides a substitute for "being," the actual effect is almost always a reinforcement of egosim of the empirical individual in his limited and closed state; and this goes against the tendency toward self-transcendence, which is the highest capability of eros. However, this situation is often to be found. In

D'Annunzio's *Trionfo della morte* (Triumph of Death), Giorgio Aurispa clings desperately to the feeling of possession in order to escape his feeling of nothingness and to fight against the irresistible urge toward suicide. And he says, "On earth there is only one lasting intoxication: absolute certainty in the possession of another creature. I am seeking this intoxication."

But in erotic experiences today we mainly find a mixture of these two contradictory moments: the impulse to have worth by possessing, and the tendency to abandon oneself during union. This contradiction has in a certain way a dialectical character, and from a metaphysical point of view the two tendencies are connected genetically and both proceed from one and the same root, being opposed to each other only in their finite, conditioned forms of manifestation.[11] Instead, in a integrated eros, the character proper to *manía* (frenzy) or to exaltation and enthusiasm will prevail under the sign of the One, and therefore there will be a movement beyond self and other, beyond affirmation of self and other, similar to what happens in heroic experience on a different plane. And the antithesis we mentioned just now is overcome. "Beyond life," "more than life," may be the principle suitable for great love, for grand passion and great desire: "I love you more than my life." The technique of an Arab love spell consists in the man's concentrating all his will in the expression of his eyes and in staring at the woman, while making three cuts in his left arm, and then pronouncing the phrase "There is no god but God. And just as this is true, so will all my blood flow out before my thirst to possess you is quenched."[12]

Phenomena of Transcendency in Puberty

Of special interest are the conditions that often accompany the first signs of the force of sex in puberty and in love.

At the stage when the state caused by the polarity of the sexes is the subject of experiments for the first time, a kind of dismay or fear or anguish is almost always felt because there is the more or less distinct sensation of the action of a new, higher, boundless force within the psychic and physical framework of the individual. It is a fear stemming from a foreboding of the crisis that the individual will undergo and of the danger he will run, this fear being mingled with lack of knowledge of desire. The expression used by Dante for the feeling roused in him by the first appearance of woman[13] delineates this point: *Ecce Deus fortior me, qui veniens dominabitur mihi* (Behold God, stronger than I, who comes and will hold sway over me): a stronger force that makes the "natural spirit" (to whom the naturalistic individual may be made to correspond) say: *Heu miser! Quia frequenter impeditus ero deinceps!* (Alas, wretched am I! For I shall often be in difficulty hereafter!) And Jelaluddin Rumi:

> Death rightly sets a term to the anguish of life.
> And yet life trembles before death. . . .
> Just as a heart trembles in the face of love,
> as if it felt the threat of its end.
> For there where love is roused,
> the ego, the obscure tyrant, dies.[14]

When examined in a proper light, the pathology of the phenomena of puberty is, in this respect, especially indicative. The appearance of the force of sex produces an upset that (if hereditary deficiencies, innate weakness of the organism, psychic trauma, or other causes prevent the individual from overcoming the crisis) provokes unhealthy symptoms, which may even lead to madness itself, a specific form of mental derangement that Kahlbaum called hebephrenia or the madness of puberty.[15] These symptoms can be interpreted as one of two malfunctions. Either too little energy has been introduced into the "circuits" in which the elementary, superindividual force of eros, transformed and reduced, gives way to the ordinary forms of individual sexuality, or else there is a structural fault in those circuits and the adjustment of the psychic and physical framework to the energy does not take place or does so only partially. Hysterical and epileptic or semicataleptic fits, forms of melancholia and depression alternating with forms of exaltation, attacks of masturbatory derangement and the like are all possible effects of the action of the new unchanneled or deviated force. Mairet states that in frenetic attacks of masturbation, as also in other acts, the individual so afflicted feels he is transported by an inner force independent of his own will, just as if he were possessed.[16] The same interpretation may perhaps be applied during the crisis of puberty to a halt in intellectual development; it is here a pathological neutralization or inhibition of the mind. But in lesser degrees it is a normal phenomenon also in falling in love and in passion. The same meaning should be attached to frequent hallucinations of sight or hearing in adolescence; they are due to a power that can disconnect the imaginative and perceptive faculty from the bonds of the senses. This has a counterpart in that magical arousal of the imagination through eros which we mentioned earlier. Last, besides conditions of energy depletion or *tedium vitae* (boredom with life), we should examine the suicidal urges that appear sometimes during puberty; here the effect is obviously one of a "passive" experience of the impulse toward transcendence, an anticipation of the sexuality-death complex, with which we shall soon deal at some length.[17] In this field, too, pathology enlarges physiology. All these possible "upsets" that take place in the crisis of puberty are repeated on a smaller scale every time one falls in love and, above all, in the first experience of love.

Marro[18] cites the clinical evidence of a youth afflicted with such troubles who said that "he felt a fluid going from his bowels up his back and reaching to his brain";[19] he was then struck by an irresistible urge to perform some violent, convulsive actions. This case gives an idea of the valuable material the psychiatrists could gather if they had adequate knowledge of the hyperphysical physiology of the human being; for it is easy to see that this testimony relates to an experience of a partial awakening of the kundalini or fundamental power latent within ordinary sexuality, which the teachings of yoga treat; such an awakening, it is said, may even have madness or death as its outcome whenever it is provoked without adequate training.[20] In its normal and nonpathological forms, which correspond to a partial channeling of energy in the individual circuits of transformation, we shall find, instead, the more or less stormy arousal of the emotional faculties during puberty.[21]

In the period of puberty, we should also consider manifestations that, though not pathological, have the same genetic origin on the spiritual plane. These manifestations directly reveal the superphysical aspect of the new force in action when free and not wholly polarized and specialized in the ordinary sexual sense. We refer to cases of a strong arousal of religious feeling and mystic tendencies during puberty. Psychologists have often noted that spiritual crises and conversions are mainly brought about during this period and accompany states that are often akin to the pathology of puberty: a sense of incompleteness and imperfection, anguish, unhealthy introspection, anxiety, disgust, insecurity, vague and inward dissatisfaction—all of these to such a degree that Starbuch could write that theology takes the tendencies of youth and builds upon them.[22] An analogy exists between the modification of feelings about the world and life that characterizes a favorable solution to a religious crisis, and the modification that is linked to the enthusiasm of a first happy love. William James wrote regarding the religious phenomenon that an appearance of newness embellishes every object, as opposed to the previous feeling of the unreality and alien nature of the world: a willingness to be, even when everything remains the same.[23] But in the same way Stendhal wrote with regard to love: "Love-passion casts before the eyes of a man the whole of nature in its most sublime aspects, just like something new invented yesterday. Man is amazed that he has never seen the curious sight which is now revealed to his soul. Everything is new; everything is alive and 'inspiring.' "[24] "*Schön wie ein junger Frühling ist diese Welt*" (Beautiful as a youthful springtime is this world), says a well-known song referring to a first happy love. "You shall see by falling in love" ('*ashiq tara*) is a Arabic saying that is said to have caused the enlightenment of a Sufi. These are reflections of the state of wholeness and of the metaphysical integration of the ego, caused by eros. The natural counterpart is the feeling of emptiness, of lack of spirit, of indifference toward everything when love has been disappointed or ended abruptly. Even the frequency of ecstasy during the age of puberty has been noted.[25]

The same situation is met on a deeper plane than that of simple psychology in the field of ethnology. In many primitive peoples the so-called sacred or initiatory diseases, which are deemed signs of being chosen, normally coincide with the arrival of sexual maturity. It has been rightly noted that the training of a shaman or wizard or priest, which follows that sign of being chosen, has nothing to do with the pathological condition.[26] It does not represent a systematic cultivation of that pathological state. On the contrary, in such a training process, a technique is used to remove everything having the nature of illness; the new force is fixed in the state arising on a spiritual plane, and therefore the symptoms of the pathology of adolescence die away automatically. The outcome is not a normal condition but something more, a capacity for real and active contact with the supersensual. In this ethnological context, there are also interesting cases of an initiation process in which youths who have reached puberty are selected before they have touched a woman;[27] the object here is to gather and fix the force of transcendent virility before it becomes specialized or sexually polarized in a strict sense.

This leads us to the so-called rites of passage that refer also to sex in an inward, spiritual sense as opposed to merely a physical one. In various cultures, special rites accompany the change from childhood to puberty, thus giving it the significance of a passage from a naturalistic level to manhood in a higher sense. Two most important points must be emphasized here.

First of all, something like death or rebirth is celebrated in these rites. Thus, one who has undergone them will sometimes be given a new name and lose the memory of his previous life or will use a new secret language and enter into communication with the mystic forces of his ancestral stock. The phenomenon of transcendency, therefore, acquires a precise physiognomy, being guided in this case by a conscious technique with institutional and traditional backgrounds.

Second, we can perceive cases of the differentiation between a spiritual virility and a virility that is only physical in that only he who has been through this rite is deemed to be truly a man and to have been "made a man." Being removed from his mother's supervision, he becomes part of the "societies of men," to which may correspond "houses of men" isolated from other dwellings which are societies having specific forms of sacred, political, or military authority over the rest of the population. Any male who has not undergone the rite, whatever his age, is not considered a real man but belongs with the women, animals, and babies. To mark the changeover symbolically, the candidate for initiation has to put on female clothing beforehand to show he has not yet been "made a man."

Therefore, we can see quite clearly that special techniques are used to gather the force of sex in the free state when it is first displayed in the individual, and to make that force act to bring about a profound change in the being. In the case of the male, the effect is the confirmation of what we called the inward manhood.[28] It is possible that the Roman Catholic rite of Confirmation, which is usually celebrated at the advent of puberty, is a last reflection of the traditional practices of the past. The first celebration of the Eucharist is linked to that rite. This sacrament in theory includes equally the ideas of transubstantiation, death, and resurrection.

This leads us now to the realm of an eros that is not profane, a realm in which sex is made sacred, but according to an undeniable continuity. In fact, the basic meanings remain the same. Here is confirmation of the transcendency of eros; for, being at the basis of the pathology of adolescence, eros, when its love is aroused within the closed circuits of the individual, characterizes the passion that overthrows and consumes, in a favorable or unfavorable sense, and takes man outside himself in a passive sense, as object rather than subject of the surpassing of the limit of the ego in ordinary lovers. The facts mentioned regarding ethnology and other facts of the traditional world, which we shall deal with, bear witness to the possibility of a conscious and active use of this potential transcendency for the purposes of special consecrations and, above all, for the realization of the nonnaturalistic aspect of the virile quality.

Love, the Heart, Dreams, and Death

The part played by the heart in the language of lovers is very well known and belongs mainly to the sphere of the most saccharine sentimentality. Nevertheless, even here, one may see a reflection of a profound fact, if one remembers what the heart has always signified in esoteric and learned traditions. More than the seat of simple emotions, these traditions considered the heart as the center of the human being[30] but also the seat to which consciousness is transferred during sleep, abandoning the seat in the head, which corresponds normally to the state of wakefulness.[31] The "conscious" equivalent of the condition of sleep is, however, as we said before, the subtle state. Especially in Hindu but also in many other mystic traditions, the inner, secret space of the heart is believed to be the seat of supersensual light ("light of the heart"). We have something more than the mere trivial and vague allusion typical of the language of lovers, something much more precise, when Dante, in talking about the first, sudden perception of eros, speaks of the "very secret chamber of the heart."[32] Nothing is more fatuous than the heart struck by an arrow (the arrow and the torch were attributed by the ancients to Eros); it is a subject preferred even for the tattoos of sailors and criminals. But at the same time, it is like a hieroglyph that has an unusual power. In its most typical forms, eros seems to be a kind of trauma at the central point of a being, which from an esoteric point of view is the heart. According to similar traditions, the bond of the individual ego is established in the heart. It must be broken to reach a higher freedom. Here eros acts like the deadly wound of an arrow. We shall see that the "Worshippers of Love" in the Middle Ages and, with them, Dante, understood this context consciously on a level beyond the profane experience of lovers. But even in mundane experience, in every love, the trace remains. The term *fat'hu-l-qalb* (the opening or disclosure of the heart) belongs to Islamic esotericism and, with the term "light of the heart," is often found in the language of the mystics. In the Corpus Hermeticum (VII, II; VI, I) we meet the expression "to open the eyes of the heart" or "to understand with the eyes of the heart." Now, it is possible to establish a relationship between this condition (which to a certain extent means a disindividualizing, a slackening of the bond of the heart) and the experience of newness (an almost fresh, active transformation of the world that accompanies the state of love); we can foresee a shadow of what the mystical language of the Sufis calls the world seen with the *ayn el-qalb*, the eye of the heart.

In the first chapter we said that erotic experience implies a displacement of the level of the ordinary, waking consciousness in the individual. This is a tendential transfer, by exaltation, toward the seat of the heart. Indeed, the condition of "exaltation" in eros, accompanied by an unusual degree of inner activity, results in the beginning of this displacement. Consciousness is retained and participates, therefore, in a certain "dreaming" enlightenment and transformation into a lucid state instead of the normal trance or sleep. Apart from the repercussions already mentioned, on perception of the outside world, this displacement is also linked to a certain aura that lights up the physiognomy of some lovers, even when their appearance usually lacks any nobility.

But if we examine the relationship of this displacement with the one that commonly occurs at night, we are led to another point that is itself indicative. In fact, the link between love and nighttime is more than a well-known theme of romantic poetry. It also has an existential substratum that is revealed in various ways. Even nowadays the night is deemed the most suitable time for sexual love. Throughout the whole world it is at night, above all, that men and women unite. Here the presence of a hyperphysical factor contradicts the findings of biology; for the best physiological conditions for "healthy and normal" love with the greatest reserves of fresh energy should exist precisely in the morning. We cannot counter with incidental circumstances belonging to our environment or way of life such as the fact that for most people there is less free time during the day; for the preference for night is confirmed as a habit even where social conditions and social status do not seem to prescribe such a preference. Indeed, among certain peoples the use of the night for sexual union is ritually and severely prescribed, sometimes in general, whereas at other times the practice is limited to a longer or shorter initial period of sexual relations. At dawn the man must leave the woman. Tantrism specifically prescribes "the heart of the night" for magical and initiatory practices with a woman, and in the *Fang-pi-shu*, the secret Chinese art of the bed, there are references to the night, which is called the time of the "living breath." It is also at night that certain orgiastic rites are practiced such as those of the Khlysti, to which we shall return later. Similarly, in the Eleusinian mysteries, the rite of sacred copulation, *hieros gamos*, was celebrated at night in an unlit place. This rite, known as Nyctelia, was not merely symbolic; it was a part of the orgiastic rite of Dionysus, and women officiated at it. In Sparta, a man could take himself a wife acquired by rape, undo her belt, and lie with her only by night or in the dark.[33] And if many women still prefer night, it is not from modesty but from subconscious memory. Hathor, the Egyptian goddess of love, was also Lady of the Night, and this theme echoes in the verse of Baudelaire: *"Tu charmes le soir/Nymphe tenebreuse et chaude"* (You charm the evening, warm and darkling Nymph).

Here are some acute factors of a cosmic and analogical type: cosmic because, as we said, it is at night that the cyclical change of condition occurs in everybody, a movement of consciousness to the seat of the heart, and therefore, even if one stays awake at night, the movement occurs and integrates the tendencies of eros; analogical because love stays under the sign of woman, and woman corresponds to the dark, underground, nocturnal aspect of being, to the vital unconsciousness, and her realm is therefore the night and darkness.[34] In conclusion, the night is indeed the most propitious time for woman's works, as a better atmosphere for the subtle developments of eros and for the evocation of profound forces below the illumined surface of individual finite consciousness. As for the extraordinary possibilities that may be realized in these states when not submerged in hazy sensual feelings, we should consider as more than mere romantic poetry what Novalis wrote in some of his *Inni alla notte* (Hymns to the Night).[35]

In reference to the heart, one last point merits attention. According to hyperphysical physiology, at the point of death or in a case of deadly peril the vital spirits flow to the middle of the human being, to the heart (they will leave this seat by following an ascending direction when death has taken place or when death is apparent, during catalepsy and during equivalent states of advanced asceticism).[36] The same phenomenon can happen in any experience of strong desire and can be aroused under some circumstances by the sight of the beloved, by evocation of an image of her,[37] or by actual nakedness. We often find in Oriental writings references to the stopping of breathing in the lover through amorous fascination, through extreme desire, or at the very moment of sexual embrace. The outward, profane, and trivial counterpart of all this is well known to physiology. The most common expression of this state is "My heart stopped beating." This symptom can also be included among the group indicated earlier regarding the potential attributes of eros. And here, too, can be established a natural passage from the phenomenology of everyday love to the sphere of a sensualism that is no longer profane. We shall see this when we come to deal, for instance, with both the *mors osculi*, the death of the kiss, mentioned by the Kabbalists, and the effect of the "greetings" of the lady on the Worshippers of Love.

One further detail may be of interest: Some French troubadours spoke of a lady seen not with the eyes or mind but "with the heart."

The Love-Pain-Death Complex

At this stage we must examine a complex of fundamental importance to the issues we are dealing with: the love-pain-death complex. In it we must distinguish the psychic aspect from one which could almost be called physical.

Regarding the first aspect, every arousal of eros in its elementary state—when not linked to a real displacement of the ego but instead remaining in the purely human circuit in feeding a passion concentrated on the loved one—will result in an abnormal saturation of the circuit. This is felt as suffering, a consuming anguish that has no outlet. Mystics often speak of this state of tension. Somerset Maugham wrote that a love like that is not joy but pain, yet it is a pain so acute that it surpasses every pleasure; it has in itself that divine anguish which the saints say pervades them during ecstasy. And Novalis wrote, "Few people know the mystery of love—they experience unassuaged hunger and everlasting thirst."[38]

It has been called "that very rare and mysterious affinity of the flesh which links two human creatures with a tremendous bond of insatiable desire." On the other hand, such cases of a great passion may also spring from an inversion; the symbol is identified with the person, and the person is loved for herself, almost "like God in the place of God." The intensity of an impulse that, in these cases, longs for the absolute is concentrated on the humanity of a given being, who thereby ceases to be a means for the lover and instead becomes the object of an idolatry or, to put it better, a fetish.[39] It is important to note that such a case is precisely the opposite of that of the sacred rites and evocations, which we shall examine later on: The partner does not acquire a different quality through real communication with a higher plane that is more than human, nor does she embody the absolute woman; rather, she usurps the attributes belonging to that plane by saturating them with the simple, fortuitous human element. In the second or physical case, one often meets a kind of vampirism that is exercised by one person on another, even unconsciously; frequently, dangerous states of sexual bondage are established.

The situation of great passion provides the favorite subject for tragic and romantic art. But in actual fact, situations of this kind can also end in crisis and breakdown. This happens through the process of idealization of the woman when she is imagined to possess unrealistic moral value that nobody can be expected to live up to. At that point, a traumatic fact can make the whole edifice tumble down, dissolving all the "crystallization" of Stendhal and leaving the disappointing reality standing in all its nakedness. This kind of trauma can even be provoked through desire for or possession of the coveted woman. Thus Kierkegaard was able to talk of the "perils of happy love" and to declare that an unhappy love and everything that a beloved woman may provide in the way of disappointment and betrayal are an essential and lucky factor in certain cases, so that it maintains the metaphysical tension of eros and avoids its sudden termination; for then a certain distance is kept and the identification producing the fetishism meets an obstacle.[40] Novalis added, "He who loves should always feel a lack and should always keep his wounds open."[41] Moreover, in medieval courtly love, the same awareness was incorporated in the seemingly paradoxical prohibition against attaining the desired woman. In fact, the courtly lover did not wish to attain this consummation; therefore, it was possible to love intensely a woman he had never seen, or one chosen precisely because there was little hope of possessing her. A foreboding of the disappointment that the actual woman by comparison to the "woman of the mind" might cause if possessed explains this. Klages rightly emphasized the importance of what he called the *Eros der Ferne* or eros linked to remoteness, to unattainability, which should be interpreted here as a favorable moment in every exercise of high erotic tension and not as the refuge of him who makes a virtue of necessity.[42]

But the ability to bear situations of this kind on a nonpathological level requires the refinement of eros and its displacement to a special realm that is no longer profane; this was precisely the case in medieval eroticism. Without such a displacement, the eros aroused in its elementary stage could only be an unquenchable and tormenting thirst. One could also consider here the changeover from the situation of a fatal passion to that of the type of Don Juan. Don Juan can be interpreted as symbolic of the desire that consumes one object after another owing to everlasting disappointment and the inability of any individual woman to provide the absolute. The lack of satisfaction is linked both to the fleeting pleasure of seduction and conquest and to the pleasure of doing evil. This is another aspect of the Don Juan archetype in some versions of the story. And so the series of Don Juan's loves continues in an endless search for absolute possession which always escapes him, just like the torture of Tantalus. His hope revives during the initial period of intoxication and seduction (which, by reaction to his intimate discomfiture, is also accompanied by a hidden loathing and by a need for destruction and defilement) but is disappointed again and leaves behind it an aversion after the attainment of what he took to be his true purpose, namely the mere pleasure of coitus. It is interesting that, contrary to other versions, in the oldest Spanish forms of the legend, Don Juan does not end by being damned and struck by lightning by the Commendatory but withdraws to a monastery. This reflects the ideal plane on which his frustrated quest could be appeased in the end; it could only be reached by means of a clean break between himself and the world of women.

Whether in the sphere of art and legend or in real life, a dramatic and tragic end for lovers seem inevitable. Even when the causes of such a tragedy seem external and extrinsic to the conscious will and human desire of the lovers and appear due to an unlucky destiny, it is the inner, transcendental logic of the situation that demands a tragic outcome. For as a poet has said: "But a thin veil divides love from death."

This is the case with Tristan and Isolde. If we wish to take the legend in its integrity, the theme of the love potion is far from being irrelevant or secondary. We have already noted that such potions are not mere fictions, for special mixtures can have the power of arousing the force of eros in its elementary state by neutralizing everything that could hinder or reduce its appearance in the empirical individual.[43] Should this happen, it awakens the love-death complex, the consuming force, the desire for death and annihilation.

The Wagnerian "O sweet death! So eagerly invoked! O death of love!" recalls a theme of "heroic love": "Dead, I live life in living death/Love has me dead,/Alas! of what a death/I who am without life or death."[44] The *music* of Wagner presents that state in a rather suggestive way (but the finale of the *Andrea Chénier* of Umberto Giordano is perhaps more musically authentic); however, the corresponding text is not so suggestive, being overcrowded with mystic and philosophic dross. The famous verses "*In des Weltatems/ wehendem All/versinken/ertrinken/unbewusst/höchste Lust*" (To sink and drown, unknowing, in the universe which throbs with the breath of the world is the greatest pleasure) give the impression of a breakdown with a pantheistic background (fusion with the "all," annihilation in the "divine, everlasting—original oblivion") rather than of a true transcendency; furthermore, the purely human element is prominent here because the desire for death is dictated by the idea of a beyond in which the absolute union of the two lovers can take place (Tristan says, "Thus we are dead to live only in love, inseparably, everlastingly joined without end, intent only on ourselves").[45] Instead, the effects of the potion in the medieval poem of Gottfried von Strasburg had already been expressed in more suitable words: "*Ihnen war ein Tod, ein Leben/eine Lust, ein Leid gegeben . . . /da wurden eins und einerlei/die zwiefalt waren erst*" (To them had been given a death, a life, joy, a song. . . . Then they who beforehand were two became one thing of the same kind).

In the case of Tristan and Isolde, mutual hatred is an antecedent to the extreme love passion that brings about their downfall. This is a situation often found; there are cases in which hatred secretly betrays the tension and sexual polarity of two individuals, ready to be expressed in the destructive short circuit of consuming love as soon as the obstacles created by the individual dispositions have been overcome.

Sensual Pleasure and Suffering: The Masochist-Sadist Complex

We have already noted that many ancient divinities of love were at the same time divinities of death. This fact can also be interpreted in a context different from that indicated earlier in this book. Love-desire negatively alters the transcendent individual metaphysically. Psychologically, too, it leads to self-destruction and suffering. It is an essential element not only in love-passion but in purely physical love as well, in the reduction of sensual pleasure to its minimum terms and to its rarest form.

Above all, it should be noted that the theme of death is not a simple element belonging to romantic literature; it is also found in the language of lovers all over the world: "I love you unto death," "I'll die without you," and so on. All of these reflect in differing degrees the ancient *cupio dissolvi* ("I long to die") as a liminal sense of experience. In his well-known poem "Amore e morte," Leopardi says that a "desire for death" is "the first effect of true and mighty love." It also occurs in the phenomenon of pleasure. After Metchnikoff, the school of Freud went on to confirm in the individual the existence of a *Todestrieb*, an urge toward death and destruction beyond the pleasure principle, which at first had exclusively occupied their attention. The biological explanation given for this urge toward death is not important,[46] just as the antagonism supposed to exist between it and the sexual urge must be rejected. Instead there remain varying proportions of a mixture of the two tendencies, the libido or pleasure element and the destructive tendency, a combination that constitutes a substratum common to the first and the second. The inscription on a fountain recorded by D'Annunzio (in the *Vergine delle rocce*) tells us how this matter had already been recognized by ancient lore: "*Spectarunt nuptas hic se Mors atque Voluptas—Unus (fama ferat), quem quo, vultus erat*" (Death and pleasure already saw themselves wedded, and their two faces made only one face). On a second level, this deals with the constant relationship existing between sexuality and pain.

In this respect it is not necessary to refer to facts that border on pathological abnormality. For instance, it would be banal to recall the similarities in moans, cries, and certain movements that the phenomenology of coitus and orgasm shares with that of suffering. We also know that, particularly among women, in love talk, the word "die" is used in many languages for the zenith of the spasm attained in full. (In Apuleius, *Met.*, II, 17, when asking Lucius to copulate with her, Photis says, "Make me die, thou who art about to die.") Moreover, the very word "spasm" refers specifically to suffering and physical pain. There is truth in the statement "Sensual pleasure is agony in the strictest meaning of the word."[47]

To see these facts in the correct light and to embody them into the general order of ideas we are dealing with, however, it is necessary to know the metaphysical aspect of suffering. Novalis wrote that in illnesses, there is a "transcendency" that includes an exalted feeling capable of translation into superior forces. More generally, that which has a negative character often contains a stimulus toward intensification of the positive.[48] In many cases this is undoubtedly true of the phenomenon of physical pain, if kept within given limits. Whatever its causes may be, from the internal point of view, every pain is a means by which individual consciousness experiences something that has a more or less destructive nature but, for that very reason, contains an impetus to transcendence as compared with the closed and stationary unity of the finite individual. Therefore, in a certain sense, what Wordsworth said is true, namely that suffering has the nature of the infinite.[49] The painful nature of pain is due to the passive character of the experience and to the identification of the ego, as if through fear, not with the force that alters its existential unity and carries it virtually beyond, but with that which undergoes the alteration; not with that which strikes but with that which is struck. If this were not so, we would have, as Novalis said, a change to positive forms of an exalted feeling.

This can also provide the key for understanding the use of physical pain as an ecstatic assistance, found in some deviated forms of asceticism. For example, the Rufai, an Islamic sect connected to dervish Sufism, inflict wounds on themselves during their frenzied rites. A sheikh declared that these wounds are made in a special state of mind such that they produce no pain but only "a kind of supreme happiness which is an exaltation of both the body and the soul." Such apparently savage practices should not be considered as such, but rather a means to open a door.[50]

Erotic sensual pleasure is a case of alteration wherein the passive nature is partly removed, and therefore the pain seems no longer to be just pain but to be mingled with pleasure. If the degree of activity in lovers were still higher, we would no longer speak of "sensual pleasure" but of a higher intoxication: that nonphysical intoxication that we have mentioned many times as the potential basis of all eros, an intoxication that, in this particular case, in the "spasm" and "death" of carnal love would not lose its quality nor be lessened but would, instead, reach its greatest intensity.

In considering the sensual pleasure-suffering complex, the libido mingled with the instinct of death and destruction, we are brought to the center of the phenomenology of transcendency presented by love in the same profane sphere. The secret of the ambivalence of the divinities of desire, sex, sensual pleasure, and, at the same time, death is revealed in its other aspect (for instance, Venus is Libitina; the Egyptian goddess of love, Hathor, is also Sekhmet, the goddess of death, and so on).

In this context, we must delve more deeply into a general fundamental element of erotic experience that forms the basis both of possession and of all strong desire. The desire for and possession of the loved one are what distinguish all sexual love from love in general as in benevolence or purely human love. The difference between the two is obvious. Pure love wants the real being of its object in a disinterested way: It affirms, it says yes ontologically to the other person as other person, as a separate being. Its model is the love of the Christian theistic God which gives existence to a free creature and desires it to live its own life without any tendency to dominate or absorb it. As against that, sexual love implies desire as a need to absorb or consume the loved being; and when possession does not have the deviated character, examined earlier, of compensation for the need of affirmation of self-worth, it has precisely that meaning.[51]

Therefore, we may speak of an ambivalence in every strong erotic impulse, because the being whom we love, we would at the same time like to destroy, to kill, to assimilate, to dissolve within us. For we feel that being to be our own complement, and we would like it to cease to be a separate being. Therefore, there is an element of cruelty attached to desire, and this element is often shown even in coitus itself.[52] We may therefore talk of "a hostile rapture of love" (Maeterlinck), of the "deadly hatred of the sexes," which is the basis of love and which, whether hidden or evident, persists in all its effects (D'Annunzio). It was Baudelaire who wrote: "Cruelty and sensual pleasure, exactly the same sensations, like extreme cold and extreme heat."[53] In fact, we can see, by derivation, in many species of animals as well, an instinct for destruction that comes into play at the same time as and mingles with the sexual urge. This instinct drives some animals so far as to slay the object of their pleasure during copulation, and this can happen in man in criminal cases of sadistic delirium. The following lines of Lucretius are significant in this respect:

Osculaque adfigunt, quia non est pura voluptas,
Et stimuli subsunt, qui instigant laedere id ipsum
Quodcumque est, rabies unde illaec germina surgunt.[54]

(And they plant kisses, but it is not a pure pleasure for there are goads within that incite them to hurt and to a frenzy from which the seeds arise.)

Spengler, who considers true love between man and woman to be an effect of polarity and an identical pulsation of a metaphysical nature, says it is akin to hatred and adds that "he who has no race does not know this dangerous love."[55] And it is very meaningful that in China the expression to indicate a person to whom one is irresistibly drawn by love means "predestined foe."

With regard to possession as a need to annihilate and absorb the loved being, psychoanalysis has spoken of an infantile oral phase and a cannibalistic phase of libido as complexes that will continue to act in the unconscious of adults and will establish relationships between the libido of the nutritive function (absorption and assimilation of foods) and that of sexual desire. The overstrained and artificial content of this concept ought not to stop us from acknowledging a legitimate analogy confirmed by more than one aspect of actual experience.

Bossuet wrote, "In the rapture of human love, who does not know that he is eating, is devouring his partner, that he would like to incorporate her in every possible way and even to take away with his teeth her whom he loves, so as to feed on her, to unite himself with her and to live as her?"[56] In Novalis the theme is the same, even though expressed at a higher level, when he links the mystery of love as an unquenchable thirst to that of the eucharist.[57] But the point that is almost never emphasized is that the food craved is also a food that destroys; within the absolute desire to destroy and to absorb is also contained the desire to be destroyed and dissolved. We seek in woman a "water of life" which is also a water that kills, a water of the kind that in alchemical symbolism is called corrosive water (which we shall deal with in its proper place). And such a condition is reached, above all, in the state of frenzy, in the orgasm and the climax, in what the Hindus call the *samarasa* of coitus.

Thus once again we have an ambivalence that arises from the potential nature of erotic transcendence in general. The suffering that can be linked to love and pleasure forces us to acknowledge a unique fact beyond the current opposition between sadism and masochism. On such a basis Schrenk-Notzing forged the expression "algolagnia," which—being formed from *álgos* (pain) and *lágnos* (to be aroused sexually)—is intended to designate pleasure obtained through sensual pain, but without distinguishing between an active algolagnia (sadism) and a negative or passive algolagnia (masochism). In the same way, the contemporary sexologists speak of one single sadomasochist complex which is not pertinent to sexual psychopathy alone because it appears with greater or lesser emphasis in other forms of sensuality as well. But in the metaphysics of sex, a refined viewpoint, we shall see that the opposite is true. It is commonly known that a masochistic predisposition is prevalent in woman, whereas a sadistic one is prevalent in man. But when we consider that state of identification and amalgamation of two human beings, without which sexual union is little more than a meeting for mutual masturbation, that antithesis is largely overcome. In reality, an erotic sadist would not be so if the suffering of his partner were completely extraneous to him, if it aroused no echo in him; instead, he identifies with the pain of his partner. Inhaling stimulates his own exalted pleasure. Therefore, he, too, is a masochist, for he satisfies at one and the same time his twofold need to suffer and to cause suffering, reducing the separation between subject and object. The same is true of a woman, who identifies with her partner's aggression in her masochistic intoxication.[58] This is largely a question of vicarious pleasure through suffering. In natural sexual sadism and masochism, that "exchange of imaginations" is acting which Chamfort examined in his definition of love: to feed reciprocally the tendential nature of self-transcendence. The latter effect is obvious in algolagnia whether it be active or passive; for in general, if pain is lived as pleasure, it is clearly no longer pain. Here, it is instead a matter of that transformation of pain into a sensation that is, in its own way, favorable and transcendent as we mentioned before.

We shall now indicate briefly what in the masochist-sadist complex belongs to psychopathology and perversion and what does not. The pathological fact occurs when sadistic or masochistic situations become necessary for the "normal" sexual process to take place. To give an example, it is unhealthy and perverted when a man can reach orgasm only by beating a woman. It is a different case, however, when sadism or masochism are magnifications of an element potentially present in the deepest essence of eros. Then the "pathological" cases represent not deviations of normal instinct but manifestations of the deepest layers of the normal instinct, which are latent in certain varieties of sexual love. This algolagnia is not exclusively sought by perverts but is used consciously by normal people to strengthen and extend, in a transcendental and perhaps ecstatic way, the possibilities of sex. And we shall see that, apart from individual cases, this situation exists in certain collective or ritual forms of mystic sensuality.

This background is useful in understanding the algolagnic potential for a woman in the loss of virginity. Because of most women's unconscious anguish and inhibitions and the carnal and impulsive primitive nature of the majority of men, some exceptional and irrevocable possibilities that the loss of virginity could provide women are wasted. Indeed, this female initiation to full sexual life, when carried out brutally, often leads to unfavorable repercussions and may even harm a woman's ability to achieve normal relations. Instead, we should think that if the state of intoxication were to be aroused in its acute form, which already contains a destructive element, the pain of the defloration together with all the subtle factors linked to it in terms of hyperphysical physiology might lead to a heightening of the ecstatic potential of that unique and unrepeatable moment. A trauma might even occur in the sense of an opening of individual consciousness to the supersensual.

It is obviously hard to gather actual documents. Only a few remnants allow us to conjecture that such a practice was at the basis of certain ancient forms of the ritual violation of virgins. More generally, procedures for the initiation of women are recorded in which the sexual act is the means for transmitting a transcendental influence; this has been said, for instance, about certain Islamic circles. Here initiation may be understood as the transmission of a spiritual influence (barakah) by the man. Görres expresses the true nature of this transmission as knowing by means of a higher light, acting and doing by means of a higher freedom, just as the normal knowing and doing are conditioned by the degree of light by the personal freedom given to every man.[59] The defloration of the virgin constitutes the best opportunity for this purpose.[60] In other cases it is possible to conceive that the whipping of the woman is used as an equivalent so as to produce the same liminal psychic climate. In this respect, too, practices continued secretly up to the present day in certain circles enable us to conjecture the same objective basis for ancient sexual rites also which are now misunderstood and have a bad reputation.[61]

Erotic Ecstasy and Mystic Ecstasy

We shall deal later with forms of sadism that have no specific sexual links. It is worth noting again the ability to convert painful sensations into sensual ones. For example, we must mention the typical historical case of Elisabeth of Genton, who through whipping was brought "into the condition of a bacchante in delirium,"[62] and also the case of the Carmelite nun Maria Maddalena dei Pazzi, who spoke of an inner fire which threatened to overwhelm her and whose eroticism is obvious from her cries while being whipped: "Enough, do not kindle anymore this fire which is consuming me. This is not the death I wish for, because it gives me too much joy and sensual pleasure." Moreover, lustful visions were appearing to her. The study of these borderlines where the factor of self-transcendence is forced rather than willed leads us to emphasize the points common to both mystic and erotic ecstasy. This commonality has been often underlined by psychologists and psychiatrists but always with the intention of denigrating some forms of religious experience and classifying them as erotic-hysterical deviations.

Objectively, we should acknowledge that these ecstasies often do have an impure and suspect nature and, except in certain cases, have little to do with true spirituality. Here we are in an intermediate sphere where an inversion may even happen, in the sense that the sexual element proper remains the fundamental one, the "mysticism" serving only to feed its deviant and exalted form.[63] In Christian mysticism this happens quite often. Just as it is characteristic of Christianity to humanize the divine rather than divinize the human, so in that mystical theology, making the sacred sensual (with a significant recurrence of conjugal and erotic symbols) takes the place of making sexuality sacred, as is done in Dionysiac, Tantric, and initiatory forms. Thus considered, the ecstatic facts of a given mystical theology may form a part of the phenomenology of transcendence proper to profane eros. The points of contact cited between "mystic" ecstasy and erotic ecstasy explain how, when these ecstasies reach a special intensity, "one of them may be the consequence of the other or else both may arise at the same moment."[64] This also clarifies the occurrence of strongly erotic images as "temptations" in the cases of the relapse of some mystics; they are forms of oscillation in the manifestations of one single energy. Typical, for example, are some of the expressions of Saint Girolamus, who in the most severe ascetic discipline and fasting felt his soul burning with desire and the heat of his lust blazing in his flesh "as though he were on a funeral pyre."

In many primitive peoples, the techniques to attain ecstasy are often essentially the same as those of some erotic rites. This is the case, first, for dancing, which has been, since the most ancient times and not only among primitive peoples, one of the most widely used methods to attain ecstasy. The sensual dances of today reflect this in a degraded form. Here we have a phenomenon with a tendential convergence of content in various forms of one single intoxication. In this phenomenon, however, we can recognize yet another sign of the virtual power of eros to carry man beyond the individual. In relation to this point, Rumi wrote: "He who knows the virtue of the dance lives in God because he knows how loves slays."[65] And this may also be said to be the key to the practices of the chain or school of Islamic mysticism that has continued down the centuries and that deems Rumi to be its master.

The Experience of Coitus

Writers have always recognized as important the sincerity that possesses lovers at the moment of sexual union. At that moment, all teasing, frivolity, meaningless gallantry, and sentimental trifling come to an end. The libertine and even the whore, unless completely anesthetized in the exercise of passive and apathetic service, are no exception to the rule. "When one is making love, one does not laugh; perhaps one may just smile. During the spasm one is as serious as death."[66] Every diversion ceases. Besides the sincerity, coitus implies a particularly high degree of concentration imposed on the lover by the very development of the process. For that reason any matter that might distract him could have an erotically or, even worse, a physiologically inhibiting effect. This is implied both emotionally and symbolically by the total giving of oneself to the other in coitus, even in the case of a casual union. This behavior, sincerity, and concentration are reflections of the deepest meaning of the act of love and its hidden mystery.

We said in the Introduction how hard it is to gather evidence pertaining to the experience of man and woman at the climax of coitus;

this difficulty is due not only to a natural reluctance to speak about it, but also to the fact that the peak of the orgasm often coincides with a state of reduced awareness and sometimes even with a break in the continuity of consciousness. And that is natural—just what we would expect during a state of partial but also sudden "transcendence" in the case of individuals whose normal consciousness is finite, empirical, and conditioned. Ordinary consciousness is hardly able to keep itself unimpaired at the highest point of coitus, whereas it can pass with full awareness over the threshold of sleep in which a similar change of state and break in level are realized. However, between the two cases there should be, in principle, a difference owing to the exaltation, the intoxication, the ecstasy that belong to an erotic state generally and that are absent during the passage to the state of sleep. Caused in the beginning by sexual magnetism, such an exaltation might support or constitute a favorable condition for the continuity of consciousness and therefore for a possible "opening." But it is hard to say when and to what extent that happens in profane love. The available documentation is insufficient for a scientific or objective examination. Strictly speaking, we should not restrict ourselves to the experiences of people of our own race or era. The inner experiences of peoples in other ages might not have been exactly the same as those of the modern European. In the matters that follow, we shall not overlook that material but shall include it and also make use of some erotic literature that confirms our empirical research.

The Upanishads[67] have mentioned ecstatic *raptus*, the ability to "suppress consciousness of both the outer and inner world" when "man is embraced by woman"; in a certain way this experience is analogous with what takes place at the manifestation of *atman* or the transcendental ego ("thus the soul, when it is embraced by the *atman*, which is knowledge itself, no longer sees inner or outer things"). When the hero of the novel *The Sorrows of Young Werther* says, "Thenceforward the sun, the moon and the stars can go forward on their path in peace, for I know not whether it be day or night, and the whole universe disappears before me," this may sound merely romantic, but in truth there is something more to it, because *raptus* is the reality of coitus confirmed in the Upanishads. At the beginning of orgasm, a change of state takes place—a further strengthing of the state that occurred tendentially at the time of falling love—and in an extreme case, during the spasm, the individual undergoes a traumatic experience of the power that "kills." This, however, passes through the individual instead of being held and absorbed.

Concerning the states that take place in the deepest structure of the individual, it is necessary to distinguish between the case of true union between man and woman based on the magnetism generated by their polarly differentiated beings, and the case of mere mutual masturbation, whose selfish purpose is the organic spasm, rather than true communication or mutual permeation. This occurs when the mere "search for pleasure" and the "principle of pleasure" overshadow the union, giving it an extrinsic character. In this case each of the two lovers is affected by a kind of impotence and only finds enjoyment for himself or herself. By overlooking the reality of his partner, the lover fails to reach contact with her intimate, subtle, and "psychic" substance, which alone can nourish a dissolving and propitiatory intensity of ecstasy. It is possible that in the Bible the expression "to know" a woman, where it is used as a symptom for possessing her, may refer to the contrary attitude in coitus. It is interesting that in the *Kamasutra* (II.x) a union with a woman of a lower caste is called "the copulation of the eunuchs" when it is made to last only until the man's pleasure has been fulfilled.

Interesting evidence is provided by a young woman who, during the sexual spasm, had the impression that she was "being transported, so to speak, into a higher realm . . . as at the beginning of narcosis brought about with chloroform."[68] Imagination has only an accessory role in descriptions such as the following which can be used as direct evidence: "He and she were now one single person. . . . He was no longer himself. He was the half of a new body; because of this, everything was so queer, up, up, up. A sudden blinding light flashed with a deafening noise which was not a noise at all; they were in a whirlpool of hues and shapes, cast into eternity; then there was a sudden shock and they fell down, down, down. He closed his eyes with fright, down, down, they would have gone on falling for ever, down, down" (L. Langley). The idea of a "deafening noise without any sound," in fact, is found in the phenomenology of initiatory consciousness, as is the sensation of falling. But it should be noted that this sensation often causes an instinctive jerk, when it occurs as we fall asleep and also during a phase—recalled by Baudelaire in his *Paradis artificiel*—in the experiences caused by hashish. A convergent thread is brought forward in the testimony of a person mortally wounded in an explosion, an experience leading to an actual "opening of the self" and "departing" as if death had suddenly occurred: "The explosion was so nearby that I did not even notice it; I might almost say that I was not aware of it. All of a sudden my normal outward awareness was cut off. I became clearly aware of falling ever further downwards with a motion which was speeded up outside of time. I felt that at the end of this fall, which did not make me afraid, some ultimate fact would be thrown wide open to me. Instead, the fall stopped all of a sudden. At the same moment I came back to myself and found that I was on the ground among wreckage, uprooted trees, and so on." These are typical feelings accompanying a change in the state or level of consciousness. The feeling described above agrees with the following one, whose second phase is interesting because of a reference to positive action on the part of the woman: "He seemed to fall headlong with her giddily as if in a lift whose steel cables had broken. From one moment to another, they could be shattered. Instead, they went on sinking endlessly and, when her arms encircled his neck, they were no longer falling headlong but dropping and rising at one and the same time beyond consciousness" (F. Thiess).

Another quotation also has value as evidence: "There are two bodies, then only one body; one body within the other, one life within the other life. There was only one need, one search, one penetration, down, down, always deeper, up, up, always higher, through the flesh, through the soft burning darkness, swelling and endless, without time" (J. Ramsay Ullman).

In connection with ever-deeper penetration and immersion into the woman's womb, several have described a feeling of union with a limitless substance, with an obscure "raw material." The dissolving intoxication of this experience can bring a person to the very ease of unconsciousness and, for some, even to the point of convulsive acceleration of the orgasm. We will see that the content of these not exceptional experiences, when they are stripped of the most superficial emotional circumstances, corresponds significantly with the elementary symbols aroused in the magical and initiatory use of coitus. The following quotation may also be of interest: "My heartbeat became faster and faster. Then I underwent a crisis which gave me the feeling of a voluptuous suffocation that, in the end, changed into an awful compulsion, during which I lost my senses and felt myself sinking" (J. J. Le Faner; a passage about a young woman).

At one point Novalis said that "woman is the supreme visible nourishment which forms the point for the passage from the body to the soul,"[69] and he noted that in the development of erotic experience two sets, in two opposite directions, converge. Starting with looking, talking, kissing, embracing, and so on up to coitus "are steps of a descending ladder by which the soul goes down" toward the body. But at the same time, said Novalis, there is another, ascending ladder by which the body goes up toward the soul. We can speak therefore of soul being made into body while the body is itself refined until an intermediate condition, neither of the soul nor of the body, is stabilized. This corresponds to the state of erotic intoxication. The removal of the boundary between soul and body comes about, then, through woman, leading to the integrating expansion of consciousness into profound areas normally shut off by the threshold of unconsciousness. The expression "to be united with life" now acquires a special importance.[70] In another passage Novalis wrote about the giddy light that can be compared to that of coitus, wherein "the soul and body touch each other" and begin a process of deep transformation. Though the physical use of women in profane love for this purpose is rare and fleeting, it is none the less real nor void of implication. We choose this passage from a writer for its significant indications: "Something mysterious happened within him, something which had never happened to him before. . . . It penetrated all his being as if a balsam mixed with a very strong wine, which made him drunk at once, had been poured into the marrow of his bones. As if in an intoxication, but without any impurity. . . . This feeling had neither beginning nor end and was so strong that his body followed it without any reference to his brain. . . . The bodies were not united but their life was. He had lost his own individuality. . . . He was transported into a state of which he could not even grasp the duration. No language has been invented to describe that supreme moment of existence, whence it was possible to see the whole of life, naked and understandable. . . . Then they descended again" (Liam O'Flaherty).

From another point of view, the idea that the free power of sex in coitus can act in a purifying and cathartic manner belongs to Dionysiac rites and all other kindred types. But certain moments of profane love may also be compared to those rites. Lawrence certainly cannot be called an initiate, but he was neither theorizing nor merely producing literature when he made one of his characters say, "He felt he had touched the most savage state of his nature. . . . How poets and all the others tell lies! They make you believe that they need sentiment, whereas the thing which they need more is that acute, destructive, tremendous sensuality . . . sensuality without phrases, pure, burning sensuality is necessary also to purify and enlighten the spirit." We have already noted that, in general, the same writer stops at a deviated mysticism of the flesh, and the phrases given above refer to a healing experience which, for a sexually deviated type—which corresponds to the vast majority of modern Anglo-Saxons—may represent a use of sex without curbs or inhibitions. Nonetheless we also have here evidence of a purification, a removal or neutralization of everything that in the life of the outer, social individual creates a barrier and hinders any contact with the deeper layers of being, even when a real transfiguring element is lacking. Therefore it is right to speak of simple "sensuality," as in fact Lawrence does. Of course, in circumstances of this kind the positive aspects are random and few, being never valued properly by their subject, and for this reason they also remain incapable of any further development or cultivation. But the ambiguity of Lawrence is that of a "pagan" religion of the flesh. Spengler saw correctly that the Dionysiac orgy considers the body as its enemy, just as ascetic practices do; and Jules Romain was right when he wrote about the "blind destruction of the flesh by means of the flesh."

In the direct evidence provided by certain lovers, we quite often find situations that recall what we said earlier about the hebephrenic case reported by Marro. Accounts of trying to prolong the sexual spasm beyond a given limit by persistent stimulating procedures speak of the unbearable feeling of a power—"like that of electricity" —which rises from the kidneys and runs along the backbone with a tendency to go upward. At this stage in most instances the experience ceases to be desirable and seems to have only a physical and painful character; one cannot bear it, and so one stops.[71] Such cases are the consequences of an inner behavior that permits nothing but physical perceptions. It is as if, at a given stage, an exclusively physical circuit replaces the psychic circuit of exalted sexual intoxication, giving rise to a deterioration in the process, as only negative sensations reach the threshold of consciousness. But behind this, perhaps, lies a phenomenology of tentative forms of the awakening of the kundalini, the supreme fundamental power to which Tantric yoga is oriented. These same forms can also appear at random during sexual union. And "the quivering, the quick devouring fire more rapid than lightning" of J. J. Rousseau is another instance of this experience. Evocatory and stimulating signs for the awakening of the fundamental power are also contained in the customs of some non-European traditions—for example, in the so-called belly dance, when performed by a woman with its true erotic background. Here we have gone outside the area of merely profane eros because this dance, of which the West has only a banal "restaurant" idea, has a sacred and traditional character. It is made up of three moments, each distinguished by the height of the arms' movements and by the expressions of the face, which correspond to three periods in the life of woman, the potential awakener of the fundamental power in coitus, and it is that time that the typical basic, rhythmic movement of the belly and loins appears. This testimony by a person (G. de Giorgio) who attended an authentic performance of this dance is of interest: "I attended a *real* belly dance, performed by an Arab woman with squatting Arabs syncopating the rhythm; I was the only European. It was unforgettable. This dance, being sacred, of course, is an uncoiling of the kundalini, with an escape from above. It is terrific from a symbolical point of view, for it is the woman who performs it and she suffers almost as much (the real dance is very difficult) as in childbirth, and it *is* childbirth; but the most beautiful and overwhelming thing is that the woman herself accompanies it with a song; songs which transport you and emphasize the escape, the cycle of articulation, the ascensional deification, the passage from ring to ring from the first to the final center."[72] If ethnological data were not gathered by incompetent people who operate with the same spirit as stamp collectors, evidence of this kind could be built up and "civilized" people would most likely find reason to be ashamed of themselves in ascertaining to what dimension their love life is in general reduced.

In the medical field, cases have been witnessed in which women, at the peak of orgasm, swoon or fall into a semicataleptic condition that can last for some hours. Cases of this kind were mentioned by Mantegazza in the eighteenth century of his *Fisiologia della donna*, whereas they are given in the treatises of Hindu erotics as normal and natural in certain types of women.[73] Some fatal consequences due to these symptoms are mentioned by D'Aurevilly in his novel *Le Rideau cramoisi*. This is not a question of hysterical facts—a generic expression which explains nothing and often only replaces one problem with another—but of phenomena that can be readily understood within the metaphysics of sex. But where there is no break of consciousness, often certain states that accompany "pleasure" and seem to be successive repercussions of the peak of the orgasm are themselves indicative enough. They are states that the following passage describes quite well: "Sometimes when between his arms, she was taken by a kind of almost far-sighted sluggishness, in which she believed she was becoming, by transfusion of another life, a transparent, fluid creature permeated by a very pure, immaterial element" (D'Annunzio, *Il Placere*). Balzac referred to a like sensation with a greater, literary and idealizing margin: "When, lost in the infinite of a swooning, my soul was separated from my body and hovered far from the earth, I used to think that those pleasures were a means to eliminate matter and to release the spirit to make its lofty flight." In actual fact a kind of lucid trance, alongside a condition of physical weariness, is common enough in lovers after coitus. Possibly it is a diffused echo of the change of state that has objectively taken place at the peak of coitus even when not perceived as such: a last thin resonance. Usually the subtle, hyperphysical element of this echo, however, is soon neutralized because either the person comes back to his sense or that element is altered by feelings of simple, human, amorous nearness.

The Metaphysics of Modesty

"He sunk in that abyss of pleasure from which love rises to the surface, pale, silent, full of a deathly sadness" (Colette). If situations like those discussed in the last section are contrasted with the depressed one described by Colette or in the well-known saying "*Animal post coitum triste*" (An animal is sad after coitus), the explanation is given by that very saying itself inasmuch as it refers precisely to animals, that is, to a human love more or less *more ferarum* (according to the customs of wild beasts). In particular, these negative or depressed states follow false unions, those occasions when one or both partners seek their own pleasure. In effect, these depressed states are very like those that tend to follow masturbation.

However, a different explanation is also possible, although it takes us outside the most immediate experience of individual consciousness and cannot be applied to the vast majority of cases. It is not the explanation given by Christian ethics which starts off with a theological hatred of sex and finds in the depression, sadness, and even disgust after "pleasure" direct evidence of its sinful nature. Certainly a confused feeling of guilt may enter into the matter, but it would be on a transcendental and not a moral plane. In this, we presuppose the existence of an ascetic predisposition, a tendency toward separation in the depths of consciousness. This concerns men almost exclusively; women very seldom feel sad or depressed after participating willingly in lovemaking; in fact the opposite is rather the case unless extrinsic, social, or other factors (such as unconscious inhibitions) are involved.

This possibility should be examined, since other manifestations that are also symptomatic of erotic behavior, among them the phenomenon of modesty, seem to lead us to the same point. To tackle this problem, we must return again to the dual character, positive and negative, of eros that we examined at the end of the previous chapter. Indeed, in this chapter we have directed our attention to those phenomena of a *positive* transcendence—delineating the metaphysics of sex via the myth of the hermaphrodite—which may figure in profane eroticism itself. But we should also consider the other possibility indicated by the myth of Pandora, namely eros as mere extroverted desire that leads to procreation and, in satisfying itself, does not suppress its existential privation but rather confirms it and perpetuates it by leading beyond the illusory "immortality of the species," not to life but to death. Since for most men and women, profane love terminates by feeding the circle of procreation, we should consider the following problem: Does man seek woman because he feels privation in himself, or does the presence of woman and her action create the privation by causing an inner yielding, drawing him out of himself, awakening in him the condition of desire and lust? We must decide, as did Kierkegaard,[74] between scenarios:

Before meeting woman, man mistakes himself for whole and sufficient. Afterward, he finds he needs her and becomes aware that he is incomplete; or is it the encounter with woman that makes him extroverted, propelling him from his proper center and harming him?

This is a complex problem. Its solution differs from one case to another, while the evaluation differs according to the point of reference. Whether he feels it or not, privation is consubstantial with the finite individual; thus the restriction of his ego cannot be deemed a value, whereas transcendence embodies a value; whence arises the order of ideas emphasized in this chapter, where we have discussed the positive aspects of erotic experience. But if we consider all the circumstances in which self-transcendence does not in any way allow for an ascent or an integration or lead to the rediscovery of Self, then in the fact of yielding to the lust for a woman one can see a fall and an alteration of the innermost being or almost betrayal of a higher vocation. Apprehension of these, even if only in a confused way, will often steer man away from the search for self-realization through the mystery of sex due to the problems inherent in this path. In this case the power and destructive charm possessed by woman, the deceitful ecstasy interposed by the intimate feminine substance may appear to be deadly, hostile, and contaminating. Without going so far as the "*Foemina janua diabuli*" (Woman is the door to the devil) of Tertullian, such as the dominating point of view in ascetic and initiatory circles. It is summarized by the biblical saying "Give not power over thy soul unto woman" (Prov. 31:3).

As indicated, the presupposition for inner reactions of such a kind is some rudimentary activation or awareness in the individual of what would be called in the Orient the extrasamsaric element, the transcendent virility, or, more simply still, the supernatural principle of the human personality. In the mass such an awareness constitutes an exceptional phenomenon. However, there exist behaviors that should be explained according to an obscure, residual shadow of that awareness.

It is in this context that we may deal briefly with the problem of modesty, but first of all we should make some distinctions. There are some general forms of modesty that have no specific relation to sex: for instance, modesty as regards certain physiological functions (defecation, urination) in addition to modesty in general concerning one's own nakedness. Some people believe that such modesty is not inborn and they cite the fact that neither babies nor certain primitive peoples show this modesty. But here we are falling into the usual mistake of deeming "natural" in man that which is merely primitive. The truth is that humanity has certain dispositions that are consubstantial with its "idea," and those dispositions may remain latent in the primitive stages and only show themselves in an adequately developed humanity when an appropriate environment is formed, which might be called civilized. In such a case we should not talk of an "acquired" sentiment but of a passage from the capability to the actuality of preexisting dispositions. In fact, it is possible to see in more than one instance that the more noble the human faculty, the slower its development.

In its more general and nonsexual aspect, the phenomenon of modesty arises from a subconscious impulse in man to put a certain distance between himself and "nature." The definition of modesty given by Melinaud is partly right, namely a shame that we feel because of the animal in us. Thus we should not expect this instinct to show itself in prepersonal stages (babies) or involuted stages (savages), for that higher principle or dimension of the ego which can bring about such impulses is either wholly latent or eclipsed.

Let us now pass on to modesty in those forms linked to sexuality. First we will consider a possible meaning of modesty related to nakedness, one different from that given just now; next we will examine modesty specifically linked to the sexual organs; and third we will examine modesty connected with the sexual act. As regards the first two, we must make a very clear distinction between male and female modesty. The deep, metaphysical significance related to the modesty of woman is generally disputed. Her modesty, just like her shyness, "bashfulness," and "innocence," is a simple ingredient of her sexually attractive quality and can be included among the tertiary characteristics of her sex. However, we shall come back to this point in the next chapter. Such an aspect of "functional" usage is, on the contrary, foreign to male modesty. Counterevidence for female modesty as a nonethical but sexual fact is that, as is well known, modesty relating to their own nakedness ends altogether when women meet each other and makes way for pleasure in exhibitionism (unless there is some inferiority complex or fear of having a less beautiful and less desirable body than the other woman) whereas it persists among man (here we leave aside what belongs to phases of a civilization that have become primitive, such as the present phase). Owing to its functional character, female modesty has, next, a psychological and symbolic meaning from which arise the variety and mutability of its main object. We know that until a very short time ago the greatest object of sexual modesty among Arab and Persian women was the mouth, so much so that, if a girl had been surprised by a man when she had only a shirt on her back, she would have used it at once to cover her mouth without worrying about showing much more intimate parts. For Chinese women, the feet were a special object of modesty, and they seldom were willing to show them even to their own husbands. Indeed, we could give other queer localities as the object of modesty, depending on the peoples and epochs. It is a fact that in this context a given part of the body has only symbolic values and to show that part and not to hide it has the implicit meaning of opening oneself. Because of the symbolic functional nature of modesty, whereby the part represents the real and most intimate being itself, we can understand the variability of its object although it would be more natural for modesty to reside in the sexual parts of the female body. This idea, indeed, is reflected in Latin expressions like "to taste" or "to use the *pudicitia*" (modesty) of a woman, which are synonymous with taking away her virginity or with her utmost erotic surrender.

The sexually functional nature of female modesty, often mistaken for having an ethical and independent character, is clearly shown by the fact that a woman displays modesty when male attention is attracted to some part of her naked body that may indeed be less than what she might proudly display in public without a shade of hesitation; for instance, she would be ashamed to show her panties by raising her dress, whereas she will display herself with shameless, animal innocence in the latest bikini. One cannot deduce a lack of modesty from revealing clothing, for special forms of modesty have been witnessed among people who go about naked or almost naked; in the same way the presence of modesty should not be inferred from the presence of clothes since the fact that a person is covered is in no way a guarantee for the presence of true bashfulness.[75] Often women use clothes only to produce a more exciting effect by hinting at what their nakedness could offer. Montaigne said that "there are things which we hide only to show them better."

We should look in a different light at the fact that throughout almost the whole world the idea of the genital organs is connected with shame (the *pudenda*, the *putende*, *les parties honteuses*, etc.). And this also extends to lovemaking, for lovers normally show modesty not only in physical union, but also in much less intimate activities. Vico went so far as to link the feeling of being seen by a god to the shame that in primordial times drove human couples to hide when copulating. Some remarks of Schopenhauer deserve attention. He asked why it is that people in love exchange their first glances, full of desire, in a hidden way and almost fearfully, and why they hide during intimacy and in the act of union, just as if caught in a misdeed. Schopenhauer remarked that this would remain incomprehensible unless the obscure, transcendental feelings of guilt or betrayal were inherent in the abandonment of sexual love; but this is inadquate for it would reduce life to nothing but misery, and since, according to Schopenhauer, the final purpose of eros is procreation, lovers would naturally be ashamed and feel guilty when they obey the procreative instinct, which is destined to perpetuate the pain and distress of the world in new beings. "If optimism were right and our existence was the gift of heavenly goodness enlightened with knowledge and therefore a precious, glorious, joyous thing, to be received with thankfulness, then the act which perpetuates that existence would have a totally different physiognomy.[76] But this is rather unconvincing. Indeed, Schopenhauer's pessimism is the product of a merely personal philosophy; the phenomena that he refers to also occur in civilizations free of pessimism and far from dualistic conceptions such as the Christian antithesis between "flesh" and spirit. Schopenhauer rightly emphasized an independent existential fact, from which derive the various pedantic and theological condemnations of sexual relations that still persist, though devoid of any deep significance. This is the ambivalence of eros which seduces us with its alluring intoxication that can surmount our finite, broken individuality, yet also poses the risk of a fall and betrayal of a higher vocation. The cause of this fall and betrayal is the illusory and uncertain nature of immediate sexual satisfaction and of everything from the value of children to the social and sentimental accouterments of love and sexual relationships which substitutes for or postpones the realization of absolute being. Last, at least in man, if not in woman, there may be an obscure premonition of the wound that desire inflicts on the supernatural principle of his innermost being whenever the poison is not transmuted into a medicine and liberating ecstasy is not derived from the adulteration. Such behavior is not associated with an idea or a concept of reflective consciousness. The symptoms of sexual modesty and the other facts mentioned above occur even among the most ordinary humanity like distant shadows of the reality of sexual metaphysics. Incomprehensible within the framework of a biological and naturalistic concept of the human being,[77] these facts have been almost ignored by the social sciences. We deem artificial the psychoanalytic interpretations of primitive sexual taboos and archaic complexes of the subconscious. The only deeper interpretation is that of Schopenhauer, who, as we have already seen, brought into play an obscure transcendental feeling of guilt; but here the reference to the idea that "life is pain" is as inadequate as the popular interpretation of Buddhism (shared by Schopenhauer himself), according to which it is the pain of existence that gives birth to the urge toward realization of samadhi—enlightenment—and nirvana.

The Meaning of the Orgy
Apart from cases of natural regression (as in certain modern and almost chaste forms of feminine lack of inhibition) or of licentious breakdown, one of the few contexts wherein eros is seen in a naked form, free of inhibition, is the collective, orgiastic rites and festivals; these are experiences, however, that take us outside the phenomenology of profane love and sexuality. On the basis of what we said before, it seems natural that the unconscious "guilt complex" linked to sex should disappear because here the oscillation of eros is resolved in a sacred manner, corresponding to the positive dimension of eros and opposed to the mere lust of the individual. Even the most primitive peoples feel repugnance toward an open and public performance of the sexual act, whereas such a feeling does not exist when that act takes place within a cultural background. Besides the ritual nakedness, a woman also performed the act called *anasúrma* in ancient Greece, in which, following a divine paradigm, she removed her clothes and revealed the most intimate part of her body, thus demonstrating how the "functional modesty" of woman can disappear altogether when a sacred situation is involved.

A reference to the metaphysics of the orgy may be timely at this point, where we are passing from the phenomenology of profane love to that of sacred, the subject of the next chapters. In effect, orgiastic forms represent something intermediate; the individual conditional qualities of eros are surpassed in them, but at the same time copulation does lead to insemination and the possibility of fertilization. However, according to the available information, fewer cases of fecundation occurred during these sacred collective orgies than would be normally expected, as though the sexual power were oriented from within in a different direction.

The most immediate and obvious purpose of orgiastic promiscuity is the neutralization and exclusion of anything concerning the "social individual." In the field of ethnology the idea of promiscuity as a "naturalistic" original stage has been largely surpassed.[78] In actual fact, promiscuity, even among savages, seems almost always restricted to special occasions linked to a ritual element. Whether they are orgies of primitive and outlandish peoples or kindred festivals of Western antiquity, the common denominator is the temporary removal of all prohibitions, all differences of social status, and all bonds that normally hinder the manifestation of eros in its elementary form. In principle, the practice of promiscuity excludes not only the conditional qualities of the social individual but even qualities of the deeper layer of the individual as a personality. It tends, therefore, to bring out an almost total freedom.

Some of these archaic festivals had a seasonal character that resulted in one-sided interpretations by ethnologists who did note that the forms that they studied were already decadent. Whether or not specific "magical" intentions were present (fecundity and fertility rites, etc.), the essential purpose of the timings of such festivals must be sought in cosmic-analogical relations. Thus the emperor Julian remembered that the date of the summer solstice was chosen for celebration because at that time the sun seems to be freed from its orbit and lost in the infinite. This cosmic background and "climate" are appropriate to a kindred tendency toward orgiastic and Dionysiac freedom. The Roman name for a festival that, except for popular license, kept partial but unmistakable features of an orgy as well was the Saturnalia. It is also meaningful from another standpoint. According to the popular interpretation, this festival celebrated a temporary return to the primordial age when Saturn-Chronos had been kind and there were no laws nor social distinctions between men. This is the exoteric interpretation of a more profound idea; it recalled a mythical past in temporal and historical terms and the participation in a state beyond time and history. Man's truest end purpose, which is to surpass in his inner being the form and limit of the individual, was presented in terms of an abolition of social distinctions and prohibitions.

Taken overall, the orgiastic festivals, upheld by holy institutional structures and in a climate suitable for collective action, tended, therefore, toward catharsis and cleansing of the mind, toward neutralizing all the layers of empirical consciousness by sexuality. We said before that this could also be brought about in cases of strong profane eros in individual unions. The term used just now, "cleansing," on the other hand, enables us to establish further symbolic associations. In fact, in traditional symbolism, the Waters have represented the undifferentiated substance of all life, that is, life in the state prior to any form and therefore free from all the limitations of individual existence. On this basis, in the rites of many traditions, "immersion in the waters has symbolized regression to the preformal, total regeneration and a new birth, since immersion is equivalent to a dissolution of forms and to a reintegration into the undifferentiated way of preexistence."[79] The Waters thus represent the element that "purifies" and, in religious and exoteric terms, "washes away sin" and regenerates; the meaning of various rites of lustration has been preserved in the Christian sacrament of baptism as well.

To anticipate the category of ideas that we shall deal with in the next chapter, we should observe next that the Waters and the deified female principle in terms of a Goddess or Mother seem to be closely linked to each other in traditional symbolism; the archaic sign of the

Waters ∇ is the same as that of the Woman and Goddess or Great Mother and is a simple outline of the shape of the female pubis and vulva. We may say that this serves to establish the fundamental character of the orgies, which is a liberating regression into formlessness carried out under the feminine sign. To bring forward facts of a slightly different nature, it may be interesting to note the connections between the Waters and the Apsarases, "heavenly courtesans" who incarnate in order to seduce the Hindu ascetics. Born from the waters, they have a name formed from *ap* (water) and *sara*, whose root is *sri*, meaning "to run" (here is the sense of "to glide" or "to flow"). We should also remember the ancient licentious Syrian festival of the Waters, Maitumas, where women showed themselves naked in the water, thus provoking rapture in the participants. It is best to keep in mind this particular point, which is not highlighted by the writer we have just quoted; nis interpretation is, however, quite suitable in other respects, provided that, for the moment, we leave aside what he has written about the magical and no longer merely inner aspect of the orgiastic experience (we shall say something about this other aspect later on): "Directly linked to the beliefs in cyclic regeneration, which is represented in the agrarian ceremonial, are numerous rituals in the orgy, in the dazzling re-creation of the primordial chaos, in the reintegration of the undifferentiated unity of times before the creation." Eliade[80] wrote, "Like the immersion in the waters, the orgy annuls the creation and, at the same time, regenerates it; by identifying himself with the undifferentiated, precosmic totality, man hopes to return to himself restored and renewed; in a word, he hopes to become a "new man.""[81]

In the significance of a cosmic-pantheistic opening that the orgy may cause the individual to experience, we may see again the positive and negative ambivalence of eros. In fact, such experiences are found in the ecstatic liberations proper to the mysteries of Woman and the Mother, to which we can oppose the purpose of the initiatic ceremonies celebrated under the Uranus-virile sign. The contact with the Waters or with the formless can have a dual outcome if we consider correctly the supernatural nucleus of the personality; it may equally loosen or dissolve that nucleus. This was seen to a certain extent by Eliade when he recalled the saying of Heraclitus (fr. 68), "For souls it is death to become water," which corresponds to an Orphic fragment, "For the soul, water is death" (*Clem.*, VI, II, 17, I).[82] These sayings are justified in relation to the solar ideal, to the "dry way" of Uranian liberation and the absolute detachment from the cycle of generation, whose substance and nourishment are the wet principle in the special aspect of the symbolism we have already discussed. For this reason, traditions have differentiated the symbolism of the Waters: The lower Waters have been set against the upper Waters. This theme appears in the Bible itself, and Giordano Bruno said, "There are two kinds of waters; the lower waters below the firmament which blind men, and the upper waters above the firmament which enlighten."[83] We shall not state our opinion regarding this point, but restrict ourselves to confirming in the orgy an intermediate form, which allows the removal of individual conditional qualities and the appearance of the transcendental moment within a holy background, the same twofold aspect found in human love.

Appendix

Marquis de Sade and the "Way of the Left Hand"

In speaking of sadism, we made the distinction between deviant sadism, a need in some neurotic or tainted individuals for cruelty as a special psychic aphrodisiac necessary to attain sexual satisfaction, and sadism understood as a natural element in eros that can be specially aroused so as to take the possibilities beyond the usual limits.

However, we must make two other distinctions. First, it is necessary to distinguish between sadism with a sexual background and sadism in the broad sense wherein the link with sex and woman may be absent or only figure in a subordinate way, and the essence of which is pleasure through cruelty, evil, and destruction per se in every form. The genetic deduction of this second type of sadism from the first, a natural sexual element, is in vogue in some psychologies and above all in psychoanalysis but must be deemed absolutely without foundation. Moreover, sadism in the general sense is part of a bigger and more important category that embraces phenomena that are quite complex and must be defined, ultimately, with an elementary existential orientation. However, to clarify this point we must make yet another distinction: we must oppose those experiences that, however liminal and problematic, still retain a genuine character, to the artificiality that marks what we call perversion. It is perversion when one feels pleasure in carrying out acts simply because they are forbidden or because, according to a given code of ethics, they are deemed to be "evil" or "sinful." Sadism can have this hue. Baudelaire's words express this attitude: "The unique and supreme sensual pleasure of love consists in the certainty of doing evil; and man and woman have known since the time of their birth that all sensual pleasure arises from evil."[84] Everything "depraved" that is displayed by so-called nineteenth-century decadents (Byron in part, then Baudelaire, Barbey d'Aurevilly, Oscar Wilde, Villier de l'Isle-Adam, Swinburne, Mirbeau, etc.) has this artificial character; it is merely literature and intellectuality. They are almost like children, who feel pleasure in doing something only because it represents the "forbidden" and because the act has the character of a transgression. However, this behavior may be an aphrodisiac for some people, and Anatole France, referring to a similar order of ideas, was right when he said, "By considering it a sin, Christianity has done a lot for love." The blasphemous scenario of the black Mass and Satanism, as a minute public has come to know it through works such as those of Huysmans, is part of this picture. It is indeed the picture of decadence. We must now determine, at this level, sadism taken in the general sense mentioned earlier. For this purpose we shall refer precisely to the man who gave his name to this tendency, namely the "divine Marquis," Alphonse François de Sade (1740 – 1814).

In considering this personality, more than one trait may cause us to think that his sadism had mainly the character of a simple intellectual perversion. It is true that, notwithstanding his social position, de Sade more than once submitted to the severity of the law and was compelled to leave France for a certain time, but what could be imputed to him was very far from all the dreadful things described in his books. Furthermore, though living through the Reign of Terror of the French Revolution, he in no way took advantage of the outstanding chances that such a time offered to a person greedy for blood and cruelty; on the contrary, he exposed himself to serious risks so as to save some friends and his own in-laws from the guillotine. The two main loves in his life were wholly normal: his wife, from whom he became separated (but not because of sadistic abuses), and, thereafter, his wife's sister, with whom he then lived. His "sadism," therefore, was essentially cerebral or, rather, imaginary; he limited himself to the stories in the works he wrote, as if for mental compensation, in his solitary life in prison and in the asylum of Charenton, where Bonaparte is said to have incarcerated him, although he was basically of sound mind, not for actual acts of cruel perversity but because Bonaparte would not forgive him for certain slanderous allusions he made in one of his pamphlets. There were many women who loved him and tried to persuade Napoleon to free "the poor Marquis."[85]

Even an analysis of de Sade's works does not provide a background that is wholly of one character. French writers who have recently re-evaluated his works have tended to see him, above all, as the champion of the "natural man" or "real man," that is, of the man who in spite of everything shows what he is really like in the wholeness of his instincts; this picture puts him on a rather insipid plane.

Moreover, there are signs in him of strange moralizing residues. It is not explained, for example, how de Sade could more than once have used the word "infamy" to describe the wicked actions committed by one or another of his characters. Then, if we read that romanticized account of things that actually happened, *La Marquise de Gange*, not only do we find a description of the sacrament of confession and of penitence which is worthy of inclusion in a religious handbook, but we also witness a moralism that goes so far as to falsify the truth of the facts by stating that one of the guilty persons was struck by divine punishment, whereas in fact, that very same person actually escaped justice and lived happily until he died.

Therefore, we must, in a way, "isolate" a given line of thought in de Sade's writings if we wish to obtain a general view of life useful as a philosophical basis and justification for "sadism." The question here is the idea that the predominant force in the world is that of "evil," of destruction and of misdeeds. De Sade admits that a God exists who is the creator and ruler of the world, but he is a wicked God, a God who has "evil" for his essence and takes pleasure in villainy, misdeeds, and destruction, which he uses as essential elements for his designs.[86] Therefore, the excess of the negative over the positive would seem to be the law of reality; nature shows us that she only creates so as to destroy and that destruction is the first of her laws.[87] But as soon as this is recognized, an inversion of all values follows; the negative and destructive element must have as much value as the positive element, for it conforms not only to nature but also to the divine will and to universal order (or, rather, to disorder); and he who instead follows the path of virtue, harmony, and good should be considered on the side of God's foes.

Another logical consequence is that, by conforming to the predominant cosmic forces, vice and misdeeds will always be victorious, happy, rewarded, and sublime, whereas virtue will always be frustrated, punished, wretched, and marked by a fundamental impotence.[88] To this is added the sadistic theme in an actual sense, the sensual pleasure and ecstasy linked to destruction, cruelty, and violation. "To doubt that man's greatest happiness on earth is irrevocably linked to misdeeds is, in truth, just like doubting that the sun is the prime cause of growth," wrote de Sade;[89] and he added, "Oh, what a voluptuous act is the act of destruction. There is no ecstasy like that which one savors when giving way to this divine infamy!"[90] The pleasure in a destructive act intended to violate the very laws of cosmic nature[91] is linked to and foreshadows the theory of the superman. "We are gods," exclaimed one of the characters in his romances.

If situations of sexual sadism predominate in his works, such sadism becomes ideally a mere episode compared with this general concept, which seems to be a deviation only if it is considered on its own and which ceases to be so if it is stripped of its perverse ornamentation and related to a broader horizon. The perverse side in de Sade lies in everything that is pleasure because of transgression or evil as such; and that implies, among other things, an open contradiction, if we examine the central idea of his philosophy. In fact, speaking about and feeling certain acts to be evil and transgressions have meaning only if we presuppose a positive order and a recognized law, whereas, as we have seen, such an order and law have no existence in de Sade's opinion insofar as evil constitutes the essence of God and nature. And so what Praz[92] noted in this respect is right, namely that, wishing to enjoy the pleasure of transgressing and doing violence to that which exists, the sadist's only possible choice is to practice goodness and virtue precisely because they signify antinature and anti-God, rebellion and violence against which, according to de Sade's premise, should constitute the final end of creation, namely wickedness. In fact, all Satanism, as such, presupposes an intimate, unconscious acknowledgement of the sacredness and law that it violates; and therefore it can be sadism only in a very refined sense, like the pleasure in violating, by acting in a given way, something that *in one's own conscience* one would oppose. There is an essential difference between carrying out an act because it is deemed to be evil or a sin (just as other persons, for the same reason, would instead not carry it out) and carrying it out because it is not felt to be evil or a sin. He who acts positively and not polemically would never speak about "evil" or "sin" or transgression; he could not find within himself any point of reference to give meaning to such words. Only a person who identifies himself with one of the forces working in the world could speak of those things.[93]

We should indicate at this stage the possibility of rather diverse horizons for experiences of this kind, and we shall do this by taking up again what we mentioned about the metaphysics of pain. De Sade was not the first person to emphasize the meaning and extent of the destructive element in the world. His ideas have a specific character only because he obtains the basis for a sort of counterreligion from the destructive element, and because of his one-sidedness and "perversity." In a complete concept three aspects are distinguished and confirmed in creation: the power that creates, the power that preserves, and the power that destroys, and these three correspond to the well-known Hindu triad, Brahma, Vishnu, and Shiva. In abstract theological terms, the same division into three is found in the Western idea of the Divinity in his threefold function of creating, preserving, and taking back to himself what he has created. But from a certain aspect or rather from the dynamic and immanent side the "taking back to himself" can also be equivalent to destroying, to Shiva's function, if we recognize in the Divinity the infinite, that which in its essence transcends all form, all law, and all finiteness. On this basis is defined the so-called "Way of the Left Hand," the Tantric *vamachara*.[94] Both the western pre-Orphic worship of Dionysus and the religion of Zagreus as the "Great Hunter who overthrows everything," and the Eastern worship of Shiva and Kali, Durga, and other "fearful" divinities, are equally characterized by the acknowledgement and glorification of destruction, violation, and incitement: they admit expression of a liberating frenzy, very often strictly linked to orgiastic experience in a ritual, sacrificial, and transfiguring framework, without connotation of sacrilege as in de Sade.

In the Bhagavad-Gita, the background of the Way of the Left Hand is given in strictly metaphysical and theological terms. It tells us that the Divinity in his supreme form (in the "universal form" that is revealed for an instant to the warrior Arjuna as a special privilege) can only be the infinite, and that the infinite can only represent the crisis, the destruction, and the breaking of everything that has a finite, conditioned, mortal character, rather like a voltage that is too high and burns out the circuit through which it passes. At this level, time, understood as the force that alters and destroys, is said to embody in a certain way this transcendent aspect of the divinity. The outcome, therefore, is that just at the moment of every destructive crisis the supreme reality can appear, the terrifying greatness which transcends all manifestation. The Bhagavad-Gita adopts this view not to justify evil or perversity, but to metaphysically sanction warlike heroism against humanitarianism and sentimentality. God himself exhorts the warrior Arjuna not to hesitate to fight and strike. "He whom thou will slay," he said, "is already slain in me; be thou only the instrument."[95] In his heroic onslaught, which takes no account of his own life or that of others, and which shows faithfulness to his own nature as a son of the warrior cast, Arjuna will reflect the awful and majestic power of the transcendent which breaks and overwhelms everything, thus foreshadowing absolute freedom.[96] In view of this and the existence of a corresponding and well-confirmed tradition, we included among Plato's divine forms of intoxication or mania, this form, not considered by him, which is based in a real sense on warrior heroism. Lastly, we believe that this state of active and transfiguring exaltation lived and shone, even at the highest moments of the sacrificial experience, in those performing bloody sacrifices, especially if they were done under the sign of "fearful" divinities or aspects of divinity, such as those mentioned before.

A last echo of this tradition is found in Novalis. We said earlier that Novalis had perceived the phenomena of transcendence hidden in suffering and even illness. According to Novalis it is with "evil" that freedom and the free will make their appearance in nature. "When man wanted to become God, he sinned." The cause of frailty, inconstancy, and death itself should be seen in the fact that the soul, though linked to nature, is yet "beyond nature," like a transcending, exhausting force that removes all conditional qualities. Such "negative" phenomena, therefore, do not confirm the power of nature over the soul but rather that of the soul over nature. "The process of history is a consuming fire," said Novalis, "and death may even represent the positive limit of this transcendence of a life beyond life."[97] The following words of Schegel can also be quoted: "Only in the enthusiasm of destroying is the sense of the divine creation revealed. Only in the middle of death does everlasting life shine."[98]

These references are not free of obscurities and show in Novalis the lack of a connection with any tradition along the lines of the Way of the Left Hand; therefore, his work remains at a level of philosophical intuition without any practical counterpart. In the "divine Marquis" de Sade, nothing any longer is divine, and the far-off reflections of such a dangerous knowledge seem highly distorted and Satanized. Even where he seems to have perceived the destruction of every limit, he is exalting only a kind of dim worship of the Superman without any light: modern commentators such as G. Bataille and Maurice Blanchot have written about a "supreme solitude" when de Sade's man inexorably precipitates a climax of violence and destruction. However, this does not annul the connection that de Sade establishes between the mysticism of negation and destruction and the realm of sex.

As the point of view mainly followed in this present study is that of the Way of the Left Hand, it is worth adding some further information regarding its cosmological background in Hindu tradition. Its starting point consists of the doctrine concerning the cyclic development of manifestation, and that development should comprise two essential phases or aspects, *pravritti-marga* and *nivritti-marga*. In the first phase the absolute soul is defined, perfected, and bound to forms and delimitations ("name and form," *nama-rupa*) which are visible in all the objects and beings that surround us. This process develops to a given limit, beyond which the direction is reversed and enters the second phase, the *nivritti-marga*, meaning a return, a revulsion from everything that is finished, formed, and manifested, and a breaking of the identification of the soul with the process belonging to the previous phase.[99]

Brahma, understood as the god who creates, and Vishnu, the god who preserves, reign in the *pravritti-marga*, while Shiva reigns in the *nivritti-marga*. The Way of the Right Hand (*dakshinachara*) is linked to the first phase, and the Way of the Left Hand (*vamachara*) to the second phase. Specific laws, rules, and cults correspond to the creative, positive, and preserving aspect of manifestation; the ethics of faithfulness to one's own nature (*svadharma*) belong to this aspect. In the second phase, the way is inverted; it is estrangement and revulsion from the first phase. This estrangement can take two forms: one ascetic and the other destructive and disintegrating. The second characterizes the *vamachara*, the Way of the Left Hand, and is linked to the Tantric practices of the "secret ritual" (the *Panchatattva*). The ascetic form is eminently represented by the laya yoga or yoga of disintegrations. The term *vama* (meaning "left") in *vamachara* is also explained by some texts as meaning "contrary"; it means the opposition to everything that belongs to *pravritti-marga*, to the creative and preserving aspects of manifestation, and therefore it is an attitude not only of estrangement but also of disdain for every law and rule. These ethics of antinomy are proper to one who place himself under the sign of *nivritti-marga*. Technically, "the method indicated by the masters [of this Way] is to employ the forces of *pravritti* [the forces proper to the positive and binding phase of manifestation] in such a way as to make them self-disintegrating."[100] The *siddha* or adept in this path disregards law and is called *svechchhachari*, or "he who can do everything he wants."

Another agreed interpretation of *vama*, or "left," is "woman," and this takes us back in particular to the part which the role of woman and the orgy (the Tantric *Panchatattva* includes the use of woman and intoxicating drinks) in the Way of the Left Hand. This way is considered as synonymous with *lata-sadhana*, an expression which includes an allusion to the special posture that the woman assumes in magical coitus within these Hindu circles.[101]

It is natural that the followers of each of the two ways should praise the one they have chosen and condemn the other. For instance, the Tantras says that the difference between the Way of the Left Hand and the Way of the Right Hand is the same as that between wine and milk.[102] But the two ways are deemed to be two different methods for attaining one single purpose. Thus it must be determined, case by case, which of the two ways is best fitted for the tendencies in the basic nature of each person. In this respect Woodroffe noted rightly that instead of "evil," each person should talk of "what is not suitable for me," and instead of "good," we should say, "what is best fitted to me"; and that agrees with the ancient saying *"Non licet omnibus Citheram adire"* (Not everyone is allowed to approach Cithera).

Last, it is best to emphasize that the Way of the Left Hand may also exist on the general plane indicated by the Bhagavad-Gita, which speaks, for instance, of the way proper to a warrior without sexual or orgiastic meanings of any kind. In the Bhagavad-Gita, this way is held to be equal, in its highest purpose, to that of faithfulness to one's proper mode of being and of turning existence into a ritual or sacred observance (the corresponding formula is *tat madarpanam kurushva*), that is, faithfulness to the *dakshinachara*, the Way of the Right Hand.

Rasputin and the Sect of the Khlysti

With relation to what we said in the last section of this chapter, it may be interesting to cite orgiastic facts wherein are gathered together in a strange manner various factors of erotic transcendence, which we examined in detail when dealing with some liminal forms of profane sexual love. These are rites performed by the Russian sect of the Khlysti, who had to keep them strictly secret. The rules and ideas of this sect could not be revealed to any outsider, not even to close relatives; outwardly the Khlysti kept the Orthodox faith, but inwardly they deemed it a "false belief."

We ought to begin by saying that the practices of the Khlysti appear highly spurious and hybrid. The rites preserve, in degraded, uncouth, popular forms, the remains of pre-Christian orgiastic ceremonies that have lost their original, authentic background and instead include some themes of the new faith in a paradoxical manner. The dogmatic premise of the sect is that man is potentially God. By developing awareness of this, he can be God in fact, taking to himself the nature of Christ (whence comes the name of the sect) if he is a man, or that of the Virgin if a woman, through the transfiguring descent of the Holy Ghost, provoked by celebration of a secret midnight rite. The participants, both men and women, wear only a white garment over complete ritual nakedness. While pronouncing invocations, they begin dancing in a circle. The men form a circle in the middle that moves quickly in the direction of the path of the sun, while the women form an outer circle at first and move in the opposite direction to the path of the sun (a ritual reference to the cosmic polarity observed by the sexes). The motion becomes more and more wild and giddy until some of the participants leave the circles and begin dancing alone, like the ancient *vertiginatores* and Arab dervishes, so fast, it is said, that sometimes their figures can no longer be picked out as they fall and rise again (the dance as a technique of ecstasy). Their frenzy becomes contagious. To increase their exaltation, the men and women, whip each other (pain being an erotic and ecstatic factor). At the peak of this exaltation, the inner transformation, the immanent, invoked descent of the Holy Spirit begins to be foreshadowed. At this point, both men and women strip off their white ritual garments and copulate promiscuously; the drive of the sexual experience and the trauma of coitus bring the rite to its most extreme intensity.[103]

A young woman is chosen on each occasion as the "personification of the divinity and, at the same time, the symbol of generative power"; she is worshipped both as Mother Earth and as the Holy Virgin of Christianity. She appears wholly naked at the end of the secret rite and hands dried grapes to the faithful as a sacrament.[104] This detail establishes a link to the ancient orgiastic rites that were celebrated under the sign of the mysteries of the Great Chthonic Goddess and of the "naked Goddess."

It is interesting to observe that in this sect sex is severely restricted to this ritual and ecstatic use; in every other respect the sect professes rigid asceticism and condemns carnal love and even marriage itself. It is remarkably similar to another Slav sect, that of the Skoptzi, in which asceticism is so extreme as to prescribe the castration of men and woman. A young naked woman also appears in the rites of the Skoptzi as the central figure. This is more likely an echo of the cult belonging to another form of the mysteries of the Great Goddess, the Phrygian Cybele, whose worship was often linked to similar mutilations carried out during ecstatic frenzy.

The staretz Grigori Efimovich, also called Rasputin, belonged to the sect of the Khlysti. Various traces of mystic orgies are also preserved in this personage, who has been talked about so much. To start with, it is meaningful that the title staretz, old saint, should be coupled with the name Rasputin, derived from *rasputnik* or "dissolute." It is hard to distinguish between the truth and the legends invented by both his admirers and his foes. The presence of certain extranormal powers in this uncouth Siberian peasant, however, is undeniable. His end amply demonstrates this; strong doses of a powerful poison, possibly cyanide, had no effect on him, and he stood up after being hit by revolver bullets fired from a close range, so that in the end he had to be slaughtered. The "religion of Rasputin" was essentially marked with the motif indicated above. His own words were "I have come to bring you the voice of our holy Mother Earth and to teach you the blessed secret which she passed on to me about sanctification by sin";[105] and in this, in fact, we can see the subject of the Great Goddess (Mother Earth) returning in a hybrid form combined with the Christian concept of the sinfulness of the flesh. In its essence, the unbridled experience of sex, the "mixture of sin" and the so-called *svalnyi grech*, was conceived as a means of "mortification" capable of causing a "mystic death," abolishing the impurity of coitus and producing a "wonderful transformation" in the individual.[106] At such a level, coitus became a kind of transforming sacrament and method of participation. In objective terms free of moral tones, the "sanctification through sin" announced by Rasputin is connected to this meaning. Instead, as regards its moral and Christian interpretation, we refer to the Lutheran "sin manfully" and to the idea, professed by Saint Augustine, that virtue can be sin when marked with the boastful pride of the fallen creature.[107] In such a context, to yield to the flesh in a way of humiliating oneself, of destroying the pride of the ego, that "obscure despot," even in its final remains, which indeed consist of pride in its own virtue. In existential and not moral terms, the pride to be humiliated by giving free rein to sex and not resisting it, by "sinning," is connected to the limitation of the finite individual, which has to be violated by means of a special paroxysmal experience of eros.

Rasputin, both personally and in his behavior, was repulsive rather than attractive; an influence of a different category, at least partly connected to the experience of the Khlysti and most likely also based on his exceptional inclinations, constituted the foundations of his power and fascination; these he exercised even in the circles of the high Russian aristocracy, which were otherwise not open to a dirty, primitive peasant. Rasputin was, to some extent, attached to the techniques of the Khlysti and often made use of the dance, which he considered a buildup to coitus; he had a prediliction for gypsy music, which, when genuine, is one of the few types that still retain a frentic and elemental dimension. It is said that the women whom Rasputin chose to dance with "had the feeling that they were taking part in the mystic influence of which the staretz had often spoken." As the rhythm became more and more frenetic, it could be seen how "the face of the woman dancing lit up, how her glances little by little became veiled, her eyelids grew heavy and, in the end, closed." The staretz then carried away the almost unconscious woman to copulate with her. In most cases, the memory that the woman retained of what had happened was one of almost mystical ecstasy. However, there were also those who brought back an impression of deep horror, and there was even one case of semimadness as an outcome.[108] On the basis of what we have already said, however, this double effect seem quite natural.

4

Gods and Goddesses, Men and Women

Mythology, Ontology, and Psychology

In traditional teachings, the theme of an original duality relates to the polarity of the sexes and recurs almost everywhere. This duality is expressed sometimes in purely metaphysical terms, at other times as the duality of divine and mythological figures, cosmic elements, principles, gods and goddesses.

Scholars of the history of religions have tended to see this as anthropomorphism; having created the gods in his own image, man also transposed and projected into them sexual differentiation. This interpretation sees all those divine dyads and dichotomies as merely the products of a fantasy that has the human experience of sex as its one and only definite content.

But the truth is exactly the contrary. Traditional man sought to find the secret and essence of sex in divinity itself. In his eyes, before physical embodiment, the sexes existed as superindividual forces and transcendental principles; before appearing in "nature," they existed in the realm of the sacred, the cosmic, and the spiritual. And in the manifold variety of divine figures differentiated as gods and goddesses, man sought to understand the essence of the eternal male and eternal female which the sexual natures of human beings reflect and manifest. This necessitates a reversal of the view of religious historians we mentioned before; instead of human sex being the foundation for the understanding of the reality of sexually differentiated divine and mythological figures, it is precisely the content of those figures that will give us the key to the deepest and most universal aspects of sex in man and woman. Only these divinities, the creations of a far-sighted intuition and even of effective individual or collective supersensual perception, can give us the meaning of what we earlier called absolute manhood and absolute womanhood in their fundamental aspects. They can also lead us to recognize and distinguish certain objective "constants" in the derived and hybrid forms in which sex appears in empirical individuals and in variations that depend on different races and civilizations. In particular, the bases for a study of the character and psychology of sex which is truly intended to plumb the depth of this subject can be drawn from sacred sexual beliefs and the mythology of sex. It cannot be overlooked even if the material we examine will contain some abstruse and novel aspects for the contemporary reader.

As a premise, we should emphasize that our traditional viewpoint is opposed to the naturalistic interpretations we cited and also quite different from recent psychoanalytical trends. Earlier, we said that the principles of absolute manhood and womanhood are not concepts, abstract and devoid of reality in themselves, though useful as standards for studying the mixed and partial empirical forms of sex; nor do we consider them as being at the level of simple "ideals" or "ideal types" which exist only because they are realized approximately in a given being. Instead, they are real principles in the meaning of the Greek word *àrkhaí*—"beings," principles-powers of a transindividual order that variously condition that by which every man is man and every woman is woman; they existed before and beyond the sphere of every mortal man and woman and beyond their fleeting individuality; such principles have a metaphysical existence. This concept has been expressed in an especially meaningful way by the Tantric and sahajiya schools, which have recognized in the division of creatures into male and female, a strictly ontological character, which springs from the metaphysical nature of the principles called Shiva and Shakti or of the mythological personifications such as Krishna and Radha.

We can therefore apply to this special realm the Platonic doctrine of ideas itself interpreted in a realistic and magical sense, namely the concept of the "idea" or "archetype" understood not as a conceptual abstract in the mind but as a root of the real and of reality of a higher category. The forces we are talking about are present invisibly in all the individual beings which they enfold and through whom they are manifested; these gods or beings of sex live and appear in various ways, in different degrees of intensity, in the multitude of men and women, in space and in time; and such manifold fleeting, approximate, and sometimes even larval forms do not touch the identity and eternity of those gods or beings.

Therefore, the divergence seems quite clear between our view and these modern trends we mentioned, for the latter operate on a plane that is not metaphysical but psychological. Though Jung did not reduce the figures of the sexual myth to mere imagination and poetic invention and though he foresaw in them the dramatization of "archetypes" of universal character and independent reality, he also understood that reality in merely psychological terms and reduced it to mental projections of the collective unconscious and to "needs" that the obscure and atavistic part of man's psyche caused to prevail over the conscious and personal part. In this, not only can we clearly see a confusion of terms, but through the misapplied concept of the unconscious and the reliance on a phenomenology of psychopaths, the general modern tendency to refer everything back to merely human dimensions is reconfirmed. If every principle having a transcendent character must be reduced to "psychological fact" so as to be subject of experimentation, yet a fundamental difference exists between psychology as an end in itself, and, instead, understanding psychology in terms of ontology. In fact, all of Jung's interpretations end on a very banal plane, and his intuition of the superindividual and everlasting reality of the sexual "archetypes" is rendered useless or degraded beause of the distortion of his professional mentality and the lack of suitable doctrinal points of reference.

The divergence of the two points of view can be seen even more readily at the level of the practical consequences. Jung had in view the treatment of neuropathic patients and seriously believed that the purpose of ancient religions, mysteries, and initiatic ceremonies was no different from his own: to heal individuals suffering from psychic conflicts and not in harmony with the unconscious part of their being. In the end, for him it was a question of "desaturating" the archetypes and ridding them of the mythical and fascinating dignity—of the *mana*—which imparts to them an obsessive character, and of reducing them to normal psychic functions, this too in the case of the male and the female archetypes as they surface here and there in ordinary consciousness.[1] In contrast, the knowledge of the metaphysical reality of the sexual archetypes traditionally served as a positive premise for the sacred rites of sex. These practices and rites were not intended to restore a divided being struggling with his "complexes" to a banal normal state, but to propitiate a system of evocations and participations extending beyond the merely human and to open the ego proper to those "dignities" that Jung reduced to unexplainable halos of the images of the unconscious.[2]

It is important to add that traditionally there existed a system of relationships between reality and symbols and between actions and myths, such that the world of divine figures not only provided a way of penetrating the most profound dimensions of human sexuality but also contained linked able to supply governing principles of the necessary relations between man and woman. On that basis such relations acquired a profound significance and conformed to a law and standard higher than the world of unforeseeable happenings, free will, and merely individual situations.

We shall consider this aspect of the metaphysics of sex briefly as well.

The Metaphysical Dyad

As regards dualities, let us first examine those which have an abstract, metaphysical character that has not yet been affected by the creation of myths and symbols.

The fundamental idea is that universal creation or manifestation takes place through a twofold condition of principles within the supreme unity, in the same way that animal procreation takes place through the union of the male and female.

As regards procreation, Aristotle wrote, "The male represents the specific form; the female represents the matter, being passive insofar as she is female, whereas the male is active."[3] This polarity recurs in the concepts of ancient Greek philosophy, having its origin in the mysteries and being applied to various forms that nowadays are no longer understood in their original, living meaning. The male is form, the female is matter. "Form" here means the power that determines and arouses the principle of motion, development, becoming. "Matter" means the material and instrumental cause of all development, the pure indeterminate capability, the substance or power that, being devoid of form in itself, can take up any form, and which in itself is nothing but can become everything when it has been awakened and fecundated. The Greek word for matter, *ûlē*, does not mean, therefore, either the matter of the organism or that of physical nature in general. It is hard for us to understand this term, but in the present context it is applied to a mysterious entity, obscure and unfathomable, which both has and does not have being, because it is the merely possible and therefore the power-substance of "nature" as change and becoming. In Pythagorean terms this is also the principle of the Dyad (of the binary, of the Two); it is opposed to the One and is presented by Plato as *déuteron* or that which is always the "other," being related to the receiving place, *khóra*, of being and to the "mother" or "foster-mother" of becoming.[4] In general, this is how the eternal male and female are presented in their most abstract expression in traditional metaphysics.

As a further determination, male and female can be made to correspond to being (in the highest sense) and to becoming; to that which has its own principle in itself, and to that which has a principle in another; to being (stability and unchangeableness) and to life (change, soul, or animating substance, maternal substance of becoming). In this respect Plotinus wrote of being, *oûsa* or *ŏn*, and of the female complement of the everlasting male *òusía*; of everlasting being and everlasting power, which is in a certain way identified with "nature" and the "divine psyche" (the Psyche of Life or Zōē of Zeus). Being, in Plotinus, is also put into relation with the nous, another word that has become hard to understand properly nowadays; it is the intellectual principle conceived as an Olympian principle, unchangeable presence and pure light, which in Plotinus also has the figure of Logos when it is considered in the action with which it fecundates and moves matter or cosmic power. In contrast, the female is the life force; as Psyche, she is "the life of everlasting being," which, when manifestation "proceeds" from the One and takes form, she develops in time, in becoming, in circumstances where the two principles are joined together and variously mixed; the male or Logos keeps himself in everything which is, which remains the same as itself, which does not become, and which is the pure principle of form.[5]

The Hellenic terms, "nature" or *phýsis* has a meaning that itself diverges from the modern, materialistic meaning; it is a meaning, however, that must be held when the female principle is identified with the "natural" principle. In fact, the supernatural principle in traditional symbolism was always deemed to be "male," whereas the principle of nature and becoming was regarded as "female." This polarity is found in Aristotle too; opposite to the unmoving nous which is pure function, there stands "nature," in which the nous with its mere presence as "moving immobility" arouses the effective movement or passage from formless potentiality or "matter" to form or individual existence. This duality is equivalent to the dyad of Sky and Earth, the polarity of the uranic and the earthly and chthonic principles as cosmic-symbolic images of the eternal male and eternal female.

Another symbol for the female, which we have already discussed, is that of the Waters. The Waters embody various meanings; first they represent the undifferentiated life prior to and not yet fixed in form; second, they symbolize that which runs or flows and is therefore unstable and changeable, hence the principle of everything that submits to procreation and becoming in the unpredictable world, which was called sublunar by the ancients; last, they also represent the principle of all fertility and growth according to the analogy of water's fertilizing action on earth and soil. On the one hand, we spoke of the "wet principle" of generation and, on the other hand, of the "waters of life" and also of the "divine waters." Let us add that the Waters were symbolically linked to the horizontal, which corresponds to the Aristotelean category of lying down or *keîsthai* and is opposed to the symbol of the vertical, the category of "standing" or *ékhein* in the specific sense of standing up or standing straight; this association with the male principle was expressed in ancient times by the phallic and ithyphallic symbolism of the erect penis.

Complementing the Waters as a female principle, the male principle was often linked to Fire. However, always we must bear in mind the polyvalence of traditional symbols, that is, their ability to sustain very different meanings, which are not mutually exclusive but follow the logic of various perspectives. The male principle as Fire has many aspects (we may recall in Hindu tradition the double birth of Agni and in classical tradition the double nature of earthly and volcanic fire and of uranic or heavenly fire), but taken in its aspect of flame that heats and nourishes, fire was adopted as the symbol of the female element, and in this aspect played an important part in Indo-European cults. Atar, the Greek *Estia*, and Roman Vesta are personifications of flame in this sense. (Ovid [*Fast*, VI, 291] says, "Vesta is *living* flame.") The fire in household and public rites, the same holy everlasting fire that burned in the palace of the Caesars and was carried in official ceremonies, the fire that every Greek and Roman army carried with it and kept lit day and night was linked to the female aspect of the divine essence, understood as the life force or life-giving element. In this context there still exists the ancient idea that the sudden extinction of the household fire is a sign of death; not the "being," but the life fails.

In Eastern traditions, we find confirmation of these symbolic aspects. Traditions of the Far East know the Sky-Earth dyad: the sky is identified with "active perfection" (*ch'ien*) and the Earth with "passive perfection" (*k'un*). In the "Great Treatise"[6] it is said, "The male acts according to the way of the creative, whereas the female operates according to the way of the receptive," and moreover,[7] "The creative acts in the great beginnings, while the receptive brings to fulfillment the things which have become. . . . The Earth is fecundated by the Sky and acts at the right time. . . . By following the Sky it meets its lord and follows its own way in conformity with order." Just as in Pythagoreanism, the binary (the Two) is linked here to the female principle, and odd numbers are generally related to the Sky, while even numbers are linked to the Earth. Unity is the beginning; Two is the female number of the Earth; Three is a male number as it represents Unity, added to the Earth (1 plus 2 equals 3), and therefore represents everything that in the world of becoming carries the sign and the imprinted form of the higher principle, as in one of its images.[8] This numerical symbolism has a universal character. We also find it in the West as late as the Middle Ages and Dante. It is at the base of the ancient maxim "God rejoices in odd numbers" (because in every odd number, One once again prevails over Two).

In traditions of the Far East, however, the metaphysical dyad is characterized by the *yang* and *yin*, which are understood as being elementary determinations and also real forces acting on every plane of being. When understood as determinations, *yang* has the nature of the Sky and everything active, positive, and male, whereas *yin* has the nature of the Earth and everything passive, negative, and female. In

graphic symbolism a continuous line corresponds to *yang* ——,
whereas a broken line corresponds to *yin*— —, indicating the idea of
the "two" and, therefore, of the Platonic power of the "other." The
trigrams and hexagrams formed with various combinations of those
two elementary signs are given by the *I Ching*, the fundamental text
of Chinese tradition, as the keys to the essential situations that reality
may display in a spiritual or natural category of the universe, as well
as in the human, individual, and collective sphere. All phenomena,
forms, beings, and changes of the universe are considered at the level
of various encounters and combinations of the *yin* and *yang*; from this
they take their final characterization. From their dynamic aspect
yang and *yin* are opposed but also complementary forces. The light
and the sun have a *yang* quality, whereas shadow and the moon have a
yin quality. Fire is *yang*, the waters are *yin*; mountain tops are *yang*,
the plains are *yin*; the spirit is *yang*, the soul and vital force are *yin*; the
pure is *yang*, the unfathomable *yin*; and so on. Lastly, it is the
predominance of *yin* in woman and of *yang* in man that make them
what they are: at this level the pure *yin* and pure *yang* appear as the
substances of absolute womanhood and absolute manhood
respectively. Besides the aspects of symbolism that take us back to
the other writers we have already examined in Hellenic tradition, it is
worth noting at this stage the attribution of the cold, wet, and dark
qualities to *yin* and of the dry, clear and light qualities to *yang*. The
cold quality of *yin* might seem a contradiction of the aspects of heat,
flame, and life already examined in the female principle, but it
should be interpreted in the same context as the cold light of the
moon and the coldness of goddesses like Diana who personify the
principle of that light; and we can see the importance of this passage
in the study of the feminine character and of woman. To the *yin*,
therefore, belong shadows and the darkness with regard to
elementary powers prior to form, which correspond in the human
being to the unconscious and to the vital, nocturnal part of his
psyche. That takes us directly back to the relationship that was
acknowledged to exist between female divinities and divinities of the
night and of the depths of the earth, the night of Hesiod, presented as
the mother of the day. Here the day is equivalent to the clear, light
("sunny") quality of the *yang*, which is the very quality proper to
manifested, definite, and completed forms that are released from the
equivocal darkness and from the indeterminate nature of the
generative womb and female substance or raw material.

We find in Hindu tradition some noteworthy details of the symbolism with which we are dealing. The Samkhya system provides us
with the basic theme in the dual nature of *purusha*, the primordial
male, and of *prakriti*, the principle of the primordial "nature," sub-

stance, or energy of all becoming and all motion. *Purusha* has the same detached, unalterable, "Olympian" character as pure light—being nonactive in the same sense as the immobile mover of Aristotle—of the Hellenic nous. It is with a kind of action of presence—with a "reflex" of itself—that it fecundates *prakriti* and that it breaks the equilibrium of *prakriti*'s powers (*guna*) and makes way for the manifested world. But it is in metaphysical and speculative Tantrism that such a concept has had its most interesting developments. That Hindu cult knew the figure of Shiva as a hermaphroditic god, Ardhanarishvara. In the Tantras the male and female of the divinity separate. Shiva corresponds here properly to the *purusha* of the Samkhya, while Shakti, understood as his wife and power, corresponds to *prakriti* or "nature"; the Sanskrit word *shakti* means both "wife" and "power." From their coitus springs the world; the formula of the texts is precisely, "*Shiva-Shakti-samayogat jayate shrishtikalpara*."[9] Just as in the Samkhya, a nonacting originating function is attributed to the male, to Shiva; he determines motion and awakens Shakti; only the latter, however, truly acts, moves, and generates. This is shown by the symbolism of a sexual union in which the female, Shakti, made of flames, undertakes the active part and moves, embracing the divine male, made of light and bearer of the scepter, who, instead, stays still. This is the so-called *viparita-maithuna*, the inverted coitus, found so often in the holy iconography of India and Tibet, especially in the so-called *yab-yum chudpa* statuettes.[10] In the field of divine personifications, the Shakti corresponds, among other things, to Kali, the "black goddess," who is also represented, however, as made of flames or surrounded with a halo of flame, joining in herself two attributes we have already examined in the female archetype, namely the darkness prior to form, and fire. In her Kali aspect, however, Shakti is mainly shown as energy that cannot be reduced to any finite form or limit and thus also as a destructive goddess.[11] Otherwise, just as the Chinese see the varied interaction of *yin* and *yang* united together and manifesting in reality, so the Hindu tradition sees in creation a varied combination of energies springing from the two principles of *chit-shakti* or *shiva-shakti* and of *maya-shakti*. Thus in one text the goddess says, "Shiva and Shakti being at one and the same time everything in the universe, you or Maheshvara [the male god] are in every place and I am in every place. You are in everything and I am in everything."[12] To be more correct, Shiva is present in the unchangeable, conscious, spiritual, and stable aspect, while Shakti is present in the changeable, unconscious-vital, natural, and dynamic aspect of everything that exists.[13] The goddess exists in the form of time, and in that form she is the cause of all change and is "all-powerful in the moment of the dissolution of the universe."[14]

Lastly, Maya is connected in speculative Tantrism to the female, Shakti. This well-known word is its most common acceptance and especially in the Vedanta is linked to the illusory and unreal nature of the visible world such as it appears in its condition of duality. However, it is also used to designate the works of magic, and the link cited above (*maya-shakti*) is correctly understood as representing the female as the "magic of the divine," the goddess as the magical generator of manifested forms, which are illusory only in a relative sense; for in the Hindu tradition the attribute of real can only be applied to absolute, bright, everlasting being that is devoid of becoming and of "sleep." In a subordinate way, however, there arises from that a connection between the female principle and the "nocturnal" world which constitutes the groundwork of a special kind of magic, enchantment, or fascination. This motif can also be found in one aspect of the Pelasgian and Greek Hecate, the goddess belonging sometimes to the underworld and sometimes to the moon, who imparted power to incantations and taught the art of magical spells to the witches and sorceresses who were under her protection or her actual priestesses (according to one tradition, Medea was a priestess in a temple of Hecate). Diana, too, like Hecate, with whom she was often identified, was said to preside over magical arts; the Hamilton vases show figures of women busy with incantations that are addressed to her. "Enchantress of the foe of the god of love" is one attribute of the Great Goddess of the Hindus.

In the context of the same Hindu doctrines belongs the concept of manifestation as a "look outward," *bahirmukhi*, namely as an outward motion or tendency, as a "going outside," a release from the One and from the Identical, this being another aspect of the nature and function of Shakti. Shakti is also called *kamarupini* or "she who is made of desire" and her sign is the female sexual organ, the upside-down triangle, which is identified with the sign of desire. This illustrates the same motif: every desire involves a motion toward "other than oneself" and toward something outside oneself. Now, Buddhism in particular has recognized desire and thirst, *kama*, *trishna*, and *tanha*, as the final basis of reality as becoming and of conditioned life, the *samsara*. In the "female of the divine," in the Shakti of Shiva, lies the root of desire, whether as cosmogonic desire or as that which is of the same substance as the Waters and "matter." It must be understood as "privation" in Hellenic terms, like Plato's Penia, devoid of being and covetous of being,[15] as opposed to the starry and motionless nature of metaphysical manhood and of the everlasting nous. On the other hand, it is said that Shiva without Shakti would be incapable of any motion and would be "inactive" just as Shakti or *prakriti* without Shiva would be unconscious or *achit*, that is, devoid of the bright element. The united divine couples of the

Hindu or Indo-Tibetan pantheon are intended to show the constant link between the Shiva and Shakti elements in everything that is manifested. Plotinus (III, v, 8) wrote that gods are defined by nous, whereas goddesses are defined by the "psyche," and to every nous is joined a psyche, and the psyche of Zeus is Aphrodite, who, says Plotinus, is identified by priests and theologians with Hera as well.

We shall not prolong this with similar references drawn from other traditions because they would add little to the basic structures we have just indicated. We shall only mention some ideas of the Jewish Kabbala and Christian gnosticism. In the former, the "female nature of the divinity," the *nubkah* opposed to *duhrah*, is generally represented by the Shekhinah, a force or principle understood as "the wife of the King," and mention is made of the holy nuptials, *zivugah kadishah*, of the King and Queen, of God and his Shekhinah.[16] It is most important to note here this aspect of the essential female principle, the everlasting womanhood under whose protection all women in the world remain;[17] according to that aspect the female principle is displayed as an equivalent of the life-giving Holy Ghost or as a power, influence, or "glory" immanent in creation, that is, a power distinct from the pure transcendence of the Divine and even able to detach itself therefrom (as we shall see to be the case with the Hindu Shakti herself in the "descending phase of manifestation"). Therefore, the Kabbala also talks of the state of "exile" of the Shekhinah. But the Shekhinah as "glory present in this world" brings us to a further corrective. In fact, "glory" was understood in ancient times not as a personified abstraction but as a divine power, or the fire in the Iranian idea of *hvareno*. This idea is akin to that of the "living flame" personified as Vesta, which, through associations brought to light by Cumont,[18] takes us back again to the idea of a complementary female divinity and efficient power, such as Fortune, especially in the guise of Fortuna Regia.

In the Christian religion, which has accumulated and absorbed motifs taken from many heterogeneous traditions, the "Spirit" has no well-defined features; it is not female when it fecundates the Virgin or when it is a principle that stands above the Waters in the Old Testament. But in Hebrew and Aramaic the word "spirit" belongs to the feminine gender, and in Christian gnosticism, the "Gospel of the Hebrews," we meet the expression, which refers to Christ, "my mother, the Holy Ghost" or Holy Spirit.[19] The Greek word for spirit or ghost, *pnêuma*, may correspond to the Hindu *prana*, or breath as vital force or life force; we can note that the descent of the Holy Ghost was represented as a descent of flames, a meaning that agrees with that of the Shekhinah itself. On the other hand, the dove was often used as a symbol of the Holy Ghost, which was already linked to the great goddesses of the Mediterranean world; the Cretan Potnia, Ishtar, Derceto, Mylitta, and Aphrodite.[20] And indeed it is the doves that bring Zeus his food, ambrosia.[21]

The female divinity of gnosticism is Sophia, a being with many aspects and names. She is sometimes identified with the Holy Ghost itself but, according to her various capacities, is also the Universal Mother, the Mother of the Living or the Resplendent Mother, the Power on High, She-of-the-Left-Hand (as opposed to Christ, understood as her husband and He-of-the-Right-Hand), as the Luxurious One, the Womb, the Virgin, the Wife of the Male, the Revealer of Perfect Mysteries, the Saint Columba of the Spirit, the Heavenly Mother, the Wandering One or Elena (that is, Selene, the Moon). She was envisaged as the Psyche of the world and the female aspect of Logos.[22] In the "Great Revelation" of Simon the Gnostic, the subject of the dyad and the hermaphrodite is rendered in terms that bear repeating: "This is he who was, is, and shall be, a male-female power like the preexisting limitless power that exists in the One and has neither beginning nor end. It was from this limitless power that the thought hidden in the One first came forth and became two. . . . Thus it happens that whatever is manifested by him, although only one, is found to be two, male and female, having the female within himself."[23]

Demeter Archetypes and Aphrodite Archetypes, the Virgin, and Ultimate Nakedness

So far we have examined the original polarity in abstract metaphysical terms. We shall now pass on to the form of actual divine figures and of appearances of gods and powers. As we said earlier, such figures stood for *arkhai* or real beings in traditional antiquity. With them we are drawing near to the existential plane or actual human sexuality since in this new sphere the meanings of the sacred myth are linked to cults, institutions, and ritual acts. To arrive at differentiated characterizations in the mythological field, however, we must be discriminating. We meet with a myriad of figures that almost always have a polyvalent character and that refract in highly varied meanings both because of their manifold aspects and because of exogenous historical reasons and the transmutation of mythical stories and different cults and civilizations.

The female principle in its manifold images and epiphanies can be classified under the signs of two basic types, which we shall call the Aphrodite type and the Demeter type, the everlasting archetypes of the human lover and human mother. They correspond to the "power of the divine," *òusía, hulé,* or Shakti in their respective aspects of force in the pure state and of force that has received form from the eternal male and has become life that nourishes a form.

The Demeter type in the ancient Western world was witnessed as early as the late Paleolithic age, continued into the Neolithic age and took shape in the pre-Hellenic mother goddesses. It reappeared in a southern strip that began at the Pyrenees, passed through the Aegean civilization, Egypt, and Mesopotamia,[24] and reached pre-Aryan India and Polynesia. The theme of fertility is displayed most obviously as a naturalistic tradition of the idea of the Goddess conceived as life itself and the origin of life. It is expressed in the shapeless idols with protruding buttocks of the Paleolithic age; but also in the late chaste form of Hellenized Demeter, it can be seen in the most ancient naked goddesses, where the most extravagant representations consist of the many-breasted goddess and of naked female images standing or lying down with their legs spread apart to exhibit the sexual organ and to release and make flow the sexual *sacrum*, the magical energy, the *mana* of fertility of the primordial Genetrix or Mother.[25]

Among some primitive peoples the same theme is mainly expressed in the stylized linear design of the womb and sexual organ, namely in the upside-down triangle, in which there is sometimes a line at the lower vertex to show the beginning of the vulvar cleft; this design acted as a symbol of a magical force intended to fertilize and, at the same time, to frighten and ward off those persons who were not allowed to draw near.[26] A similar meaning can be seen in the female act of *anasúrma* or pulling up her clothes and showing her sex, which also could frighten, as for instance when that act was used by the Lycian women to cause the threatening waves of Poseidon to retreat,[27] and when in the Islamic cycle, together with the removal of her veil, it was used by the ancient moon goddess al-Uzzos to stop the emissary of the Prophet, who wanted to fell the trees that were sacred to her.[28]

This is not the time to cite the manifold names of the Great Goddess or Magna Mater Genetrix, the image of the Demeter principle, but also very real power and force. She is Mother Earth. She is the Iranian Ardvi, whom Ahura Mazda called his "Water," linked to a mythical river coming down from the heights. From that river springs forth the waters of the earth in their symbolic meanings of life-giving energies and forces of fecundity and fertilization. Here the wet principle constitutes the elementary substance of the Goddess, and a Neoplatonist etymology also emphasizes the other aspect of that principle when it derives the name of one of her manifestations in the shape of Rhea, from the word *rein*, meaning to flow. For this reason we see goddesses of the Demeter type, such as the Argive Hera, and also of the Amazonian type, such as Pallas Athena, recover their virginity by diving into the water consubstantial with their original substance, renew them, and reintegrate their nature.[29] The mysteries of Hera relate how she always emerges a virgin again from her ritual bath in the spring waters of Kanathos.[30] We should also bear in mind the link between the Roman cult of Vesta and spring water or flowing water; it alone was used as "living water" in certain purifying rites performed by the vestal virgins—*aqua vivis fontibus amnibusque hausta* (water drawn from the living springs and rivers).[31] So Ganga, the Hindu Great Goddess, manifests in "liquid form" as the sacred river whose waters wash away all sins.[32]

The supreme essential principle in the world of such figures is the Great Goddess, who, like Hesiod's Gaia, procreates without a husband or by having herself fecundated by a husband who is at the same time her son. In this case her mate is subordinate to her and only instrumental. He is often a short-lived being who dies and arises again thanks only to the goddess (Tammuz and Attis in respect of Rhea-Cybele and Ishtar) because in her alone lies the true principle and spring of life. We are here on the borderline of those scissions and absolutes which make way for Demeter as gynecocracies (not necessarily in the form of social sovereignty by woman but, more generally, in the form of a preeminence of everything linked to her as mother) or those regressions that lead to the idea, cited earlier, of earthly immortality or the immortality of the Mother. It is within the framework of these absolutes that the female principle, connected mainly to the earth, can also assume the figure of a heavenly sovereign divinity, the Great Mother of the Gods; this is a transformation that we can see especially in the person of the Egyptian Isis. Isis, who was originally an earth goddess—in cosmic-naturalistic symbolism, the black earth of Egypt, watered and fertilized by the streams of the Nile representing the male Osiris—is, in fact, introduced into the heavenly world and becomes "the Lady of the Sky" or "She Who Gives Light to the Sky" or "the Queen of All the Gods."[33] In the same way, the goddess of the Elamites wears the tiara of sovereignty and holds in her right hand a cup, from which she gives mortals the vital intoxicating fluid to drink, and in her left hand a ring as a symbol of the unending circle of generation. When the Great Goddess passes on from being Mother Earth and takes on, in particular, the form of a moon goddess, we can see another expression of the basic meanings mentioned earlier. In fact, the moon is the planet that changes. Being linked to the force at work wherever there is change, alteration, and transformation, it reflects in some way the very nature of the Waters and of cosmic ūlē (matter). Star of the night, lady of the night—in the moral transposition, "changeable and inconstant star"—by way of this connection the moon is associated with the divine female archetype; thus the sickle of the moon is also represented as an attribute of the Iranian Ardvi, who, we said, is the "Water" of Ahura Mazda.

Perhaps in the Hindu manifestations of the Great Goddess (in Kali, Bhairavi, Karala, and above all in Durga, all various forms of the wife or Shakti of the "divine male") is seen the best expression of the Aphrodite principle of primordial womanhood as the dissolving, overwhelming, ecstatic, and unmeasurable force of sex, in opposition to Demeterian womanhood. In the Mediterranean world such features belong mainly to the goddess Ishtar, goddess of love, together with many other goddesses, such as Mylitta, Astarte, Tanit, Ashera, and Anaitis. One fundamental characteristic ought to be examined here: the name of Durga, the corresponding Hindu goddess, means "the Inaccessible One," but she is also the goddess of orgiastic rites. The Mediterranean goddesses cited just now often have the attribute of "virgins," *parthénos*. Ishtar is a "virgin" but at the same time the "Great Whore," the "Heavenly Prostitute."[34] Kali is deemed a "virgin" in the aspect of Adya-Kali; she is *kumarirupa dharini*. Aphrodite goddesses who have lovers are thought of as virgins, and so are goddesses of the Demeter type who are mothers. Porne, Hetaira, and Pandemos were names that in the Aegean and Antolian world were compatible with their opposite, "virgin." Shing-mu, the Great Goddess, the Chinese Virgin Mother, is at the same time the patroness of whores. To move to another cultural field, the heavenly Islamic houris, who offer themselves continuously to the embraces of the chosen, are described as being always virgins again. In a materialistic transposition, an echo of this idea can even be found in the Christian belief that Mary, besides having conceived as a virgin, remained so even after giving birth. This most profound meaning has been missed by those who explain it only in terms of the many connotations that the word "virgin" had in ancient times, for it designated not only a woman prior to sexual experience, but also an unmarried woman, a girl who had intercourse with a man out of wedlock, but shunned the bonds and vassaldom of wedded life.[35] Rather, emphasis is to be placed on the capacity of the "raw material" to receive and be impregnated with every form without wearying or being possessed in its ultimate root.[36] Virginity is therefore deemed to be the quality of the "divine female." It constitutes the "Durga" (inaccessible) aspect of the divine female and is also linked to the cold quality, which can exist alongside the gleaming and fascinating quality of the Aphrodite archetype and of the courtesan. In the most common representation of the sirens, who were said to be virgins as well as enchantresses, their lower part is shaped like a fish and is wet and cold.

A similar example is the female goddesses of the Amazonian type, whose chastity or virginity in the modern meaning of the word was often just a later accretion to ancient figures in an attempt to make them seem moral. Thus, for instance, it is known that Artemis-Diana and Athena, who were essentially conceived by the Hellenic world as virgins, were mother goddesses of the foregoing type when they were pre-Hellenic and Pelasgian divinities. In this context the virgin goddesses and Ishtar herself, virgin and whore at one and the same time, could also be presented as goddesses of war and victory (the Venus Victrix, Ishtar invoked as the "Lady of Arms," the "Arbiter of Battles"). In the following invocation addressed to her, one sees the duality of motifs: "Thou art strong, O Lady of Victory, who canst awaken my violent desires."[37] Przylusky correctly called attention to the fact that the Great Goddess was also the goddess of fighting, because in such a case war is considered essentially under the sole aspect of action that destroys and slays.[38] It is at such a level that Aphrodite takes to herself, as *areía*, the characteristics of a warrior goddess with the esoteric meaning of power or shakti or Ares-Mars. Here, therefore, emphasis is given to the ambiguity of a power that is at one and the same time a power of life and death; indeed it was said that Astarte is "Goddess Astarte, the life and safety of gods and men, and she who is also destruction, death, and annihilation."[39] She is the shining moon goddess whose other face, however, is the "black" unfathomable goddess, the Mother of Darkness, Hecate of the underworld (the virgin Artemis also sometimes takes on the aspect of Hecate), Juno of the netherworld, the Lady of Pluto (Virgil), Ishtar, and Kali, "Dreadful Mother"; these are archetypes in which also converge the symbolism of derived figures, such as the virgins of battles and storms, the Nordic Valkyrie and the Iranian Fravashi. Men seek to employ and arouse the goddess, as unchained power and the power of death, against their foes; then indeed she takes on the characteristics of a goddess of war and of the Promachos (champion) fighting like a lion with javelin and bow. And when this power leads to victory, the Virgin appears in the end like a goddess of victory too. Thus Durga is also the black virgin, *krishna kumari*, invoked as she who gives victory in battle.[40] There is a netherworld aspect to this which is interesting to observe, in the Roman *devotio*, for example, a gloomy rite in which a general offered himself of his own free will as a victim to the forces of the netherworld so as to unleash them against the foe. In the invocation proper to this rite, after the litany of luminous divinities including Mars, comes the name of Bellona, who is precisely a goddess of war in the sense we mentioned but is also identified by ancient writers with other forms of the Great Goddess.[41] We must also cite the Egyptian Sekhmet, the lion-headed goddess of war, who rejoiced in bloody sacrifices and was said to copulate with the victors.

On the moral plane, cruelty is attributed to the goddess in her Durga aspect in various mythical tales that have constellated around figures of this kind. The goddess takes delight in blood and death. This can be seen very clearly in Kali. But human sacrifices were offered in ancient times to the divine Virgin, Artemis Orthis, who was called Taurian Artemis, at several places in Greece, at Sparta, Brauron, and elsewhere. After these sacrifices were stopped, a trace of them still remained at Sparta during the festivals of the goddess in the rite of the diamastigosis or whipping of adolescents so that their blood bathed her altar, for the virgin goddess loved blood. In other Greek cities, too, the worshippers of Demeter whipped each other in turn. The festival of Cybele at Rome, inspired by the worship of the Great Goddess, was held from the fifteenth to the twenty-seventh of March, the latter date being marked in the calendar as the *dies sanguinis* or day of blood. On that day the priests of the goddess whipped and lacerated themselves, uniting their cries to the sound of the flutes and kettledrums. Then, after a mysterious vigil, it was believed that the initiates copulated with the Great Goddess.[42] The orgiastic rites dedicated to the goddess Ma, who was also a goddess of war, had the same character. In the same context, the performance of bloody sacrifices was often entrusted to priestesses; this was the case among the Gauls and in America. In an archaic Roman rite performed by the vestal virgins, sacred guardians of the flame of life, twenty-four dolls were thrown into the Tiber, yet it is the prevalent opinion that human victims originally were thrown instead of dolls.

We must distinguish the meaning of the nakedness in the Durga aspect of the goddess as opposed to the nakedness of the Demeter-Mother archetype, principle of fecundity. The first is the Aphroditic "ultimate nakedness." The strongest and most expressive symbolic and ritual expression of this is linked to the sacred dance of the seven veils. The teaching of the mysteries included the symbolism of passing through the seven planetary spheres and freeing oneself little by little of the various determining and conditional qualities related to those spheres, which were conceived as being so many clothes and covering to be thrown away until a person reached the state of the "ultimate nakedness" of absolute and simple being, which is only itself when it is beyond the "seven." In this context, Plotinus[43] cites those who ascend by degrees in the holy mysteries, laying aside their clothes and advancing in nakedness, whereas in Sufism a parallel exists in the *tamzig* or tearing of clothes during ecstasy. In the opposite realm, that of "nature," the corresponding process is the stripping of the feminine power of all its forms until it appears in its elementary character or virgin substance prior and superior to all form. It is precisely that which is made perceptible by the progressive freeing of the woman from the seven veils until she is shown utterly naked, just as, in the Egyptian invocation cited earlier, Isis is desired to appear and as in the myth of Ishtar also, who descends to the netherworld and leaves a part of her ornaments and clothes at each of the seven doors through which she goes. This is the reverse of uranic nakedness. Ultimate female nakedness can also act in a deadly way: the sight of naked Diana killed Actaeon ("invulnerable and mortal Diana"), while that of naked Athena made Tiresias blind. The prohibition or taboo of nakedness that is met with in certain traditions and customs, even among primitive peoples, stems from earlier rituals. The sight of wholly naked images in the Greek mysteries corresponded to the highest grade of initiation or epopteia, and in the ritual of Tantric sexual practice, the woman to be used appears as the embodiment of *prakriti*, the divine female and primordial substance hidden beneath the numberless forms of manifestation. The naked woman represents this very substance freed of all form and in its "virgin and ultimate state." On the other hand, female nakedness is graduated in the rite; the use of a wholly naked woman is not permitted to everyone, but only to Tantric initiates of a high grade. Only these were allowed to see ultimate nakedness, to possess the naked Virgin without deadly peril or profanation.[44] A similar meaning may be found in the paradoxical ritual union between an ascetic and a whore in the Mahavrata festival; as though for a woman reduced to her primal state, the inaccessible substratum of all form (the "prostitute"), the only fitting mate would be one who by asceticism had been reintegrated into his own principle or into the opposite primal state of transcendental manhood. Symbolically connected to this is the Hermetic saying that the bride and bridegroom should remove their clothes and bathe thoroughly before entering their nuptial bed where the *mysterium conjunctionis* is performed.[45]

But we shall deal with these ritual complexes later. We shall end now by indicating the specific feature that is highlighted in appearances of the Great Goddess as Varunani. This Hindu divinity, also known as Varuni or Sura, appeared as a goddess of the sky, of the waters, and of intoxicating drinks. The word *varuni* in Pali designates actually either an intoxicating liquor or an enraptured or possessed woman, and Varuni or Sura in epic poetry is the "daughter" of Varuna, the male uranic god, who brings happiness and intoxication to the gods. In India the link between Varuni and intoxicating drinks is certain (so much so that, in some writings, to drink *devi varuni*, the manifestation of the goddess in liquid form, means to drink an alcoholic beverage). Sura is also one of the names of the Great Goddess in Iran.[46] Even in the hymns of the austere Shankara, the goddess is described with intoxicating drinks and holds up the goblet or is herself inebriated.[47] In this divine archetype, therefore, the aspect of the female as the principle and cause of intoxication is established. And that intoxication can have the lower, elementary, Dionysiac, savage, and maenadic form or the higher form of a transfiguring, enlightening intoxication.

Christianity was obscurely fixed on this second aspect in the figure of the Virgin Mother who stands above, her foot on the sickle of the moon or even the serpent, which, as Nahash, symbolized in Hebrew esotericism the elementary, cosmic principle of desire. To that may be linked the division existing in the ancient mysteries of the Mother, wherein the lesser mysteries of Persephone of the netherworld, who is connected also to Aphrodite, were celebrated in the spring more or less at the same time as the various orgiastic, chthonic festivals, whereas the Great Eleusinian mysteries were celebrated in the autumn. We may also bear in mind the Aegean goddess, Our Lady of the Waves and Stella Maris, in her twofold aspect of goddess who descends from the skies and goddess who appears from the nether regions, one the "goddess of doves" and the other the "goddess of snakes" and panthers.[48]

As a last point, if we consider the cosmic substance or power in its aspect fixed to a given form in which it remains held in its fluid, fleeting, unrestrainable character, we have the Demeter principle in the form of female figures as "brides" tied to a god by the bonds of one single marriage or one single being; the substance then is no longer the "Virgin" or the "Whore" but is the divine wife as a "sealed fountain" who, when viewed on the moral level of the archetype, has the characteristics of chastity and faithfulness such as to hide her original nature (the Great Goddess as Hera). In the myth, the divine sexed couples paired in a relationship of relative harmony and equilibrium correspond to this ontological situation.

Typical Differentiations of Manhood in Myth

Typical figures in myth that embody the male principle act in a certain way as counterparts to the appearances of the female, first according to the pure Aphrodite aspect, then to the Durga aspect, and last to the Demeter-Mother aspect.

Bachofen partly sketched this morphology, starting with mythical tales from Mediterranean antiquity clustering around the figure of Dionysus. His method of associations, which at first gives the impression of a confused attempt at harmonization, actually uncovers profound significances.[49]

First we should consider, as a lower limit, the Chthonic-Poseidon form of manhood. At this level Dionysus was linked to both Poseidon, god of the waters, and to Osiris, conceived as the stream of the Nile, which waters and fertilizes Isis, the black earth of Egypt. At a higher level Dionysus is linked to Hephaestos-Vulcan, the god of the fire of the netherworld. In the first of these mythical tales there is a displacement of the symbolism of the Waters since they now designate the wet principle of generation related to the merely phallic concept of manhood; the god is the male considered only according to the aspect of the being who fecundates the female substance and, as such, is subordinate to her. The changeover to the god of the fire of the netherworld takes us only one step forward since we are dealing with an earthly and still dim, savage, elementary fire, whose counterpart is still the Aphroditic womanhood in her state of weakness (Aphrodite as the unfaithful wife of Vulcan).

A higher appearance of the male principle is indicated by Bachofen at the point where Dionysus is seen as a bright and heavenly nature because of his link with the moon god and with the sun and Apollo. But the fact that Dionysus in these same mythic forms is always joined with female figures related to the archetype of the Great Goddess signifies a limit that is evident in the fact that, even when Dionysus is seen as the sun god, as the sun itself, he is considered not in the aspect of pure, unchangeable light but as the star that dies and rises again. This is precisely the central theme of Orphic Dionysiac worship, which in this way fits into the background of the religion of the Mother and comprises the same situation as Attis and Tammuz, male mortals gods whom the immortal Goddess always causes to rise again (in fact, instead of Attis we can also find Sabazius alongside Cybele; and Sabazius is often identified with Dionysus); in the same way the sun sets and rises again, and its light is still not the steady, abstract light of pure being or of the pure Olympian principle.

Development of the series involves passing on to another mythical complex beyond the one based on Dionysus. The connecting links can be identified as Dionysus in the guise of a foe and conqueror of the Amazons and also the treachery of Aphrodite in coupling with Ares, the god of war. Ares, the Hellenic Mars, has features that embody a savage manhood which is heroic and no longer phallic nor Dionysiac in a promiscuous and elementary sense; but the embodiment of such manhood is Dorian Heracles. Heracles, too, was a conqueror of the Amazons, and moreover a foe of the Mother (of Hera, just as Roman Hercules was the foe of Bona Dea), from whose bonds he freed himself; but he still possessed her principle in obtaining Hebe, everlasting youth, as his wife in Olympus after attaining the way to the garden of the Hesperides and plucking there the golden apple, itself a symbol linked to the Mother (the apples had been given by Gea to Hera) and to the life force.

The representations of ascetic and Apollonian manhood must be deemed still higher than Heracles with the symbolism of his labors, which emphasize heroic manhood and, to some extent, resistance to the dominion of women (we shall talk about the important symbolism of the garment of Nessus in its proper place). Here we can consider Shiva as a connecting element, as the god of a cult and not as a metaphysical principle; if, on the one hand, in the Alexandrine period, he was taken to be the same as Dionysus, god of the orgiastic rites, on the other hand, he was also thought of as the great ascetic of the high peaks. He had a wife, Parvati, but was not held in bondage by her, for he was able to strike with lightning the god of love, Kama, when the latter sought to awaken in him desire of need, privation, thirst, and dependence. (In Hindu myth, Kama was revived by Shiva through the intercession of divinities, such as Rati, who personify forms of pure erotic experience, free of conditional qualities.)

Above all the ascetic struggles, manhood, next, has a typical symbol in Heruka, whose severe and imposing heroic beauty is sometimes even frightening. He is the naked divinity and shining scepter-bearer of the Hindu-Tibetan pantheon; here nakedness expresses a meaning opposed to that of female ultimate nakedness and represents pure being in itself, the "purity" or dominating uranic simplicity which is dangerous for woman (to see man in such "nakedness" may signify that she will lose him forever, which is another well-known theme in the saga). But Shiva often already had the same attribute, namely *digambara* or "the naked one."

Therefore, to go back to Hellenic themes, the series can have as its upper limit the Apollonian manifestation of pure manhood. Here Apollo is the embodiment of Olympian nous (perception) and of unchangeable uranic light, freed from the earthly element and also from his connection with goddesses in some spurious historical varieties of his worship. At this level Apollo, as the god of "pure form," was conceived without a mother and was "born by himself," *amētōr* (without a mother) and *autophués* (self-growing), being the Doric god who "produced form geometrically." (The determination of plastic matter is proper to the male and to form, whereas the indeterminate nature of plastic matter and the limitless, *ápeiron*, belongs to the female.) In the opinion of Orestes, Apollo defends the principle opposed to that of motherhood without a husband but also to Demeter or Aphrodite womanhood. Orestes said that it is actually the father who generates a child, whereas the mother is only the "foster-mother" of the child.[50] This is the affirmation and corroboration of the relationship given in metaphysical terms between the everlasting male and the everlasting female. But in the Apollonian symbol there is something besides reaffirming order "according to justice" between the two principles, which takes us beyond the whole world of the Dyad. Therefore, let us establish the principal types of male in this order; first, phallic and earthly manhood; next, Dionysiac manhood in a strict sense; third, heroic manhood; fourth, ascetic manhood; and last, Apollonian or Olympian manhood; for they are the centers of mythical stories and can be found in endless varieties in widely differing traditions, as the counterparts of the chthonic Mothers, Demeter goddesses, Aphrodite goddesses, and, last, of the ambiguous, unfathomable, Amazonian, and destructive "Virgins."

Male and Female in Manifestation

In the preceding sections we have passed more than once from the male and female principles as static categories or divine forms to a consideration of them as dynamic powers standing in varying relationships to each other. To deal in greater detail with this special aspect, we must first state an important definition.

No complete metaphysical and traditional doctrine has ever considered the Dyad as the highest reference point for a view of the world. Beyond the yin and yang, the traditions of the Far East recognize the "Great Unity," T'ai-chi or T'ai-i. Plotinus wrote of the One superior and prior to the divine duality of nous (perception) and ūlē (matter), of "being" and life force. Tantrism knows Nirguna-Brahman or another equivalent principle beyond the Shiva-Shakti Dyad, and so on. This signifies that the two principles cannot attain an equal rank. The male principle of the Dyad—yang, Shiva, or being—reflects the One or transcendental being; it represents and embodies this One in the process of universal manifestation and in the relativity and tendency of forms (in Plotinus, in the form of logos or reason). As regards "nature," we may say in theological terms that it is not a principle that coexists with God but that it springs from God and therefore has a "second reality."[51]

Hence the male has an ontological or metaphysical preeminence of right over the female; but we do not say that such a preeminence always exists in actual fact. On the contrary, the first phase of manifestation must be characterized by the freeing and acting of the awakened female power, which gains the upper hand over the principle of pure being and of the identical. It keeps that upper hand throughout the whole descending or emanatory phase in the próodos or progress of Plotinus, or in the pravritti-marga which we spoke of when dealing with the Way of the Right Hand and the Way of the Left Hand.[52] This phase continues until a limit marked by an equilibrium of the two principles, after which there is a turning point, a crisis or breaking point. The power of Shakti can be dissolved or lost in the infinite, or be recovered in steps and governed by the opposite principle. Then the male forever has the upper hand to a greater and greater extent until there is a full, clear possession of that which has "become." Brought by the female, it is vested in the male as the awakener of becoming, until there is a higher synthesis that reproduces the primordial unity in a certain way. After the lowest point of the cycle, the ascending arc turns toward that which in Christian terms may be called the "consummation." It can be linked to the Way of the Left Hand and stays under the sign of Shiva as a god of "transcendence," whereas the first phase is under the sign not only of Shakti but also of the gods of creation and preservation, Brahma and Vishnu.

It is important to recognize that these various phases are not a temporal succession but manifold possible circumstances with varying relationships between male and female, form and matter, Sky and Earth, *yang* and *yin*, with now one and now the other principle predominating. These circumstances can be found everywhere: in the cosmos and its periods; in history and its ages; in the structure and spirit of cults, civilizations, and societies. Consider the opposition between civilizations of the Father ruled by men and those of the Mother ruled by women, between institutions based on paternal right and those governed by the matriarchal principle. In individuals, too, it is the predominance of one principle over the other that leads to sexual development (as sex of the body and also of the soul). Thus, seemingly abstract concepts actually provide basic leads to orient ourselves in the perception of every reality.

It may be noted that behind various figures in the myth of the "Fall" is often hidden the idea of a loss of the male principle in the female one (or "cosmic" one) or an identification of the male with the female so far as to assume its way of being. That is what happens of necessity in the first phase of manifestation, which for pure being must have the sense of a progressive darkening or oblivion (the Hindu *avidya* or, in Plato's myth, the drunken and fainting Poros copulating with Penial, the nous (perception) which is swallowed by darkness in the embrace of the *physis* (nature), the melting away of Narcissus, and so on. In the *Corpus Hermeticum* we find: "Although male-female [hermaphrodite] like the Father [as the One, of whom the male is the reflection] and superior to sleep, it is dominated by sleep."[53] The awakening or revival (in soteriological terms, the "redemption" or "salvation") can happen in the circumstances of the second, ascending or Shiva phase. The presupposition for this is the passing of the turning point and the overcoming of the resistance offered by the female binding force or force tending toward the limitless; it is the breaking of the "cosmic" level.

A list of the typical myths that have given meaning to this context would be too long to cite. For instance, we have already cited the kabbalistic idea of the exile of the Shekhinah symbolic of "breakage" in the realm of the divine powers (it is the phase of the dissolving or of being, as if on its own, of the cosmogonic Shakti), and we have also mentioned the corresponding idea of the everlasting Sabbath (understood as the reunion of the Holy One with his Shekhinah) in which everything will be referred to its original root. The wedding of the Holy One with his Shekhinah will also restore the unity of the Divine Name, which had been destroyed by the Fall. According to the tradition in question, every holy precept should have this as its aim, and so the formula that the Hasidim recite before fulfilling each commandment is "In the name of the unity of the Holy One, blessed by he, with his Shekhinah."[54]

A similar motif in Christian gnosticism is the changes in fortune of cosmic Sophia in the netherworld until she was married by Christ (or Logos—reason—namely, he who reflects or "bears" the One, the "son" of transcendental being) and was brought back again into the world of Light.[55] The symbolic context is clear when Simon the Gnostic indicated the embodiment of Sophia in the woman he had with him, in Elena (Selene, the Moon), who had been a prostitute before and had now become his wife. More generally, we have the following important fragment of the Gnostic philosophy of Marcus: "I am the son of the Father, who is beyond all existence, whereas I am in existence. I came [into existence] to see [the things] which are mine and not mine [and which are to be referred to the male and female of the primordial Dyad respectively] and are not wholly mine [in the emanating phase] because they belong to Sophia, who is my female counterpart, and she made them for herself. But I derive my birth from him who is beyond existence, and I return again to the beginning whence I came."[56] The various phases are shown clearly in the mystery teaching as reported by Ireneus,[57] about Adam, the "unbreakable," who was also called "the foundation stone" and "glorious man." Here it is a question of the barrier behind which, in every man, is the inner man who springs from the heavenly archetype, Adam, who "has fallen in a work of clay and chalk and forgotten everything." Classical mythology speaks of the ebb and flow in opposite directions of the Ocean and the Waters, bringing forth the birth of men in one case and in the other the birth of gods (a clear reference to the descending phase and the ascending phase in which the Waters are stopped and taken back on high, bringing the "kingdom of woman" to an end). It is said: "First there is the blessed nature of man from on high, Adam; next there is mortal nature down here; and third there is the race of those without a king who have ascended up above where Mariam is, she who is sought [the female as principle of reintegration]." The being produced by the current thrust back on high is called the "hermaphroditic man [*àrsenóthlus*] which is in everyone." Last, there is talk of two statues of naked ithyphallic men (with erect phalluses) at the temple of Samothrace. One is interpreted as the image of the primordial male, Adam, and the other as the image of the reborn man "who has, in everything and for everything, the same nature as the first." This same knowledge continued unchanged in the Hermetic tradition, in the Middle Ages, and up to the early modern epoch. Pernety wrote of the "Whore," identified with the Moon, whom the Royal Art brought back again to the state of the Virgin, the "Virgin who, animated by the seed of the first male and united with a second male [man as representative of the primordial male who fertilized the life substance in the beginning], will conceive again through the bodily seed of the second male and will beget in the end a hermaphroditic youth who will be the source of a race of very powerful kings."[58] Essentially, this is the same mystery that we mentioned when speaking of the Far Eastern tradition and that we called the "Mystery of the Three" through which the One, being united with the female Two, returns to itself. Implicit in the rectification or transmutation of the feminine polarity are both the Hermetic symbol of the "Son who generates the Mother" and also the strange expression of Dante regarding the Virgin, "Virgin Mother, daughter of your son."

The importance of such traditions lies in their direct relationship to both the world of the ancient mysteries and also to the theme of the hermaphrodite. They also provide us with a way to approach a world of actions and realizations.

The first of these two points relates to the theme found in Plato which has served as a basis for understanding the metaphysics of eros, namely the myth of the hermaphrodite. It is shown integrated into a context of universal character and defined against a cosmic background. It may be interesting to provide some further documentation in this respect.

The *Corpus Hermeticus* speaks of the state of original hermaphroditism, which at a given moment ceased, "as its period was completed"; then the male on one side and the female on the other took shape.[59] Apart from the doctrine of the Shekhinah, the kabbalistic interpretation of Genesis contains the same theme. According to the *Bereshith Rabba* (I, i, 26), primordial man was an hermaphrodite. The woman taken from Adam was called Ayesha because she was taken from Ayesh ("man"); then Adam gave her the name Eve ("life," "the living") because he could return to the unity through her.[60] In this text, as also later in Maimonides,[61] we meet the same Platonic tale of the being broken into two parts and also the theme of the being "who in some respects is one and in others is two." Leo the Hebrew (Jehuda Abardanel) also referred explicitly to Plato and tried to relate his doctrine of the hermaphrodite to the biblical myth of the Fall, thereby retaining Plato's interpretation of eros's most profound meaning. The fact that man leaves his father and mother and unites himself with woman, forming one single flesh with her, as the Bible says, is explained by Leo the Hebrew as an impulse of the two parts to re-create the original unity since the two "had been separated out of one and the same individual."[62]

This story taken from the mysteries was not unknown to the Greek fathers, and from them it was passed on, most likely through Maximus the Confessor, to Scotus Eriugena, to whom we owe a version that is worth telling. Scotus taught that "the division of substances starts in God himself and is defined in a progressive descent as far as the limit which is the separation of man from woman. Therefore, the reunification of subtances also must begin in man and retrace the same steps until it reaches God, in whom there is no separation because in him everything is One [equivalent to the level of the One in Plotinus or of the Great Unity of the Far East, etc.]. The unification of creatures, therefore, begins in man." Both in Plato and Scotus the metaphysical theme is set forth in moral terms, related to the "all" (we have already seen that this concept corresponds metaphysically to the ontological and dynamic situation proper to the descending or emanating phase). Scotus taught in this way that "if the first man had not sinned, his nature would not have undergone sexual differentiation," and that this differentiation only took place with the Fall.[63] From this comes the eschatological counterpart: "The reunification of the sexually divided human being into his original unity, in which he was neither man nor woman but merely a human being, will be followed by the reunification of the earthly sphere with paradise at the consummation of the due period of time."[64] Christ must have foreseen this restoration of the original ontological status of being. Scotus recounts the tradition, which draws its origin from circles belonging to the mysteries cited earlier, but for which he mentions Maximus the Confessor as the source, according to which Christ must have united the divided sexes in his own nature and must have been "neither man nor woman" at the resurrection, although "he was born and died man."[65] Through the grace of the redemption, man has also been made virtually capable of the same.[66]

In Scotus Eriugena these views have a simple theological and eschatological doctrinal character. There is no reference to eros as a possible tool for the reintegration or to any concrete proceedings. On the other hand, there is reason to believe that the mystery of the hermaphrodite, with greater adherence to the initiation tradition where it had already taken shape before the arrival of Christianity, was assumed on an operative level by Hermetic and alchemic tradition, which, from the very beginning and since the Hellenistic texts, had traced back the essence of the Great Work to the union of male with female. In medieval literature as well as in extensions of it up to a relatively recent period, the Hermetic and alchemic tradition also gave great importance to the enigmatic symbol of the "Rebis" in alluding to the "double being," the hermaphroditic being which unites in itself the twofold nature, male and female, solar and lunar. From this literature we can pick out as particularly suggestive the hermaphrodite figure corresponding to epigram 33 of Michele Maier's *Scrutinium chymicum* with the caption "The hermaphrodite, lying like a dead man among the shadows, needs Fire."[67] We shall come back at the proper time to the practical teachings that refer to this, those teachings capable of being applied practically in terms of sexual magic. To end this digression, we shall only say that, along the lines of this same tradition, the link established by Scotus Eriugena between Christ and the hermaphrodite crops up again in Khunrath. In illustration II of his *Amphiteatrum eternae sapientiae* (1606) we can in fact see Adam-Eve regenerated in the shape of a hermaphrodite and bearing the caption "The man who rejects the binary [Dyad], clothed with Christ and imitating Christ." The same theme is given more explicitly in illustration III of the same work, where the philosopher's stone is shown. In the middle part of it is the Rebis Man-Woman, Sun-Moon, with the proverb "The world too shall be renewed by Fire."

Lastly we may note this fact: it is hard to deny the existence of eso-tericism in Leonardo da Vinci. Indeed, the theme of the hermaphrodite has an obvious emphasis in his paintings, especially in the most significant of them, which refer to Saint John and to Bacchus (Dionysus). Furthermore, there recurs enigmatically in them, almost like a monogram, the theme of the columbine, a plant that was deemed to be hermaphroditic.

On the Daemonic in the Feminine and the Symbolism of the Inverted Coitus

It is well known that the female principle has been linked in the traditions of many peoples not only to the principle of "seduction" but also to a daemonic element. According to the Kabbala, the daemonic indeed springs from the female element,[68] and from the *yin* principle in Chinese Taoism, while in the Egyptian tradition the personification of the antisolar forces was mainly female; Isis herself sometimes had this character, as can be seen in the legend where she is given the traits of an enchantress who takes possession cunningly of the "name of power" of Ra so as to make him her subject.[69] It would be easy to gather further data from different traditions on this aspect of the female. This must be understood not on a moral but on an ontological plane with reference to the natural partiality of the Shakti or principle of "matter" and the "Waters," whenever we consider manifestation in its dynamic and dramatic aspects as well as in the everlasting emanation process of a kind that is almost Spinozan.

This brings us to an esoteric teaching very like the metaphysics of human sexuality. The female partiality toward the daemonic is shown in the attempt to catch and to absorb the principle of transcendental or magical manhood, linked to that which in the male reflects the supernatural element prior to the Dyad, and to what in nature is higher than nature and should have the power to "make the stream of the waters flow back on high" and to break the cosmic bond. This is the exact meaning of the word *virya* in technical Buddhist terminology, whose root is the same as the Latin word *vir* ("man"); it designates manhood in a lofty and transcendental sense as that which is brought into action in the ascent on high and can lead us beyond the region of "becoming" or *samsara* by "stopping the flow." According to the polyvalence of the technical terminology of Tantrism and hatha yoga, however, the same word *virya* can also designate the male seed, which in a more general context connects with the theory that to man as such, owing to the simple fact of his manhood, or *purushamatra sambandhibhih*, has been granted the potential to attain the supernatural completion of himself.[70] Now, it is part of the female nature to tend to enslave and absorb this principle in her Demeter or Aphrodite function, but not so much on a material and human plane, with reference to procreation and to the bonds of the flesh and desire, as on an occult level. In that she shows her essential daemonism and her antagonistic function. She is oriented toward keeping that order which Gnosticism, in a dualistic background, called the "world of the Demiurge," the world of nature as opposed to that of the spirit. Thus it was possible to talk of a "draining death" that comes to man from woman because losing his *virya* or manly magical principle while mingling with the female substance of desire means for man "being erased from the Book of Life." Here, therefore, we have the theme of a natural "inexorableness" of the female principle and of a metaphysical "war of the sexes" beyond the sphere of merely human, individual, profane, and social relationships.

Meyrink emphasized this category of ideas and showed their most drastic fulfillment in the ancient mysteries celebrated in Pontus under the sign of one variant of the Great Goddess, Isais.[71] But it is in no way foolhardy to attribute a similar meaning to the mysteries of Rhea-Cybele as well. The "holy orgy" celebrated under the sign of that goddess burst out in such an unmanning ecstatic intoxication that in its degenerate forms at the peak of the frenzy, the participating men sacrificed to the goddess the actual physical expression of the principle of their manhood through castration and wearing women's clothes. Besides, in these and in other cults of the same cycle (the mysteries of Hecate of Laguira, of Astaroth, of Astarte of Hieropolis, of Artemis of Ephesus, etc.), the priests of the goddess were castrated or wore women's clothes.

In the pre-Orphic worship of Dionysus, the female element prevailed. Besides the public cult, mysteries were celebrated from which, in some cases (as in the early bacchanals at Rome), men were excluded and only women were initiated. The Dionysiac woman exercised sovereignty over mere phallic manhood, whereby the exciting, accomplishing, and absorbing of that manhood were in practice the same as harming and breaking the transcendental manhood in accordance with the ambivalence of eros.[72]

However, the partiality of woman for the daemonic is acknowledged just as much in these "lower" forms as in the "heavenly" ones, which themselves involve a "cosmic" limit. Although "woman" can give life, yet she shuts off or tends to shut off access to that which is beyond life. This, too, is a subject that we often meet in the world of legends and heroic myths. Typical is the myth, for instance, about a heavenly woman who, even if she helped and protected the shaman, yet sought to have him for herself alone in the seventh heaven and fought against the continuation of his ascent. She told him that life beyond was cut off and tempted him with heavenly food.[73] In the heroic legends the love of a woman with more or less supernatural features was often presented as more of a hindrance and peril than as a help for the protagonist.

It is essential to distinguish two kinds of mysteries, which we may call the greater and lesser mysteries or the mysteries of Ammon and the mysteries of Isis, which, however, have no strict historical links with the actual outward form of the ancient holy institutions which were given that name more on the basis of a general morphological definition. The lesser mysteries or mysteries of Isis may therefore be defined as the mysteries of the woman, those whose purpose was the "cosmic" reintegration of the individual and his union with the female substance, life force, and substratum of manifestation. Such mysteries can have either a bright or a daemonic nature, depending on their functional character. The daemonic forms and circumstances indicated earlier occurred when the female principle of the mysteries was made absolute and activated in a function antagonistic to the supercosmic. As we said, this tendency may be always directly visible; but even when the principle of the Woman and Mother is transformed into the terms of a Divine Mother or Mother of God—a theme present earlier in ancient Aegean times and in the cult of Isis itself, which represented the goddess with a baby—similar to the Christian motif *ianua coeli* (Gate to Heaven), even then the limit remains.

The great mysteries or mysteries of Ammon may be defined as those linked to the "reascent" or to the waters flowing back on high and to the surpassing of the "cosmic" level; they are, therefore, under the sign of transcendental manhood and mark the beginning of that manhood's gaining the upper hand.

One meaning in particular of the archetypal myth of incest can be fitted into this context. The woman, who had the function of the "mother" who gave the "Water of Life" and of resurrection to the divided being (this is the "second birth" of the lesser mysteries), was possessed by him to whom she had given birth in a certain way and who was her son. Although related to the Royal Art (which is said to reproduce the work of creation in its phases), this symbolism in alchemic Hermeticism was presented in a severe form. It is said that there was a first phase or regime of woman, of the Waters or Moon or whiteness, in which woman had the upper hand over man and reduced him to her nature (lesser mysteries); after the man had been dissolved in the opposed principle, however, the so-called regime of Fire or the Sun or redness came about, and in it the man regained the upper hand and reduced the woman to his nature. To indicate this second phase the texts sometimes employed the symbolism of incest between the son and mother.[74] When these two phases are considered, not in succession, but in opposition to each other, they correspond in their essential content to the two opposed forms of ecstasy or to the two traditions of the mysteries or the "births," as we have seen.

If we look through the rich and manifold traditional symbolism and imagery, we find a rather expressive sign concerning this opposition in the contrasting meanings of one and the same curious theme, that of the "inverted coitus." One of those belongs to Egypt; the ancient Egyptian goddess Nut is a representation of the female that, like Isis herself, seems in the beginning to have had a chthonic character but thereafter to have assumed a heavenly and absolute one. Identified by Plutarch with Rhea, Nut appears as the "Great Lady who gives birth to the gods," the "Lady of the Sky," the "Queen of the Sky and Sovereign of the two Earths," who bears the papyrus scepter and holds the Key of Life. In one of her most frequent representations, Nut is "she who bends herself"; "being almost always naked, she bends her body until she touches the ground with the tips of her fingers, and her legs and arms seem to be the stands or pillars of her horizontally positioned body." In this posture Nut is the Sky and beneath her lies Seb, a god of the Earth, with his manhood erect. This grouping leaves no doubt that Nut is ready to lower and spread herself on the supine god, to copulate with him, taking him into her flesh in the holy union of Heaven and Earth. Pestalozza observed quite rightly that the unwonted, inverted position of the goddess in the coitus hinted at a very precise meaning; we meet with this position not only in the Egyptian figures but also in the Sumerian era and even in late Paleolithic times, as has been shown in the bas-relief of Laussel. The principle of female dominion has an odd, drastic expression in it. The position of the goddess above the god expresses the preeminence of the female principle in forms of civilization oriented toward rule by woman. Her dominion is witnessed and proclaimed in the very act that perpetuates life.[75]

However, the same symbolism of inverted coitus performed by divine figures can be found in civilizations oriented toward rule by men, and then it has a totally opposite meaning. We should mention in passing that this type of coitus among Islamic people is marked with a precise symbolic context according to the proverb "Cursed be he who makes of woman the Sky and of man the Earth." Whereas in the Hindu Indo-Tibetan world we can very often find plastic representations of the *viparita-maithuna* or else of a kind of coitus characterized by the male staying still while the female moves, which partly repeats the situation of the Egyptian representation of Nut but expresses the opposite idea of male dominion. The god here is Shiva or another equivalent divinity of a *purusha* type, and his lack of movement expresses the character of true manhood, which, as we said, does not "act" in the proper meaning of the word but only arouses motion in *prakriti*, in "nature" or Shakti, which is the woman, so that she "moves" and develops the dynamism of creation. To use an apt expression of T. Burckhardt, we are dealing here with the "activity of the unchangeable and the passivity of the dynamic." Tibetan representations of the divine pair joined together in this kind of coitus often bear the name of "the god who possesses the Mother,"[76] which repeats the symbolism of the incest we have already met in the Western hermetic traditions, likewise drawn from the mysteries.[77] It is worthwhile to observe next that the position of the *viparita-maithuna* belongs to a framework that is essentially holy and ritual. In fact, texts such as the *Kamasutra* make it clear that that position was not particularly used in India in the sphere of profane love, because profane relationships have no bearing on the symbolism proper to that position. Apart from iconographic representations and statues it seems to have been used, above all, as *lata-sadhana* and *lata-veshtitaka* in the secret rites of Tantric sexual magic, and not without reason. For in those rites man is believed to embody Shiva and thus to adopt toward woman that inwardly active behavior of which there is hardly a trace in the lustful rapture of the normal act of physical love, but which is the precise "mark" of the *viparita-maithuna*.

Note how the deepest meaning of male stillness found in this sexual symbolism is connected to the kindred significances of hieratic stillness and royal stillness, both clearly reflective of transcendental manhood.

The Phallus and Menstruation

We shall end this exploration by touching on two particular sides of the sexual *sacrum*.

We shall deal first with the worship of the phallus. In the history of religions this worship has almost always been given a merely naturalistic, if not indeed obscene, meaning and has been reduced to a cult of fertility and pandemic begetting manhood. But such a view basically concerns only its most outward, degraded, and popular side. The phallic symbol has also expressed the principle of transcendental, magical, or supernatural manhood, which is something very different from the merely priapic varieties of male power. Thus the phallus was linked even to the mystery and hope of the resurrection and to the power that can bring it about; for this reason the phallus can be seen in the art of the graveyard and was often put on the tombs in Greece and Rome. We have already mentioned texts in which the ithyphallic god, or the god with erect phallus, is linked to the image of one in whom there rises again and is reconfirmed the nature of the primordial being, of Adam, of "him who cannot be broken in two." In further evidence coming from the same source this being is also called "he who stayed on his feet, stays on his feet, and will stay on his feet," and the ithyphallic symbolism, being based on the upright, indeed expresses the idea of standing upright as opposed to the condition of him who has fallen or been knocked down.

The text refers explicitly to the metaphysical context indicated earlier when it talks of "him who stood on his feet up on high in the power of the Godhead and who stands on his feet down here as he has been generated by the [image] brought by the Waters";[78] the text then passes on at once to speak of the ithyphallic Hermes. In the Egyptian world (in its "solar" aspects as opposed to those which found expression in the symbolism of the "goddess who bends"), the ithyphallic god Osiris symbolized, not the fertility, birth, and death linked to animal procreation and to the wet principle of generation and desire, but resurrection from the dead. "O gods who sprang from the phallus, stretch forth your arms to me," reads an Egyptian inscription near the figure of a dead man who is rising from his grave, and we can also read, "O Phallus arising to slaughter those who rebel [against the sun god]! By virtue of your phallus I am stronger than the strong and mightier than the mighty!"[79] In various statues and representations, Osiris himself holds or points to his phallus, alluding to his resurrection as a prototype for his worshippers. In Egypt, moreover, there existed phallic mysteries in which, as Diodorus Siculus tells us, those who wished to become priests of particular cults had to be initiated. Last, a fact especially worth mentioning is that the phallus or *lingam* in India is one of the symbols of Shiva and that a pendant which reproduces its shape is worn by ascetics as their token. This symbol relates not to Pan or to Dionysiac procreation but to the force of the *virya* or awakened manhood, which becomes active through ascetic detachment from the conditioned world.

Now, there is a hidden connection between this meaning and the degradation of the same symbolism that we find in the ancient Roman world where the image of the phallus was used by the lower classes as a talisman or amulet against lucky influences and harmful spells—though even this echoes the significance of triumphant and luminous manhood, which disperses everything underhanded and demonic. Thus the iconography of the phallus in some temples (not only of Bacchus, Venus, and Priapus, but even in temples of Jove, Apollo, and Hermes) was present to purify and neutralize any adverse force. The walls of ancient Italian towns had a phallus to evoke a magical protective force, and the phallus as an amulet is widespread among other civilizations, especially in Japan. On the other hand, we see the phallus represented in emperor worship after, as Pliny says, the emperors had already placed it before their triumphal chariot. But according to the ancient Roman mystical theology of victory, it was Jupiter, the shining uranic principle, who caused emperors to be victorious. This complex, removed from the naturalistic and priapic, integrated the symbolism and cult of the phallus as known by the traditional world. But the history of religions only acknowledges its lowest values. Only in the decadent phase of classical culture did the phallus become a symbol of wantonness and take on an "obscene" connotation.

Turning again to Egyptian traditions, we find the myth of Osiris, the primordial god, who was torn to pieces. The various parts of his body were found and he was put together again; however, his phallus was never found. This dismembering symbolizes the passage from the world of the One to that of manifold natures and individual existence. In the latter world, the primordial being in man tends to be recomposed. But still man lacks the phallus, not that of physical manhood but that of transcendental manhood and of creative, divine, and magical power. He will find it and become whole only as an initiate or as a "being made into Osiris." This myth of the phallus of Osiris is thus another thematic variant of something lost and found again, the holy word lost or forgotten, the true heavenly liquid draught no longer known, the Grail itself become invisible, and so on.

The male aspect of the sexual *sacrum* can be contrasted with the ambiguous and even perilous aspect attributed to the female principle in a group of traditions that are in agreement with each other. It is not only within a background of puritanical religions hostile to sex that woman was thought of as the principle of "impurity"; the commandment to be "pure and innocent of woman" can certainly be found in a much wider system of rituals and faiths. Such "impurity" is not thought of in moral terms but refers to the objective and impersonal quality of a given influence linked to an essential side of female nature. The same idea lies at the bottom of various concepts and beliefs concerning female puberty and, above all, the menses.

This idea may have found its most extreme expression in the primitive customs of certain savage peoples among whom young girls were segregated and even kept away from the group[80] at their first sign of puberty. They were then deemed to be "charges of a powerful force which, unless kept within given limits, could destroy not only the girl but also all the people with whom she came in contact." Therefore, she was considered to be taboo as the bearer of a mysterious energy, which in itself was neither good nor evil but capable of acting in either way, depending on the applications and circumstances involved. The initial isolation of the girl on the appearance of the first menses might even be repeated at every occurrence. The influence was thought of as objective and almost "physical," so that on the first occasion her very clothes were burned because impregnated with that influence.[81] Among certain peoples the same danger and impurity were attributed to women who gave birth, and they were isolated and purified. Along with the shedding of blood and the contact with dead bodies, childbirth was similarly a contaminating situation that necessitated the rite of lustration. Women in Hellas were forbidden to give birth in the sacred enclosures or holy precincts of the temples. Among other peoples, cases of abortion were thought to involve an especially high degree of danger, based on the idea of an energy that had started to act but had not been exhausted because of the interruption of the process of gestation. Furthermore, the Roman Catholic and Anglican churches have recognized a special service, called *rélevailles* in French, that can be considered "the survival of an ancient belief that a woman who had brought a child into the world should be cleansed, not medically, but religiously [spiritually]." Popular superstition here and there continues to hold to the idea that "if a woman has not been to church to be purified after childbirth, it is very dangerous for her to leave her home."[82]

The interesting point here is that the ambiguous and perilous side of the occult female substance seems connected not to the Aphroditic capability but to the Demeter or maternal capability of woman. This is confirmed by the fact that in almost all traditions, the idea of the magical peril acquires its greatest importance in connection with the menses, which is linked to the maternal and not to the Aphroditic nor Dionysiac capability of woman. This influence is able to paralyze everything sacred and strikes at the most profound nucleus of manhood. Thus, the Laws of Manu state that the knowledge, strength, force, might, and vital energy of a man who lies with a menstruating woman disappear wholly. North American Indians believe that the presence of a woman in that state can sap the power of a holy man.[83] At Rome, the virgins actings as vestals had to suspend this task during their menstrual period; among the Medes, Persians, and Bactrians, menstruating women were isolated away from holy elements and especially from fire; among Greeks of the Orthodox church women in that condition were forbidden to communicate and to kiss the icons in church. In certain parts of Japan as well, they are strictly prohibited from visiting the temples and praying to the gods and the good spirits; according to the *Nitya-karma* and *Padmapurana* in India, the commandment is "In that period a woman must not think of God nor of the sun, nor of sacrifices nor prayers." Among the Hebrews even the death penalty was contemplated in certain instances for men who joined themselves in the flesh with a menstruating woman, and for Zoroastrians this was a sin for which there was no remission. The Islamic code of Sidi Khebil said: "He who touches a woman during her menses to satisfy his own pleasure loses the force and tranquillity of the spirit." An old English rhyme, cited by Ellis, says: "O menstruating woman, thou'rt a fiend / From whom all nature should be closely screened!"[84]

An especially indicative value lies in the Hindu concept that a menstruating woman of any caste has the substance of an untouchable during her period, and this quality weakens in her only as her period declines. The interesting point here is that according to Hindu beliefs the untouchable represents the chaos or devilish element, which is more and more curbed the higher the caste involved. In this context menstruation undoubtedly is connected, above all, to the negative aspect of *mana*, the mysterious force borne by and contained in woman; this aspect appears by contrast, when it interferes with a sacred quality having a truly supernatural manly character. Menstrual blood has played a part in the magic of incantations and love potions as well as in witchcraft. In medieval Europe its use in certain potions was said to have the power to make people idiots and hypochondriacs or, in other cases, to create mania and catalepsy (the same effects as found in the pathology of adolescence). When mixed with wine, it was supposed to make people walk in their sleep or go crazy with love.[85] The "superstition" is still widespread that when a man was made, unawares, to carry the menstrual blood of a woman on his person, it would bind him irrevocably to her. According to the gypsies, menstrual blood mixed with certain drinks provokes a loss of control that can cause a man to become alcoholic; they also believe that women who celebrate the Sabba on the "Mountain of the Moon" confirm their pact with the Devil every seven years by means of their menstrual blood.[86] Superstition or not, the link between the substance of woman, through her menses, and the world of nocturnal (non-Apollonian) magic is significant, as are the psychically arousing and disintegrating influences.[87]

As with everything having the character of "man," here, too, a certain ambivalence can be witnessed. A positive use of the perilous force is possible. Thus Pliny[88] wrote that favorable influences as well as harmful were attributed to the menses, as a power effective against the elements and natural phenomena. Their use for therapeutic purposes against epilepsy is mentioned. In the *Getreuer Eckarth*, special magical virtues are attributed to the first menses of a virgin, as a capability belonging to every power when manifested for the first time. Among ancient Nordic populations, the Finns and Goths, it was used for victory in competitions, good luck in games, and counterenchantments in the hazards of navigation.[89] But in these traditions the unfavorable aspect of the mystery of the Mother prevails, an aspect that was dimly felt wherever there was an apprehension of the essence of its opposite (the higher values of the phallic symbol).

All of woman's secretions have an erotic power by reason of the fluid that is linked to her, with the exception of menstrual material. A woman's period almost always exercises a decidedly antierotic effect on man. We may deduce a metaphysical background for this based on the idea that, while the Aphroditic potentiality of woman is the one that corresponds to the possibility of integration, of life-giving and even of ecstatic transcendence, her maternal capability, which has in menses and in menstrual *mana* its crudest manifestation, shows an exclusively naturalistic character and is therefore unable to activate the higher values enclosed in all male eros. It is claimed that menstruation ceases entirely in young girls employed in sexual magic.

Male and Female Psychology

We said at the beginning of this chapter that from the structures of the mythology of sex it would be possible to deduce the general principles for a psychology of man and woman. This psychology would be normative and deductive rather than empirical and would examine the fundamental morphological traits beyond any possible variation, modulation, or distortion due to accidental or environmental facts of psyche and behavior of the sexes.

We know that up to a relatively late period the Roman Catholic theologians were wondering whether woman should be acknowledged to have a soul; it seems that Augustine declared, "Woman is not made in the image of God." The thesis that "women are not men" was discussed again 1555 in the sense that they cannot be true human beings but must belong to another species. A like theme is found in Islam, while in the traditions of the Far East it was taught that women were not found in the "Pure Earth" or so-called Western Paradise because women worthy of being welcome there would first have to be "reborn" as men. The Council of Mâcon debated the question whether on the day of the resurrection of the flesh, deserving women, before passing into the Kingdom of Heaven, ought not to be changed into men. Consider the link between these ideas and those in Plato's *Timaeus*, where he poses the possibility that, owing to regression and to the identification of his spiritual principle with the sensitive and sensual element, a man might reappear on earth as a woman instead of going back to the uranic being whence he had come.

Taken as a whole, these ideas were more than mere historical curiosities. In our time Otto Weininger has taken up ideas of the same kind in his highly interesting application of the transcendental philosophy of Kant to the psychology of the sexes. The principles set forth in the preceding chapter may clarify the actual state of things. As she reflects the essence of the eternal female, each woman belongs ontologically to "nature" in the widest and "cosmic" but not simply material sense of the word (as in the Greek *phýsis* or nature). By contrast, in each man, since he embodies the opposite principle, there is virtually present, besides "nature," that which transcends nature and is higher than and prior to the Dyad. If we say that woman lacks a soul, we have expressed nothing more than just that, but such a wording, of course, lends itself to ambiguity. If the word "soul" is taken in its original meaning of "psyche" or principle of life, it should signify in fact that woman not only has a soul but is eminently "soul." What by nature as "absolute woman" she lacks and what she cannot have as woman and not man is not a soul but a "spirit" (nous and not psyche). By "spirit" we mean here the supernatural principle that Roman Catholic theology refers to when it speaks of "soul" and when it upholds the belief that, contrary to woman, man is made in the image of God. It has been said that "the spirit is the male principle in us, whereas sensuality is the female principle."[90] We shall come back to the question of sensuality. Meanwhile, the point we believe settled is that woman is a part of "nature" (in a metaphysical sense she is a manifestation of the same principle as nature) and that she affirms nature, whereas man by virtue of birth in the masculine human form goes *tendentially* beyond nature.

Weininger seems to be more radical in asserting not only that woman has no soul but also that she has no ego or "being," and in declaring the decisive factor between masculinity and femininity to be the possession or lack of "being."[91] The whole of this has a scandalous and paradoxically misogynous character only because of another ambiguity of words. In fact, when Weininger speaks of ego, he means, following the philosophy of Kant, not the psychological but the transcendental ego, which is apprehended by intuition and is above the whole world of phenomena (in metaphysical terms one would say "above all manifestation," like the Hindu *atman*); and when he talks of "being," all natural and empirical reality is nonbeing in the opinion both of Parmenides and the Vedanta.

Whether every man in actuality has such an ego and being is another question. In fact, it is rather obvious that by far the greatest number of men do not possess such a principle. But that man is ontologically linked to that principle, even though he has no clear awareness of it, and that, as Far Eastern traditions put it, it is the "Heavens" that produce men, are decisive factors for all male psychology and for the possibilities open in principle to man as man, whether he makes use of them or not. Absolute woman not only does not possess that ego but would not know what to do with it if she did. As she is unable even to conceive of it, its presence would act in a highly disturbing manner toward any genuine expression of her most profound nature.

Furthermore, such an ontological status has no prejudicial effect on what women in some epochs and especially in the present may choose as the object of their mistaken claims; a woman can build up an ego that is "intellectual" and practical in the modern sense almost as well as a man by way of a layer placed on top of her deepest nature. The female quality of being consubstantial with "nature" has not prevented women in past civilizations from having access to functions of a sacred character, in connection with much more interesting callings than those for which feminists in the West are fighting so hard. When writing about the mysteries of the Mother, however, we remarked that the "cosmic" limit is not removed with that. Nowadays it is hard to accept this fundamental point of the ontology of the sexes. As we have almost no idea of the truly supernatural, so the type of the absolute man has almost disappeared. Borders that were clearly demarcated in other times have today become unstable through disintegration.

The symbolism of the Waters and lunar changeability, which are essentially related to the female archetype, also give us the key to the most elementary psychology of woman. But we must underline here a basic point of a general kind; the characteristics with which we shall deal now and hereafter do not concern a person as such; they are not "qualities of character" or "moral qualities" for which one or another female individual is responsible. Instead, they are objective elements working in individuals almost as impersonally as the chemical properties inherent in a particular substance. It is effectively "nature proper" which acts in a more or less exact and constant manner. So let it be said once and for all that it makes no sense to formulate value judgements or to speak of "good" or "bad."

Having made this point, it would be trivial to dwell on the fickleness, changeability, and unsteadiness of female character (and also of male character wherever man has something of woman in him) as the outcome of her "wet" (watery) and "lunar" nature. This "essential deduction" was already known to some authors of the Middle Ages. Thus a certain Cecco of Ascoli gave the following explanation for the lack of "steadiness" in women and for their shifting now here and now there like the wind: "Each of them, of course, is wet, and wetness does not keep its form"; and he links to the same cause another female trait with which we shall deal shortly: "Broken faith is in her by nature."[92]

Furthermore, we may also point to the prevalence in female psychology of the emotional part, which has passive, "lunar," and discontinuous characteristics. As a physiological counterpart, the great changeability of woman's expressions, which belong only to her surface, is the changeability of a mask without any deep counterpart, which would in any case be impossible. Here it is almost a question of movable surface waves that do not "penetrate" into the physiognomy, as happens in the male mask; in this there is more mobility than true expressiveness of character, linked to a greater neuromuscular ability to become excited; here we may think of how women blush and smile. It is for this reason, too, that the art at which women excel most is that of the theater and that in every actor there is always something feminine.[93]

In a wider context, it is necessary to consider what arises, for a woman, from the fact that she reflects the cosmic female according to its aspect as material receiving a form that is external to her and that she does not produce from within (*natura naturata* or *natura signata*—"natured nature" or "impressed nature"). This gives rise to the great suppleness, credulity, impressionability, and adaptability of the female psyche and woman's natural disposition to accept and assimilate ideas and forms coming to her from outside, although a possible rigidity may follow the reception of ideas due precisely to the passive way she has adopted them, which may appear under the guise of conformity and conservatism. In this way, we can explain the apparent contrast inherent in the fact that female nature is changeable, yet women mainly show conservative tendencies sociologically and a dislike for the new.[94] This can be linked to their role in mythology as female figures of a Demeter or chthonic type who guard and avenge customs and the law—the law of blood and of the earth, but not the uranic law. This aspect is reflected on the biological plane in Darwin's observation that the female tends to preserve and lead back to the average type of the species, whereas the male has a greater power of physio-anatomical variation. Here we are faced with two opposed kinds of changeability. One of them, female changeability, springs from the material and plastic principle and has as its counterpart the force of inertia or static fixedness as soon as the material has been "shaped" (the Demeter aspect of the female, opposed to the Aphrodite aspect). The other, male changeability, is instead linked to the creative "seminal" principle, which is a principle of activity in a free and proper sense. The contrast between the two aspects of female nature, fickleness and inconstancy alongside conservativism, is therefore only an apparent one.

Of those modern writers who have tackled sexual psychology, Weininger is perhaps the only one who has risen above the level of banality. We can refer to him again for some other essential points. First, Weininger established an organic relationship between memory, logic, and ethics on the basis of the link between each one of them and the "transcendental ego." This concerns essentially the psychic structure of the absolute man. "Being" tends to support its own unity in the world of "becoming." On the psychological plane this is revealed in the memory, which, as a synthetic function, opposes itself to the dispersion of consciousness in the fluid and instantaneous multiplicity of the contents of that consciousness; on the plane of the intellect, the same impulse is shown in logic, which has as its basis the principle of identity: A equals A. The ideal of logic is to bring the unlike back to one. As such, both memory and a logical nature have a guiding ethical value because they express the resistance of being, its effort to stand upright, identical to itself, and to assert itself in the stream of inner and outer phenomena. According to Weininger, as the absolute woman is devoid of being, she could have neither memory, logic, nor ethics. Incapable of a logical or an ethical imperative, she would be wholly ignorant of the precise, vigorous, imperative nature of the purely intellectual function of judgment, which has a distinctly male character.[95] Bergson distinguished between two separate kinds of memory. One is the "vital" and is linked to "duration," or the flow of experience (this memory is connected to the subconscious and at given times throws up distant recollections unexpectedly and involuntarily; the same memory may recall the whole content of a life instantaneously when death threatens). The other memory is determined, organized, and dominated by the intellect. Woman lacks this second memory owing to her "fluid" lunar nature, whereas she may be more generously endowed with the first kind than man. But the first memory lacks the ethical capability of which we spoke earlier, and it proceeds not by the presence but by the lack of a "transcendental ego."

We have to bear in mind two differing sides of logic. We are not dealing with everyday logic, which woman, when necessary, knows how to use "instrumentally" with undoubted ability and ingenuity, even if the method is not straightforward but polemical and fleeting, like a guerrilla or a sophist. Instead, we are dealing with logic as a love of pure truth and inward coherence, which leads to a strict and impersonal style of thought that constitutes a sort of inner imperative for the absolute man. Woman is almost incapable of this logic, and it does not interest her. She has as a substitute her intuitive and sensitive qualities, which are linked to the fluid element of life, the *yin* aspect, as opposed to the precise, steadfast, enlightened, Apollonian (but often also dry as dust) forms of nous (perception) and logos (reason), the male intellectual principle.

Weininger's statement that the absolute woman is not aware of the ethical imperative has a greater weight. Woman, insofar as she is woman, will never know ethics in the categorical sense of pure inner law detached from every empirical, eudemonistic, sensitive, sentimental, and personal connection. Nothing in woman that may have an ethical character can be separated from instinct, sentiment, sexuality, or "life"; it can have no relationship with pure "being." It will almost always have a naturalistic character or will be a sublimation with a naturalistic content, as we shall see when we come to deal with the traditional ethics of the mother or female lover. Apart from this, the question here is not of an ethical nature but, at most, of morality, which in woman is a superficial thing, received from the world of man and often only conformist. This is the way we should think, for instance, about female ideas regarding "honor" and "virtue" and many other qualities in "social ethics," which are not true ethics but mere habits (of the Demeter woman as the guardian of habit). Woman may even prize in man some qualities that have an ethical value: justice very seldom, but often heroism, the power of command and decision, and in certain cases even an ascetic disposition. But that feminine recognition is concerned not with the inner ethical element of such behavior but with the personal quality that is sexually attractive in a particular man. In other words, these qualities meet with a response from the sexuality of woman and not from an ethical nature.

That telling lies is an essential characteristic in female nature has been acknowledged at all times and in all places by popular wisdom. Weininger relates this trait likewise to the absence of being in the absolute woman. In fact we can see in this a disposition that is a special, possible outcome of the existential weakness of woman, a weakness that reflects that of her "raw material" or of *ŭlē* (matter), which according to Plato and Aristotle is the principle of the "unlike," nonidentical, alteration and "decline." Weininger observed that nothing is more baffling for a man than a woman's response when caught in a lie. When asked why she is lying, she is unable to understand the question, acts astonished, bursts out crying, or seeks to pacify him by smiling.[96] She cannot understand the ethical and transcendental side of lying or the fact that a lie represents damage to being and, as was acknowledged in ancient Iran, constitutes a crime even worse than killing. It is nonsense to deduce this trait in women from sociological factors; some people say that a lie is the "natural weapon" of the woman and therefore used in her defense for hundreds of years. The truth, pure and simple, is that woman is prone to lie and to disguise her true self even when she has no need to do so; this is not a social trait acquired in the struggle for existence, but something linked to her deepest and most genuine nature. Just as the absolute woman does not truly feel that lying is wrong, so in her, contrary to man, lying is not wrong, nor is it an inner yielding or a breaking of her own existential law. It is a possible counterpart of her plastic and fluid nature. A type such as D'Aurevilly described is perfectly understandable: "She made a habit of lying to the point where it became truth; it was so simple and natural, without any effort or affectation." It is foolish to judge woman with the values of the absolute man even in cases where, by doing violence to her own self, she makes a show of following those values and even sincerely believes that she is following them.

Woman as Mother and Woman as Lover

We said earlier that in the sphere of manifestation and nature, the male is metaphysically the complementary correlative of the female, but beyond that, he also reflects the character of that which is higher and earlier than the Dyad. The outcome on the human plane is that, whereas all relationships based on the Dyad have an essential character for woman and fulfill the natural law of her being, the same is not true for man insofar as he is truly man. Such relationships are the sexual ones in a strict sense, and the relationships between mother and son as well. It is not wrong to say that in every higher civilization man has never been deemed to be truly a man as long as he submits to the double bond of mother and wife and exhausts the sense of his own existence in that sphere. We mentioned earlier that in the very rites of passage or of puberty among primitive peoples the consecration of manhood and admission to a "society of men" were shown as a surpassing of that naturalistic sphere. Rachel said in the Bible, "Give me a son or else I shall die." There are Buddhist texts that underline the "inexorable nature" of woman as regards motherhood and sexuality, of which she can never have enough.[97] Not so much as a person, but rather owing to a metaphysical impulse, woman will always tend to lead man back under the yoke of eros or domesticity.

In characterizing man and woman, Weininger was right to say that absolute woman is nothing but sexuality, whereas the true man "is sexual but something else as well." We concur with that writer in seeing the profound symbolic meaning in the anatomical and bodily facts that the male sexual organs seem to be something limited, detached, and almost added on to the rest of man's body from the outside, whereas the sexual organs of a woman go deep into her innermost flesh. As there exists in man a certain gap between himself and sexuality, he can "know" his own sexuality, whereas woman can be unaware of it and deny it, for she is nothing other than sexuality and is sexuality itself.[98] A Hindu name for woman is *kamini* or "she who is made of desire," and that expresses the same meaning as the old Latin proverb *"Tota mulier sexus,"* "The whole of woman is sex." Among other things, there is a link between that and the provocative character often shown, without the least intention, by very young and "innocent" women and even by baby girls. We should note, next, in a not dissimilar context, a special and almost unconscious narcissism within every woman which lies in her feeling of the potential pleasure that she can constitute for man. This she can relish by imagining that pleasure, even outside of any real sexual relations. Moreover, Ellis was right when he wrote that woman thrives on sexuality and motherhood, which make her proper being function. There is no correlative of this for man (let us add, unless he reaches in some way the higher dimensions of sexual experience); on the Aphroditic side, the counterpart in man may rather be a certain loss of manhood, even if we leave aside the occult question, with which we shall deal in the next section.[99] On the Demeter side, the obscure and predominant desire of woman to be a mother does not meet in man a kindred elementary need to beget. Where such a desire exists in man, it belongs to a different plane, which is ethical rather than naturalistic (the idea of the continuation of the stock, family or caste, and so on).

What the Greeks called "heterity," that is, being connected to another or being centered on someone other than oneself, is a characteristic proper to the cosmic female, whereas to have one's own principle in oneself is proper to the pure male. At the psychological level that fact leads to qualities in woman which can be readily seen in everyday life: female life is almost always devoid of an individual value but is linked to someone else in her need, born of vanity, to be acknowledged, noticed, flattered, admired, and desired (this extroverted tendency is connected to that "looking outside" which on a metaphysical level has been attributed to Shakti). The practice of wooing, gallantry, and compliments (even insincere ones) would be inconceivable if separated from the obligatory basis consisting precisely of this inborn trait of the female psyche, which man has had to keep in mind at all times and in all places. Let us remark in passing that the values of female ethics are very different from those of male ethics, and this can be seen at once in the fact that a woman ought to despise a man for such fawning behavior, which is often pursued just to possess her body; yet exactly the opposite happens.

The two basic capabilities of feminine nature are determined on a less frivolous plane, one corresponding to the Aphrodite and the other to the Demeter archetype, namely woman as lover and as mother. In both cases we have to deal with a being, a will, an attainment to self-confirmation that depend on someone else, either lover or child. This fulfills the being of woman at a profane level (but will continue to a great extent at the sacred level). From the viewpoint of moral obligation, her law and her possible ethics are determined within this framework.

We owe to Weininger once again a classical typological and existential description of these two fundamental capabilities of female nature. But, as with all of what that writer says about woman, here we must discriminate the real from the distorted, which springs from his unconscious misogynous complex with its rather puritanical basis. Indeed, Weininger sees the fundamental womanly capability in "prostitution," to which he gives a deprecatory and degraded meaning. Instead, we are dealing here with the pure type of female lover and her corresponding Aphroditic calling, and professional prostitution does not enter into the question at all, unless in a very minor and conditioned way, for prostitution is often made necessary by environmental, financial, and social circumstances without being linked to an inner predilection for it. At the most, we might talk here of the type of ancient or Oriental courtesan or of the "Dionysiac" woman. Every true man knows at once that there is a contrast or antagonism between the real Aphrodite attitude of woman and the maternal attitude. At their ontological bases these two opposed types are reconnected to the two main conditions of the "raw material," to its pure and dynamically formless state tied to and oriented toward a form and nurturing a form. Now that this point has been cleared up, the differential characterization of Weininger can be accepted as accurate; it is the relationship with procreation and with the child that distinguishes the two opposite types. The "mother" type seeks man for the child, whereas the "lover" type seeks him for the erotic experience by itself (in lower forms, for "pleasure"). Thus the maternal type fits specially into the natural order of things—if we wish to refer to the biological myth, we can say that that type fits into the law and end-purpose of the species—whereas the pure "lover" type transcends this order in a certain way (a meaningful sign is the sterility often found in the types of the pure lover and the "prostitute"),[100] and we would say that, rather than a principle that befriends and affirms the physical, earthly life, the lover type is potentially hostile to that life because of the virtual content of transcendency proper to the absolute display of eros.[101] Thus, although it may disappoint bourgeois morality, it is not as a mother but as a lover that woman can approach a higher order in a natural way, that is, not on the basis of ethics but merely by arousing a spontaneous disposition of her being. However, an ambiguity lies at the base of the statement that the maternal type should feel a strengthening of existence in coitus whereas the Aphrodite type should have a desire to feel herself destroyed, annihilated, and crushed by pleasure.[102] But this is wrong from two points of view: first because the "deadly rapture of love" as a wish to destroy and be destroyed in ecstasy is quite common in both man and woman in all strong and higher forms of erotic experience; and second because the aforesaid disposition of the lover concerns at most the superficial psychic layers of the Virgin or Durga substance of the Aphroditic woman, and the opposite is true on a more profound plane.

But whether a woman is of the mother type or the lover type, existential anguish, fear of loneliness, and the feeling of an uneasy emptiness if she does not possess a man are characteristic of her. The social and even financial conditions that often seem to form the basis of that   ＊ feeling are actually circumstances that only favor its existence but do not cause it. Instead, its deepest root is precisely the essential dependence of woman on another being, the feeling of "matter" and of Penia, who without the "other" and without "form" is nothingness and therefore, when left by herself, experiences the fear of nothingness. Weininger assigns to this metaphysical content also the frequent behavior of woman in coitus: "The supreme moment in the life of a woman, when her original being and elementary pleasure are revealed, is the moment when she feels the male seed running inside her; she then embraces the man tempestuously and hugs him to her; it is the supreme delight of passivity. . . . the matter which, indeed, is formed and does not wish to abandon form but to keep it everlastingly bound to herself."[103] The situation is the same for a woman nearer to the Durga type when, at the same moment, she does not embrace but is almost motionless and her face shows the feelings of an ambiguous ecstasy that have something of the inscrutable smile of some Buddhas and of certain Khmer heads. It is at that time that she receives something more than just the material seed and that she absorbs the *virya*, the magical manhood, the being of the male. It is here that we meet the aspirating quality, that "draining death which comes from woman" of which we spoke in company with Meyrink in connection with the occult side of every normal lustful coitus, a side that may find its symbolic manifestation and echo in the physical outward appearance.

What D'Annunzio said in his *Il Fuòco* (Fire) about one of his female characters—"as if the whole body of the woman had assumed the quality of a sucking mouth"—not only takes place on a subtle plane but in reality makes the erotic practice of fellatio seem the best expression of the ultimate essence of woman. Actually, the ancient world had already recognized a special active participation of woman in coitus, and Aristotle talked of her aspirating the seminal fluid.[104] This theory was taken up again by Fichstedt toward the middle of last century and is now acknowledged to be accurate as regards its physiological side; the existence is admitted of rhythmic contractions of the vagina and uterus, like an aspiration or suction, and of spasmodic automatic movements with their own special wavelike contractions based on particular slow rhythmic tonic waves and having, in fact, the function of absorption by aspirating or sucking. This bodily behavior can be ascertained now only in highly sexed women, but the people of ancient times were right in deeming it to be a general phenomenon. In fact, we believe that during the course of history a physiological atrophy has occurred in feminine sexuality.[105] In Oriental women, who are closest to the ancient type, this physiological behavior in coitus is still almost normal and is joined to physiological capabilities that have become unusual in European women, who nevertheless must have possessed them in ancient times.[106] We are dealing in this regard with a physical symbol or reflection of an essential significance. At this level of physical reflex, the comparison with sucking has a liminal expression in a fact that still remains physiologically obscure, namely the smell of sperm which sometimes is given off by a woman far from her genital parts shortly after coitus; a poet, Arturo Onofri, even went so far as to speak of a "spermatic smile."

Pity, Sexuality, and Cruelty in Woman

A Persian legend indicates the ingredients of which a woman is composed as "the hardness of a diamond, the sweetness of honey, the cruelty of a tiger, the warm brightness of a fire, and the coolness of snow." These ambivalences, the same as those met with in the archetype of the Divine Woman, lie at the basis of another set of traits in feminine psychology: the coexistence of a disposition toward pity and a disposition toward a special cruelty. Lombroso and Ferrero observed some time ago how woman is simultaneously more pitying and yet more cruel than man, for her capacity for a loving protection and compassion is often accompanied by a lack of feeling, ruthlessness, and destructive violence that, once let loose, take a far greater hold on her than they do on man; history bears witness to this in collective forms when rebellions and lynching have taken place.[107] As it is obvious and rather trivial for us, in company with the two writers just cited, to link feminine pity to the maternal disposition or Demeter element in woman, her cruelty must instead be explained by referring to another of her aspects, namely to the most profound essence of female sexuality.

The link between cruelty and sexuality was dramatized even in classical antiquity in the type of the bacchante and maenad. However, it is important to note the presence of this characteristic (which is not unrelated to the "sucking" quality mentioned earlier) behind even the profane and not just the exalted forms of feminine sexuality. This is the "cold" dimension of woman as an earthly and human embodiment of the "Virgin," of Durga and as yin; and it is here that the characteristics shown by the most superficial psychology of the sexes are inverted. We must distinguish two forms of the Aphroditic female type. The lower of these is "female" in a primitive or "Dionysiac" sense, in the popularly accepted meaning of the word, whereas the higher form by contrast has subtle, remote, ambiguous, and apparently chaste features. The figure of Dolores was called "Our Lady of the Spasm" and "daughter of Death and Priapus" by Swinburne, who wrote with reference to her: "I penetrated by the last portal as far as the chapel where sin is a prayer; what does it matter if the rite is mortal, O Lady of the Spasm? What does it matter? The last goblet that we were emptying is all yours, O terrible and wanton Dolores, Our Lady of the Spasm." This characterization is mostly the cerebral surmise of a decadent and "perverted" literary romanticism.[108] However, we are getting nearer to actual circumstances when D'Annunzio writes, "Cruelty is latent at the base of her love, he thought. There is something destructive in her, which becomes more evident as her excitement amid the caresses grows stronger . . . and he saw again in his memory the fearful image, almost like a Gorgon, of the woman as she had appeared to him on several occasions, between his half-shut eyelids, convulsed in a spasm or inert in his extreme weakness" (from his *Trionfo della morte*).[109] This cruelty is not due to inversion or to a masculine trait in women; indeed the opposite is the case. The fact is that, however sweet and loving she may be, every woman's expression has, in moments of desire, something cruel, hard, and ruthless; along with sweetness and tenderness and abandonment coexist an insensitivity and a subtle selfishness beyond the personal essential relationship with her elementary Durga substance as lover. Viazzi rightly noted that such traits are not foreign even to the most ideal type of girl, the romantic Mimi as Murger described her: "She was twenty-two. . . . Her face was like a sketch of an aristocratic figure; but her very refined lineaments, sweetly brightened by the sparkling of her clear blue eyes, took on, at certain moments of boredom and ill temper, a character of almost savage brutality, such that a physiognomist would perhaps have seen the signs of a profound selfishness and a great lack of feeling." And Viazzi noted how often this sign appears "in the most genuine attitudes of a woman in love."[110] The subtlest and deepest feelings in a woman's "abandonment" are seldom understood or seen. But it was a woman and, moreover, a psychoanalyst who commented, "It is rather seldom that we meet men who stay cold in an erotic situation, whereas there are numerous women who are as cold as stockbrokers even when in an erotic relationship. The coldness of the moon and the hard-heartedness of the Moon Goddess symbolize this side of female nature. Notwithstanding its lack of warmth and feeling, and perhaps even owing to its indifference, this impersonal eroticism in woman is often attractive to man."[111]

Besides, it would be hard to say whether outside economic and

social circumstances alone determine the fact that, in spite of everything, a woman in love can aim at a positive and practical objective.
She may show, more than man, a calculating attitude that can be assigned to an instinctive nature and an irresponsible search for pleasure. Leaving that aside, the element of cruelty and coldness in
woman can be shown on the moral plane, for if there are some women
who are proud of a heroic man and the extraordinary deeds he does
for love of her (because these deeds enhance her worth indirectly),
there is also the type who deems her lover's renunciation of all higher
manly valor and his possible fall into ruin on her behalf the strongest
proof of his love for her. One of Don Byrne's characters said that the
man who lost himself wholly in a woman was not a man, however
strong his love for her; the woman would despise him. But the
woman in the book retorted that it was true that the woman would
despise him but that she would also love him all the more. It was not
in regard to the so-called vamp but in general that Remarque adopted
the fable of a rocky boulder that the wave loved: "The wave foamed
and whirled around the boulder and kissed it day and night, and
hugged it with her white arms and begged it to come to her. She loved
it and tossed around it and in this way slowly sapped it; until one day
the boulder was wholly worn away at its bottom and yielded and fell
into the arms of the wave. And for some time there was no longer any
boulder to play with or love or dream of. There was only a stone
drowned at the bottom of the sea. The wave felt disappointed and set
herself to look for another rock." Women, wrote Martin, are ruthless
about the evil they do to men they love.

The Fascination of Woman and Activity and Passivity in Sexual Love

The metaphysical trait of the eternal woman as witch, as Maya and
maya-shakti, the cosmogonic enchantment of the One, corresponds
in general to female fascination. The association of the Aphrodite
type with the type of the witch is often to be found in myth and saga.
Both aspects were assigned, for instance, to Calypso, Circe, Medea,
Isolde, and even Brunhilda in some versions of the saga. At Rome,
Venus Verticordia was conceived of as skilled in the arts of magic.
Minoan figures of women with magic wands in their hands are well
known. A great deal of similar evidence could be readily collected.
That woman is more closely linked to "earth," the cosmic and natural
element, is demonstrated on the material plane by the various effects
that she undergoes owing to the periodic rhythms of the cosmos. In
times of yore, however, this link was referred more to the *yin* aspect
of nature, to the nocturnal and unconscious supersensual field, irrational and unfathomable, of the vital forces. Whence there arise in

woman certain powers of magic and prophecy in a restricted sense (opposed to the male and Apollonian characteristics of high magic and theurgy), which are liable to degenerate into witchcraft. In the trials of the Inquisition, by comparison with men, women figure as the accused in the overwhelming majority of cases; in A.D. 1500, Bodin reported fifty trials of women and only one of a man relating to witchcraft and the occult arts. One of the most widely read treatises of those times on the subject of devils, the *Malleus maleficarum* (Hammer of the Witches), dwells at great length on why witchcraft was undertaken mainly by women. In the traditions of many peoples, this type of magic is related to an archaic feminine and lunar tradition. It is of interest that in China the character *wu*, used to designate a person who exercised the arts of magic in a strict or "shamanic" sense, was originally applied only to females. The techniques employed by the *wu* to contact supersensual forces were sometimes ascetic and at other times orgiastic; in the latter case it seems that in the beginning the *wu* officiated wholly naked. The *wu* had to have youth and fascinating beauty as preliminary qualifications for her work, and the meanings of the characters *yao* and *miao* as "queer" "disquieting," and "mysterious" refer to the type and qualities of the *wu*.[112] One text says that the nonuranic forces brought down by their rites "eclipsed the sun."

But what interests us here apart from these specific references to the supersensual is the magic of woman and the sense of her natural fascination and power of seduction. We find the following sentence in Daudet: "I felt myself invincibly attracted by her; only an abyss can cause such fascination." We dealt earlier with the symbolism and the rite of disrobing and discussed the ultimate expression that this process had, for women, in such forms as the dance of the seven veils. We are concerned here with a woman stripped not of the material clothes that hide her body but of her individual identity as an empirical being and particular personality, until she can be seen in her elementary and uttermost substance as the Virgin, as Durga, as the woman prior to the manifold varieties of mortal women. The fascination exercised by all female nakedness in its final root is that it hints in an obscure way, which only the senses perceive, at this other nakedness. It is not a question of "beauty" or of an animal summons of the flesh; and what Paul Valéry wrote is only partly right: "The influence of nakedness should of necessity arise from the value of the 'hidden' and of the accompanying peril imparted to it by its quality of ill-omened revelation and deadly means of seduction." It is true that the fascination of woman's nakedness has a dizzying aspect like that caused by emptiness and the bottomless, under the sign of *úlē*, the raw material of creation, and of the ambiguity of its nonbeing. This characteristic belongs to female nakedness alone. The effect of the naked male on woman is not only small in comparison but, where it exists, is of a special kind and essentially physical and phallic; it only effects her in the trivial meaning of a suggestion of the muscular and animal efficiency of the "male." Not so in woman; in a fully naked woman Durga is dimly felt by the man; she, goddess of orgiastic festivals, is the "inaccessible," the Prostitute and the Mother who is also the Virgin, the Inviolable, the Inexhaustible. It is precisely this which awakens in man an elementary desire united with vertigo; it is this, too, which drives desire to a paroxysm, accelerating the rhythm until priapic man precipitates himself into the subtle and sucking ecstasy of the motionless woman. If man in general finds pleasure in defloration and rape, everything that in that pleasure can be related to the instinct or pride of first possession is only a surface element; the deepest factor is the feeling, even if only illusory, that the physical act gives him of violating the inviolable and of possessing her whom, in her ultimate root, in her "nakedness," will never be possessed by the lust of the flesh; it is the desire to possess this "virgin" that acts obscurely in the desire to possess the physically intact woman or the woman who resists. Moreover, there is no difference between that and the root of a specific element of sadism, which is linked to the act of defloration and also exists in almost every coitus; it is different from the ambivalent "algolagnia" of which we spoke earlier and is much more profound; this cruelty and ferocity act as a counterpart to the transcendental and fascinating intangibility, "coldness," and insatiability that belong to the elementary female substance. There is a wish to "kill" the hidden and absolute woman contained in every female being, and a futile sadistic desire for "possession."[113] It is for this reason, too, that, as a rule, nothing stirs a man more than feeling the woman utterly exhausted beneath his own hostile rapture in the coitus.

When treating the myth of Pandora, Kierkegaard[114] wrote that the last gifts, to crown all others, donated by the envious gods to the "woman of desire" sent to Epimetheus so as to strengthen her power were her innocence, modesty, and resistance. We said before that modesty in woman has a character that is not ethical but merely functional and sexual; it would be equally banal to show that all shyness and resistance in woman most often have a similar functional purpose of sexual excitation.[115] These features play a great part in the field of individual conscious behavior. Moreover, beyond the flirtatiousness, modesty, and rationalizing devices used in presenting herself and proper to accomplished femininity, there is a more subtle and impersonal factor that consists of the fascinating sexual element belonging to innocence and chastity. A woman who shows her desire openly can surprise and even disgust any man who has more than a merely animal nature and who, instead, is attracted by innocence,[116] because the "pure" girl embodies to a greater extent a challenge for man inherent in the Durga substance. We ought to examine an objective and impersonal side of this general effect. Ignorance of occult law obscures recognition of the true meaning of female purity and the secret of her potential fascination. This law requires that all inhibited or withheld energy be strengthened by translation into a more subtle and invisible influence that is nevertheless more efficient. Hindu terminology calls it transmutation into *ojas* force. Well, in normal purity and chastity, there is no evidence of the "inborn tendency of womanly nature toward purity" imagined by some Roman Catholic writers who have forgotten the very different views of their predecessors. In any event, woman continues to be the *kamini*, she who has sexuality as her substance, she who, beyond the threshold of her most peripheral consciousness, "thinks about sex, thinks of sex, thinks sex, delights in sex." She shows the impersonal, "natural" inhibition of this disposition in the form of a subtle, magical power that forms the special aura of fascination that surrounds the "chaste" and "innocent" kind and has a greater effect on every differentiated man than any coarsely sensual feminine behavior. It is precisely when no trick or conscious moralistic inhibition is in question and when we are only dealing with her elementarily existential nature, whose root is the archetype, that woman has at her disposal this more dangerous force.[117]

This leads us to one last fundamental point concerning the less visible side of the ordinary relations between the sexes. If, from a metaphysical point of view, the male corresponds to the active and the female to the passive principle, such relationships are universally inverted in so-called natural sexuality. The man very seldom goes to the woman as a bearer of the pure principle of "being" or as an emanation of the power of the One but, as a rule, seems to "undergo" the magic of the woman. The relationships are inverted and are shown in a meaningful way by a dictum of Titus Burckhardt that woman is actively passive, whereas man is passively active. The "actively passive" quality is the substance of woman's fascination and is activity in a higher sense. Common parlance alludes to this in attributing the power of "attraction" to a woman, this attraction being the power of the magnet. In such a regard, woman is active and man is passive. "It is said and generally admitted that in the struggle for love woman is almost passive; but this passivity is far from real. It is the passivity of the magnet, whose apparent stillness attracts iron into its vortex."[118] It is remarkable that within the strongly patriarchal social system of the Far East, there was a tradition that knew the concept of "acting without acting" (*wei-wu-wei*) and understood that "in her apparent passivity and inferior status the female is superior to the male."[119] Paradoxical though it may seem, it is always man who is "seduced" in the strict, etymological meaning of the word; his active enterprise is reduced to that of approaching a magnetic field, the force of which he will undergo as soon as he has come within its orbit.[120] Woman always and decisively has the upper hand over any man who desires, that is, over mere masculine sexual need. Rather than give herself, she "makes herself be taken." A. Charmel in his *Dernière semaine de Don Juan* gave meaningful expression to this: all the women Don Juan had possessed were revealed as being so many different aspects of one single woman without a face (the eternal feminine or Durga) who had really wanted the words and gestures with which he had "seduced" each one of them. He had desired these women "just as iron desires the magnet." It was by making Don Juan aware of this that the Commendatory made him kill himself.

Thus priapic man is quite deluded when he assumes and boasts that he has "possessed" a woman just because he has been lying with her. The pleasure a woman feels in being "possessed" is an elementary characteristic; "She is not taken but welcomes and, in welcoming, wins and absorbs" (G. Pistoni).[121] For this there is also a biological analogy in what happens between germinal cells: the movement, activity, and initiative of the fertilizing spermatozoon, itself lacking vital substance and nutritive plasma, succeeds in overcoming all the other spermatozoa poured into the vagina. It penetrates the attracting ovum, almost motionless and rich with vital foods; it opens a breach, which shuts behind it, imprisoning it as soon as penetration is completed; after that there occurs the mutual destruction of the two kinds of cells, male and female, which have come into contact inside the womb. The woman knows a yielding so full that it should be deemed more active than the onslaught of the man, as Aldous Huxley said. Lastly, if we examine the experience of coitus in its innermost psychological side, the situation of the "magnet" is very often repeated; in fact, it seems that the most differentiated man is mainly passive in the sense that he forgets himself, and all his attention, as if he were fascinated, is drawn irresistibly to the psychic and physical conditions that are brought about in woman during coitus, especially as they are reflected on her physiognomy ("the tragic mask of her, laboring under the rhythmic caress"—A. Koestler); and it is precisely this that forms the strongest aphrodisiac for man's rapture and orgasm.

In the Mediterranean cycle of the Great Goddess, the "nonacting" power or magic of woman was represented by Potnia Theron or

Queen of the Wild Beasts, a goddess who rode a bull or held him on the leash, and Cybele, who had herself drawn in a chariot by two tame lions as a symbol of her sovereignty; Durga seated on a lion with a rein in her hands is the corresponding Hindu goddess. The same theme crops up in the kabbalistically inspired symbolism of card XI in the game of Tarot, where Force is shown with the figure of a woman who is holding the jaws of a raging lion open without any effort. Every woman, inasmuch as she shares in the "absolute woman," possesses that force to a certain extent. Man knows it, and often owing to a neurotic unconscious overcompensation for his inferiority complex, he flaunts before woman an ostentatious manliness, indifference, or even brutality and disdain.[122] But this secures him the advantage, on the contrary. The fact that woman often becomes a victim on an external, material, sentimental, or social level, giving rise to her instinctive "fear of loving," does not alter the fundamental structure of the situation.

On a subtle plane, the passivity of man increases the more the material aspects of the "male" and the instinctive violent and sensual traits of manhood are predominant in him. As a rule, the man poorest in inner manliness is the very type that the Western world has adopted as the ideal of manhood. The activist man busy with doing and producing, the *Leistungsmensch*, the athlete, or the man with an "iron will" is among the most helpless of men before the more subtle power of woman. Civilizations such as those of the Far East, India, and Arabia have a more accurate understanding of what is truly manly. Their ideal of manhood differs widely from that of the European or American ersatz male with regard to physical and psychological, spiritual and character traits.

In general, we may summarize the possible forms of actual relationships between the sexes by saying that activity in man and passivity in woman concern only the outer plane; on the subtle plane it is the woman who is active and the man who is passive (the woman is "actively passive" and the man "passively active"); especially when union leads to procreation, it is the woman who absorbs and possesses. This is the situation in profane eros, and thence arises its ambiguity. In situations of this kind, erotic ecstasy only randomly and tangentially involves the phenomenon of transcendence, which seldom takes effect between ordinary lovers. Only when eros is used for sacred purposes are the relationships between activity and passivity changed so fundamentally that they reflect the proper metaphysical status, whereby the man becomes truly active with respect to the woman. This is self-evident because only in the spirit and under sacred conditions is it possible to arouse the higher potential rank of man. The polarity is then inverted and a third level or erotic experience is determined, which is symbolized by the Tantric *viparita-maithuna* or inverted coitus in ritual expression. The stillness of man is the chrism of the higher activity and of the presence of the *virya*, which the magic of woman no longer endangers and the sight of "naked Diana" herself no longer threatens.

As regards the psychology of the sexes which we have sketched in the foregoing pages, it is best to recall once again its ontological background. We have dealt less with individual qualities or "characteristics" than with objective components and manifestations of the nature of absolute womanhood and absolute manhood in individuals according to the fundamental aspects, deducible metaphysically and dramatized in myths. These superindividual "elements" or "constants" of sex may be present in individuals in various degrees of purity and strength; moreover, they manifest differently depending on the race and type of civilization. We may also speak of structures and capabilities of the deep consciousness that the more superficial and social consciousness—the level where personality is determined (cf. chapter 1)—does not always recognize or admit and that the "person" never activates fully in the profane sphere. Thus Harding wrote quite rightly that it is too dangerous for women to recognize what they are in their own depths; they prefer to believe that they are what they seem to be, within the facade of the outer consciousness that they have constructed for themselves.[123]

We must remember that what we confirmed as constituting a true difference between the natures of man and woman in no way implies a difference of worth. As stated already, the question of sexual superiority or inferiority makes no sense. Every judgment of worth between aspects of the male and female psyche must show signs of bias toward one sex or the other. Let us note that certain psychological aspects of the "absolute woman" might superficially appear pejorative, for example, an inclination to lying, "passivity," fluidity, a lack of the logical and ethical imperative, and an extroverted nature. This apparent lack of worth is only relative and appears as such because we are used to the man's point of view in a society ruled by men. But, in Far Eastern terms, "passive perfection" is no less perfect than "active perfection" and has its own place alongside the latter. What may seem negative has its positive side when considered from the point of view of its own principle, in the ontological aspect proper to "its own nature."

Last, we must bear in mind that, aside from their elementary sexual development, almost no man is only and in every respect a man, and no woman is only and in all respects a woman. We said earlier that cases of full sexual development are seldom found. Almost every man bears some traces of femininity and every woman residues of masculinity according to proportions varying over a wide range. We must take into account all consequences arising from this fact, especially when examining the psychic field, in which that range of proportions varies widely indeed. Thus, the traits that we deemed typical for the female psyche can be found in man as well as in women, particularly in regressive phases of a civilization. Weininger, who made evident the reality and importance of "intermediate sexual forms," did not take that sufficiently into account. To give one instance, Weininger thought he could attribute to woman the inner propensity for telling lies (in the extreme, a hysterical or neurotic propensity) because of her passive internalizing of the values and rules of society in contrast to her own sensual nature. Psychoanalysis has clearly demonstrated how often this is the case with men too, especially contemporary men; psychoanalysis even makes the point that what is sometimes thought to constitute the essential nucleus of the male psyche, the so-called superego, dominating, criticizing, and avenging the instinctive life, is nothing but the artificial product of "introjected" social conventions, which causes neuroses and wounds of all kinds. We ourselves have spoken of a "race of escapist manhood,"[124] with regard to the characteriological, psychological, and moral traits that typify men since the last war, and then we can see how little the "liquid" characteristic of woman is restricted to women alone.

However, one point must be kept firmly in mind. It is arbitrary to judge woman on the basis of man or vice versa, whenever the sexes are considered in themselves, but such a judgment is legitimate when considering the components or dispositions of the other sex that a man or woman may develop within himself or herself. In this case, it is a question of imperfections as compared with type, of a lack of "form," and of the hybrid nature that characterizes an incomplete or corrupted being; and, from the point of view of traditional ethics, that which in woman is man and in man is woman, is wrong and worthless.

The Ethics of the Sexes

This final comment leads us to mention the problem of the ethics of the sexes, which we can only touch on briefly here for two reasons. First, according to traditional ideas, ethics do not constitute an independent sphere, as many people today think. If ethics are to have a real governing value, they must be based on the realm of the holy and the metaphysical. Second, we have already dealt elsewhere[125] with sexual ethics considered according to this outlook. Therefore, we shall only skim this subject here, partly as an introduction to our examination of sexual forms that have been made holy.

Assagioli:
(Italian idealism?)

All true ethics, which is to say traditional and not "social" or abstract and philosophical ones, are founded on the elevation, in a form as free as it is absolute, of the actual nature proper to each being. An element that is "naturalistic" in origin loses that character and takes on an ethical value when it becomes the content of a pure act of will. The formula of all ethics is summarized in the dictum "Be yourself" or "Be true to yourself," wherein the self is to be understood as one's own deepest nature or one's own "idea" or the quality of one's own type.

Now, if we have recognized the elementary characters of manhood and of womanhood in a "being by itself" and a "being that depends on another being," it seems evident enough what the respective ethics of man and woman are; they will be the pure, unconditional assumption and development of those dispositions by the empirical individuals of one or the other sex. As types of pure manhood who realize "being by itself," we indicated the warrior and the ascetic, whose ideal genuine female counterparts are expressed in the lover and the mother.

idea of connection
less invidious

Taken in themselves, neither the Demeter nor the Aphrodite dispositions have any ethical worth or moral imperative; both confirm that woman belongs to mere "nature." Though that is generally acknowledged with regard to the Aphrodite disposition, there is a marked tendency, entirely without foundation, to glorify the maternal disposition. We speak of the "sublime function of motherhood," whereas it is hard to show what precisely is sublime about motherhood. The female of the human species shares this motherly love with the female of various animal species;[126] that love is an impersonal, instinctive, naturalistic trait of woman devoid of any ethical dimension, and it can be displayed in clear contrast to ethical values. Such a love does not in any way depend on higher principles,[127] but rather is blind and can be unjust. A mother loves her child only because it is her child and not because she sees in it the embodiment of what is worthy to be loved. The absolute mother will be ready not only to give her own life (thus far there would be a naturalistic basis for an ethical attitude) but even to stain herself with crimes unforgivable from an ethical point of view to save or defend her child. The most thoroughgoing example of this type of mother is found in the tale "Imant and His Mother" by Aino Kallas: having learned that her son is risking his life in a plot against his master, she does not hesitate to betray all the conspirators on condition that the master undertakes to spare her son. All his companions are slain and her son is saved, but, of course, as soon as he learns the truth, he cannot help killing himself. The contrast between male ethics and maternal love is shown here in its crudest form.

A woman would have to sublimate her individuality and possess a heroic and sacrificial disposition for her natural tendencies as a mother and lover to take on an ethical character. When such is the case, it is a question no longer of blind love, instinct, or compulsion that leaves no opportunity for choice, but of a free act and a far-seeing love in which would remain woman's natural dependency on another (here, the son) but which is also united with an ability to distinguish and with a positive will capable of transcending her naturalistic substratum, so far perhaps as to even desire the death of an unworthy son. Some Spartan, ancient Roman, Iberian, and Germanic types of mother can provide example of this first ethical potentiality of woman.

The second ethical potentiality of woman corresponds to the type of the lover and is realized in the "being dependent on another" and in living for another[128] in a heroic and transfiguring environment in which man is desired as her own "master and husband" but is also venerated almost like a god; this capability overcomes all exclusiveness and all selfishness and turns her self-offering into an almost sacrificial act. She conserves the disintegrating, life-giving, and "demonic" potential of the absolute Aphroditic woman but frees it of its destructive and "sucking" side, as we mentioned earlier. In our book cited earlier, we dealt with institutions of the traditional world that presupposed this possible ethical change in woman as a person not of a Demeter nature but of an Aphroditic and Dionysiac one. The perfection of this way is woman who wants to follow her own husband beyond the limits of her own nature, even into the flames of a funeral pyre (a custom mistakenly assigned only to India, for a similar custom, inspired by the same spirit, existed among the Thracians, Wends, ancient Germans, Chinese, and Incas).[129]

We shall restrict ourselves in this book to this very sketchy outline of the ethics of the sexes. We will leave aside altogether the "problems" of woman and of sexual relations, as people think of them nowadays in relation to marriage, divorce, emancipation, free love, and so forth. These are all spurious problems. The only true problem is to what extent in a given society and epoch man can be himself and woman can be herself in an accurate approximation of their respective archetypes, and also to what extent the relationships of man and woman reflect the natural and unchangeable law rooted in the very metaphysics of male and female. This law is "reciprocal integration and completion together with a subordination of the female principle to the male." Everything else, as Nietzsche would say, is nonsense; and in the introduction we observed in what a state the modern Western world finds itself in relation to man, woman, and sex thanks to our so-called "progress."[130]

[margin annotation:] vB

[handwritten at bottom:] claims (1) archetypes
(2) female principle subordinated to male principle

5

Sacred Ceremonies and Evocations

This chapter involves the problem of what point of view to adopt vis-à-vis the subject we shall treat. Its essence belongs to experiences proper to human beings different from the people of today with respect to their civilization and the world they inhabited; for their world had another dimension. They understood the supersensual as a fundamental part of reality and moreover felt it as a "presence." We cannot follow the method used in modern "neutral" researches restricted to the gathering and ordering of the facts of ancient and foreign traditions in their obscure external appearance. Instead, we shall go forward with an interpretation that considers, first, the inner dimension of such facts, bearing in mind that such an interpretation, in practice, implies an unavoidable margin of speculation. The ritual and evocatory side of eros in sacred ceremonies and in the nonnaturalistic use of sex has always played a fundamental role. But, especially in dealing with institutional forms that have now disappeared, it is almost impossible to ascertain to what degree the examples we shall discuss preserve a genuine depth dimension, retaining the ritual element involving actual evocations, or whether instead they have become reduced to mere formal custom. Second, our investigation is hampered because our knowledge is often based on fragmentary evidence and forms that were already quite removed in time from their original sources. However, we shall seek, as best we can, to set in order the essential materials available to us.

To guide ourselves, we shall first distinguish the nonprofane forms that sexuality has assumed.

1. The transformation of sexual union into a holy institution
2. Evocatory and sacramental forms given to cults of sexual union
3. Ascetic detachment of the sexual drive from the plane of the Dyad and its inner transmutation for the purpose of spiritual realization
4. The special practice of sexual union for the purpose of ecstatic or initiatory breakthrough in existential level
5. Each of these possibilities may lead, in addition, to active (magical) applications beyond the pure fact of inner experience. We may distinguish (a) primitive sexual magic (fertility rites and holy orgies), (b) individual active sexual magic in a strictly ceremonial sense, and (c) initiatory sexual magic.

Wedlock as "Mystery" in the World of Tradition

It has been generally acknowledged, especially since the fundamental work of Fustel de Coulanges, that the family in ancient times was an institution with a religious basis as well as a natural association. But, more generally, the family has a religious foundation in every proto-original civilization and all great traditional cultures. It was impossible for this holy character not to affect the intimate relations and the conjugal use of sexuality.

It should first be observed that the individualistic factor in marriages was quite unimportant and certainly not the determining one. Inclination and affection were only accessory elements, and the stock carried the most weight. The *dignitas matrimonii* in Rome was linked from the very beginning to the idea of ancestral descent. Thus, not only in Rome but also in Greece and other traditional civilizations, the woman selected for the *dignitas matrimonii* was chosen with this end in view. The man was perhaps allowed the privilege of having other women at the same time for the purpose of mere erotic experience (thus arose the institution of concubinage, which was recognized by law alongside the family system as its complement). Moreover, the wife herself often distinguished between her merely erotic role and her role as childbearer. When a man lay with his wife with this purpose in mind, a ritual was often carried out with lustration or propitiation ceremonies and special methods were used in the practice of coitus. Often a period of abstinence would precede the act (in ancient China the man withheld his seed during this period); one ritual even considered exorcising the devil of lust, who was thought to hold the woman in his power; in some cases, prayers and invocations were made to the gods, a favorable date was chosen, and finally the persons were isolated. Elements of a special science are recorded which define the circumstances suitable for influencing the child's sex at conception.

Next it is important to emphasize that, beginning with the totemic societies, the concept of procreation transcended the naturalistic idea of the biological survival of the species; the purpose of generation was deemed essential to preserve and hand down over the ages the mystical force of one's own blood and clan and, above all, the force of the primordial forefather, inborn as the *genius* or creative spirit of the stock and symbolized in classical antiquity by the everlasting holy fire of the household. Participation in the rites of a family created new kinsmen or admitted an outsider to the family, and certain extant indications lead us to believe that the woman in traditional antiquity, before belonging to the husband, was wedded by this mystical force of the stock. It is meaningful that in Rome the "thalamus" or marriage bed was called the *lectus genialis* or "bed of the *genius*." More precise evidence concerns the Roman wedding custom according to which a woman had to unite herself to the god Matitus, the priapic Tutinus, who was fundamentally the same as the *genius domesticus* or *lar familiaris* (god of the household), before lying with her husband. Upon entering her husband's house, the new bride had to sit on the ithyphallic image of the god before going to her marriage bed, just as if the god were to deflower her first ("so that the god seems to have been the first to savor their modesty").[1] Similar rites could be found in other civilizations. The real purpose of marriage was to produce the "son of duty," as the first-born male was called in India; with a prayer that he should be a "hero," the final wording of the wedding ceremony, *shradda*, was as follows: *viram me datta pitarah* (O fathers, make my son a hero).[2]

In the sacred ceremonies of the family, the polarity of the sexes was played out, emphasizing their complementarity. Hence developed the part often played by woman in Indo-European household cults in connection with the fire, of which she was the natural guardian since, in principle, she had the nature of Vesta, the "living flame" or fire of life. In a certain way woman was the living upholder of this supersensual influence and thus acted as a counterpart of the pure male principle, of the *pater familias*. Thus it was the woman's duty above all to see that the flame stayed pure and did not go out; she invoked its holy force when offering sacrifices in the fire.[3]

The same complementary system was in force in Rome for the priesthood. There, if the wife of the flamen or priest (the *flaminica dialis*, or wife of the priest of Jupiter) died, he had to relinquish his office just as though his power had been lessened or paralyzed through the lack of a life-giving complement. Similar evidence has been gathered from other traditions, such as that of the brahmins, where, however, further meanings have been emphasized. The woman, joined to the man by the sacrament, *samskara*, was presented as the goddess of the house, *grihadevata*, and originally was associated with her husband in the cult and rites. The woman acted as the heart, *kunda*, and also as the flame of the sacrifice. People are advised to meditate on the woman, who is thought of as a fire, *yoshamagnin dhyayita*. Within this framework, the union between man and woman was conceived as a great rite or *vajna* and as an equivalent of the sacrifice in the fire, *homa*. It was said, "He who knows woman in terms of fire attains to freedom"; and the *Shathapata-brahmana* makes the woman say, "If you make use of me in the sacrifice, you will obtain through me any blessing you may call for."[4] The fruits of one form of the sacrifice of the soma (*vajapeya*) were said to be equal to those produced by union with a woman when that union was accomplished with a knowledge of the correspondences and cosmic equivalents in her and her body. The womb, as the center of woman, was indicated as the sacrificial fire.[5] In another traditional text, all the phases of coitus were made to correspond to an act of public worship, suggesting the possibility that the latter was carried out in conjunction with the former.[6]

Wedlock would generally show the characteristics of a "mystery" in a system practicing rituals. In Greece, the goddess of wedlock was called Aphrodite Teleia, the Fulfiller, her attribute coming from *telos*, a word used also for initiation. In a well-known Indo-European ritual linked to the act of procreation, the conscious identification with the cosmic male and female, the Sky and the Earth, was confirmed openly:

> Then the husband should draw near to her and pronounce the formula "I am He and you are She; you are She and I am He. I am the song [*Saman*] and you are the refrain [*re*]; . . . I am the Sky and you are the Earth. Come, embrace me, let us mingle our seed for the birth of a male and for the richness of our home." Next, making [the woman] open her legs, he should say, "O ye Sky and Earth, mingle yourselves!" Then he should enter her and with his mouth joined to hers stroke her three times from above downward and say, " . . . Just as the Earth welcomes the Fire to its bosom, as the Sky shuts Indra within its womb, and as the cardinal points teem with wind, so I leave in you the seed of [the name of the child]."[7]

Manhood, therefore, was under the sign of the Sky and womanhood under that of the Earth. In Greece as well, according to Pindar, when referring to the foundation of their deepest nature, men in love called on Helios, the Sun, whereas women invoked Selene, the Moon.[8] We should also note that in almost all the Hindu dialects having their origin in Sanskrit, women were called *prakriti*, a word that, as we saw earlier, was the metaphysical designation of "nature" and also of the female force of the impassive god, the *purusha*.[9] The background of marriage as a holy ceremony was destined to become slowly obscured, although to this day positive traces of it still persist which can only be explained by supposing its prior existence. It was only preserved with precise divine and cosmic relationships in the cultural domain, in a specific sense, in connection with varieties of the *hieros gamos*, the ritual holy marriage or marriage to a god, as we shall recount shortly. In ancient times, it was rightly said that a people who made wedding customs into a rite that conformed to the eternal laws formed a great magical chain binding the material realm to higher realms.[10] Novalis was right when deeming that marriage as it is known nowadays is like a "desecrated mystery"; with the passage of time it has been reduced in effect to nothing more than the only alternative provided by society against fear of loneliness. And the fact that Claude de Saint-Martin certainly did not understand the importance of his words and had no vision of the situation in which those words are true, does not lessen their accuracy: "If mankind knew what marriage is, it would have at one and the same time an extraordinary desire for it and a tremendous fear of it; for by means of it man could once again be made like God or could end in total ruin."[11]

In the framework of the creationist religions, however, the generic concept of the sanctity of the procreative act has persisted. It is considered and experienced as a reflection, an extension or reenactment of the divine creative act. In the Mazdaism of Iran we can note an ancient wedding rite in which the idea of divine grace is linked even to the maximum intensity of coitus.[12] An Islamic ritual that partly recalls the Indo-European rite we just mentioned demonstrates how foreign to such traditions is the idea of sexuality as something obscene and sinful. According to this ritual the husband says when he is entering the woman: "In the name of Allah the merciful and kind, *Bismillah al-rahman al-rahim*. Then both the woman and man say together, 'In the name of God,' and lastly, when he feels the woman climaxing and is about to bathe her with his seed, the man alone says the remaining words of the formula, ' . . . merciful and kind.' "[13] The great Sufi teacher Ibn Arabi went so far as to talk of contemplating God in woman, in ritualized coitus conforming to metaphysical and theological values. In his treatise *Fusus al-hikam* he wrote, "This [conjugal] act corresponds to the projection of the divine will on that which He created in His own image, at the very moment when He created it, to recognize Himself in His own form. . . . The Prophet loved women precisely because of their ontological station and because they are like a passive receptacle of his own act and lie in the same relationship to him as Universal Nature [*tabi'ah*] stands to God. It is in Universal Nature that God makes the forms of the world reveal themselves by means of His will and by means of the divine act, which is manifested as a sexual act in the category of forms constituted of the elements, as spiritual will [*himmah*—it is that which we have called transcendental manhood elsewhere] in the world of the spirits of light, and as logical conclusion in the category of reason." (It would be possible here to refer to logical strictness as the main expression of the male principle. Cf. chapter 4.) Ibn Arabi said that he who loves women in this way and evokes such significations in union with them "loves them with a divine love." For him who, instead, only obeys sexual attraction, "the sexual act will be a form lacking any spirit; of course, the spirit always remains immanent in the form as such, but it will be imperceptible to him who lies with his wife or with any woman just for sensual pleasure, without recognizing the true object of his own desire. . . . 'People know that I am in love but they don't know with whom!' This verse can be applied to him who loves only for sensual pleasure or to him who loves the giver of that pleasure, namely woman, without any awareness of the spiritual meaning involved. Were he aware, he would also know by virtue of what and whom he enjoys this pleasure, and he would then be spiritually perfect."[14] In this Sufi theology of love we should see only a broader, more elevated and precise awareness of the ritual mode in which men of this culture have more or less clearly understood and conceived of conjugal relationships, beginning with the blessing conferred by the Law of the Koran on the sexual act in a polygamous system. Hence arises the special meaning of procreation, understood as the extension of the divine creative power in man.

Judaism did not take an ascetic or puritanical stand on sex. Wedlock was thought of not as a concession to the law of the flesh, but as one of the holiest mysteries. For the Kabbala, every true wedding was in fact a symbolic re-creation of the union of God with the Shekhinah.[15]

Last, the Chinese doctrine of royal unions is worth mentioning. The king had 120 women besides his wife, and his method of consorting with them had a ritual and symbolic meaning. The royal women were divided into four groups in an inverse relationship between their number and value. The largest group consisted of women deemed less noble. These were only allowed to go to the king on given nights before the full moon and were sent for during nights that were almost dark and without moonlight. The last group of only three women had for themselves the two nights before the sacred night of the full moon. On that night, when the full moon in all its splendor faces the sun macrocosmically, the queen alone faces the king, the Unique Man, and is united with him. This is the idea of a union that is absolute at the midpoint and then becomes more and more attenuated as multiplicity dominates and the rank is lower, precisely like the force of the One in fertilizing matter; these conditioned reflections which take place in the holy marriage of the royal couple are based on a system of participations that follows a cosmic model.[16]

Christianity and Sexuality

The sacred institution of marriage in Catholicism has a hybrid character because of the ethics chosen by that religion. We can see in Catholicism the outcome of the unruly interplay between principles and rules of two very distinct planes. Traditional religions based on a creationist belief have always recognized two laws. One of them concerns the fallen original "being." In fact, when reproducing the biblical passage that speaks of the two becoming one flesh and leaving father and mother, Paul added, "This is a great mystery" (Eph. 5: 31–32). The precise word used here is "mystery" and not "sacrament" as written in the Vulgate. In Paul's epistles there is a reference to the double status, male and female, and implicitly to the corresponding ways for man and woman in the words "Forasmuch as [man] is the image and glory of God; but woman is the glory of man" (1 Cor. 11: 7), and also the mystery of the conversion or "redemption" of the female through the male principle (Shakti led back by Shiva), with the commandment that a man should love his wife as Christ loved the church, giving himself for it "that he might sanctify and cleanse it with the washing of water by the word"; this is followed by the words "So ought men to love their wives as their own bodies. He that loveth his wife loveth himself" (Eph. 5: 25–28). But Paul's epistles, in contradiction, also deny all higher capabilities of sexual experience that is taken as "fornication" and shamelessness, while marriage is deemed to be a mere makeshift. We also read, "It is good for a man not to touch a woman. Nevertheless, to avoid fornication, let every man have his own wife, and let every woman have her own husband"; and further on, "But if they cannot contain themselves, let them marry; for it is better to marry than to burn" (1 Cor. 7: 1–2, 9).

It was precisely this latter view which was taken as the basis of postevangelical Christianity, for which sexual life in general is a sin.[17] It is not lawful for Roman Catholics to have sex except in wedlock and only for the purpose of procreation. We know, however, that marriage as a regular "sacrament" and not as a generic blessing of the spouses only appeared at a late stage in Christianity (about the twelfth century) and that even more recently, the Council of Trent in 1563 imposed the religious rite for every wedding that was not to be viewed on the same level as concubinage. This sacramental, posthumous aspect has a purpose that is fundamentally secular rather than spiritual. As the idea of the sinfulness and simple "natural character" of sex remains and since sex is not acknowledged except as a means for procreation, marriage here is shown to be exactly what Paul has disparagingly conceded it to be, just a lesser evil, a "cure for the sickness of lust" for men and women who are incapable of choosing celibacy and succumb to the flesh; it was Saint Thomas who said that "the act of marriage is always a sin." The canonical idea that marriage as a sacrament "confers the grace needed to bless the lawful union of man with woman by perfecting natural love and giving it a character of indissolubility which was lacking beforehand" is therefore reduced to the mere form of a superstructure. It is in no way a rite intended to establish or promote the deeper, transfiguring, sacred dimensions of sexual experience, because, as a principle, theology has condemned anyone who, even in wedlock, broadens this experience without having procreation as his essential goal and detaches himself from a practice of "chaste unions." This involves the mistaken belief that eros and the "instinct for reproduction" should be one and the same thing. Moreover, we should bear in mind the disappearance, in a society controlled by this dogma, of everything that in the ancient family could impart to procreation the higher meaning referred to earlier, which is linked to familial and ancestral cults. In practice, the Christian point of view prevents sex from becoming a sacred ceremony, which leads to its repression and nonconsecration because of the hybrid nature of this point of view. For it has laid down as a general rule, still valid in our times, that detachment from sex should be viewed in the light of ascetic transformation and not as a puritanical repression of the sexual drive. Thus, the Christian religious rule has only bequeathed us social restraint and the simple mediocre and dull fettering of the human animal, which is devoid of any interest to us. Only with the marginal updating of Vatican Council II has the point of view of the church been modified somewhat and a certain emphasis given to sexual union in wedlock, although the same relationship to procreation has been kept.

The rule of celibacy of the priesthood in Roman Catholicism arises from a similar confusion. The type of the priest (secular clergy) has been confused with that of the ascetic (monk). Most traditional civilizations with long priestly dynasties separated these distinct roles. The continuity of blood acted as a natural upholder and carrier of the continuity of supernatural influence transmitted down through successive generations of a given stock. Moreover, a law intended for persons who live in the world and not for the ascetic must have been very like that expressed by Ibn Ata: "Men of devotion and austerity execrate because they are far from God; if they saw Him in everything, they would not execrate anything."[18]

A different attitude toward sex has only been adopted by certain decidedly heterodox and outlawed Christian doctrines or in a few random cases. In the first of these two categories we should call to mind the doctrines of the Americans, Beghards and "Brothers of the Free Spirit" (twelfth to fourteenth century), who drew from the idea of divine omnipresence conclusions about sex similar to those of the traditions referred to earlier. In such doctrines two religions were distinguished, one for the ignorant, the other for the enlightened who could reach such a state that they could see God acting in themselves and in everything. For him who attains such a state, sin disappears and the ascetic rule loses all meaning, for even the actions of the body glorify God and, whatever they may be, are felt to be carried out by God in human form. It was stated that the enlightened man who was free in spirit could not sin; it was even said that women were created to be used by those who live in such a state of freedom; moreover, even freedom from law was claimed, which went far beyond anything needed to surmount the Christian concept of the essential sinfulness and impurity of sex, for such a freedom would lead to complete license. The following proposition is attributed to some followers of this belief: "He who is thus free cannot sin . . . and if his nature should be disposed to an act of love, he may lawfully do it with his sister or mother and at any place, such as altars."[19] But in such circumstances, we must distinguish what the enlightened actually professed in secret from what their orthodox foes slanderously attributed to them. From our research, we believe that this was mainly a matter of doctrine, or principles that were not necessarily put into practice.

As an example of random individual experience, let us use the one cited by Woodroffe concerning the outcome of an inquiry carried out in the eighteenth century in the Convent of the Dominicans of Saint Catherine at Prato because of the scandal caused by the mystical sensualism practiced there in secret. A declaration of the young abbess of this convent is meaningful: "As our spirit is free, it is only the intention that can make an action wicked. It is enough, therefore, to lift ourselves in our minds up to God, and then nothing is sinful." She added that to be united to God was to be united as man and woman; the everlasting life of the soul and paradise in this world consisted in the "transubstantiation of the union that man makes with woman." The "enjoyment of God" was reached by the act that united one with God, and this was effected "by the cooperation of man and woman, of the man in whom I recognize God." She concluded: "To practice that which we mistakenly call impurity is true purity, which God wishes and bids us to practice and without which we have no way of finding God, who is truth."[20] But we have now said enough on this subject, because in cases of this kind we are no longer dealing with sacred ceremonies in a formal and institutional framework, but with marginal experiences having a free and mystical background. We shall encounter them in other traditions as well. However, in this unusual case, we are struck by its likeness to the ideas that elsewhere have marked the ritual nature of marital practices free from the onus of sin.

We have already mentioned the collective rites of the Slavic Khlysti, which involved the sexual union of men and women, men being considered the embodiment of Christ, women the embodiment of the Virgin Mary; but it is obvious that the Christian element in these rites is a mere whitewash superimposed on survivals and revivals of previous heathen rites.

Sacred Prostitution and Holy Marriages

Traditional cults aim essentially at manifesting the real presence of a particular supersensual being in a specific setting and at the reception by an individual or group of that being's spiritual influence. This transmission has occurred through rites, sacrifices, and sacraments. Sex, too, has been used to this end in various civilizations.

One of the most typical cases occurs in the framework of the mysteries of the Great Goddess, within which erotic practices were intended to evoke the divine female principle and revive her presence at a specific place within the community. This was one of the true purposes of the rites of sacred prostitution in the temples of the many Aphroditic goddesses in the Mediterranean cycle, such as Ishtar, Mylitta, Anaitis, Aphrodite, Innini, and Athagatia. We must distinguish two different sides of this practice. On the one hand, there was the custom that every girl on reaching puberty had to give up her virginity in a sacred ritual context rather than a profane one before she could be wedded; she had to give herself in the sacred enclosure of the temple to any stranger who made a symbolic offering and invoked, through her, the Great Goddess.[21] On the other hand, there were temples with an established body of temple slaves for the service of the goddess. These priestesses practiced a form of worship that the modern world would call "prostitution." The mystery of carnal love was celebrated not in a formal and symbolic rite but in a magical, operative rite, to nourish the current of psychism which manifested itself in the presence of the goddess and, at the same time, to pass on to the men who copulated with the priestesses the goddess's influence or virtue as in a sacrament. These young women, called "virgins" (*parthenoi hierai*), pure ones, or blessed ones (*qadishtu, mugig, zermasitu*), were deemed to embody the goddess and to be the "bearers" of the goddess, from whom, in their specifically erotic duty, they took their name, Ishtaritu.[22] The sexual act thus performed had both the general function proper to sacrifices intended to evoke or revive divine presences and a function structurally identical with participation in the Eucharist. Ritual sex was the instrument for man's participation in the *sacrum*, in this case borne and administered by the woman; it was a technique to make an experiential contact with the divinity and to receive her. The trauma of the coitus, together with the interruption of individual awareness that it caused, formed an especially favorable condition for that contact.

Such a use of woman was not limited to the mysteries of the Great Goddess of the ancient Mediterranean world; it was also witnessed in the Orient. The ritual offering of virgins is encountered in the Indian temples of the Juggernaut and had the purpose of "feeding" the divinity or effectively arousing his presence. In many cases the temple dancers had the same priestly duties as the temple slaves of Ishtar and Mylitta; and their dances, punctuated with *mudra*, symbolic evocatory gestures, generally had a sacred character; and their "prostitution" also was holy. Even well-known families, therefore, deemed it an honor that their daughters should be consecrated to this duty in the temples from their earliest years. Having the name of *devadasi*, they were sometimes considered the wives of the god. In this case they were not the bearers of the female *sacrum* who initiated men into the mysteries of the Goddess, but served generically as fire in sexual union. Traditional Hindu texts had held it equivalent to sacrifice in the fire, as we have already seen.

Moreover, there is reason to think that even outside of these cultic and institutional frameworks courtesanship of ancient times and in the Orient had aspects that were not merely profane, for the women were taught to bring to the act of love dimensions and results that have been lost today. Knowledge of what we may call hyperbiological and subtle physiology has been found in courtesans of the Far East, who were often formed into guilds, having their own heraldic arms, symbolic insignia, and ancient traditions. There is reason to believe that in some cases the profane *ars amatoria* are decadent forms of the external elements of a specific science based on traditional priestly wisdom; we cannot overlook the possibility that among the postures shown in works such as the forty-eight *figurae Veneris* of Forberg there may be some that originally had the meaning of *mudra* or magical and ritual postures used for the sexual act, since these meanings have endured even in the practice of sexual magic among modern circles, as we shall see later on.

We dealt earlier with love potions, whose meaning has also been completely lost, for we know only degraded uses of them or their equivalents in popular supersitition, mystifications used by worthless sorceresses. The authentic ones were intended to provide sexual experience with dimensions transcending those of ordinary eros rather than to awaken common passion. Demosthenes caused a lover of Sophocles who had the reputation of being a compounder of love potions to be condemned, but during the lawsuit it became known that she had been initiated and had attended circles close to the mysteries. In general, many courtesans or women of their type, even in sagas and legends, were described as enchantresses not only because of their womanly fascination but also because of their specific knowledge of magic. The *Kamasutra* (I, I) list of the skills in which a *ganika* or high-class courtesan was obliged to be expert is long and rather vulgar, but nonetheless it significantly included the magical arts, the art of drawing mystical evocatory diagrams (*mandala*), and that of preparing enchantments.[23] When the renowned Phryne showed herself naked at her trial, Atheneus relates, her defenders emphasized not so much the aesthetic aspect of her profane beauty but rather her sacred and Aphroditic aspect: "The judges were seized with holy fear of the divinity; they dared not condemn the prophetess and priestess of Aphrodite." She also appeared naked to the initiates of Eleusis and thereafter at the Poseidon festival of "Waters"; the deep, magical, and vertiginous side of woman's nakedness was undoubtedly emphasized here. We believe that originally the courtesan's duties covered the administration of the women's mysteries activating her aspect as an embodiment, individualization, and living symbol of the essence of womanhood.

In these ancient ritual complexes we must consider the possibility of a transcendental sexual development or of the momentary or quasi-permanent embodiment, in the priestess-prostitutes, of the divinities or archetypes of their sex. This would be actuated in precisely the manner by which Catholicism, through consecration of the Communion wafer, actuates the divine presence therein. In many Aegean monuments the representations of the priestesses are often confused with that of the Great Goddess,[24] which leads us to believe that the former were actually worshipped by a sort of divine proxy. Living images of Ishtar, Isis, and other goddesses of the same type can be seen in historical Mediterranean and Oriental queens. Those momentary embodiments of a divine being in a given individual, determined by a magical and ritual atmosphere, are a *mysterium transformationis* similar to the mystery of the Catholic Mass itself.

A similar mystery imbues the *hieros gamos* or holy marriage, the marriages of gods. These ritual or religious unions of man and woman were intended to celebrate and renew the Mystery of the Ternary or union of the everlasting male to the everlasting female (Sky with Earth), whence should arise the central current of creation. The corresponding principles were embodied and activated, and their momentary physical union became an effective and evocatory reproduction of divine union beyond the realms of time and space. The purpose of such rites, therefore, was different from those mentioned above as rites of participation in the substance or influence of one or another goddess. Here it was the Three, the Ternary beyond the state of Two, which was called forth by the nuptial act so as to awaken a corresponding influence periodically in a given community; this awakening was carried out against a background of ritualism and not of individual initiatory experiences.

Rites of this kind can be gleaned from the traditions and religious beliefs of highly diverse civilizations. As one salient example, we shall cite the ancient mystery wherein once a year the high priestess personifying the goddess copulated with the man representing the male principle in the holy place. When the rite had been consummated, the other priestesses took the new sacred fire, which was deemed to have been born from that union, and with its flame lit the hearth fires of every household in the community. It has been rightly observed that this rite resembles the one celebrated even now at Jerusalem on Easter Saturday. Moreover, the Easter rite of consecration of the water, celebrated in particular by the Orthodox church, preserves visible traces of sexual symbolism: the candle, which has an obviously phallic meaning, is dipped three times in the font, symbol of the female principle of the Waters; the priest touches the water and blows on it three times, making the sign of the Greek letter *pi*; the consecration words pronounced at this juncture include the phrase "May the power of the Holy Ghost descend throughout the whole depth of this font . . . and fertilize all the substance of this water for regeneration." In the East the very widespread iconography of the *lingam* or phallus put within the lotus (*padma*) or the overturned triangle (the sign of the female *yoni* and symbol of the Goddess or Shakti) has the same meaning; and, as we shall see later on, this symbolism may also allude to actual sexual practices.

In fact, the original rite of the holy marriage has often been preserved in forms where a symbolic rite or simulation takes the place of the real sacred sexual union of a man with a woman. While dealing with actual usages, we may mention the so-called seasonal sexual fertility rites. These are one of the warhorses that contemporary ethnology first associated with the "solar myth," passed on next to totemism, and now explains as "agrarian."

In reality those rites are an example of applied and operant magic belonging to the context noted earlier. We mentioned the experimental contact with the primordial that orgies may have enhanced in the spirit of the participants. Owing to its very nature and the change in existential level that it implies, this state may allow an effective extranormal insertion of man's force into the cosmic web, into the order of natural phenomena, and, in general, into every cycle of fecundity, as an application of a higher strengthening and galvanizing power along the same basic direction of the natural process. Therefore, what Eliade wrote in this respect is correct: "The orgy corresponds generally to the holy marriage. The limitless genesiac frenzy on earth must correspond to the union of the divine pair. The excesses play a very precise part in the arrangement of the sacred; they sunder the barriers existing between man and society, nature and the gods; they help in circulating the force, life, and seeds from one level to another and from one zone of reality into all the others."[25] This is, in fact, one possible meaning of some of the vast collection of "agrarian" rites gathered by Frazer. But, when one is dealing with historical traditions in which the collective orgiastic facts are replaced by isolated and well-circumscribed forms of the sacred marriage, one should not generalize but distinguish the meaning of the magical (and, in a way, "naturalistic") rite from a higher meaning belonging to the mysteries and linked essentially to the task of inner regeneration, even though in certain cases, the more evolved rite may have embodied both meanings. This seems to have been the case in the Eleusinian mysteries where the rite of plowing was linked to the holy marriage as an initiatory rite. To overlook this twofold meaning is typical of research that unconsciously chooses the tendency of modern profane sciences by referring the higher to the lower or emphasizing only the lower wherever possible.

Depending on the case in question, it may be either the man or the woman who is the source of holiness in the sexual rituals. We may find, therefore, holy marriages in which only one of the two persons is transformed and takes on a divine and suprahuman character. In these cases the union may be intended not as a mystical participation but for procreation. The recurring theme in many legends of a woman possessed by a "god" or of a man who possesses a goddess are too well known to be recalled here. We need only mention a few cases in which such connections are presented against regular institutional backgrounds. Thus in ancient Egypt the pharaoh was united with his wife not as a man but as the embodiment of Horus so as to continue the line of his "divine royalty." In the Hellenic festival of the Anthesteria or Feast of Flowers, the sacrifice made by the wife of the king-archon to Dionysus in his temple of Leneum and her copulation with the god were the high points of the ritual. In the rite of holy union celebrated at Babylon, a chosen young woman ascended by night the seven floors of the terraced tower of the holy ziggurat to a nuptial room above and awaited coitus with the god. It was also believed that the priestess of Apollo at Patara passed the night on the "holy bed" in union with the god.

The symbolization of the god as an animal led both to an uncouth literal interpretation and to stories of copulation between human beings and holy animals. Thus Herodotus tells of the sacred ram of Mendes, called "the lord of young women," to whom the women in Egypt gave themselves in order to have a "divine offspring"; echoes of these same themes persist even in Roman traditions. Ovid speaks of the divine voice which bade the Sabine wives to let themselves be fertilized by the sacred he-goat.

This doctrinal foundation underlies the idea that human and individual limits can be overcome and that a "real presence" can, under certain conditions, be embodied or aroused in a man or woman through transubstantiation. This concept seemed natural to people in ancient times owing to their innate idea of the world; but modern man takes it as an illusion and accepts it only as a psychological phenomenon devoid of reality, an eruption of archetypes from the unconscious. It will be even harder, therefore, for him to understand the reality present in traditions dealing with integration through the female principle, in which an actual woman takes no part, not even as a symbol for ritual evocation; instead, these traditions involve an "invisible woman," an influence that does not belong to the world of phenomena. We shall now speak of this more direct and nonindividual manifestation of the power imaged in the mythology of sex.

Incubus and Succubus; Fetishism and Evocatory Processes

We are now presented with all the rich, strange material of the sagas and heroic myths in which a supernatural woman is shown as the giver of life, wisdom, salvation, mystical nourishment, holy force, and everlasting life itself. As such, she is often linked symbolically to the tree: in Egyptian representations, for instance, the goddess who has the "Key of Life" or "Draught of Life," Nut, Mait, or Hathor, is often confused with the sacred tree, shown as the tree of temptation in Hebrew myths, as the tree of enlightenment in Buddhism, or of victory and empire in the legend of the priest Gianni.[26] We mentioned these sagas elsewhere[27] and indicated the meaning of the heroic myths. We shall highlight two specific examples here.

According to the Hindu doctrine of royalty, the chrism of power is given to a sovereign by his wedding to the goddess Lakshmi (conceived of as his wife among all his human spouses), who takes on the supernatural animating force of "royal good fortune" (rajalakshmi). The king would lose his throne were she to leave him. We also see in the Mediterranean cycle representations of goddesses who hand kings the "key of life" (an ideogram having the sound ankh, "to live" or "living") while speaking words such as those addressed by King Ashurbanipal to the goddess, "From you I invoke the gift of life," and those of the Zohar (III, 51a, 50b), "The path which leads to the great and mighty Tree of Life is the Mistress (equivalent to the Shekhinah as wife of the king).

We may even hear a last echo of this in Christianity, for in the Virgin, conceived of as the almighty mediatrix of grace, appears the theme of a female principle from which arises a supernatural influence added to the merely natural forces of man, besides the attributes we cited in the example of the Byzantine hymn.

We shall have to come back to this subject for the background of possible erotic experience it presents. Now we shall just say that it is not foreign to magic. One of its dark aspects appears in the phenomena of possession by succubi and incubi, which have been recorded since the days of the Sumerians. Let us cite the following passage from Paracelsus: "This fantasy arises from the astral body as if by virtue of heroic love; it is an action that is not fulfilled in carnal union. In isolation such a love is, at one and the same time, father and mother of the spiritual seed. From this psychic seed spring the incubi which oppress women and the succubi which attack men."[29] This is what the Germans called the *Alpminne* in the Middle Ages. Paracelsus was alluding here in a cryptic language to the evocatory power of the imagination that can lead to psychic contacts with the supersensual capabilities of sex, and awaken feelings of such intensity that they can cause hallucinations. The less dark and involuntary varieties of this phenomenon are understood thus by De Guaita: "The incubus and succubus are two ghostly forms of a 'convertible hermaphroditism,' which is now predominantly phallic and now predominantly in the form of the female sexual organs."[30] This is a matter of special impelling forms of absolute union of the male and female principles, the union developing, however, along an obsessive line[31] because of the subject's passivity vis-à-vis the development of the experience itself, which does not take place on the material plane. In actual fact the same result, almost an obsession, also can result from the initiatory forms of sexual magic when they fail or are deflected from their real purpose; this is an interesting similarity because in this case the intention and aim are clearly known. In these circumstances real and objective forces play a part. We can distinguish between the sexual fantasies common to certain schizophrenic states and possession by incubi or succubi, by the extranormal phenomena that frequently accompany true "possession"; this explains the events that happened as late as the eighteenth century in the Convent of the Ursulines at Loudun. Such "prodigies" were recorded during the arousal of maenads and bacchantes who felt themselves possessed by the god; Pliny and Euripides, for example, mention ruptures of level by means of sex which sometimes involved a removal of the boundary between ego and nature, resulting in interpenetration of the two spheres ("prodigies" in the former case and "hysterical obsessions" in the latter). In general it is necessary to remember that what is seldom fulfilled on the material plane can reach forms of arousal on the subtle and hyperphysical plane, with all the related consequences.

We have seen that beyond all incidental conditional qualities, the foundation of all important erotic experience is the relationship established between a person and the essence or "being" of an individual of the opposite sex. This implies an evocatory process that in profane eros differs only because of its weaker degree and instinctive and unconscious form. Krafft-Ebing rightly saw in all love a phenomenon of "fetishism" but recorded that this word, originating in the Portuguese language, really meant "enchantment"; it should be understood as referring to an emotion "which is in no way justified by the intrinsic value or reality of the symbolic object," namely of the person or part of the person or thing that provokes the erotic arousal.[32]

Havelock Ellis took up the same idea. After recognizing that in "erotic symbolism" the part can represent and evoke the whole and explaining the basis of amorous fetishism in a specific or perverse sense (the aphrodisiac effect caused by a part of a woman or even by an object or garment belonging to her), he went a step further and saw the same phenomenon repeated on a large scale when the beloved "being" as a whole becomes a symbol that leads beyond her mere person.[33] If a woman or just her body excites and intoxicates, it is because she dimly calls forth something that transcends her; thus "fetishism" is a normal and constant fact, whereas abnormal, pathological fetishism represents only a deviated variety, which, however, has the same inner structure.[34] Evocation and fetishism are constant facts in every passion and all deep love and are connected to the lover's tendency to "idealize" the woman he loves as if she were a divine being and to make her the object of worship and veneration, even if in actuality she in no way deserves it. A deflection, however, takes place in the cases mentioned earlier (chapter 3) where the woman who is the cause of the evocation inverts the relationship and has such an intense life of her own that she absorbs, devours, or burns the image. This is what lies at the basis of the phenomenology of sexual slavery, whether psychic or physical. This phenomenology is unavoidably interwoven into love as we experience it today, and it paralyzes every "anagogic" capability of that love.

We have just indicated a phenomenon of infatuation and of unwarranted "projection of value" (dictated, according to Schopenhauer, by the "genius of the species" for its own ends). When the intoxication of the first love is dissipated and desire has been fully satisfied, the true reality of the idolized being should reappear in all its banality. This interpretation is opposed to another that does not exclude the possibility that there may indeed be present in varying degrees a process of evocation or magical fantasy, which is not limited to subjective daydreaming but is a kind of sixth sense allowing us to perceive that which is hidden and seems unreal but in fact has a higher degree of reality. In such cases the "woman of the mind" or "secret woman," of whom we wrote earlier, truly transports and fascinates us, and her being acts only as a means for the experience of her arousal. The primordial image that we bear deep within ourselves is activated by a certain person under certain circumstances, leading to a powerful, enraptured trance. The image that we have within us is also the eternal female perceived objectively in the beloved being, which then undergoes a very striking process of transubstantiation and transfiguration as in an epiphany or in a sacred manifestation of power.[35] This dangerous contact with the supersensual can last for one single exceptional moment or for an extended period of tension; however, in normal lovers it is not usually based on the awakening of strong emotional conditions. In love at first sight and in the so-called *coup de foudre*, the process is short-circuited. This state of affairs can also be brought about unexpectedly in a one-night encounter with a stranger and even with a whore. Such a miracle may never be repeated in a whole lifetime, notwithstanding all relationships of affection and human closeness to other women or the transparent nature of the beloved, and the action of her higher power in an "exalted" atmosphere of evocation and revelation may be stabilized for a certain length of time.

As we said earlier, random causes should not be confused with essential facts, and it is necessary to bear in mind the margin of chance involved in externalities that enhance or condition the phenomenon. It may happen that the process is set off only in relation to a precise person. Here the most immediate biological, physical, and social qualities are obvious. An important part will be played, above all, by the ideal, not of an abstract beauty (the Platonic "beautiful in itself"), but of the type of beauty proper to a given race. For instance, it is unlikely that a man will find in a woman of a different race the incentive and basis to arouse the primordial image he has within himself. We should also consider the obvious conditional qualities of a biological character: aging, a fate to which man and, even more so, woman are doomed. With old age and the weakening of the physical basis of sexual love, the very prop of magical evocation changes and fails, and everything lasting will have a different and only human quality. Thus one of Barbusse's characters, when talking about time "which is bound to us inside like an illness," says to the woman that she is precious in only one given moment. "I think that this moment will not last any longer and that you will have to change and die, and that you are going away now even if you are here." This is the existential tragedy of all true love. In fact it is between given limits of age that a woman especially is suitable for her possible metamorphosis (by means of the "attractions" she possesses during this period, woman seeks to bind to herself, as an empirical person, a man forever, generally by means of marriage). However, this concerns neither the reality of the archetype nor that of its evocation and perception, in its timeless essence, where it is not linked to the incidental and to the empirical and finite individual; it concerns only the circumstances necessary for the apparition but not the principle, which appears and which can withdraw once again, just as fire becomes invisible and returns to its potential state when the conditions for combustion are no longer present. It is natural, then, that the prosaic reality of a person resurfaces, but this does not justify interpretation of these phenomena as mere illusion and empty romanticism.

In "Epipsychidion" Shelley wrote words to this effect: "Look there where a mortal divine form arises; life, love, and light belong to it, and a motion which may change but not be extinguished, the image of some bright eternity." Carpenter also expressed it fittingly:

The young man sees the girl; it may be an ordinary face, a random figure from the most trivial background. But that sets things going. A memory, a confused recollection arises. The outer mortal figure is pervaded with the inner immortal one and then there emerges in the consciousnes a bright and glorious form not belonging to this world. . . . The arousal of that image intoxicates man and it shines and burns within him. A goddess, perhaps Venus herself, is standing in her holy temple; a feeling of splendor and awe invades him, and the world is transformed for him. . . . He makes contact with the very real presence of a force . . . and feels this vaster life within himself, subjective and at the same time intensely objective. In fact, it is also evident that this woman, the mortal woman, who provokes such a vision, also has a close relationship to it as much more than just a mask or an empty formula that brings that vision to his mind. Inside her, as in the man, deep unconscious forces are acting, and this ecstatic appearance of the ideal in the man is linked to that force which (as an objective archetype) has acted so powerfully in the heredity of the woman and contributed to the molding of her form and figure. We should not wonder, therefore, that her form reminds him of it. In truth, when the man looks into her eyes, he sees a life much deeper than she herself realizes and which belongs to him as well, an everlasting and wonderful life. That which is immortal in him looks at that which is immortal in her, and the gods descend to meet in them.[36]

The chapter from which this passage was taken is entitled "The Gods as Apparitions of the Race-Life." Apart from the idealizing and poetic ornamentation and the inherent biological emphasis, it expresses the archetypes in their aspect of molding forces of life, race, and species.

There is, therefore, a continuity between that which happens to a certain degree in strong profane love and that which belongs to a plane of real and secret evocation. It has been called quite precisely *coup de foudre*. These erotic flashes and hermaphroditic closings of circuits have the power to take us beyond, to a higher consciousness, just as certain initiations do. We have defined these facts in their most hermetic meanings when dealing with the liminal phenomenology of profane eros and through our study of the practices of ancient sacred ceremonies. We can now give an adequate interpretation of the "platonic love" of the Middle Ages; this is an interesting example in which the phenomena we are dealing with are not exhausted in exceptional, individual, and random experiences but are offered within the framework of a tradition.

Our next two sections will look at the chivalrous cult of women and the experiences of the "Worshippers of Love."

Evocation Processes in the Chivalrous Love of the Middle Ages

First of all, let us circumscribe the areas that interest us. There certainly existed a tradition of troubadours and "courtly love" that is well understood by the historians of medieval customs and literature. There also existed real "courts of love" (A.D. 1150 and 1200), which centered upon well-known women who actually lived, such as Queen Eleanor, the Countess of Flanders, the Countess of Champagne, Ermengilda Viscountess of Narbonne, Stephanetta of Baulx, Odalasia Viscountess of Avignon, and so on. In these courts the cult of women had a settled, stereotyped character, derived at least in part from the lack of understanding by certain circles of an esoteric doctrine to which they faithfully adhered notwithstanding. The role of women in chivalry differed from their role in the courts of love and in the lays of the troubadours. For in the latter, women performed their role even to its ultimate conclusion. It is best to highlight the contrast between this part and the role of the majority of women of the era. In the Middle Ages women were not generally "idealized" and in fact were rather mistreated. The behavior of their husbands was generally very rough, if not actually brutal. The women's habits could be quite free and were in no way fitted to the ideal of modesty and bashfulness; epic tales of the early Middle Ages often speak of women who undertook amorous adventures or courtships, while their men remained indifferent or merely acquiescent. Leaving aside the promiscuity of the baths (a duke of Burgundy described how the baths of Valenciennes provided everything for the needs of Venus, including brothels), young women were apt to undress the knights given hospitality in the castles and to keep them company in bed at night; a certain Gilbert of Nogent in the twelfth century deplored the extent of female shamelessness. As regards the behavior of men,

Meiners observed quite rightly that "in the Middle Ages there were never so many ladies and girls kidnapped and raped as in the fourteenth and fifteenth centuries when chivalry was at its height. During those two centuries, warriors had the right in war to violate the women and girls and to kill them thereafter. It was precisely the knights who ravished and slew the women and daughters of their foes and subjects without worrying that they were laying their own women and daughters open to the rights of reprisal."[37]

This picture may be a little exaggerated, yet overall the difference between actual sexual relations in the Middle Ages and the part that women played in certain knightly customs is indisputable. Therefore, it is likely that the knights had as their focus not real women but rather a "woman of the mind" linked to a practice of evocations, a "lady" who basically had an autonomous reality independent of the physical individual who could act perhaps as an aid and, in a certain way, embody her. The "lady" was actually imaginary, and it was on a subtle plane that the knight brought his love, desire, and exaltation into action. This is how we must understand everything that we have studied so far; in fact, the woman to whom a knight dedicated his life and for whom he performed dangerous undertakings was often chosen in such a way that the possibility of actually possessing her was excluded from the very beginning. She could belong to another man, and therefore hope of marriage was impossible; she might be renowned for cold unapproachability, though her "cruelty" was accepted and even exalted; she could even be the image of a woman who indeed existed but had never been seen. Nonetheless such a woman fed men's desire and drove them to service leading even to death, while in any other respects such men, as warriors, feudatories, and knights, obeyed no other law but their will, were not used to subjection or renunciation, and were averse to any sentimentality. In certain circles in Provence the name *donnoi* or *donnei* actually meant a kind of erotic relationship that, in principle, shunned the possession of women. In one illustration of the time, a man has his hands tied symbolically, and it was said that "he who wishes to possess his woman wholly, knows nothing of *donnoi*." In other cases, the man already had and possessed a woman, but she was not the object of such an eros.[38] As we said earlier, we must think here of a silent will to prevent concrete erotic relations from marking the end of the inner tension (Rilke observed quite rightly that it seemed men feared the success of their courtship more than anything else); but, on the other hand, we should remember the facts that fit into the system of evocation of the female as such and of the absorption of the female and self-integration with her on a superphysical and invisible plane; such a state is an approximation, albeit confused, to absolute possession of the "inner woman" and runs parallel to a constant urge toward self-transcendence (heroic undertakings, dangers, adventures, and every fanatical action done for the lady). For example, it is meaningful that the Crusades were often included among such deeds. The theology of the castles and courts of love commanded faithfulness to both God and "woman" and affirmed spiritual salvation of the knight who died for the woman of his mind; this takes us back to the idea of the immortalizing power belonging, in the end, to eros. Moreover, some information concerning the Templars is interesting as regards occult and hermaphroditic integration. It is said that "demons" came in the form of women to the Templar knights who practiced chastity, and that every knight had his own demon.[39] We can see clearly here the theme of the union with the female on a nonphysical plane, a theme that we also meet in certain magical traditions and also mentioned by Paracelsus. Moreover, we should note that the "idol" used as the center of the secret rites of the Templars, Baphomet, was said by some people to resemble a hermaphroditic figure or even a Virgin.

We should note that the Worshippers of Love, like the Templars (to whom they may have been linked historically), were an initiatory organization. A systematic and well-documented survey, which we owe mainly to Valli and Ricolfi, has confirmed and made public details that have been passed on among select circles about the basis of the poetry of the "sweet new style." The "sweet new style" of poetry employed a secret language that was fully understandable only to the initiates. The love exalted in that poetry was something other than idealized or uplifted profane emotion, and the women glorified in it were not actual women; this begins with Dante's Beatrice and the love described in his *Vita nuova*.

We have already written about this subject elsewhere and will therefore content ourselves here with setting out the problem according to the special point of view that interests us.

The proposition of Valli can be summarized as follows: "These poets, who lived in a mystical and initiatory environment and were seeking an art that was in no way art for art's sake or expressions for expression's sake, were wont to make out of all their feelings of love and of the true emotions which they felt in their love life a 'material' to express mystical and initiatory thoughts. The reality of their loves as men may have provided some true source of some image for their verses but was filtered through symbolism in such a way that this material of love came to have a 'truthful meaning,' that is to say, a significance of profound truth which was mystical and initiatory. A stream of initiatory thoughts was introduced at a certain point into the poetry of love (of the troubadour type) and pervaded it little by little to such an extent that the great central nucleus of the poets of love that existed around Dante employed an artificial 'jargon' for the language of symbolic love."[40] Such was Valli's opinion. For our part, we propose to add the following observations.

First, Valli gives too much emphasis to that which in this poetry may have been linked to the militant wing of the Worshippers of Love. Starting with Dante, those poets were at the same time almost all party men and foes of the hegemonistic intrigues of the church. As to the essential nucleus of their works, it is wrong to say that it is merely an information bulletin produced among the members of the sect under poetic disguise (as Valli believed). They did not need to wait for inspiration nor to write in verse; other forms of secret communication would have been much more convenient and safer than poetry, which, although in code, was yet always available to everyone.

The other and more important point is that there is no need to go beyond reason with a merely symbolical explanation, as Valli is inclined to do. The various women celebrated by the Worshippers of Love, whatever their names might have been, were one single woman, an image of "Blessed Wisdom" or Gnosis, an image of a principle of enlightenment, salvation, and transcendental understanding. However, we are not dealing here with allegories or mere personified doctrinal abstractions, which the school of Dante had already supposed in Beatrice. The plane is that of an actual experience, as in the ancient mysteries and secret rites of the Templars. At the same time, we should understand that the choice of the symbolism of the woman and love was not accidental or meaningless; for they could have used any other material to express what they wanted to say and to mislead the profane crowd, as did the alchemists, for instance. Contrary to the beliefs of Valli (and of Rossetti, Aroux, and Guénon as well), in this case the experience for lovers was not limited to supplying random material for an artificial and symbolic language which would hide a true meaning, itself unrelated to eros (such as, for example, in the ecclesiastical use of amorous language in the Song of Songs); we should not therefore think that the words themselves might be transposed from an erotic to a mystical level. Some Eastern texts lend themselves to such a practice: the title of the *Ananga Ranga*, a treatise that is more than crude eroticism, can be translated as "The Bodiless One or the Hindu Art of Love" and its every stanza can have a sacred as well as a literal meaning.[41] Although here it is essentially a matter of the "initiatress" or "glorious woman of the mind" (as Dante called her and added, "She was called Beatrice by many who did not know what her name was"), this woman was not reduced to a symbol among the

Worshippers of Love; instead we believe that contact with the occult force of womanhood played an essential part. Love aroused by real woman could be employed to develop the initiatory process. Only by looking at the question in this way can we take into account everything that these poetic creations offer in terms of their lively, open-hearted humanity, pervaded with directness, spontaneity, and drama. The explanation of the "woman" as Blessed Wisdom personified or as a mere secret abstract doctrine (or as symbol of the organization that safeguarded it, according to Valli) does not in itself clarify the strong emotional experience and *coups de foudre* described suggestively in this literature. It is unlikely that the Worshippers of Love sexually used women to obtain this experience, as in the rites of Dionysus or Tantrism; no such information has come down to us, and the erotic references in almost all these poems are very restrained and far from daring.

We must be dealing here, therefore, with the intermediate level we mentioned (neither that of mere uplifted human love nor that of sexual techniques) wherein the real woman is important but secondary because she merely acts as an aid to contacting the immaterial power of which she is, in principle, the living embodiment. Opposed to knightly devotion toward woman and their relative "exalted" states, the initiatory phenomenology and arrangements among the Worshippers of Love can be clearly seen. It was not a matter of sporadic and isolated cases devoid of awareness of the process. Rather it was an orientation of a chain of practitioners, the full extent of which is perhaps unknown to us, for it may have included men who have left nothing behind them, neither verses nor other tangible traces.

The Initiatory Experiences of the Worshippers of Love

We must reiterate what we have set forth in other books on the essential experiences of the Worshippers of Love.[42] The emergence of the initiatress through the ordinary woman was expressed clearly in some verses of Guido Cavalcanti, who seems to have been one of the heads of the organization: "I seem to see such a beautiful woman coming out of her lips that my mind cannot understand her, and that at once another woman of a new beauty is born of her, in which it seems that a star is moving and says, 'Your salvation has appeared.' "[43] Besides Cavalcanti, Dante and Cino da Pistoia say that it is "by the virtue which my imagination gave to her," that Love takes a hold on the soul of its worshipper. We must also observe the ambiguity of meaning between *salute* (salvation) and *saluto* (greetings) in almost all the poetry of the New Style. The "greeting" of the mysterious woman, shown as being the end of love (*Vita nuova*, 18, 4), always confers "salvations" on him who receives it; it favors an experience and provokes a crisis from which spiritual salvation may come. Its power tests the lover's force and often even surpasses that force. In fact, Dante wrote, "He who is able to stay and look at [the woman] will become a noble thing or will die; and when she finds someone worthy to see her, he can prove thus the strength of his virtue, for that which gives "salvation' is happening to him."[44] Linked to this is the vision in which Love is shown with the unwonted characteristics of a "Lord of awesome countenance." In his arms, said Dante, "I seemed to see a person sleeping 'naked' except that she appeared to be slightly wrapped in a bloody cloth, and looking at that person I knew that she was 'the woman of Salvation,' who had deigned to greet me the day before."[45] To arouse by love this woman who had been seen naked and sleeping and therefore latent—Hermetism calls her "our hidden Eve"[46]—means to allow a power to act on oneself which is capable of killing and provoking an initiatic death. In this literature, when the "woman of the mind" appears, "the heart is dead." On seeing the woman and receiving her "greeting," Lapo Gianni said: "Then I forced myself not to fall down; my heart, which had been alive, became dead." Guido Guinizelli spoke of a greeting and a deadly look and compared himself to one "who saw his own death. It passes through the eyes just like thunder, which wounds through the window of the tower and breaks or cleaves in twain that which it finds inside."[47] Love warns him who wishes to see the woman: "Flee unless you want to die."[48] In such an experience, therefore, death should not be feared; in fact, a deep inner fracture may be its outcome. A song, perhaps written by Cavalcanti, spoke of "a new passion, such that I remained full of dread; a brake was applied to all my virtues suddenly, so that I fell to the ground, 'by a light which struck me in the heart'; and if the book is not mistaken, the stronger spirit trembled so greatly that it seemed 'that death had come for him in this world.' " Dante described this experience in similar terms: on perceiving the sudden approach of the "woman of the miracle," he felt all his spirits destroyed by the force of Love; there remained only his sight, which, however, was sundered from his physical organs, as in ecstatic rapture. Thus it seemed to Dante that he was falling to the ground, and he said, "I kept my feet on that part of life 'beyond which one cannot go if one wishes to return' "; later on he wrote about a "transfiguration";[49] in yet another passage he returned to the theme of the "destruction" worked by love.[50] Moreover, the teachings of the medieval Kabbala mention the *mors osculi* or death through the kiss, and similar expressions are also found in Arabic and Persian Sufi poetry.[51]

If we look at the writings of the Worshippers of Love as a whole, it seems that sometimes it is the direct action of the woman (her appearance) and at other times her indirect action that produces these effects. Her image, her "greeting," and her idea transform Love from a potential state to an actual state in terms of a force that arouses fear and causes initiatic death. In this respect Cavalcanti spoke of an action on the "potential intellect," a term taken from the Aristotelianism of Averroës, where he called by the name "nous" the intellectual principle in its transcendental aspect, which in an ordinary man exists only potentially.[52] According to the path followed by a true Worshipper of Love, therefore, it is by means of the woman as life that this potential is actualized or becomes real in his consciousness and transforms him. Cavalcanti wrote of "you who pass through my eyes to my heart and awaken the intellect that was asleep," and he added that "Love takes up its place and dwelling in the potential intellect as a subject." Guinizelli indicated the "heart" as being the seat of the "nobility," which becomes real through women. In the development of the experience, therefore, the emotional and traumatic moment seems to change into a pure intellectual act (the "rebirth of the intellect" of which the *Corpus hermeticum* wrote). This nobility (Love, too, is called the "Lord of nobility"), actualized by woman in the ecstasy that she provokes, is an ontological perfection linked to the reawakening of the intellectual essence; in everything, said Dante, who also cited Aristotle,[53] nobility is the perfection of its nature, and in this regard the act of denuding and the symbolism of nakedness are again mentioned: Love has the power to make the spirit come out from its "lodging" and to "make it fly without covering."[54]

In general, the recurring theme with these writers is a crisis followed by the beginning of a new or transformed life, and explicit references to the mystery of the hermaphrodite are often present. Da Barberino[55] made Love say, "Something of such a strong nature struck him that some people think he died because of it; but he found himself again in a higher life." He ranked degrees of experience in a hierarchy. In an illustration in his book *Love Documents*, we can see symmetrical male and female figures which, as is obvious and as Valli had already noted,[56] are taken in pairs. Men and women are struck by the arrows of Love more or less heavily; in the beginning they fall to the ground, but as they draw near to a central figure, they stand up and hold roses as a symbol of their initiatory rebirth. After the last couple, who bear the inscription "From this death life will follow," there are no longer a separate man and a separate woman but one single hermaphroditic figure, above which Love, himself holding some roses, takes off in flight on a white steed. The hermaphroditic figure has an inscription with the words "Love, you have made us one instead of two with higher virtue through wedlock." The key meanings could not be given more clearly: after the crisis, which even in the first degrees wounds, topples, and slays, the union with the woman and the "higher virtue of wedlock" lead to the hermaphrodite (which in the picture is represented exactly like the hermetic Rebis), a state after which Love will develop the higher experience in a flight or transcendental rapture. In fact, another Worshipper of Love, Nicoló dé Rossi, when dealing with "grades and virtues of true love," considered their zenith to be the ecstasy which is called death of the mind and adds, "just as Paul was carried away," which means the opening of the spirit to superindividual and supernatural states of being.

It is interesting that Dante linked to the action of Love a fettering and enthraldom of the "vital spirit" or naturalistic, *yin* part of being, which he made to exclaim, "Behold the God who is stronger than I and, coming, will govern me."[57] It is as if, through the awakening of a higher principle (the "potential intellect" or nous, realized the "nobility" or, in Hindu wording, the luminous Shiva principle), a new precedence of rank were established among the various powers of the human being. In the *Symposium*, although an allegoric and learned interpretation predominates over an anagogic and initiatory one (it is at the former that Dante said explicitly that we should stop), the "miraculous woman of virtue" is said to arouse a "straightforward appetite," which "upsets and destroys its opposite"; from her issues a fire "which breaks the inborn or natural vices" and she has the "power to renew the nature of those who look at her, which is a miraculous thing."[58] The "salvation" achieved through the awakening and renovation of the inner power of being ensures participation in everlasting initiatory life. We have already mentioned the established etymology, which a Provençal exponent of the same faith, Giacomo di Baisieux, used in identifying love with the "deathless" and with the destruction of death; he spoke of lovers as "those who die not" and will live "in another century of joy and glory."[59] In any event, among the Worshippers of Love the concept remains well established that the union with woman leads to the possibility of a higher life, so that if she were to be separated from man, he would again face the shadow of death.[60] In fact, Cecco d'Ascoli said, "I am transformed into the third heaven in this Woman, so that I know not who I was. Wherefore I feel more blessed every hour. My intellect took form from her as her eyes showed me salvation, as I looked at the virtue in her countenance. Therefore I am She; 'and if she sunders herself from me, I shall then feel the shadow of death.'"[61]

We shall end this section by mentioning two more points. The first concerns the symbolism of numbers. We know the part played by the number three together with its multiples both in the principal work of Dante and in his *Vita nuova*. In the latter, the first power of three (three squared), or nine, is given particular importance. At the first meeting, the woman was nine years old (and that, given the traumatic effects produced by the sight of her, should be enough to set aside the literal interpretation of Beatrice as a young girl of that age). It was at the ninth hour that the greeting took place, as also did one of the most significant visions recounted by the poet. The name of his own woman, Dante tells us, "could not bear to be in a number other than nine." The number nine reappears as the duration of a certain painful illness of Dante.[62] In explaining this, Dante only says that "the number three is the root of nine and makes nine by itself (i.e., multiplied by itself) without needing any other number." As regards three, he refers to the Christian Trinity and calls it the "factor by itself of miracles" and ends by saying, "This woman was accompanied by this number, nine, so as to give us to understand that she was a nine, that is, a miracle, the root of which is only the wonderful Trinity."[63] This is basically only half of the matter, for a more precise and universal side of the symbolism of three and its powers was undoubtedly known in Dante's circles. We have already noted how three is the number of *yang* and how it also meant that which arises from the union of the One with the female number, the Two, and then leads back beyond the Two to unity.[64] In ancient Egypt three was the number of lightning but also that of vital force and of the invisible life-being enclosed within the body, the *ka*. Moreover, nine was also linked to *yang*, as also was eighty-one, so much so that the latter number plays a strange part in a detail of Taoist sexual techniques. The significance of nine lies in it being the first power of three, whereas the importance of eighty-one is that it is the perfect power of three (3^3). In a certain way, eighty-one takes us beyond the experience of the "woman of the miracle," and it is important that Dante himself in the *Convivio* spoke of it and gave it as the "age" of a perfect and completed life; he recalled that it was Plato's age and even said that Christ would have reached that age if he had not been crucified. But this symbolic age figures in other traditions too, and the same age was attributed to Lao-tze. Overall, this relates to cycles of fulfillment of the One, which is renewed through the Dyad or female, developing as the act or power of itself until it is identical to this particular power of itself and is established in "nobility." Now, Dante, who made Beatrice die on the ninth day of June, also observed that in Syria, June is the ninth month, and he noted lastly that her death happened when "the perfect number, nine, was fulfilled," that is, in '81 in the thirteenth century.

The other point we wished to mention concerns the death of Beatrice. First Perez and afterward Valli[65] linked this death to that of Rachel in the Bible and recalled how Agostino and Riccardo of San Vittore assumed the death of Rachel as a symbol of ecstasy, the *excessus mentis* or death of the mind. Valli thought that the woman's death in the *Vita nuova* was "a representation of the transcendence of the mind beyond itself during the act of pure contemplation, a mystical representation of the mind which is lost in God."[66] But we do not agree, for it only concerns more than the merely mystical plane, which is not that of the Worshippers of Love, but also, in our view, actually inverts the situation. It is certain that the woman's death marks the last phase of the experience that began with her "greeting," and there are some enigmatic expressions concerning this in chapter 27 of the *Vita nuova*. After having referred to the death of Beatrice, Dante added the mysterious words "It is not fitting for me to talk of that event because, if I were to do so, I should have to praise myself," just as if the event, Beatrice's death, would resound to his glory. The mystical interpretation put forward by Valli does not fit the circumstances, for if it had been a matter of the death of the mind ("the killing of the intellect," of the *manas* of yoga terminology), we would have merely been dealing with one of the effects of woman and Love on the lover, leaving aside the point that death, interpreted as a mystical shipwreck, would then concern not the woman but the Worshippers of Love; whereas the opposite is stated, and it was the woman who died, to the glory of the Worshippers of Love. We do not deem the opposite idea too rash, namely that the last term of the experience is represented by surmounting the woman in the fully realized reintegration. This is what corresponds in Hermetism to the "Red Interaction" (or Red Opus) after the "White Interaction" (which is preceded by the "Black Interaction" or death or dissolution), namely a condition of manhood reestablished beyond the ecstatic opening. This is the final state for which, also in Hermetism, there was sometimes mentioned a killing of her by whom one had been killed but also been "regenerated." Furthermore, as we have seen, besides the number nine, Dante made eighty-one the number for the death of the woman.

We are also led toward this explanation by a point that has not been sufficiently emphasized: in Christian mysticism the soul acts as a female who is the "fiancée" of the heavenly bridegroom; in all this literature and in the symbolism of woman recorded in sagas and myths, the parts are generally reversed, and it is the subject of the experience who has the male quality;[67] nor, indeed, could we expect anything else if the Worshippers of Love were an organization for initiation and not mysticism. One last anomaly is significant: Guido Cavalcanti, who must have been one of the leaders of the organization, stated that Love arises from and dwells in the sky of Mars, not of Venus ("who comes from and dwells with Mars"); and it seems that Dante shared this opinion tacitly. The significance of this will not escape anyone.

We have dwelled somewhat on the subject of the Worshippers of Love because they enable us to establish to a certain degree a bridge between some of the main themes emphasized in our own investigation and the field of profane love as well. Speaking of profane love, Knut Hamsun went so far as to call it "a power that can bring man down to nothing and then raise him up again and mark him with its scorching brand." Stendhal uses the following words for an actual case of the *coup de foudre*: "A higher force of which I am afraid took me out of myself and out of reason." On feeling the breath of Lotte, Werther said, "I feel myself thrown down as if struck by lightning." The Worshippers of Love shared the same experiences and developed and integrated them outside of any sentimentality. This subject is precise and recurs in their works. Other recurring themes include rapture and death, the profound significance of the heart, trauma in the heart considered as a secret place ("the very secret chamber of the heart," as Dante said) and as a place to be purified ("the tender heart") because it is in the heart that the dazzling mystery of the Three will begin, owing to the effect of the woman-miracle and of the "Lord of nobility."

In conclusion, we must reject the aesthetic and literal interpretations that attempt to link everything to real women and to experiences of merely human love transposed, uplifted, and expressed in high-flown language by the poet. We must also reject merely symbolic interpretations that only introduce learned abstractions or even personifications of an Understanding ("Blessed Wisdom") as an enlightening power, which, nevertheless, is unrelated to the power of femininity. This last interpretation was followed not only by Valli but also by Guénon and Reghini; these explanations may be acceptable in the case of mystical teachings based more or less on Neoplatonism (including Bruno's) or even in the case of the Arab and Persian poetry that flourished between the ninth and fourteenth centuries, but they are not complete, in our opinion, as regards the Worshippers of Love. For them, the alternative is transcended, and we should consider their essential basis to be the possibility of evocations and contacts for initiative purposes with the occult female principle in a liminal and nonmaterial field. Beyond this, there is only real sexual magic, an extreme development of the capability of eros at a nonprofane level. This sphere remains to be dealt with. The third of the solutions listed at the beginning of this chapter is that of the transmutations of the force of sex through asceticism and yoga.

Besides, in evocation and participation we can distinguish two paths that run under the signs of Demeter and Durga, the two basic female archetypes. The first is based on the mother-father principle considered as the source of holiness, and leads toward life everlasting, peace, and light. In the profane and human field, this can come to a man who takes shelter near a maternal woman; Pythagoreanism recognizes in woman a special holiness and even talks of the "initiatory mother," *tē mētrí teleíē* (perfect mother); this trend is manifested in the fact that after his death Pythagoras' house was turned into a shrine of Demeter. This feminine archetype finds strong expression in the myth of the heavenly Virgin and divine mediating Mother. The other path runs, instead, under the sign of Durga, the depthless Aphroditic female, and may either be the road to perdition or the means of surpassing the Mother under the sign of the Great Mysteries.

Appendix

The Meaning of the Sabbat and the Black Mass

As a supplement to what we have written concerning supersensual evocations with an erotic basis, we may touch briefly here on the content of the experiences of the Sabbat and the so-called Black Mass.

The demonology of past centuries is in general an interesting field, but it has never been studied from the right perspective. The correct point of view is neither that of theologians who ascribe everything to Satanism, as did the judges of the Inquisition, nor that of rationalists who blame everything on superstition, psychopathology, and hysteria. Psychiatrists and psychoanalysts have sought to eliminate any theological and supernatural interpretation. They argue that simple psychotherapy has led to the disappearance of phenomena formerly attributed to diabolical influence. This confirms the superficial nature of what the general consensus deems "scientific" or "positive." Certain individuals show real psychic disorders and have defective constitutions, which allow for supersensual manifestations. Moreover, in these cases, it is obvious that when one succeeds in "healing" the individual, the basis of these manifestations will disappear and they will end; but that will teach us nothing about their true nature or their profound dimension.

As regards the Sabbat, even if we give a wide margin to what has been attributed to mere superstition and suggestion (either autosuggestion or brainwashing applied to defendants in trials), yet certain facts of inner "experience" with a sufficiently constant and typical structure have been witnessed. In order to "enhance" these experiences in certain individuals, who may or may not have been predisposed toward them, substances were used which had effects like those of love potions. From the material point of view we find aphrodisiac powders and also narcotic and stupefying substances. The texts of the day speak of deadly nightshade, opium, wolfsbane, four-leaf clover, henbane, poplar leaves, certain kinds of poppies, and so on, mixed with special animal fats and made into an ointment that was absorbed through the skin, causing a twofold intoxication: either deep sleep, which liberated the plastic power of the imagination to produce images, lucid dreams, and visions, or the reawakening of the elementary sex drive and its arousal on this ecstatic, visionary, and imaginative plane. Furthermore, the writers speak of a ritual consecration of these substances. For example, it was said: "In this composition they do not forget a special invocation of their devils and of magic ceremonies instituted by them."[68] This obviously alluded to a secret operation intended to give a special "direction of efficiency" to the action of the drugs in question. This factor clearly must have had a fundamental importance. Whether or not we acknowledge its reality will depend on the extent to which we believe, for instance, that the sacraments are more than merely symbolic ceremonies. It is most likely that we owe to that factor the difference between the generic and disorderly action that some drugs and aphrodisiacs produce today and the specific action that led to the experiences of the Sabbat. Another essential factor must have been the existence of a "tradition"; a determined set of images must have been evoked through a collective psychic current, into which the individual was introduced through joining the group of practitioners. This explains the considerable agreement regarding the fundamental experiences. Contrary to Bodin, Johannes Vierus in his *Daemonomania* upheld the proposition that these experiences, although having a supernatural influence (the Devil) as their basis, took place in a state of trance, the body remaining motionless although the subject believed he was physically present at the Sabbat. Görres recorded certain experiments conducted in the fourteenth century by a Benedictine monk (other men later repeated them, including Gassendi himself) on persons who, after carrying out the ritual preparations to go to the Sabbat, were tied to their beds and observed. They often fell into a lethargic or cataleptic sleep so deep that not even burns or pin pricks could wake them. It has always been insisted that "to betake oneself to the Sabbat" it was neccessary to fall asleep after being anointed and reciting specific formulas. Thus the simplest interpretation is that of orgies of the erotic imagination experienced during sleep. But traditional Hindu teachings differentiate mere subjective illusion or dreaming from a change in level of consciousness or the virtual displacement of consciousness to the "subtle." De Nynauld described certain ointments capable of causing "a transport that does not take place merely in an illusion, for a state of deep sleep exists"; that is, an out-of-body experience.

To accept this, we must first accept the premise that such phenomena have been accounted even in the lives of some Christian saints.[69] However, we should note that in the experiments we mentioned earlier, more cases of double existence were confirmed at least in the sense that a person lying still and senseless on his bed owing to the effect of drugs could sometimes tell exactly what was happening in his environment (Görres). Therefore, we should not exclude the possibility of experiences that, although of an essentially psychic nature, are not merely subjective dreams or the hallucinations of schizophrenics but possess an objective dimension of their own.

Nor should we exclude the possibility of very ancient, ecstatic rites that continued to be practiced in the Middle Ages and culminated in the sexual act, as if in a sacrament, which had many of the characteristics attributed to the Sabbat. Thus a horned god by the name of Cernunnos was celebrated; an altar dedicated to him has been found beneath the foundations of the Cathedral of Notre Dame de Paris.[70] Moreover, we should note that spontaneous confessions were made without torture by participants in this ceremony, who died without fear or remorse, convinced that they had gained everlasting life. Some young women declared that they had gone to the rite because their hearts and wills had been enraptured by the god. They stated that he was the "supreme religion," that the Sabbat was the true paradise which bestowed indescribable pleasures so ecstatic that they had shed the weight of their bodies and taken new bodies like "those of the angels"; they were proud of their experiences and met their deaths with the same calm steadfastness as the first Christians.[71]

But we are dealing here essentially with hazy evocations of archetypes and ritual conditions imitating ancient orgiastic cults. If we so wish, we can relate these to the collective subconscious considered as a receptacle of images capable of being reawakened and revitalized on the subtle plane; however, remnants of every kind in the individual subconscious are mingled therewith, for the subjects of such experiences belonged to the general populace and had neither training nor tradition comparable to those of the ancient mysteries. Moreover, we should take into account here the fact of a specific distortion or degradation due to the milieu of Christianity, which assigned a sinful character to everything linked to sex. Under such circumstances and in a system of confused and disorderly evocations, "devilish" forms and forms of antinomy may well be brought about in the manifestations. Demonism is often only a distortion of themes and figures belonging to a previous, ousted cult against the background of the new one that replaced it. Many examples of this can be found in the history of religions. In the mechanism of the subconscious, when psychic remains of such a kind are revitalized, it is easy for them automatically to assume antagonistic, devilish, and even satanic images.[72] Therefore, we should deem that in the case of experiences such as those of the Sabbat, anyone who underwent them took little account of their real content and only experienced that content indirectly through the swiftly changing images of the witches' Sabbat, so that he made confessions in good faith which conformed precisely to the diabolic scenario already made up by the judges of the Inquisition.

Last, we ought to refer to the animal element present in such phantasmagoria. We should bear in mind here also the effects of an agitation of the deepest and prepersonal layers of being, where there are latent animal potentialities excluded from the evolutionary process. These potentialities, which play an important part in the totemism, can also be activated and involved in the evocatory process so as to produce by projection human-animal images or animallike deformations of the human figure which correspond generally to the more degraded and formless content aroused in the overall process. But from every other angle this process can be considered like the Dionysiac rejection of inhibitions and the ancient rites of erotic and orgiastic initiation.

Using information provided by writers who have dealt with this subject over past centuries, such as Buguet, N. Remigius, Bodin, Del Rio, Binsfeldius, and Dom Calmet, De Guaita actually reconstructed the prevalent structure of the experiences of the Sabbat in the following terms.[73] At the diabolical meeting the "queen of the Sabbat" appeared as a young naked woman, often a virgin, having a particular beauty and borne on a black ram (Pierre de Lancre wrote, "All of those whom we have seen chosen for the title of queens were sweet and were more marked for beauty than the others"). The virgin was initiated by the persons officiating with successive sacraments, was anointed, and was then violated on an altar. According to a witness, this made her undergo "a wonderful and dreadful torment." A general orgy followed in which the antagonistic mode of manifestation of elementary eros in the free and formless state ended in adulterous, incestuous, or unnatural unions and a gang rape of the new priestess. On her supine body, as if on a throbbing altar, the he-goat of the Sabbat, now in human or semihuman guise, officiated, offering grain to the "Spirit of the Earth," the principle of all fecundity. Sometimes birds were released as a symbolic rite of liberation for the attendants of the Sabbat (an evocation of the "devil of freedom" perhaps; but one name of Dionysus at Rome was also "Free"). A cake was sometimes kneaded to carry out a wedding offering or a communion by shared consumption of the cake. It is said that at the end the queen of the Sabbat rose and, as a triumphant victim, called out formulas such as "Lightning of God, strike if you dare" (in a similar rite with a sexual background, observed in Slavonia until the twelfth century, it is related that the formula was "Let us be merry today, for Christ is conquered").[74] An objective element existed in that anyone who took part in this orgiastic initiation obtained the secrets of compounding love potions, poisons, or elixirs. The possession of such gifts is strongly attested.[75] According to information available from the trials, Diana was often invoked in the Sabbat (until the sixteenth century, *"ire ad ludum Dianae"* or "to go to Diana's game" meant the same as going to the Sabbat) together with Lucifer, a clearly "inverted" transposition of the male god of light.[76] As is well known, a certain figure in the Germanic World was Vrowe Holda with her ambivalent characteristics, gentle and dreadful, bestower of grace and destroyer, characteristics already noted by us in the female archetype. The mountain of the witches' Sabbat and the night of Valpurga were confused with the mount where Venus abode, the mountain being transformed into a devilish place of sin according to Christian views. It is not devoid of meaning that the actual rites should be held near the ruins of heathen temples or ancient ruins (for instance, the summit of the Puy-de-Dôme in Auvergne, where the remains of a temple of Hermes are situated) or dolmens and other megalithic monuments.

It has often been observed that in the scenario of the phantasmagoria of the witches' Sabbat the *hircus sacer* reappears in the form of the he-goat, the holy symbolic animal (identified by the Greeks sometimes with Pan and sometimes with Dionysus) who possessed young women in the sense of a holy marriage in one of the cults of ancient Egypt, whereas the naked woman worshipped as the living goddess is a variant of an ancient Mediterranean theme. We have already recounted how in the Aegean area, for instance, the cult of the goddess was confused with that of her priestess and how similar traces persist in the secret orgiastic ceremonies of certain Slavic sects. Even if only tendentially, ritual structures like those of the Sabbat have been attributed to the Gnostics. Thus it is related that Marcus the Gnostic violated some young girls who had been persuaded to climb on an altar, and in this way he consecrated them and made them become prophetesses. Where such cases had validity, it was obviously a question of technique of sexual initiation. As regards the ancient world, moreover, Pliny[77] has told us of witches' Sabbats by night on Mount Atlas, with unbridled dances and an orgiastic unleashing of the elementary forces of man together with the presence or manifestation of ancient nature gods and goddesses. We should think, therefore, of the basis of the Sabbat as a reactivation of these ritual structures based on an obscure liberation of energies on the subtle plane, whereon archetypal forces can work effectively and forms of ecstasy can occur that can seldom be attained within the field of normal waking consciousness. Furthermore, we shall prove that, if rites carried out with human persons, material actions, and physical accessories have any efficacy, it is because consciousness is transported onto the subtle plane.

We have already remarked on the technical reason that makes the experience diabolical, owing to the part played by Christianity's repression and theological condemnation of sexuality. But in principle we should also consider the possibility of a conscious "instrumental" use of everything having the character of a devilish and formless substratum held in check by the forms of a given religion; such a use would be arranged for the purpose of a special transcendence of these forms and a potential participation in a state free from conditions. We should be able to say, perhaps more clearly, that in such cases where the form is presented as a limitation, that which is "below" the form is called into use daringly as a means "against form" so as to reach that which is "above" form (to this there correspond, particularly in the theistic religions, special divine figures, dogmas, positive rules, prohibitions, and so on). In anomalous cases where, notwithstanding everything, we remain in the psychic current of the corresponding tradition, such a technique from the outside can actually show the characteristics of a counterreligion, inverted religion, or Satanism.

In such a context we may refer to a particular detail. In a description of the Sabbat it is said that an obscene kiss, *osculum sub cauda* or kiss below the tail, which those taking part should have given to the god of the rite, to the image or the man who was officiating and representing the god, was a chrism of their "satanic" faith. Other witnesses, however, said clearly that no such rite was required. In this we may be dealing with an unbelievably and obscenely twisted version of something wholly different. De Lancre wrote that the actual thing in question here might be another face, a black one, which the idol or person officiating had behind him, perhaps like a mask attached to the nape of the neck, as if on a head of Janus.[78] This symbolism is clear enough; if the light-colored face at the front represented the "outer" manifested God, the rear black face represented the depthless, formless divinity ranking higher than the outer God. In the Egyptian mysteries, the formula of the ultimate secret referred to Osiris as a black god; besides, we can find accurate references to that divinity in early Greek Christian patristics, which was influenced by the teachings of the mysteries and Neoplatonism (Dionysius and Areopagite, for instance). And so this matter may have been distorted into an obscene rite of witchcraft instead of a true profession of faith or "worship" of the formless divinity which employed the lower to reach the higher, namely the "black God," the *Deus Ignotus* or Unknown God. But it is hard to say to what extent this may be the case in some ceremonies and obscure cults, among which may be numbered the Black Masses themselves.

If the information at our disposal regarding the actual celebration of the Black Mass is scanty and untrustworthy, yet the technique of a diabolical inversion of the Catholic ritual is the subject of adequate evidence. We may set aside here the merely blasphemous, ludicrous, and sacrilegious version belonging to descriptions such as the fanciful version of Huysmans. The little that we do know concerns actions having purposes that were vilely magical rather than ecstatic, as was the case in the Black Mass that Catherine de' Medici caused to be performed. The structure of the ceremony shows traces of similarity to the ancient rites of the Aphroditic mysteries, and what was experienced in the phantasmagoria of the Sabbat was partly carried out here on the plane of reality. Indeed, the center of the rite considered of a naked woman stretched out on the altar and herself acting as an altar. The position she sometimes assumed, with her legs spread open so as to show her sex, the *os sacrum* or "sacred mouth," in the words of a Hermetic witness, was the same as in the representations of some ancient female goddesses of the Mediterranean. Besides the inverted performance of the Mass, it seems that the rite consisted of the same developments as those we described earlier with regard to the Sabbat. The most abominable detail, namely the possible sacrifice of a baby before the altar, was not only a devilish imitation of the Eucharistic sacrificial rite of the Mass but also referred to the theme of the sacrifices and pouring of blood in which the Goddess, in some forms of the ancient belief, took delight. On the other hand, this might be a magical technique intended to provide a body for for the real presence of that goddess. A detail that is important not only as regards this particular point but in general is as follows: it was deemed absolutely necessary that the rite as a whole should be performed by a properly ordained priest. In fact, according to

Catholic doctrine, apart from a man who may be directly consecrated by the Lord, only a priest can effect the mystery of transubstantiation by means of an objective power which he may be forbidden by interdict to exercise but which cannot be destroyed or revoked owing to its indelible character established by ordination. Now, the rites we have mentioned can possess some efficacy only on condition that the person officiating has the same power of transubstantiation, a power that can call forth and awaken actual presences in susceptible species, not only in inanimate things (as in the host of the Eucharist) but also in human beings. A "mystery" of this kind is supposed to take place in the very person of the naked woman lying on the altar, so that there is provoked in her a momentary, magical embodiment of the archtype, the power of transcendental woman and the goddess. If we suppose that this supersensual force was evoked, then an operational use of it could be imagined. We need only think that the employment of the technique of the counterreligion together with the arousal of everything formless and "hellish" which is held in check by a historical tradition, involves a heavy risk and presupposes in the persons officiating a specific and exceptional skill so as to prevent it from becoming truly satanic in the worst meaning of the word. The danger is less where such rites of sexual magic fit into the background of a sympathetic tradition and do not have recourse to the technique of inversion, and are thus devoid of an antinomial character, as we shall show shortly.

It seems that the divinity in the practices of black magic in the seventeenth and nineteenth centuries was female. She was called Astaroth, a name having the same root as Astarte, Ashtoreth, Attar, Ash-tur-tu, and so on, which leads us to believe that it was linked to Astarte-Ishtar (in Semitic languages *oth*, as in Astaroth, is a plural ending), even if the sex of the divinity was not determined. Sometimes women officiated at the Black Masses.

As a last point concerning only the Sabbat, we shall observe that, besides using the same means, experiences of this kind on the subtle plane are hard for modern man to conceive of, since they are more than mere orgies in dreams belonging to the individual erotic imagination, but rather imply real contacts and evocations. The necessary psychic atmosphere is no longer available, and a process of increased attention to the physical has shut the individual within himself in his mere subjectivity. Apart from truly exceptional cases, the only plane nowadays for possible experiences beyond the normal psychic processes is such that, as a rule, those experiences are suited to banal interpretations such as that of Jung or else fit into the "psychedelic" sphere because of the profane and disorderly use of certain drugs.

The Doctrine of the Hermaphrodite in Christian Mysticism

We saw in Scotus Eriugena that the doctrine of the hermaphrodite had appeared within the framework of Christian theology. Without any visible link to Scotus but beginning, instead, with Jakob Boehme, the same theme comes to light again in a little-known group of mystical and explanatory writers who, while remaining essentially within the fold of Christianity, sought to show the differentiation of the sexes as an outcome of the fall of primordial man, who had been created by God in the beginning in his own image, male and female, and therefore a hermaphrodite.

We mentioned that the Kabbala had already sought to give this meaning to the biblical myth, and in particular that Leo the Hebrew had attempted explicitly to make the biblical myth correspond to the myth in Plato's *Symposium*. In developing similar ideas, but without referring to Plato and holding instead to the Bible alone, these Christian writers, beginning with Boehme, were driven to make sophistical and unnatural speculations so as to provide some unity for themes of diverse origins which exist in the biblical myth in the state of a harmonized blend. In fact, Genesis, as opposed to Plato, spoke first of the original being created as a hermaphrodite and then described the appearance of the sexes not as the effect of sin but as the work of God, who became aware, as it were, of a fault in his seven days' work of creation. Finding that it was not good for Adam to be alone, God divided him and formed Eve out of him. Last, with the sexes already existing, Genesis spoke of Adam's sin, for which it could not, as we noted earlier, give a sexual reason since the commandment to multiply and the saying that man will form one single flesh with woman came in Genesis before the story of the disobedience and Fall of Adam.

The theory of the hermaphrodite, however, had such an influence on some Christian mystics and writers that they passed by these obvious discrepancies and sought to make that theory equal in worth within the biblical framework. Boehme, who inaugurated this strand of thought, not only was aware of Hermetic speculation but had also adopted from alchemical Hermetism a part of its symbolic terminology (thus Boehme made Sulfur, Mercury, Niter, Water, Fire, Salt, and so forth into symbols of cosmic and spiritual powers). It is likely that he took the story of the hermaphrodite not from the secret Jewish theology of the Kabbala but from Hermetism, which already possessed it in the forms of the Rebis through an independent tradition derived from the mysteries and Gnostic circles.[79]

Boehme's arrangement of the biblical myth was as follows. In the beginning, one hermaphroditic being was created and combined within itself the male and female principles (called by Boehme the

Hue of Fire and the Hue of Light). The slumber of Adam was not the state into which God put him when, of God's own will, he wished to take Eve from Adam, but was conceived as the symbol of the first Fall. In Boehme this slumber alludes to the state in which Adam found himself when he misused his freedom, sundered himself from the divine world, and "imagined" he was in the world of nature, thus degrading himself by allying himself with the earth. Some of those who continued the work of Boehme linked this slumber to the dizziness that overcame Adam when he saw the animals copulating and longed to imitate them. The appearance of the sexes would therefore have been the outcome of this original Fall; but there should also have been a divine remedy, just as if God saw the state of privation and desire of the fallen being and gave him the woman Eve to avert a worse outcome.[80] Leo the Hebrew had already been teaching that the original purpose of man was not procreation but divine contemplation, which would have ensured everlasting life without the need to procreate. It was when man became mortal owing to his sin that God gave him the power to reproduce himself by providing Eve as his mate so that in one way or another mankind should not perish.[81]

Let us go back to Boehme: the story of the apple and the serpent (the true sin, according to the orthodox story) should not be referred to a second Fall or second phase of the Fall. J. J. Wirz, a follower of Boehme, recounted the birth of Eve in the following way: after having seen the animals copulating, Adam begat Eve first as a magical image (we might say, as a feverish image projected by his own desire), which he then endowed with earthly substance. Last, God intervened to breathe a divine spirit into her and gave her a true being, so that the two then made one.[82]

In such speculative thinking we find a typical double nature of the female principle in relation to the doctrine of Sophia or the wisdom of the divine Virgin. The undivided original being should have been united inwardly "in a holy and hidden blend" to the "dazzling body of the heavenly Sophia." Joined to her, Adam could communicate with God and perform all miracles.[83] Gichtel spoke of this Sophia as the "light of the fiery soul" in the original being; when he considered Sophia as the "fiat or sanction with which God created everything"[84] or as the "power" of God, he made her appear as almost the equivalent of the Hindu Shakti. She was also assimilated to the Tree of Life and called the Water of Life (M. Hahn), and here we find links with traditional symbols of the female, already known to us.[85] Finally, Sophia was also thought of as "heavenly knowledge." Boehme and Gichtel also described the Fall in the following way: like Lucifer, the primordial being wished to dominate the Virgin, who then sundered herself from him so that there remained in him only the fiery principle, dry and thirsty and devoid of light. Other writers (e.g., Gottfried Arnold) believed that it was carnal desire itself that caused the original being to lose his "hidden wife."[86] However, even in the degraded state in which he loved women, it was, secretly, always that Virgin whom he desired; he always hungered for her even when he believed he was glutted with carnal and earthly pleasure. The "weak" earthly woman was only a substitute for her. The completion of being that she seemed to offer was an illusion. Boehme made the biblical exile from Eden with its Tree of Life into a symbol of the impossibility of reaching man's goal through the union of the earthly sexes; it was like touching a fruit that the gardener snatched at once from man's hand because man had replaced Sophia with Eve or had replaced the Virgin with the *matrix Veneris*, which had attracted him with false desire.[87] Wirz[88] thought of the fire of the sword of the angel placed on guard at Eden as being that which should destroy, root and branch, the animal principle of desire in those who truly aspired to the reintegration of the divine image. From this we pass on next to the study of the doctrine of the Virgin Mary, in whom is fulfilled not only the birth of the Son but also the rebirth of the Soul.

Thus, in this school of thought, which seeks a link to the Hebrew biblical myth supported by Christianity, the doctrine of the hermaphrodite is shown as the key to the mystery of the reciprocal attraction of the sexes. Franz von Baader made the decisive pronouncement that "only the theology that indicates sin as the disintegration of man and presents redemption and rebirth as this reintegration will rise victorious over all its foes."[89] Otherwise the doctrine of Sophia has led mainly to the dualism of a puritanical asceticism; he who wishes to reach Sophia again must renounce Eve, the earthly woman, for the one excludes the other. Sophia, moreover, is sometimes confused and identified with Mary and at other times with Christ (who, according to Scotus and these writers, should have renewed in himself the unity of the two sexes); she is desired not only by man but also by woman, just as if she, Sophia, embodied the One. This leads toward the plane of mere religious mysticism. We do not know if these speculations led to the practice of actual evocations, except perhaps in the case of Gichtel (he was perhaps the exponent nearest to esoterism in the whole of this school, for we find in his writings, among other things, a doctrine of the secret centers of the body like that of yoga and Tantrism).[90] Gichtel wrote, "We have a starry body within the one composed of the elements, and that starry body is also spiritual and has a hunger for Sophia and continues to attract her with this hunger."[91] But in general we can find nothing in this school linked to a definite initiatory use of sex. At the most we arrive at an idealizing justification of wedlock instead of an ascetic denial of it.

This justification is to be found, above all, in one of the later exponents of this school, Franz von Baader, who wrote, "The purpose of wedlock as a sacrament is the mutual restoration of the heavenly or angelical image in man as he should be, namely he who inwardly or spiritually is no longer a male animal, and also in woman as she should be, namely no longer a female animal, for it is only in this way that they both should have fulfilled in themselves the idea of mankind."[92] "It is only at this level," added Baader,[93] "that we can understand the sacramental element in such a union [marriage], for only such an end leads us beyond time into everlastingly true being, whereas that which is merely earthly or temporary cannot, as such, possess the character of a sacrament, nor does it need such a character." Therefore, "the higher meaning of sexual love, which should not be identified with the instinct for reproduction, is nothing other than the need to help both man and woman to become integrated inwardly (in soul and in spirit) in the complete human or original divine image."[94] This hermaphroditic image, which became noncorporeal after the Fall, should be embodied, fixed, and established in two lovers so that "the two do not merely reproduce themselves in a third being or baby and so that, although they themselves remain what they are (unregenerated), yet they are both reborn inwardly as children of God."[95]

However, apart from this abstract sketch, Baader did not conceive of a real initiatory path for sex, even in theory, for he remained tied to Christian dualism and asexual mysticism. For instance, we find him propounding the strange and somewhat comical theory that a mere embrace of lovers that involves only the area of the breast should be contrasted to actual coitus, "which, taken by itself in the abstract, is so little an act of union and love (or marriage) that it expresses rather the opposite, the greatest mutual reinforcement of selfishness (or nonlove), which ends not in union but in indifference and in the separation of two despiritualized poles and indeed in the reciprocal loss of the one within the other and even in the torpidity which is the brother of death, for it is an animal act that can only be exorcised through embracing, that is, through love."[96] Baader linked this contrast to that existing between the mystical Christian doctrine of the androgyne and the "heathen" theory, which, according to him, concerned the hermaphrodite:

In sexual relations taken by themselves or considered without the exorcism carried out by love—by religious love as the only principle of every free association which enhances the link imposed by passion until a free union is accomplished—we do not find at all that which the thinkers and philosophers dealing with the nature of paganism supposed, namely an urge to go back to the hermaphrodite, as if to the integration of human nature in man and woman; there is rather, physically and psychically, the same orgiastic, loveless, selfish impulse in both man and woman to arouse in themselves individually the double hermaphroditic desire and to take from each other what each of them needs for that arousal, so that in coitus without love the uttermost selfishness of both man and woman seeks its own satisfaction, the woman acting here as an instrument for the man, and the man for the woman; and therefore the satisfaction of sexual instinct is fulfilled not only by disdain but even by hatred toward the other person.[97]

Anyone acquainted with the doctrine of the hermaphrodite and the metaphysics of sex in their proper context can readily see the confusion and one-sidedness of Baader's opinions. Like the other writers cited earlier, he may have some understanding of the deepest cause of sexual attraction, but he still ends in a vague mysticism that always reflects the inborn Christian hatred of sexual experience. Like so many theorists of love, Baader seems to understand very little of the real values of such experience. The forms in which this experience is reduced to the mutual greedy, sexual selfishness of lovers are the lowest even in mere profane love. We have already seen how in orgiastic experience, just as in all known experience of sexual union, the destructive factor, which involves a rupture of the individual ego (existentially, the opposite of selfishness or *Selbstsucht*), is instead fundamental, while the reader already knows the deepest meaning of the hatred that Baader mentions. The mythical story in Baader, as in Boehme, is acceptable to the effect that, since the primordial being sundered itself from the Father, its "fiery quality" took up the form of a false being as the ego in manhood and that this form was extrinsic and degenerative and had to be overcome and slain and to disappear. But he said practically nothing[98] about the practice of a love able to restore the One as if through a mystery. In these writers the general picture does not differ too much from orthodox doctrine, which urges believers to repress sexuality as much as possible (understanding it as animal in nature). It confines sexuality to "chaste unions" of spouses who should, above all, love each other in God and in this way forget their sexual characteristics. The latest exponent of this Christianizing view, Berdyaev, conformed to Russian mentality in shifting the problem onto an eschatological plane and relegating "the man with a transfigured sexuality" and the "revelation of heavenly hermaphroditism" to a future world epoch.[99]

In conclusion we may say that, overall, this speculation adds nothing to Plato's development of the subject; indeed the opposite is the case. To begin with, the references to Christianity and the confused biblical myth hinder us from extracting the principles of the real metaphysics of sex. Only these are able to give us a basis for the system of holy marriage and for the practices we shall deal with in the next chapter, which are based on the phenomena of transcendence that nonmystical but real sexual love can provoke. It is a fact that in Christianity the doctrine of the hermaphrodite represented an alien seed cast onto unsuitable ground in which it could not bear fruit. The ideas we have just summarized can, at most, help one who does not seek Sophia through Eve but tends to call upon her and be united with her at a mystical level, assisting himself with the forms to which the concept of the female archetype or "woman of God" has led in a certain school of Christianity that reflects Gnostic influences.

In passing, it would be interesting to find the origin of the Mormon belief that a man, when dead, cannot reach the seventh and highest degree of holiness and become a divine being unless he has been married to a woman.

6

Sex in the Realm of Initiations and Magic

Transmutations and the Commandment of Chastity

Let us now briefly consider the fourth solution to the problem of sexuality: the ascetic transmutation of the sex drive in relation to supernatural phenomena.

In the great majority of ascetic and initiatory traditions we meet the commandment to be chaste and to abstain from dealings with woman. In general this commandment is not properly understood because a moralistic meaning is attached to it. It is mistakenly believed that the exclusion or elimination of the sex drive is desirable ("to make ourselves eunuchs for the Kingdom of Heaven," as Matthew said). Sexual drive lies at the very root of the living individual, and to believe one can truly suppress it is self-delusion. At best it can be repressed in its most direct manifestations, but this will only lead to the neurotic and divided existence on which modern psychoanalysis has cast so much light. The only alternatives in coping with the sexual drive are to assert it or to transform it. When transmutation is not possible, repression is inadvisable from a spiritual point of view, for it may lead to inner paralyzing contrasts, to dissipation of energy, and to perilous displacements. Sufficient examples of this exist in emotionally based Christian mysticism.

It is to the second possibility, transmutation, that the ascetic or initiatory commandment of chastity or continence is really addressed. Here it is not a question of eliminating the sexual energy but of relinquishing its use and dissipation in ordinary carnal and procreative intercourse. Its potential is conserved, but it is separated from the plane of duality and applied at a different level. We have repeatedly considered what eros can provide on the dualistic plane in relations between man and woman besides mere lustful sensuality (and we shall refer shortly to further and more precise teachings on this subject). The mystery of transmutation is concerned with a different field of capabilities, techniques, and inner procedures. However, we must first get a clear idea of what we are dealing with, especially because ambiguities may arise from the widely held views of contemporary psychoanalysis.

First, when esoteric doctrines speak of sex, they refer to the manifestation of a deeper and more elementary force than that which in the teachings of Freud is called libido or the pleasure principle; they refer to a force having a potential metaphysical value, as we made clear in examining the myth of the hermaphrodite.

There is another point that is no less important: the transmutation involved in the higher practice of asceticism must not be confused with the displacements and sublimations that psychoanalysis is occupied with or the techniques that it employs to overcome personal sexual problems; for that is a matter not of real transmutation at the root level but of peripheral phenomenology on the edge of ordinary, profane life, concerned above all with pathological situations that hold no interest for us. When conscious yogic techniques are applied, transformation can take place, if the spirit of the practitioner possesses a truly transcendental reference point capable of absorbing the whole of his being. This is the case in the higher practice of asceticism but not in the therapy of psychoanalysis. This condition is more than natural; if we acknowledge the deepest metaphysical meaning of eros, we shall readily understand that only in the former case can the diversion or revulsion of sexuality from its most immediate object not leave remains, for it will take place exactly in accordance with the deepest meaning. Instead, the transformation of the normal sexual force will happen by itself, without violent and specific occurrences, when the whole spirit is truly focused on something higher. This happened in the past to the saints, mystics, and ascetics of high rank who, after an initial period of self-control, had no reason at all to fight against the "flesh" and "the temptations of the flesh." This category of things merely ceased to interest them; they no longer felt the need for a woman because the integration of being in them took place in another, more direct and less perilous way. The most certain mark of this attainment was not a puritanical dislike of sex but merely indifference and tranquillity toward it.

This is no concern of psychoanalysis; the purpose of such transformation is not to "heal" a sexual neurotic struggling with his complexes, severe or mild. Instead, its purpose is the transcendence of the human state, real regeneration, and a change of ontological status. The transmuted force of sex should lead to this end. In such a context the ascetic, yogic, or initiatory commandment of chastity is justified in technical rather than "ethical" terms. The teachings of the mysteries spoke of one single current with a double flow, symbolized by the Great Jordan and the ocean, which, flowing downward, leads to the generation of men and, flowing upward, to the generation of gods.[1] This teaching makes evident the double capability inborn in the force of sex, depending on its polarization. This is the basis of the practice, or mystery, of transmutation, to which the figure on Tarot card XIV ("Temperance") refers. On that card a woman with wings is pictured decanting liquid from a silver into a golden receptacle without spilling a drop, while some flowers can be seen sprouting from the ground nearby which symbolize inner and upward growth.[2]

Furthermore, the same expression, "upward flow" or *urdhvaretas*, recurs in the terminology of yoga. We shall come back to this shortly. In the meantime, it is worth distinguishing once again between the highest purpose just indicated and other incidental purposes sometimes confused with the former in certain Hindu texts that treat the vow of *brahmacharya* or celibacy. The fact that sexual abuse can lead to nervous prostration and have a bad effect on the mental faculties, intelligence, and character is rather banal and well known and only of interest in relation to the personal psychic well-being of a normal man in common life. But the possible significance of sexual experience may cause many people to neglect such consequences, as pointed out in the discussion (in the appendix to chapter 2) of the values of erotic transcendence in the profane sphere. Besides such misuse, a possible depressive effect resulting from the practice of sexuality depends to a great extent on the system of coitus used, as we also saw. Finally, the more specific decision not to waste vital, nervous energy but to save it by restricting one's sexual life is, from a spiritual point of view, of little interest unless one has in mind a higher use for that energy.

We are now ready to take up the theory of *ojas* and *ojas-shakti*. We can see the point in question even in a modern writer like Sivananda Sarasvati, although his considerations are often intersticed with matters of health and ethics. He wrote, "The seed is dynamic energy which has to be converted into spiritual energy" (*ojas*), and added, "He who seeks divine realization with true zeal should observe strict chastity."[3] Here we must make a distinction. On the one hand, what Sivananda said concerns a force that springs from all self-control and from all active inhibition. That law is in action which creates that most subtle and efficacious power of seduction exercised by the "chaste" type of woman. It is, therefore, not a question of sexuality alone. Sivananda acknowledged that "even wrath and muscular force can be transformed into *ojas*."[4] It is an ancient esoteric teaching that the mastery of every impulse of a given strength, even if merely physical, frees a higher and more subtle energy; therefore, the same must be the case with sexual impulse and desire. As an outcome of the buildup of *ojas* in this way, there is contemplated, among other things, the formation of a special "magnetic aura" in a "personality that inspires a kind of holy awe," together with the power of influencing other people by words or a mere look. The same energy, *ojas* or *ojas-shakti*, can also be employed for contemplation and spiritual realization.[5]

In this connection we may add that the chastity which warriors undertook in various traditions, often among savage peoples, too, can be linked to this complex of ideas. It was a question less of saving physical energy than of accumulating a force that was to some extent supernatural and magical, in the same sense of *ojas*, for integration of the natural forces of the warrior. Such a context is explicit, for instance, in a well-known episode in the Mahabharata.

We must now distinguish between the generic notion of *ojas* as a subtle force, which can even be produced by controlling elementary impulses other than sex, and *virya*, or spiritual manhood, which if lost or wasted results in death and if withheld and conserved leads to life. *Virya*, as we said earlier, is linked to the seed, to such an extent that in the technical and mystical terminology of Hindu texts the word is often used to designate both. In this context we can understand the concept of the "aspiring death that comes from woman." From metaphysical and ascetic viewpoints, that which is wasted in animalistic and lustful unions is not mere vital or nervous energy but rather the "being" principle of man, his transcendental manhood. It was in this connection that we recognized a higher form of manhood in the ascetic. This background is consistent with the specific doctrine of transmutation and the upward flow of force, which flows downward in merely natural sex; this transmutation comes through practicing chastity and then making this force change its polarity. Now we can see why the commandment to practice chastity is also found in operational magic. Eliphas Lévi rightly said that for a "wizard," nothing is more deadly than the desire for sensual pleasure. Here the purely technical and nonmoral end purpose of the commandment to practice continence seems quite clear. The force gained through active inhibition and transmutation of sex in terms of transcendental manhood can also be used for "wicked" purposes. The commandment of chastity may be equally strict in operations of "white" or "black" magic.

The Techniques of Endogenous Transmutation in Kundalini-Yoga and Taoism

A distinction like the one we have just made is also necessary in the sphere of yoga itself. In contrast to asceticism and mysticism, yoga is an exact science of techniques for controlling processes in the service of specific ends. Yoga is in essence, however, a secret doctrine for which the principle of direct transmission is the rule; and so, although a great deal has been published about it and many classical texts have been translated in the West in recent years, it is not always easy to glean an adequate understanding of some fundamental points of its teachings.

Yoga, especially in its Tibetan adaptation, seems to have envisaged and taught a transformation of sexual force in the generic sense of *ojas*. This is certainly at issue when *tum-mo* or "mystical heat" is spoken of as an energy that can also produce extranormal phenomena of a physical and physiological nature.[6] In the same way, when this heat is assigned the function of arousing the kundalini, it is obviously only an aid or an instrument. But it is better to refer to the actual Hindu teachings of Tantric kundalini yoga, where a clearer doctrinal picture of the whole can be found.

The field of yoga in Tantrism is separate from that of the sexual practices we shall detail later on, in the sense of two paths that may lead to the same goal but are applicable to men of different gifts and viewpoints in their most profound nature.

Whether the path of yoga that excludes woman is recommended, or instead the one that includes her, will depend on the predominance of *sattva* (the luminous principle of "being") or *rajas* (the principle of excitability, transport, and fire or passion in the individual aspirant). The two human types based on these principles are also called the spiritual (divine or *divya*) type and the heroic (*virya*) type respectively; both of them equally tread the path of Shiva and are distinguished from the person who restricts himself to the ritualistic practice of traditional religion.

The spirit of Tantric yoga itself is characterized best by these words from a text: "What need have I of an external woman? I have a woman within me."[7] This alludes to the female principle contained in the depths of a man's being which corresponds to "our Diana," to "Eve," and to "secret Hebe" of Western Hermetism. According to Tantrism, this Goddess is present in the human organism itself in the form of an elementary force which is given the name of "she who is wrapped" (this is the meaning of the word *kundalini*). This yoga, therefore, considers an inner process; the union of male with female and the surmounting thereby of the Dyad are carried out in one's own body without recourse to another individual of the opposite sex as an embodiment and living symbol of the opposite principle. Hyperphysical physiology now comes into play with its subtle forces and elements acting behind the material structure of the organism and below the threshold of normal waking consciousness. Two streams of vital energy, called *ida* and *pingala*, which normally run in coils on both sides of the backbone, one linked to the negative, female, lunar principle and the other to the positive, male, solar principle, play an important role. They are manifestations and analogues of the Dyad or elementary polarity in the human body. A yogi can divert these streams by certain strenuous techniques, preventing them from following their two lateral, winding directions and making them flow together. This diversion and union bring about a closure of circuit that can lead to the awakening of the kundalini.

We said that the kundalini represents the Goddess or primordial Shakti within man for the followers of Tantrism. It is the "dazzling" life force which has organized the body and continues to dwell there secretly as the root of all the subtle, vital currents in the body. It is called "she who is wrapped" to indicate that in ordinary human existence its true nature is invisible; it "sleeps" in a subtle center located at the base of the spine. There is an essential relationship between the expression of thoughts, the fire of desire, and the sexual functions.[8] As the potential bride of the primordial male, the kundalini is expressed by the symbolism of a serpent wound around the *lingam* or phallus of Shiva in the lowest center. When the streams on the two sides are halted, the kundalini awakens and "unwinds" itself. A change of polarity in the basic life force of man then occurs, and the kundalini flows upward, running along an axial "duct" up the line of the backbone, called the *sushumna* (it is also called the "path of Shakti" and, in Buddhist Tantrism, "the path of nirvana"). From its original seat in the profane, the kundalini goes upward to the top of the head. A fiery nature is attributed by analogy to the aroused force, and therefore some texts describe its arousal and ascent in terms of a fire that burns everything it meets and eliminates all conditional qualities. In this respect we may speak of the *sushumna* as the dazzling path of unity inasmuch as the ascent occurs under the sign of an advancing union of the male and female, the union being made perfect and absolute at the end of the path of the *sushumna* at the top of the head. Here there is the *excessus*; Shiva and Shakti, the god and goddess embrace and are united; there is complete fusion and resolution of the *shakti* principle in the *shiva* principle, equivalent to the Great Liberation, the transcendental reintegration, the surmounting of the dual state and, in general, of the cosmic bond.

References to the organism in this should not make us think of processes that are exhausted within the individual physical structure. The body in Tantrism is "made cosmic" and is conceived of in terms of principles and powers that also act in the world and in nature in accordance with the traditional correspondence between macrocosm and microcosm. Thus the ascent of the kundalini in a yogi involves a set of supersensual experiences and a passage through the "elements" (as in the ancient mysteries) and also through manifold states of being symbolized in various ways according to different schools and, in this particular yoga, linked to various centers arranged along the axial path and awakened by the kundalini as it contacts them.[9]

In this type of yoga, the key to the whole process is the arousal of the basic energy, which also continues to be the operational power until the final resolution. Speaking of the relationship that this force has to the sex urge and animal generation in a normal man, a text states that this force, the kundalini, produces slavery in the ignorant and freedom in the yogi.[10] There is obviously a twofold polarity. From the change in polarity arises the mystery of transmutation and awakening. The texts speak openly of a saving of the force of the seed, the *virya*, of the "backward practice" (*ujana-sadhana*) and of the "causing of an upward flow" (*urdhvaretas*).[11] The operation of "causing the seed to flow upward" was mentioned in the Upanishads (cf. Maitri-Upanishad VI, 33; Mahanarayani-Upanishad XII, I) as well as in hatha yoga in general. In the Dhyana-bindu-Upanishad (86), we read, "He in whose body the seed remains need not fear death," and in the "Chandilya-Upanishad" it is written, "Either we succeed in overcoming the *bindu* or the Yoga fails," *bindu* being one of the words to describe the force of the seed or the *virya*. According to Tantric teachings and symbolism, as long as the kundalini sleeps, it stops access to the central path of *sushumna*, which is the same as saying that the force oriented to normal sexuality forms an obstacle for the process that should lead to initiatory rebirth instead of animal generation. In this way, the sleeping kundalini is also represented as blocking the opening of Shiva's phallus, so that the seed of rebirth on high cannot be emitted. On the other hand, it is said that when vital energy no longer runs along the two lines on the sides, as happens in the ordinary existence of a normal man, but, with the obstruction removed, enters the central duct or *sushumna*, the conditional quality of the time is suspended and "the fire of death blazes"; that is, a rupture of level takes place equivalent to the crisis that in many traditions is generally called "initiatory death." "You who ascend like a streak of lightning," says a hymn of the Goddess, who is manifested in this.[12] Therefore, it is natural that the practices in question should not be free from grave perils; the texts say that he who awakens the kundalini without the necessary skill and the knowledge of a true yogi may meet not only serious disturbances but even madness and death (actual death, not initiatory death). Therefore, the strictest disciplines of self-control, mental concentration, and purification are the indispensable precondition for kundalini yoga. Only a man who has realized in himself his true nature as Shiva is capable of not being overthrown when he arouses, exposes, and activates the Goddess. One text, in fact, gives the symbolism of a widow (who represents the force in its state of separation from the One during the descending phase, bereft of its counterpart, the male principle) seated by two rivers, which represent the two streams (*ida* and *pingala*, which in the human framework reflect the principle of the Dyad), violently stripped and possessed, the text tells us. She will then lead to the highest seat.[13]

Kundalini yoga extensively uses a technique of breathing linked to special magical positions of the body (*asana*). A system of breathing, which includes the total cessation of breathing, facilitates the desired diversion of the subtle energies.

Given the scope of this book, we must limit out discussion of kundalini yoga to this brief sketch and direct our readers for further information to the book of ours cited earlier. We have referred to this yoga as an outstanding and well-attested example of the "endogenous" method that has rigorous chastity as a prerequisite. It arouses the force that woman bears and embodies in the conditioned world, that is, the Shakti, in the form of the kundalini; in the same way, within a yogi the magical coitus and marriage to the divinity are realized after preliminary ascetic discipline has led him to realize the opposite principle, the principle of the absolute or transcendental male, the Shiva nature or the Vajradhara (Bearer of the Scepter), according to the Tibetan name.

The mystery of transmutation is found in other secret traditions as well. Taoism knows of it, and the alchemy of both the East and West often alludes to its techniques, as well as to the problematical transmutation of metallic substances, by means of a symbolic jargon. Precisely because of the potential polyvalence belonging to all esoteric symbolism, the outline of the fundamental operations in alchemical hermetism can admit an interpretation in terms of sexual techniques as well. However, such an interpretation is not the only one, nor is it a binding one; indeed, with the possible exception of Nicola Flamel, no information has come down to us from the golden period of this tradition concerning teachers who worked on this plane with the assistance of women. Later we shall refer to that interpretation only from a secondary point of view by considering some evidence in modern writers who have made use of hermetic symbolism in relation to these realizations. The interpretation of the *opus transformationis* in merely initiatory terms instead falls outside our subject; however, we treated it in full in another book.[14]

As regards the operational Taoism of the Far East, it is necessary to make the same distinction as in the case of Tantrism, for here, too, a kind of endogenous transmutation of the yoga type is contrasted with a category of explicitly sexual practices; we shall come back to the latter shortly. As regards the former, there are not always explicit references to sexuality as the raw material for the transmutation. We shall therefore restrict ourselves to a brief note on the basis of the teachings contained in a rather late text, the *T'ai I Chin hua Tsung Chih*, which has been translated in some European languages as "The

Secret of the Golden Flower,"[15] by reason of some interesting likenesses between it and kundalini yoga.

This Taoist text also starts with the primordial duality, of the *yang* and *yin*, which is present in each individual and not in two separate persons of opposite sexes. In man the *yang* or male principle is present in the form of the luminous *hun* element situated in the head and precisely between the two eyes. The *yin* or female principle is present, instead, in the form of the obscure *p'o* element located in the lower part of the body in an area called the "space of the force," and this brings us back again to the idea of the female as Shakti. In Chinese teachings the duality is also indicated as that of the *hsing* and *ming*, words meaning "being" and "life," which refer to one of the most essential aspects of the Great Dyad. It is said that with the birth of individual existence, "being and life are separated and see each other no more from that moment onward," naturally, wherever the initiatory procedures described in the text do not take place, procedures which have the purpose of leading the center of the human being back to the Great Pole (*t'ai chi*) or "Great One" or "State without Duality" (*wu chi*), which takes back to itself both the being and life, the *yang* and the *yin*.

The condition of an ordinary man is that of a being in whom "the center is no longer defended" and where the female *yin* principle (also called the "lower soul") subjects the male *yang* principle (also called the "higher soul"), compelling it to serve her and directing it outward. This outward direction is called "straight and irreversible" (like someone who is thrust irresistibly forward) and involves the dispersion and dissipation of vital energy and of the "original seed." The starting point for reintegration, therefore, is an action intended to turn energy back upon itself and "to make the light circulate" (or crystallize), and for this purpose systems of spiritual concentration are required (the so-called fixed contemplation or *chih kuan*) together with breathing exercises, as in yoga. When the change of direction has been brought about, the straight outward compulsion is stopped and replaced with a backward movement and thereafter with a movement of "rotation"; then other systems tend to make the consciousness descend to the "space of the force." At this point the rupture of level and the union of the two opposed principles take place, with the final meaning, however, of a "distillation of the *yin* in pure *yang*." To the restoration of the original state "without duality," which is also called the "sprouting of the Flower of Gold," is linked the birth of the *kuei*, a word that can be translated as "active divine being." Observe that the Chinese character *kuei* also means lightning; we noted earlier the relationship established in other traditions between the mystery of reintegration, the number three, and lightning.

Taking possession of the "original seed" and withholding it are a central theme in such teachings. But in this text only a few scanty allusions can lead us to believe that this seed is the equivalent of the Hindu *virya* and therefore has a specific reference to the secret force of manhood, which is normally received by a woman when the male seed runs onto her innermost flesh in the act of love. At one point the fundamental principle of sexual magic is actually expressed, namely the principle of the transmutation, into a beneficial thing, of that which in itself should have a toxic character, when it is said, "Here we allude to the sexual union of man with woman from which sons and daughters are born. The madman squanders the most precious jewel of his body in unbridled pleasures and knows not how to save his seminal energy, with the exhaustion of which the body collapses. Those who are learned have no way of conserving their life other than by eliminating pleasure and conserving their seed."[16] Here the end purpose is the prolongation of existence symbolized in the alchemic elixirs of long life (a recurring theme in Taoism also), rather than the initiatory reintegration of the being. In relating the alleged use of women to obtain the elixir by P'eng, an ancient teacher, the text states that this did not involve actual sexual copulation but the union and sublimation of the two principles, that of the crystallized light, *yang*, and that of the wet force, *yin*. Therefore, these teachings refer to the plane of endogenous processes, on which the mystery of transmutation is fulfilled directly within a single being ("in one single vessel," to use the expression of hermetism) and not in operations to be conducted in copulation with a woman ("operation with two vessels"). We shall write shortly about more ancient Taoist texts wherein this second possibility is, instead, considered openly; in their case, however, the doctrinal assumptions are not different from those just indicated in referring to the teachings of the Secret of the Golden Flower.

Sex in the Kabbala and Eleusinian Mysteries

We still must examine the techniques used to bring about an ecstatic, mystical or initiatory rupture of level through special methods of sexual union. Moreover, we shall comment briefly on some possible applications of "operational" magic.

This sphere is different from that of sacred ceremonies and ritual unions in that it places greater emphasis on pure experience than on the realization of symbols and cosmic analogies. It is not that the one excludes the other; indeed, we shall see that the practice of evocations and transmutations often constitutes a strict premise for these experiential techniques. In essence, however, the purpose is different. It is not concerned with holy ceremonies and participations that can be carried out within the framework of institutions and cults, but is an absolute fact of individual experience that can eliminate the conditional qualities of the ego. Here everything is directly considered, assumed, aroused, and strengthened which, as a phenomenon of partial or conative transcendence, we have already seen to be present in profane sexual love itself. As a source of information, what has leaked out from the secret traditions of various civilizations can be supplemented with the more serious and trustworthy contents of some writings referring to circles in which knowledge and practices of the same kind seem to have continued up to our own times.

As an introduction we shall mention the ideas that in Jewish eso-terism and, above all, in Hasidism lead us into this sphere. In the Zohar (I, 55b) we read, "The Holy One, may He be blessed, does not choose to dwell where the male and female are not united." A saying in the Talmud is "Three things have in themselves something of the beyond; the sun, the Sabbath, and sexual union."[17] Again, we find in the Zohar (III, 81a):

> The King [God] seeks only that which corresponds to him. Therefore the Holy One, may He be blessed, dwells in him who (like Him) is one. When man, in perfect holiness, realizes the One, He is in that one. And when is it that man is called one? When man and woman are joined to-gether sexually. . . . Come and see! At the point at which a human being as male and female is united, taking care that his thoughts are holy, he is perfect and stainless and is called one. Man should therefore act so that woman is glad at that moment and has one single wish together with him, and both of them united should bring their mind to that thing. For thus has it been taught, "He who has not taken a woman is as if he were only a half" (Jebamoth, 83). If, however, man and woman are united and be-come one, body and soul, then the human being is called one, and the Holy One, may He be blessed, takes up his dwelling in this one and generates for him a holy spirit.[18]

Beginning with these views, in which occur again the theme of the hermaphrodite. we find that practices of sexual magic were not foreign to certain trends of Kabbalism. We should consider as an appearance of one of these practices the information that has come down to us regarding the sect of the Sabbatians with regard also to the doctrines set forth by Jakob Franck. The "advent of the Messiah" is here given an esoteric interpretation and is considered not as a historical or collective fact but as a symbol of inner individual awakening and of the enlightenment that frees men and leads them beyond the Law. To this is linked the specifically sexual theme whereby the mystical force of the Messiah is situated in woman, and it is stated that the mystery of the awakening and salvation is fulfilled through sexual union with woman. In fact, Franck said, "I tell you that all the Hebrews are in great ill luck because they are waiting for the coming of the Savior and not for that of the Woman." By altering the doctrine of the Shekhinah somewhat, we find that this Woman or Virgin is in the end the female archetype, the Woman present in every woman and behind every woman, for it is said, "She has in her power many young women, all of whom receive their force from her, so that, when she leaves them, they have no more power." In Franck's opinion she "is a door of God, through which one enters into God," and he added, "If you were worthy to take this Virgin, in whom all the force of the world dwells, you would also be able to fulfill the Work, but you are not worthy to take her." Here "Work" means the celebration of an orgiastic sexual mystery, of which it is said, "By means of this Work we draw nearer to the thing which is all naked and without covering, and therefore we ought to be able to fulfill it." It may be possible to see in this a likeness to the "sight of naked Diana" of which we spoke earlier; however, from the grace lavishly bestowed by this Virgi of the Kabbala, diverse powers and revelations can spring depending on the "rank" of each person.[19] Ideas of this kind ought to be linked to an original initiatory teaching.[20] Their widespread dispersion ended, however, in misuses and deviations, as indeed was the case with Sabbatism where, among other things, the doctrine of the "messianic mystery of the awakening" and of the realization of the One seems to have led to orgies with mystical purposes centering on a naked girl worshipped with various deviant forms of sexuality. Such orgies have been rightly seen as a twisted revival of ancient cults of the Goddess, such as those of Ishtar. Just as among the Tantric Kaulas and among the Brothers of the Free Spirit of the Middle Ages, so also among these Jewish sects which made use of woman and sex there recurs the theme of the impeccability of the Awakened One, referring to a Kabbalistic doctrine regarding that principle in the human being which cannot be punished, whatever it does, for if it were punished, "it would be as if God punished himself."

In the mysteries at Eleusis of classical antiquity, holy union had not only the generic value of ritual and symbolic holy matrimony, but also alluded to the mystery of rebirth within a context that originally must have included sexuality as a means; here, too, emphasis was on the female principle, the divine woman. The purport of the evidence of some Christian writers in this respect cannot be attributed to derogatory intentions and puritanical scandalmongering alone. Clement of Alexandria, Theodoret, and Psellus agree in declaring that in those mysteries the female organ, called mystically and euphemistically the "woman's comb," was shown to the gaze of the initiates as if to indi-

cate the instrument needed to activate the mystery. Gregory Nazian-
zienus, when referring to Demeter as the goddess of these mysteries,
said he was ashamed to "expose to the light of day the nighttime
ceremonies of the initiation and to make a mystery of the
obscenities." He also included a verse in which Demeter was
described as *anasuramete* (that is, she who shows her sex by lifting up
her clothes) so that "she might initiate her lovers to those rites which
are still celebrated symbolically even nowadays."[21] All this would
leave us to suppose that the meaning of the symbolic ceremony of the
mysteries, the ceremony alone having remained in evidence at later
times, was to recall, behind the ritual holy matrimony itself and the
sexual union of the priest and priestess (which was only simulated
later on,) the mystery of the resurrection which can be brought about
through sex and woman, the latter being considered the embodiment
of the Goddess. Thus, at Eleusis, after the rite of the wedding had
been fulfilled in darkness, a great light was lit and the high priest
announced in a voice of thunder, "The Great Goddess has given birth
to the holy Son; the Strong has generated the Strong"; and the ear of
corn shown at this point to the onlookers as a symbol of the holy
initiatory rebirth is strictly related to the primordial hermaphroditic
man and to his resurrection.[22] And then it was said, "August indeed
is spiritual, heavenly generation from on high, and strong is he who
has been generated in this guise." It is possible, therefore, that under
the sign of the mystery of the Great Goddess the ancient world of the
Mediterranean also knew the secret doctrine of sexual initiation.
What we know about the Eleusinian mysteries may only be a
displacement of that doctrine onto the spiritual plane by a cult that no
longer actually performed sex but employed other initiatory and
mystery techniques. Little by little, these were reduced until these
mysteries were a religious cult open to almost everybody.

For specific information about the sexual techniques it is necessary
to refer to the Orient and, first, to Tantrism in the Way of the Left
Hand and the "secret ritual." As we mentioned, this ritual is
restricted to those whose qualification is "manly" or "heroic" (*virya*)
and who are *dvandvatita* or capable of overlooking all dualities, good
and bad, merit and guilt, and other similar opposites in human
values.

Tantric Sexual Practices

We said in the Introduction to this book that the practice and
philosophy of Tantra is set within a specific historical context. It
starts with the concept of an increasing involution through four
successive eras in the present cycle of mankind, and it maintains that
we have now reached the last of these eras, the so-called dark age or

Kali Yuga, which is a period of dissolution, of the prevalence of elementary forces, and of a Shakti no longer restrained within bounds, whereas the spirituality of mankind's origins has been almost wholly lost. According to Tantra, the path most suitable for such circumstances is one characterized in the directive "Ride the tiger." In other words, rather than avoid or directly oppose a dangerous force, one should grasp it and hold it tight with the idea of getting the better of it in the end. The arrival of the Kali Yuga effectively cancels the bond which in other times imposed secrecy regarding the doctrines and practices of the Way of the Left Hand because of their perilous nature and their potential for misuse, deviation, and distortion.[23] The fundamental principle of the secret teaching, which is common to both the Hindu and the Buddhist circles of the Tantras (the latter circle corresponds essentially to the Vajrayana) is the transformation of poison into medicine or "nectar," the use, for the purposes of freedom, of the very forces that have led or can lead to man's fall and perdition. "Poison as an antidote for poison" is a frequent maxim. Another Tantric principle is that "fruition" and "freedom" (or release, renunciation) do not necessarily exclude each other, as the one-sided ascetic schools believe. Their purpose is to realize both, to nourish passion and desire while at the same time remaining free. Teachings of this kind had earlier been deemed unsuitable for general publication. One text states that this path is as difficult "as walking on the edge of a sword or keeping a tiger on a rein."[24] In view of this difficulty, we may indeed wonder how well the Tantric methods are suited to today when the vast majority is wholly lacking in the training needed to face such risks. Anyone who thinks that Tantrism provides a convenient spiritual alibi for sensual abandonment is sorely mistaken. These teachings presuppose a preliminary initiation and consecration, an introduction to a community or chain (*kula*) that can provide protective force and a special course of asceticism and self-discipline. Furthermore, the same premise was in force in other teachings that proclaimed anomy and the freeing of the spirit from all bounds, rules, and mores of the times. Such was the case with the Ishmaelites of the period of the Sheikh of the Mountain, the Brothers of the Free Spirit, the Beghards, and the Ortlibians, of whom it was written, "Before reaching the point where all pleasure was allowed to them, they underwent very hard trials; their life was that of the strictest orders; they aspired to break their own will and eliminate their own person so as to find it again as pure glory in divine splendor. . . . They had to pray, meditate, and exercise themselves in the deeds that disgust us most. But as soon as they had reached the freedom of the spirit, everything was permitted."[25]

Tantrism is rooted in the archaic substrate of aboriginal India, to which belongs the central theme of goddesses of the Shakti type as well as an assemblage of orgiastic practices and cults. Shadowy forms of Tantrism are found in rites bordering on witchcraft, whereby, to obtain special powers, man sought certain elementary female entities, *yakshini, yogini, dakini,* sometimes considered the servants of the goddess Durga and at other times her emanations. The Tantrist often interpolated animistic themes and used spells on those entities to subjugate them by incantations in the person of an actual woman, intoxicating himself and possessing that woman carnally in wild places, in a graveyard or wood.[26] However uncouth, these practices represent the use of evocations, which we examined in their manifold varieties in the preceding chapter, with the difference that in this case the sexual act really took place. The young woman who had first to be "demonized" and then violated not only constitutes the basis of the shadowy rites just mentioned but is also the fundamental theme of the higher forms of Tantric and Vajrayanic sexual magic.

In these forms, moreover, the concept of the human couple, transformed into a momentary embodiment of the everlasting divine couple, moves from the generic ritual plane of holy marriage to the operational plane. The ontological principles of Shiva and Shakti or of other equivalent deities present in the bodies of the man and woman are realized; it is necessary to arrive ritually and sacramentally at a state where the man actually feels himself to be Shiva and the young woman Shakti. This is the precondition of a sexual union that must transcend the limitations of physical and carnal nature and assume a magical character. Its center of gravity must be transferred to a subtle plane where the mutual magnetisim of intense sexual love and desire consists in an "intoxication or congestion of astral light." Its "climax" and supreme ecstasy correspond to the rupture of level of individual consciousness and the sudden realization of the nondual state.[27] This is the ultimate goal of that path of desire or *kama-marga* which has been considered in Hindu tradition alongside the other paths of liberation—the path of knowledge, the path of action, and so on.

Let us investigate these various sides of Tantric practice more closely.[28] The starting point is the capacity for a particular feeling or perception of female nature, related to what we said earlier about the nakedness of woman. According to these teachings every woman embodies Shakti or Prakriti; therefore, a naked woman ritually expresses this same force in its pure, elementary, and primary state, not bound to form and not hidden by an individual condition. When a woman removes all her clothing, she is offering this essential state to the gaze of the onlookers. Therefore, Eliade was right when he wrote, "The ritual nakedness of the *yogini* or companion of the *vira* has an intrinsic mystical value; if in the presence of a naked woman we do not feel arising in our deepest being the same awesome sensation which we feel before the relevation of the cosmic Mystery, then there is no rite [in the union with her]; there is only a profane act with all the unfavorable consequences that flow therefrom; for instead of loosening the chain which binds us to our conditioned existence, the use of woman will strengthen that chain."[29] This subjective condition (linked to a practice of intense visualization and of mental projection of a vitalized cult image into the woman) acts as a counterpart to a procedure technically termed *aropa*, which is in its own way objective. *Aropa* means "establishment of a different quality" or, in a strict sense, "transubstantiation" in the same accepted meaning of the word employed in Christianity for the mystery of the Eucharist where the priest invokes the actual presence of Christ. In this respect the Hindu writer we cited said that by means of *aropa* the physical form (*rupa*) of the woman is not denied, but every atom of it is pervaded by the *svarupa* or primordial, nonphysical element that ontologically constitutes its essence.[30] To be qualified for the sexual practice, a young woman must be duly initiated and trained in the art of the magical positions (*mudra*). Her body is aroused and made living by *nyasa*,[31] a sacramental procedure by which a "divine fluid" is laid upon, emitted into, or aroused in various points of the body (in her "points of life"). This is an equivalent of the "demonization" of the woman belonging to the shadowy practices mentioned earlier, intended to strengthen the natural fluid that feeds the sexual magnetism of a normal woman and is the basis of her fascination. Besides, one name of the young women used in these rites is *mudra*. This has left the Orientalists perplexed, although it is clear enough; *mudra* (meaning, literally, a seal) is the name of the magical and ritual gestures or postures taken up by the yogis to activate the circuit or cause the closure of the circuit of certain currents of subtle force in the organism. This same part is played to a high degree by woman in magical coitus, and therefore the same name is transferred to her (perhaps in relation also to the real meaning of *mudra*, the special positions used by her during the act of love).

At this level the young woman used in these practices is differentiated from the women in the mere promiscuous orgiastic rites, just as the system of coitus is different in the two cases. Just as the Worshippers of Love spoke of the "woman of the miracle," here the term used is "woman of exception" or *vishesha rati*, coming from the same substance as the transcendent or divine woman, Radha, Durga, Chandali, Dombi, Sabaja-Surdari, etc. (she is sometimes identified with the kundalini itself in the personified form of a goddess). It is

said that it is with her and not with a common woman or *samanya rati*
that coitus can attain to what certain schools call the *sahaja* or
nondual primordial state that produces freedom even in life.[32]
However, it would be a mistake to think this entailed a vague
idealization of the woman. In circles of this kind, dissolute girls of a
low caste are sometimes exalted and indicated as the most suitable,
even if a symbolic justification is adopted for the purpose; for by
living outside social and ethical systems and the rules of the
prevailing religion these young girls reflect in some way the state of a
"raw material" not tied to a form.[33] This constitutes a specific
difference with the wedding rite and unions of a holy rather than
magical nature against a background of institutions and castes, of
which we spoke earlier. Moreover, the special concept of virginity
explained earlier returns when the girls used in the Kaula cult (a
subdivision of the Tantric cult) are called the "virgin whores" or
veshya kumarika. The followers of Vishnu, according to Tantric
practices, deem the highest kind of love to be the *parakiya* or
unlawful love, referring to union with a very young girl or with a
woman who is not one's own wife (or, to be more accurate, who is not
one of one's own women, seeing that polygamy is lawful in this
civilization). In rhetorical debates carried on in Bengal, just as in the
Western medieval courts of love, the supporters of conjugal unions
have always been defeated by those of free unions (also called
marriages of Shiva) or unlawful unions; and therefore a couple who
are unlawful and adulterous, such as Radha and Krishna, have been
often upheld as a divine model which a human pair should emulate
and embody.[34] This has been justified, first, by the psychological
reason that a conjugal union cannot be expected to provide emotional
intensity and passion as great as that aroused in the irregular or
exceptional circumstances we have mentioned; and second, by virtue
of the adaptation of the reality to a symbol; the aim of a union is the
unconditioned state, and a secret union that is free from or even
violates all sanctions or social ties symbolizes better "the rupture
imposed by all genuine religious experience" (in truth it would be
better to say "initiatory experience").[35] Eliade noted in this
connection that to Hindu eyes the conjugal symbolism (the
"Bridegroom" and "Bride") in use in Christian mysticism does not
sufficiently underline the separation from all ethical and social values
which is imposed on him who tends toward the absolute; and
therefore arises the choice, as an ideal model of the myth, of a couple
such as Radha and Krishna[36] and, as companions of the Siddhas and
Viras, of young women without restrictions as regards caste, whose
person will be less important than a certain power or special fluid in
them able to feed an intense "searing" process. A man of weak

disposition is forbidden other women than his own, but this restriction, according to the predominant opinion of the Hindu Tantras, is withdrawn, and no extrinsic restriction is imposed if the state of *siddha-vira* is reached. We have already spoken of the symbolism in graduated degrees of woman's nakedness and stated the fact that only an initiate of a high grade can utilize fully naked women.

Another word used to designate a young woman is *rati*, which means literally the object of *rasa*, intoxication or strong emotion. The Sahajiya school distinguishes three kinds of *rati*: the *sadharani* or normal woman, who seeks only her own immediate satisfaction in coitus; the *samanjasa*, who seeks to participate with the man; and the *samartha*, who is capable of total and superindividual abandon. Only the last type, it is said, is a suitable young woman.[37] Desire or *kama* in its various grades is also made the subject of elaborate distinctions in some texts. In essence, animal desire is contrasted with that which might be called "the Great Desire which unites body with spirit well beyond the union of bodies in the Little Desire."[38]

Next there is an interesting detail that indicates the exclusion of the Demeter (motherly) capability as compared with the Aphrodite or Durga capability in the young women concerned; women who have been mothers are not allowed to take part in practices of a Tantric nature. A saying of a modern writer[39] sums up the theory that is most likely the basis for this rule: "Just as a woman loses her physical virginity in her first coitus, so she loses her magical virginity when she becomes a mother." When she becomes a mother, her employment in practices of a higher type ends.

Tantra holds that the act of human love reproduces a divine action. In Tantric iconography, the predominant type of union between god and goddess would lead one to suppose that Tantrism of the Left Hand adopts as its fundamental ritual position the *viparita-maithuna*, which is characterized by the man's immobility. Besides the symbolic reason already given, its choice may also be practical. During coitus, the man must be allowed to exercise a special concentration of his mind on what occurs and takes shape in his consciousness, so that he can react suitably, and this is certainly easier for him if his body stays still. Moreover, the position in question is confirmed by one of the names given in these circles to both the woman, *lata*, and the activity, *lata-sadhana*, for *lata* (literally "liana" or "creeper") is linked to one of woman's positions proper to this inverted form of coitus (the treatises on profane erotics have, in this regard, names such as *Lataveshtitaka* and *Vrishadhirudhaka*). The expression we generally find in the texts is "embraced by the woman" but not the opposite; and this, too, leads us to believe that the woman plays the active part. Thus, on this plane as well, metaphysical significances are activated which correspond to the essence of the male and female.

Tantric Sexual Practices and Their Dangers

We have already observed that the initiatory forms of Tantrism are differentiated from the orgiastic ones by a particular system of coitus. The special method consists in preventing ejaculation and withholding the seed at the moment when all the emotional and physiological conditions exist for the seed to be injected into the woman. This point is often expressed in coded and mystical terms, but there is fundamental agreement in the main texts of these schools, such as the *Hathayogapradipika*, the *Goraksha-samhita*, the songs of Kahna, and the *Subhashita-samgraha* as well as various works of the Vajrayana. The first of these texts directs that, when in the progress of coitus "the *bindu* [seed] is about to be injected into the woman, it must be forced to reascend with an extreme force. . . . The yogi who withholds his seed in this way overcomes death because, just as the seed when ejected leads to death, so the seed when withheld leads to life."[40] This is abviously connected to the doctrine of the *virya*, the hidden force of manhood. Thus we should not take at face value some expressions in the texts that seem to suggest a merely physical and physiological process, as if it were only important to save the material substance of the seed. Such references in Hindu Tantric writings and also Chinese Taoist books should be taken with a grain of salt. Rather drastic measures are prescribed, such as manual action in Taoism and, in the Hindu work mentioned before, an auxiliary strangulating action exercised by the female organ on the male organ at the moment of emission, a normally counterproductive action because it usually arouses feelings that lead to ejaculation. Both the *Hathayogapradipika* and the Dhyana-Bindu-Upanishad recommend the suspension of breathing by means of the system called *khechari-mudra*, with which fakirs and yogis can also enter into a cataleptic state. Under this condition, the texts state that ejaculation should not take place "even if a man is embraced by a young and ardent woman." It is hard to conceive of a man attaining such a state without isolating himself completely from any erotic situation, which would destroy the basic process of fluidic amalgamation and turn everything into a rather insipid exercise of skill. Directing the mind to something else and stopping the breath are methods considered by the Hindu writings on profane erotics to hinder or retard the emission of seed. But the operations of yoga are carried out differently. Without doubt, breathing is controlled so that coitus does not reach its usual outcome and "the seed does not flow downward";[41] but in this case it is not a question of paralyzing the inner process by means of a temporary halt or withdrawal. It is rather a matter of releasing the liminal erotic emotion from its almost forced physiological, conditional quality, consisting precisely in ejaculation, in the normal man.

In such a context success in retaining the seed can have the significance of both cause and effect. It is an effect where there is desire which is particularly aroused and refined (and we shall hear shortly from a witness that in Tantric circles an actual preliminary training is also provided for arousing such a desire). In the sphere of profane sexuality, cases exist where a high degree of desire in man can hinder the normal physiological outcome of coitus. Furthermore, this same phenomenon is brought about every time consciousness is displaced to the subtle plane, since the displacement involves a certain separation of the psychic processes from the parallel organic processes. This also takes place in the profane field; the use of drugs and alcohol (material means to bring about a partial and passive displacement of ordinary consciousness toward the subtle plane) sometimes affects ordinary man so that he cannot ejaculate in coitus or can do so only with great difficulty. In such conditions he may experience a pervasive, ecstatic, and prolonged form of "pleasure" such as is sometimes found in dreams, a condition that corresponds to the subtle state. It is precisely for this effect that the ancient or Eastern profane *ars amatoria* employed certain drugs. Given the premises and prerequisites, the sexual activity of the Tantras is fulfilled, like all magical and ritual activity, not in a state of ordinary awareness but in one of clear-minded rapture or trance ("intoxication with astral light"), which involves the arousal of the subtle state and therefore prevents the physiological crisis of ejaculation. This condition, which is undesirable and may even cause neurosis in the normal lover intent only on speeding up his own physical orgasm, is instead a favorable condition in these Tantric practices because it assists inner and not merely physiological inhibition and the consequent transformation both of the aroused force and of the entire experience brought about by woman and coitus.

At the same time we should bear in mind the other aspect: that the stopping of the seminal emission is the cause of the displacement of consciousness and, at its ultimate, of transcendence. The violent preventive action of the man who "must not lose control of himself at all levels of emotion" may produce at the highest level of coitus and amalgamation with the woman a traumatic breakthrough in level of consciousness, like a flash of lightning representing the highest degree of the crisis produced in profane erotics, even though close to a condition of passivity, of reduced awareness, and of physical orgasm in the partner. The same is the purpose of the technique of stopping the breath at the moment before the seminal emission, since the corresponding physiological process is already in process; here it is desired to release the force aroused by this physiological conditional quality and make it act on a different plane as a force that for one moment destroys the individual limit effectively and "kills" or "halts" the mental faculty.

In the commentaries on a text mentioned by Eliade[42] it is in fact said that by halting the seed the thoughts also are halted. The "mental faculty" (*manas*) is "killed" (*excessus mentis* in the form of an active ecstasy). But it is precisely at that time, the commentary adds, that there also begins the absorption of the "pure grain of the lotus" or of the female *rajas*.

We shall come back to this last point later on. In the meanwhile, it seems clear that the essence of these practices is the highest and most conscious arousal of "physical" love as a "force that kills" (it "kills the obscure tyrant," the individual ego, as Rumi said).[43] With her fluid and her "fire," woman provides a substance that dissolves and liberates, the poison being transformed into Water of Life. Therefore, the texts of Buddhist Tantrism attribute to the yogini, the female companion of the yogi, the power of "freeing the essence of the ego," and a Buddha is presented to us who achieves the awakening and attains nirvana in this way by using the woman.[44] In this respect, the point of complete amalgamation is decisive, the so-called *samarasa*, a word which was translated incorrectly by Shahidullah, in an almost profane way, as "identity of enjoyment" in coitus.[45] In fact, it is a matter of something much deeper and more radical because its counterpart is said to be the stopping, immobilization, and union of *shukra* and *rajas*, words that mean the male "seed" and the female "seed." Just as in practices that belong to yoga alone the suspension of breathing plays a part in the techniques used for the awakening of the kundalini, so the same power is assigned to the stopping of breath and the seed at the highest point of erotic amalgamation; and by means of this power it is also possible to arouse the kundalini and cause the ascending lightning current in the act of union. It then happens that "the identity of enjoyment" (of the two) ceases to be the spasmodic and carnal identity of a few moments, after the attainment of which the process is ended and the union ceases. Instead of being an end, the identity is a beginning, and for the *sukha* or pleasure, too, an *aropa* or transubstantiation takes place. The pleasure is "fixed" in a state that in its own way is continuous ("devoid of growth or falling off") and that represents the transcendent dimension of all experience. As regards this, it is as if the union took place on a nonphysical plane without being restricted to one single moment; mention is made of *sahaja-sukha* or nongenerated or nonconditioned pleasure-ecstasy, an idea that can be understood only by referring to the traditional theory of the everlasting and omnipresent elements. According to this theory, fire, for instance, exists everywhere as an element, identical to itself, outside space and time; the processes of combustion do not "produce" it; they only provide the conditions that are normally needed for its manifestation at a given place and time. But a yogi can also call upon the fire "in himself" apart from these conditions. In the same way a nongenerated continuous pleasure is thought of, outside space or time, connected to the everlasting union of the cosmic male and female mythologically, of the God and Goddess, of Shiva and Shakti, of Radha and Krishna. Of this pleasure, "which neither comes nor goes," the pleasure felt at a given moment by a pair of lovers can only be a particular fleeting apparition in time, linked to the physiological and to the psychic and emotional conditional qualities of human coitus. Now, the magical and ritual Tantric unions produce the occurrence of a timeless "pleasure in itself" linked to the nondual state, the highest unity, the unconditioned.[45a] The peak that is experienced hazily in normal coitus for one single moment when the seed is emitted into the woman and held by the woman is "fixed" or stabilized in a Tantric coitus by the change of plane; it leads to a state of a considerable length ("without end") which is no longer physiologically conditioned and is considered, above all by Buddhist Tantras, as the threshold of the Great Freedom and "perfect enlightenment." The wave of pleasure that arises becomes exactly the same as that of the enlightenment-thought (*bodhichitta*) which is lit and goes up from below toward the head, as in yoga.

This continuity is fed, like the flame of a fuel, by the subtle substance of the woman; and here we are dealing with what the text cited earlier called the absorption of the *rajas* during the state in which the seed is stopped. Thus there develops the stationary, motionless alchemic union of Shiva with the substance of his bride in an active sense, which in the end leads beyond the solely ecstatic moment itself.

The texts do not state clearly whether the technique of the stoppage should also be exercised by the *mudra* or *shakti* during coitus. A corresponding technique, the *amoroli-mudra*, is prescribed for the woman, but it is mentioned separately by enumerating the special powers that it provides for the woman without any mention of synchronizing it with the analogous act of the man.[46] In any event, this technique contemplated for the woman confirms the nonphysiological side of such procedures. In fact, in the case of a woman there is no need to inhibit a process of ejaculation or to withhold a substance comparable to the male seed; as is known, a woman has vaginal and some uterine secretions, especially those of Bartholin's gland (secretions that the Hindu writings on profane erotics call "water of love" or "water of the god of love"), which normally are activated with her general state of sexual arousal without being restricted to the point of crisis, as is the case for man. The word *rajas* used frequently in Tantric texts has more than one meaning; one indeed is "menses"; obviously there can be no question of stopping menses during coitus, and it most likely refers to the force whose effect is felt bursting out at the erotic peak that the woman, too, has built up and held. This force in woman is the counterpart of the *virya* or transcendental manhood. In woman it bears the same relationship to the menses as the *virya* bears to the seed as sperm. It is the force that ancient peoples thought of as the "female seed" and which they believed necessary for procreation. Some have been in too great a hurry to declare that the concept of "female seed" is mistaken and fanciful, although it was acknowledged in Europe also, up to the eighteenth century, because the thing in question was casually linked to the menses or vaginal secretions. Like the *virya*, the "female seed" has a hyperphysical nature; but in considering everything in general that normally constitutes in woman the means needed for generation, we may well speak of a physical and psychic whole that also includes the menses and secretions on its physical side. When the Tantras speak of the male seed and female seed as of two principles which, by uniting, generate the ascending current of enlightenment in the same way that in normal coitus the sperm and the ovum, by uniting, generate the first nucleus of the embryo, they are actually referring to the hyperphysical counterparts separated, withheld, fixed, and brought to amalgamation; and it is for good reason that the texts of the Vajrayana establish likenesses between these and the two currents, *ida* and *pingala* or *lalana* and *rasana*, which in ascetic yoga are halted and caused to flow together, as we have already noted.[47] If we wish to translate *rajas* as "menses," it should be understood in the meaning of the ambiguous magical force or special *mana*, which we mentioned earlier (see chapter 4). To withhold the menses should be related to the full conversion of the motherly capability of woman into the merely Aphroditic capability, with the consequent effect of creating an extreme sexual fascination and demonic saturation. But there is another meaning of the Sanskrit word *rajas*. Besides "red" (whence arises the link with the menses), besides the philosophical meaning proper to it in the traditional doctrine of the *guna*, and besides the meaning of the pollen of a flower (especially of the lotus), *rajas* is synonymous with *tejas*, fire or radiant energy. This meaning is pertinent to the nature of the subtle substance of the woman. The ancient texts reflect this connotation when comparing sexual union to a sacrifice in the fire and woman and her sexual organs to the flame of the fire itself.[48] *Rajas* is the substance that feeds the process of dispersion and of ecstatic union during magical coitus. The following saying in an ancient Egyptian text may have a meaning that is not only profane: "A woman's body burns like fire."

To clarify the theory that the transcendent state is achieved by means of the union of the *shukra* with the *rajas*, we must first recognize that in this context these words cannot be taken in their literal meanings of sperm and menses. They refer to the two principles, male and female, which must be conserved and fixed by hindering their dissipation and degradation in the animal, physiological process. Then the woman performs a simultaneous action in the *samarasa*. Indeed the *Dohakosha* say that not only the *shukra* but also the *rajas* (female seed) must be immobilized to achieve the desired state.[49] It seems that this is not always the case in Taoist sexual practices, which are partly aimed in another direction. At one point Paracelsus wrote, "God preordained birth in such a way that fantasy is hidden in two persons, the imagination in one of them being adapted to the imagination in the other, the imagination of man being adapted to that of woman, and vice versa. For man has only a half imagination, but has a whole one together with woman."[50] This idea could be fittingly applied to the situation we are discussing; the integration of two living imaginations, which are magnetized by desire and which meet each other, is the inner counterpart of the Tantric system of coitus.

Finally, the participation of the woman in the fixation process would seem necessary for a practical reason as well. The *mudra* adopts the inverted ritual position and plays her active part. If she were to abandon herself in climax, she would be unable to go on playing her part, and her orgasm would bring the process to an end.

Furthermore, some curious expressions of the Sahajiya school regarding the system of coitus may be of interest: "In love dwells the shiver of joy, and above this shiver is the flow [the beginning of the continuous state] and above the flow is the flow [the arrival of the new state through fixation]." "There is water on the earth, and above this water rises the wave; love remains above this wave [this is a reference to the surpassing of the point of the erotic crisis]; is there anyone who knows this?"[51] And also, the phrases "to immerse oneself in the depths of the ocean without becoming wet" and "to tie an elephant with a spider's filament"[52] are references to details of the inner art. We have already discussed the metaphor of riding the tiger, a situation in which dismounting entails grave consequences, for then the tiger would seize the rider and destroy him. We shall deal later on with the consequences of the failure of the method of coitus.

We must comment briefly about the kind of training needed for the higher forms of these practices. The rule is that the young woman is first "adored" and then possessed (in the ritual, two different positions are indicated for the couple; in the first phase the woman is on the man's right, in the second on his left). "To adore," in its highest degree, means "to make an object of worship" by invoking in the woman the presence of the goddess Tara, who gives salvation, or of other images of the female principle. Here there is a certain similarity to the adoration of woman proper to the medieval Worshippers of Love. An interesting detail is that in the phase of adoration, the nature of Radha, a woman, is often attributed to the man although his essential nature is Krishna, the divine male. While the man remains in the profane sphere, he belongs to the female nature and does not possess true manhood; he has to set aside the presumption that he is already a *purusha* (the embodiment of true manhood, without motion) if he wishes to enter into the sphere of the everlasting.[53] In mysticism, a feminine role is often attributed to the soul, as the bride or beloved of the heavenly lover. In Vaishnavic Tantrism this relationship sometimes holds, but as an exception or splinter of the central concept. The process develops as a surmounting of that condition and inversion of polarity. The woman is adored first as a living embodiment of the goddess and a bearer of the supersensual, the health-bringing and enlightening force, as we said; then she is possessed and made to pass from the right to the left.

It is possible to glean some interesting data regarding the preparations for the sexual rite from a Bengali manuscript summarized by Mahindra Mohan Bose.[54] A long and hard discipline is required to nourish the desire and, at the same time, to keep it in check. During a first period, the man must serve the young woman (technically equivalent to the medieval "service of love") and sleep at her feet in the same room. Next he will share her bed for four months, keeping her on his right, a position appropriate to the phase of "adoration." He will then sleep with her for another four months, keeping her on his left, always desiring her but having no physical contact with her. It is only after this period that coitus is allowed. This rather formal procedure has a twofold purpose: on the one hand to refine and heighten desire for the woman without actual contact (as though the quintessence of platonic love is made into a technique); on the other hand, to develop control to such a degree that in coitus and in the dispersive integration with her fluidic substance, her *rajas*, it will be possible to halt the seed and to deviate the wave of feeling at the peak of the erotic crisis.

We may, therefore, speak of a preliminary discipline in an unusual form of asceticism just as we may talk of a superascetic achievement different from mystical ecstasies in relation to the highest purpose sought with these techniques. This was particularly emphasized in Buddhist Tantrism, the Vajrayana. These teachings went so far as to conceptualize a Buddha very different from his usual image, a Buddha who had conquered Mara, the goddess of the earth and death, and attained to absolute enlightenment through the rites of sexual magic and union with women ("Women are divinities, they are life," the Buddha said, according to one text).[55] Moreover, this is not just a question of sex thought of as one means to achieve nirvana. The specific point we want to emphasize is that in the Vajrayana the highest state of the *mahasukha*, when the Buddha is copulating with Shakti, is positioned in rank beyond the state of nirvana itself considered unilaterally, that is, as ecstasy separated from the world. This is the essence of the doctrine of the "fourth body" of the Buddhas, called *mahasukha-kaya*; united with their Shakti, they are united in her with the root of all manifestation, and that means that they are lords both of immanence (*samsara*) and of transcendence (nirvana), words that in these teachings no longer form an antithesis. As regards experience, therefore, we may think of a surpassing of the ecstatic state or of mere *excessus mentis* (death of the mind), when understood passively or "mystically." Furthermore, this is a purpose that was consciously supposed in other trends of Hindu metaphysics. For example, it was said, "Do not allow the intellect to enjoy the happiness that comes from the ecstatic condition [*samadhi*] but, by means of the practice of discrimination, free it from the love that it feels for that happiness."[56]

Like meanings can, in general, be found behind the symbolism and terminology of the teachings we are speaking about. If it is thought that every man is potentially a Buddha, then the female participant, besides being called *mudra* and *shakti* (because she embodies Shakti in the flesh), also has the name of *vidya*, which means "knowledge" in a sense often confused with *prajna* or enlightenment. This signifies that the woman embodies the principle that can arouse the potential Buddha quality in man. In the same context for which the woman of the Worshippers of Love awakens *Madonna Intelligenza*, the health-bearing Understanding, the Holy Wisdom that activates the "capability of intellect" present in a lover, she is here the living symbol of the *prajna* (enlightenment) and enfolds the *prajna* in the depths of her own being. Furthermore, in these schools the mystery of the fulfillment is often presented in the symbolism of the union of *padma* and *vajra*; these are two polyvalent words, since they have both an abstract, metaphysical, and doctrinal meaning and a concrete sexual one. They can allude to the female and male sexual organs (the "matrix of the Buddhas") or to the scepter-lightning and diamond (symbols of the force and the fixed, incorruptible and sovereign principle of being). In other cases, the two words used are *prajna* and *upaya*—namely, the enlightenment force or else the technique, the "suitable means," or the "acting power"—which unite and lead to the highest achievement. Once again, we are dealing with a union that is thought of sometimes in only abstract, metaphysical, and spiritual terms and at other times within a background of the sexual act, for once again there is an ontological, magical, and analogical likeness between those principles and everything designated by the foregoing terms (*upaya* and *prajna*).[57] Now, the point that can be deduced from this context and that we want to emphasize is the accentuation obtained by the male principle owing to the fact that a female character is given to the enlightenment force which in the symbolism of the holy marriage takes the part of the woman possessed by the male in coitus, for it is generally acknowledged that the *vajra* may also assume a phallic significance.[58] This is an indication for the "magical" purpose of such teachings; in a certain way we are brought back to what we said earlier about the deaths of Beatrice and Rachel and the Hermetic symbolism of incest.

We may ask ourselves to what extent the Tantric sexual practices lead to the same results as the purely yogic awakening of the kundalini. The writings show clearly that the awakening can be brought about by means of woman. We directed the reader's attention to phenomena of profane sexuality (e.g., certain cases of hebephrenia) that can be explained as effects of a partial awakening of the basic force. The hyperphysical physiology of yoga indicates a center near the one in which the kundalini sleeps, called the *yonishthana*, and it is said that herein, under the sign of carnal desire, a union of Shiva and Shakti can be produced, almost like a foretaste or reflection of that highest union which, according to the teachings of yoga, will be fulfilled in the corona region of the skull. This also makes us think of the possibility of a convergence of the two techniques. Besides, there are texts in which the woman loved and possessed is shown as the living symbol of the same kundalini or *chandali*. The predominant view, however, is that through sexual practices it is possible to arrive only in passing at the *sahaja* or highest nondual state beyond the ego and nonego, but that this achievement is hard to stabilize and is, as it were, only a surprise feat, and that it is impossible to proceed with all the operations contemplated by yoga with the kundalini ascending. Indeed, this is precisely the objection raised by the adherents of pure yoga against the practices just mentioned.[59] In conformity with this, the writings of Buddhist Tantrism, too, often speak of teachers who, after attaining enlightenment by means of sexual practices, keep far away from women and follow another path, proclaiming a strict doctrine. However, this is not the case with the Siddhas and Kaulas, nor with groups among whom such practices are even considered as operational magic.

If, as we have seen, the possible outcome of a badly performed awakening of the kundalini in yoga may be illness, madness, or death, it should be obvious that the same risk is present to an even greater extent in Tantric sexual practices, because the process is harder to direct and control in the right way owing to the intrinsic nature of human sexuality. If the *bindu* (the seed and its corresponding principle) falls during coitus, the consequence will be a more fearful bondage.[60] In particular, the danger may be complete sexual intoxication, for the female force will have been absorbed in the deepest layers of the man's being and the elementary energy of sex and desire will have been aroused. If the transmutation or inversion of polarity does not then take place because the tendency toward mere lustful pleasure has remained predominant, even if only unconsciously, the result may be an irrevocable intoxication of the man's real being. In such a case a man may be degraded to the level of a "devil" or an instrument of the force that he had set out to master. This is also the risk involved in what some people call "red magic." Whereas the real purpose of Tantric practices is to use the experience of sex as a means to establish contact with the supersensual, the real purpose of red magic is the opposite: to use supersensual contacts (sometimes with the help of drugs) to intensify the sexual experience and, especially, to prolong abnormally the duration of the orgasm and pleasure but without changing its nature in the sense indicated above. The risk of Tantric practices lies indeed in remaining on that plane, even without understanding the fact properly.

The Greek myth of Nessus' cloak imaginatively depicts that abortive outcome. To bind Heracles to herself with love and desire, Deianeira sent him a magnificent cloak that she had obtained from Nessus and that was soaked with a love potion; but the love potion was in fact a philter of death. Heracles felt his body poisoned and his veins burning with unquenchable fire that even Deianeira's suicide could not expiate. Only by his own sacrificial transfiguration in the fire on Mount Aetna could Heracles be saved. The fire was replaced by divine lightning, which transported Heracles to Olympus, where he obtained Hebe, everlasting youth, as his bride. The meaning of this legend is clear: the elementary woman who is evoked and absorbed can become the starting point of a deadly and unquenchable thirst. At that stage, only an Olympian "flash of lightning" can take one back to the original immortalizing purpose of the union.

The obsessive situation was well illustrated in a romance of Meyrink with precise reference to the ideas of Tantrism. He described a character who was subjected to the power of the goddess aroused in a woman as in one of her previous incarnations to such an extent that he lost the principle of supernatural manhood (here symbolized by a spear-dagger, which can be made to correspond to the scepter-diamond or *vajra* of the Oriental doctrine). The woman, who had already been possessed physically, then went on to act in a hypersensual or subtle form as a kind of fascinating and bewitching image "of her eyes and body and all her ruthless being." Meyrink's character expressed himself thus: "The succubus took complete possession of my sense . . . it was like a continual deadly thirst up to the point where either the goblet broke in pieces or God himself opened the prison. . . . My torment increased a hundredfold because Assia had, so as to speak, gone on to act on a more profound plane; she was less tangible to my senses but alway made her consuming presence felt. If at first my will sought to rid myself of her, yet the same will turned back against me and I felt myself burning with desire for her." There now appeared to him in a thousand enchanting images "the Naked One, the Sucking One, the Dissolving One," and, staying exactly the same in all these manifold images of fever, desire, and nakedness, the woman began to "enfold him within her aura and permeate into him, growing within him and around him" until he felt he was at the edge of perdition and "on the border of what the Wise Men called the eighth world or world of total destruction."[61]

Let us, finally, bear in mind that according to Hindu texts, he who wishes to set in motion the sexual techniques that lead to the *mahasukha* must have not only perfect self-control but also a healthy body strengthened with the disciplines of physical yoga; otherwise the *mahasukha* or ecstasy of the condition of union will lead to a darkening of the senses, "something like a swoon."[62] This detail is important; we can see how it is linked to the unfavorable states that in profane erotics, and particularly in woman, take the place of the transfiguring experience during coitus.

We have dwelt somewhat on the subject of Tantric sexual rites because they demonstrate all the main themes we encountered in considering the metaphysics of sex both in the profane sphere of unintentional, passive, and tendential forms and in the sphere of traditional sacred ceremonies. We have found again in these rites the practice of evocations and the appearance and arousal of the power that constitutes the deepest nature or ontological root of individuals of both sexes. We have considered as a part of the whole the practice of "platonic" desire, the refined psychic condition of rapture that is the essence of all eros. An exact premise in the practices is the potential independence from the ordinary physiological conditional qualities both of this desire and of the peak of "pleasure" itself which is brought about in coitus. The link between death and love (the love that slays, the death of love, the "death" in the spasm, in the orgasm, and in the bodily delirium) passes here from the romantic and solely emotional plane to the real and objective plane of an initiatory technique in an experience wherein the break in continuity and the submersion which in most cases corresponds to the trauma or final crisis provoked by union with a woman are replaced by a presence that is accompanied by or actually determines the breakthrough of level, the "slaying of the intellect" and the stroke of lightning of the "enlightenment thought" beyond the dual state. Finally, both the doctrine of the hermaphrodite as a key to the metaphysics of sex and also the idea that sexuality as a merely animal, procreative function represents a fall are confirmed by the techniques of the inversion of polarity and the withholding of seed. They are also confirmed by the concept of the kundalini, which, when aroused, becomes the force that, rather than feeding the circle of generation and reinforcing its bond, leads toward the *sahaja*, toward deathlessness, toward the unconditioned. In these traditions we encounter the various elements like so many links in a chain, which provide us with a picture of the whole that we must have to obtain the deepest understanding of the individual phenomena, aspects, and capabilities of eros and sexual love.

In what follows we shall provide information about other secret traditions on the same lines as the Tantric teachings. The new data that can be gleaned, however, are more fragmentary, and we shall not always find the same clarity and level as regards the highest purposes of the procedures.

Secret Sexual Practices in Chinese Taoism

The main source of information for the sexual practices of Chinese Taoism is material gathered by H. Maspéro in a long and well-documented essay, to which we shall continually have recourse here.[63] As a background, however, we should also keep in mind the "secret art of the alcove," common in ancient China, which was dealt with by Robert H. van Gulik.[64]

First of all, it is best to make clear what realizations Taoism sets forth. Although Maspéro is an authority in Sinology, we believe he is wrong in saying that the most general concept in Taoism concerns the immortal sequel linked to the "dissolving of the corpse"; this is the case where, when the Taoist initiate dies, he does not leave a body behind him, but causes a sword or wand-scepter to be found in its place and arises again in an everlasting body, which is an essential transformation of his short-lived body. Instead, acording to Maspéro, the Taoist esoteric teaching should concern practices regarding breathing and sex. This is not actually the case. The "dissolving of the corpse" has also been considered in other traditions, not as an ordinary religious idea but as the highest goal that an initiate of the topmost rank can hope to reach. Christianity itself asserts that Christ rose again and his body disappeared from the tomb. It also includes the doctrine of the "body of resurrection," which Paul certainly took from the mysteries. In many traditions and legends is found the subject of mythical figures stolen or mystically vanished. The Taoist doctrine of dissolving of the corpse forms a part of this same category of ideas.

The secret practices mentioned by Maspéro may be procedures for accomplishing the transmutation of the body until its natural corruptibility is eliminated, so that it can then "dematerialize," leaving no residue. Or such practices may aim at the attainment of "everlasting life," in the sense of a "long life," *ch'ang-sheng*, or of a kind of extranormal extension of individual existence with a reduction of the ordinary processes that alter the physical-vital and subtle framework of the organism. We would interpret in this way the operations of withholding, fixation, and nutrition of the original life principle, described in the treatise *The Secret of the Golden Flower*. If such is the case, these Taoist practices would be sharply differentiated from the Tantric and Hindu yogic practices, since these aim at the surmounting of all conditional qualities and at the Great Liberation. However, there is a definite ambiguity, for the Taoist practices also emphasize the union of the male and female, the *yang* and *yin*, an equivalent to the attainment of the nondual state. The unresolved ambiguity may be attributed to the fact that "the most important instructions of Taoism are not found in the written texts of books but in formulas passed on by word of mouth."[65]

Maspéro distinguished the practices connected with breathing from those which employ sex as a means. It will be enough here to mention the former because they concern teachings like those we considered earlier when dealing with endogenous transmutation. Thus the notion recurs of the "space of the force" located in the *yin* region of the body (the part of the body above the diaphragm is *yang* or male and the part below *yin* or female), to be exact, "three inches below the naval"; it is now properly called "the field of the lower vermilion," *tan-t'ien*. Access to this field is blocked (by a threshold that "the divinities do not open readily"). Essentially the practice consists in controlling the breathing, in gaining possession of the vital principle of the breath, and, when the obstacle has been removed, in making the breath reach the field of the lower vermilion. The breath then meets the essence, also called "the breath of the mysterious woman"; being integrated in this way, the breath is "closed," or held for a long time, and leads to a special hyperphysical energy, which spreads and circulates throughout the whole body like a fluid, thereby regenerating and vitalizing the body. Sometimes an ascending process is also considered by means of which the force from the lower center is taken toward the so-called field of the upper vermilion (situated in the head). It is then transformed into a fire "by which the body is set ablaze, so that the body has the brightness of fire." This is linked to the "melting of [physical] form" or of the body itself—being a melting, it is said, by analogy with the change of state worked by fire in solid metallic substances. We are thus brought back to the idea of a transformed body that overcomes death.[66] In this we find certain similarities to the teachings of kundalini yoga: the lower center, the fiery nature of the kundalini, the obstruction of the threshold of the axial path, the ascending process and the union of the male and female (in yoga, Shiva and Shakti) at the top of the head.

Let us now pass on from the Taoist breathing practices to the sexual ones belonging to the same tradition. In the handbooks on sex the term *yin-tao* ("hidden way") designates sexual union. Like Tantrism, Taoism lays down the principle that, while the use of sex may be harmful for some people, it may be a means of spiritual attainment and health for others who have knowledge of its use. "To be united to a woman," it is said, "is like riding a horse at the gallop with rotten reins." But he who knows will experience no harm from copulation with women; indeed, he even obtains a benefit. "The Yellow Emperor," we read in the *Yu-fang che-yao*, "lay with 1,200 women and became immortal; the common people only have one woman each and [in enjoying her] destroy their own lives. To have or not to have the knowledge; how could opposite results not arise from that?"[67]

The knowledge concerns a secret doctrine; thus in the same text it is written that the procedure "is transmitted by the Immortals to each other; they drink blood when swearing an oath not to transmit it at random." The scholar Teng Yn-tse repeats it: "This technique is absolutely secret; never transmit it except to wise men!"[68] Another Taoist scholar, Ko Hong (of the fourth century), after having underlined the great importance of the "practices of the alcove" (*fang-*

chong-che-fa) said of the highest purpose to be pursued with them, "This recipe is passed on by the True Men to each other by word of mouth; in origin it was not written down. If a man does not know this efficacious procedure [the practice of sex] he cannot attain to ever-lasting life even by using the most famous drugs" (*Pao-p'u tsu*, 8, 3b). We should not think, therefore, that texts alone will provide full clarification of this matter.

Ko Hong actually cites various ends pursued by those who make a nonprofane use of sex. For some it is a matter of restoring depleted vital energy and of obtaining long life; others wish to strengthen their *yang* and disperse their *yin*; but the most important purpose should be to "make the essence return again to restore the brain." This is how Maspéro's translation runs;[69] but whether or not the word "brain" was actually used in the text, it is obvious that the operation refers to the breathing practices we have just considered. This is not a question of the physical brain but of the "field of the upper vermilion" situated in the head. Indeed, we must generally remember that in teachings of this kind, all references of an apparently physical or physiological nature actually refer to a hyperphysical "anatomy" and physiology.

Even if we distinguish among these various end purposes, the general background of the practices always continues to be the union of the *yang* and *yin*, the male and female principles. It seems that the purpose attained in coitus depends on the varying arrangement of the state of union. A strange but also suggestive expression used for the sexual practice is "the coiling up of the dragon and the game of the tiger." The dragon symbolizes the *yang* and corresponds to the man; the tiger symbolizes the *yin* and is embodied in the woman. It should be borne in mind that, unlike other traditions, Chinese tradition considers the dragon a dual-natured creature, not only chthonic but also heavenly and kingly. Since the dragon symbolizes man according to its twofold nature, the developments of inner experience in the "game of the dragon and tiger" could perhaps be connected to the six situations of the *yang* attributed by the commentary to the six *yang* signs of the first hexagram of the *I Ching*. Starting from the bottom, the dragon passes from the phase where it can be seen and little by little hurls itself onward, rises into the sky, and disappears.

Age is important in the selection of the woman. She should not be older than thirty and is best if younger than eighteen or nineteen. As in Tantrism, she should not be a mother nor have had children: "Even if she is young, she cannot be used if she has had a child" (*Yu-fang pi-kiue*, Ia). A special feature here is the commandment to change the female partner; a whole group of texts emphasize this point as essential. "It is necessary to change the woman after each excitement; it is by changing the woman that one attains everlasting life," says the text cited above, and it adds, "If we are united always with the same woman, the breath of the *yin* will diminish, and the yield will be scanty. . . . the essence and the breath of the woman will become weak little by little, and she will not be able to render great benefit to the man."[70] This is even interpreted in the sense of using many young women, one after another, and in another text we can read that "when the woman is changed several times, the benefit increases, and if the woman is changed ten times in a night, the highest and best degree [of the operation] will be reached."

This, however, sounds less like an initiatory purpose or transcendence than sexual magic bordering on male "psychic" vampirism. This idea comes to mind from references in some texts to long life, to the absence of illness, and to the body "becoming light" or being "made subtle" as an outcome of such practices.[71] Further evidence shows that the texts sometimes recommend that young women who already know the technique should not be employed lest, according to P'eng-tsu, the woman should obtain advantage from the coitus to feed her *yin* and become immortal; a girl who has the knowledge will seek her own development and will not be of benefit to her companion.[72] Here there is no longer a two-sided game or experience from which both parties can obtain advantage by fusing themselves in the states that develop during the act of love. Rather, in this case, the man merely seeks a complementary fluidic substance to absorb or to use to excite himself, strengthening his *yang* or dragon quality, the principle of his manhood, against the yin or tiger quality of the woman; and so he would prefer a companion not initiated into the secret and magical meaning of coitus so that he, not she, will obtain the benefit and so that the *yin* will not prevail. Moreover, in the treatises on the profane art of love, an antagonism is emphasized and the woman is called the "foe" because she tends to take away the *yang* from the man.[73] Thus it is easier to understand the use of many women, when the man's goal is to absorb the female fluid and, vampirelike, to feed his own vitality. Sexual techniques are also known in India and Tibet for prolonging life within a similar framework. To do this it is essential that, when a man copulates with a woman and brings about her orgasm, he should not participate in the pleasure in any way; this allows for the vampirelike absorption of the vital female energy.[74] Furthermore, even in the Upanishads there are traces of an analogous "aspirating" procedure intended to remove "the seed" from the woman during coitus, preventing her from conceiving. The text says that for this purpose the man should join his mouth to that of the woman, penetrate into her, let out his breath, and then breathe in again (and, most likely, hold his breath), at the same time realizing in his mind the formula "With my force, with my seed, I do take her seed." (We spoke about the "female seed" earlier.)[75] This text even mentions something analogous to that considered in Taoism: the advantage of the man or of the woman depends on the possession of knowledge when they are joined together sexually; the man takes advantage of the "good works of the woman" with whom he is united if he has the knowledge; or the woman takes possession of the good works of the man if he lacks the knowledge and is unaware. The text adds that even men of the brahmin caste are without virility when they copulate with a woman without having that knowledge.[76]

However, everything does not end on such a problematic plane in Taoist secret practices. In actuality, the main technique does not differ much from that of Tantrism. The first phase of it is called the real art of equalizing, harmonizing, or mingling the breaths, or *chang-k'i chen-chu*; this is the technical name of the erotic preliminaries intended to revive the natural magnetism, kindled by the *yin-yang* relationship, to a special degree of exaltation and harmony of the two. It is only after this state has been reached and nourished for a certain time that the two proceed to unite their bodies (*Yu-fang che-yao*, Ib). It is possible that the aim of these preliminaries is to reach the condition that, according to the Tantric ritual quoted earlier, is attained by passing a certain period of time with the woman in intimacy but abstaining from physical contact. Likewise, as we said, the practice of the coitus, *huo-ho*, is not very different here from the Tantric practice; in possessing the woman, the man should not reach the point of emitting his seed,[77] and should the process of ejaculation become activated, he must prevent it and bring his seed back so as to "withhold the essence"; this essence corresponds to the *virya* and the *bindu*, the principle of the magical manhood in Hinduism. The *Su-niu-ching* indeed says: "The essential basis of the technique consists in copulating with many young women without emitting the essence."[78] It is a matter here of reawakening the primary force (the essence); as soon as the development of the love act has set that force in motion (one text says, "It should become very excited"), the process of ejaculation should be halted, and in some texts physical devices are even recommended for that purpose. Then the backward process takes place; the aroused and withheld essence goes up along the spinal column toward the "brain." This is called "the art of making the essence return to reintegrate the [center located in the] brain"—*huan-tsing pu-nao* (*Yu-fang che-yao*, Ib).[79] "Penetrate only without emitting" is the repeated advice. The instructions of Lieu King are, after the breaths of the man and woman have been harmonized, to "penetrate when [word missing] is weak and withdraw when it is steady and strong," whereas another text says, "He who enters strong and withdraws weak will perish even when he has had the best destiny" (*Yang-sing yen-ming lu*, II, 13 a,b). Maspéro suggests "phallus" as the missing subject of the clause in the foregoing proposition. In these texts the male organ is called the "jade stem." But this interpretation seems to us rather awkward. Among other things, it would be difficult to imagine how this would work in practice on the physical plane. We suggest that a state and a force were originally implied. Not the sexual organ but the *yang* principle of the man should be "weak" at first and gradually strengthened during the development of the magical operation until it gains the upper hand over the *yin* and can be withdrawn "hard." For this is one of the explicit purposes indicated by the texts. The ritualism is applied here so thoroughly that to perfect the practice, the "jade stem" should perform eighty-one strokes within the "strings of the lute," eighty-one being the complete *yang* number.[80] This must seem a paralyzing mechanical process except under those very special circumstances in which, without wishing it, the intensely experienced realization of a significance leads spontaneously, we might almost say magically, to a corresponding precise symbolic structure in the physical act.

Teng Yu-tse, the legendary figure of an "immortal" who seems to have lived under the Han dynasty in the second century, defined the twofold purpose thus: "to lessen the *yin* so as to strengthen the *yang*" and "to coagulate the liquor of the essence" (to fix the *virya*).[81] Maspéro repeats the warning that, as with breathing techniques, these practices should not be undertaken without adequate training. Moreover, to dedicate oneself to them one must choose the right days, for a group of prohibitions founded on astrology exists in Taoism. For instance, the first and last days of the month, the periods of the first and last quarters of the moon, and the period of the full moon are forbidden, among other dates and unfavorable circumstances; in practice about two hundred days in the year are excluded for the "magical union of the dragon with the tiger."[82] Also, certain times are deemed favorable: being sober and unencumbered with too much food, the man should operate with the woman in the "hour of the *yang* living breath after midnight"—another link in the thematic chain of woman, eros, and night. The practice assumes the ability to meditate and concentrate. Preliminary rituals for making the union sacred, as in India and elsewhere, are not envisaged, but it is explicitly stated that the operation should be carried out in a frame of mind different from that of normal waking consciousness. "Every time the practice is undertaken," said Teng Yu-tse, "it is necessary to enter into meditation; it is necessary first to lose awareness of one's body and then of the outside world."[83] This means that one must enter into a state of active trance so that, while carrying out material actions and without losing the sensation of the woman, the experience may proceed substantially on a subtle and hyperphysical plane. The ascent of the essence toward the higher seat, after the aroused force has been stopped and diverted from the normal direction of emission, should be accompanied by a mental projection that guides and directs the process.[84]

Teng Yu-tse also refers to an invocation[85] at the end of which "the men will keep [their spirit fixed] on the kidneys, steadfastly withholding the essence and distilling the breath, which follows the spinal column and ascends against the current toward the *ni-huan*; this is what is called 'causing to return to the Origin,' *huan-yuan*. The women, on the other hand, will keep [their spirit fixed] in the heart and nourish their spirits, distilling an unchangeable fire [the *rajas* as *tejas* in Hindu terminology] in their hearts and making their breath descend from their breasts to their kidneys, whence it will ascend again along their spinal column to arrive also at the *ni-huan*.[86] This is called 'transformation of the Real,' *hua-chen*. Transcendence is reached after one hundred days. By practicing for a long time, one becomes spontaneously a real man, and the centuries will pass by with everlasting life. This is the method for 'not dying.' "[87] Regarding this "not dying," we find the ambiguity we noted earlier. It is hard to see whether it is just a matter of acquiring long life and compounding a kind of alchemic elixir (in fact, we sometimes even find expressions of the following type: "Whether you be young or old, you will become youths again")[88] or whether a sort of reintegration of a physical and "vital" nature is considered a consequential effect of a realization of a higher category, namely the realization of transcendent and everlasting life in a real sense. When faced with an ambiguity of this kind, we must always bear in mind the warning of the texts that the essentials of such initiatory teachings were only passed on by word of mouth.

The information gathered by Maspéro gives no indications of dangers involved in the sexual practice of union of *yin* and *yang*. However, these practices expose the participants to the risk of erotic intoxication if the man ejaculates during the magical coitus and the *yin* or tiger quality gains the upper hand over the *yang* or dragon quality. We reiterate that this may be why it is advised not to use young women initiated in the secret side of the practice lest they profit by a perilous development of the *yin*, which would completely invert the polarity of the practice.

Besides individual sexual unions carried out by couples in isolation, some Taoist texts hint at collective practices that seem to have been a combination of ancient seasonal orgiastic rites (belonging to the spring or fall) with the real initiatory techniques mentioned before. For these collective rites, the days of the new moon and full moon are stated to be favorable, although these same days should be avoided for individual sexual rites. The purpose of these collective rites of freeing the participant from his sins and keeping away bad luck that may arise from his own needs according to the "law of concordant actions and reactions" is similar to the purification or catharsis obtained by immersion in the formless (the "Waters"), which we discussed when dealing with the ultimate meaning of orgiastic rites in general. But there is a difference from these collective practices: the rule that the seed should not be emitted during coitus must be observed. The *Siao tao luen* states: "Those who take part in the practice fulfill the true formula in the field of the vermilion; but they take care of the defended secret and do not let it out on their way."[89] The principle is that of promiscuity; indeed, nothing must hinder the exchange of women. The same text also hints at ensuring a protective (lucky) force for oneself against all danger, hostile influence, and devils. In the desired effect, the attainment of the pure male *yang* quality, we might recognize a parallel with the ancient ideas of the magical and exorcising power of the phallus. But it is difficult to conceive of a practice of collective orgies consistent with the retention of semen. At best, we can conceive of the framework of a magical chain suitably organized and articulated (like the Tantric "circles" to which we shall refer later on), a concept quite different from actual promiscuity. However, "things which cannot be set forth in all their details"[90] are alluded to, and there is no doubt that such collective practices must have degenerated, as evidenced by writers who deplored the fact that in the age after the Wei and Tsin periods the practices led to the birth of children among the Taoists,[91] which implies that the participants let matters take the normal "wet" course of human coitus.

Arab Sexual Practices and Hermetic Symbology

Orgiastic practices for mystic purposes have also been found in the Arab-Persian region, but information about them is confined to a few comments by writers and travelers who were scandalized and unable to examine the corresponding traditions intelligently or understand their implications. Direct information regarding sexual practices that have continued into our own times among Arab circles in North Africa can be found in a report that is part of a recently published collective work.[92] Union with a woman is one of the means employed to arouse the power of a spiritual influence (*barakah*) after its potentiality has been established in the man by ritual initiation. It should be noted that this technique is chosen only for persons who are particularly drawn toward sex by their temperament; thus the predominating inclination forms a kind of raw material.[93] Another interesting detail is that the ability to prove that the person in question cannot be hypnotized is an essential qualification.[94] This is a precaution against passivity or even susceptibility to a spell when the man enters into relations with the woman. We should recall here that Tantrism also warns of the danger that a fainting state or lassitude may take the place of the active ecstasy of the *mahasukha*. In the report, we find the unnatural method of semen retention: "The rule is that the union with the woman is to be performed so that in no case is its normal final end attained, that is, the seed must not be ejaculated. The organizations with which I came in contact had Berber girls at their disposal who were skilled in these practices. I believe that on each occasion they underwent an occult preparation. Furthermore, formulas (*dhikr*) were provided and no girl agreed to be used for the practices when these formulas were not used. During the whole night throughout which the experience had to last, Arab tea was used as a kind of strong concoction to which were added successive infusions of various herbs, which must have had some relationship with the level and progress of the experience."[95]

The reporter continued, "The practice seemed to have a twofold purpose. Above all, there was self-control, different from mere resistance to temptation because all the normal physical and psychic conditions of bodily union with a woman were acceptable, nor was there any commandment to suppress the feelings that are usually aroused therein, with the sole exception that the emission of seed had to be controlled and prevented. Instead, the girls employed had precise instructions to use every means available so that that very thing would not take place. There was one queer detail: I happened to see these girls weeping when they succeeded in this 'spoiling' action and apologizing, for they say that they had had to obey an order." But the end to be attained through resistance and self-control was also a means, in that the forces awakened by the coitus performed in this way had to cause the trauma needed for enlightenment and contact with the suprasensual.[96] It is interesting to observe that, apart from these sexual practices, the author of the report was trained in rites of evocatory magic, which aimed not at the production of paranormal phenomena but at the development of self-control and power of command, since it is said that in evocatory experiences of the kind, without right attitude, one may meet madness at every step, and that is a risk that we have also seen indicated as regards sexual practices.[97]

To establish a link between the practices in this report and the way of Sufism, we might emphasize the "extinction," or *fana*, which is followed by "stability," or *tasis* or *baqa*. We have already quoted Ibn Arabi as regards the system for making a union holy and the ritual identification of the woman with "cosmic nature." We can cite here another passage from the same scholar: "When the man loves the woman, he desires the union, namely the most whole union possible in love; and in the [bodily] form composed of elements no union exists which is stronger than that of the conjugal act. In it, the sensual pleasure spreads throughout every part of the body, and it is for this reason that holy Law bids us to wash the whole [of our bodies after the sexual act], for the purification should not be less whole than the wholeness of the extinction of the man in the woman during the ecstasy provoked by the sensual pleasure. Therefore, God, being jealous of His servant, does not suffer him to believe that he takes delight in a thing which is not He. Therefore he purifies his body [with the prescribed rite] so that he may turn in his vision toward Him in whom he has in reality been extinguished, there being nothing other than this."[98] Therefore there is a transposition of self-dissolution through the woman into self-extinction in the divinity through surmounting the illusory fact of individual and bodily sensual pleasure; this seems to be the key to the Islamic technique.

It is hard to verify the existence of circles where analogous procedures were put into operation in medieval Europe or after. We have already written about special kabbalist groups and the Brothers of the Free Spirit, but in these cases it was a question of simple mystic sensuality, and we can find no signs of a special initiatory method of coitus. It is not impossible, however, that such a method was practiced in other, more secret surroundings. In another book[99] we cited a hermetic-kabbalist text, the *Esh Mezareph* (Fire of Purification), which has been attributed to Isaac the Dutchman; in it the symbolism of the blow of the spear of Phineus, which pierced the sinning couple in the moment of coitus, thus leading to prodigies, may recall the Tantric and Taoist technique of halting the *virya* during the love act. A similar meaning could be deduced from one of the *Chiavi* (Keys) of Basilius Valentinus, namely the eleventh. In it, two women are represented astride two lions, which devour each other in turn; the women bear a heart where the fluid of the Sun and of the Moon are poured and mixed. Nearby a warrior can be seen, fully armed and with his sword uplifted, ready to strike (and halt the process).[100]

The hermetic-kabbalistic interpretation applied to Tarot card XV, "The Devil," suggests sexual procedures.[101] The central figure has the features of Baphomet, the secret goddess of the Templars. The hermaphroditic figure with a ram's head has a pentagram marked on its forehead. The right and left arms are associated respectively with two alchemist-hermetic formulas, *Solve* and *Coagula*. In its right hand the figure bears a lighted torch that, representing *Solve*, might allude to the inner fire illumined during the operation. The left hand holds the ancient symbols of the male and female sexual organs united, and the corresponding *Coagula* might refer to the magical action of fixation that generates the hermaphrodite. Moreover, a he-devil and a she-devil can be seen low down in the hieroglyphic, tied to the stand on which there rises the central figure, which acts as the key for the whole. The two devils may correspond to the man and woman taking part in the operation under the sign of the central figure, the hermaphrodite bearing the sign of the pentagram. The man, with his left hand turned upward toward the lighted torch, is making the ritual sign of benediction, while his right hand is laid on his genitals; whereas the woman is touching the lower part of the hermaphroditic figure with her right hand and has her left hand on her own sexual organ. As she is on the side of the *Coagula*, this might allude to another meaning of this formula, "the coagulation of astral light," the state of fluidic intoxication that forms the woman's contribution to the operation. Thus, although embedded in the various parts of an abstruse and ambiguous hieroglyph intended to convey polyvalent meanings, a figure of this kind may allude to the various moments in the procedure of initiatory sexual magic.

Concerning the actual hermetic art itself—and we mean here the secret doctrine that was transmitted in the West through the symbolic and elusive language of alchemical procedures—we have already said that the sexual interpretation is a possible one for the operations that the texts describe; but it is only one of the manifold number of planes to which every initiatory symbol, by its very nature, may refer simultaneously. In hermetic doctrine, erotic symbolism plays rather an important part, and the procedures it deals with might also be applied, in their outline, to the sphere of sexual magic in particular. We have already observed the importance which the symbolism of the hermaphrodite, the Rebis, has in this tradition. Starting with ancient Hellenistic texts, it is stated that the essence of the *Opera* (Work or Interaction) consists of the union of male and female.[102] From the alchemical viewpoint, the male is Sulfur, a force linked to the ego principle and to the divine (the Greek word for Sulfur, *theîon*, also has this meaning). The female principle has a number of designations: it is Mercury, the Water of Life, the Raw Material, the Universal Solvent, Divine Water, and so on. It is the Woman of the Philosophers, which is needed by "our Gold"; Gold can also signify the male in his "being" principle. "Our bodily

Gold," said Philateles,[103] "is as if dead before it is united with its bride. Only then does the inner, secret Sulfur develop." A treatise by Ostanus said, when referring to the Woman, "In thee is hidden all the dreadful and wonderful mystery."[104] The first effect of the "hidden union," however, is dissolution, for the Female or Mercury acts as a solvent. From this point begins the phase called Black Opera or *nigredo*, in which the male, "Our King," dies.[105] Moreover, this crisis is undergone appropriately by the "bodily Gold," also called "common Sulfur"; it is the conditioned form of appearance of the principle of the personality, which can be called the "physical ego." By uniting itself to the Mercury or Divine Water, its enclosure is removed. Thus, after the crisis, the ecstatic condition appears, the light rises, and the "doves of Diana" are seen in the so-called *albedo* or White Opera (White Work or Interaction), which should be considered as the positive (transmutation of the negative) aspect of the "system of the Woman" or "of the Moon." But it is essentially for the purpose of the overall affair that the man should have available what the texts call the "Steel of the Wise Men," the "seed of the Gold" or the "Incombustible Sulfur," names alluding to a power that is not "lit" (it does not let itself be transported) nor altered (Steel) but is conserved throughout these changes of state and, when the time is ripe, forms the beginning (seed) of a new development. This development corresponds to the third essential phase of the *opus alchemicum*, which is the Red Opera (Red Work or Interaction) or *rubedo*, in which the condition of mere ecstatic opening is surpassed. Now Sulfur and Fire become active again; the male becomes alive and reacts on her who had dissolved him; he gains the upper hand over the female (the *Turba philosophorum* or Turmoil of the Philosophers said, "The Mother is always more kindly toward the Son than the Son is toward her"), absorbs her, and transmits his own nature to her. It is then that the union of the King and Queen, the two persons washed and stripped naked, also called "Incest," gives way to the person who is beyond the two, that is, the Rebis or crowned hermaphrodite, Sun and Moon together, who "has all power" and is immortal.[106]

Although the texts emphasize the fact that these procedures of the hermetic art as applied to man reflect the very process of creation and cosmic manifestation in its essential moments (and we noted this earlier), yet on the other hand it seems clear from this brief treatment how aptly the hermetic symbols and operations lend themselves to application on the plane of sexual practices. But, as we said, we believe that, notwithstanding the wide use of erotic symbolism (sometimes in the most open ways; we find in the texts representations of the coitus of the King and Queen naked with their organs variously intertwined),[107] in practice the ancient masters of hermetic doctrine did not follow the path of sex, and in order to reintegrate themselves with the female principle, to strip their Diana naked, to possess their Hebe, and to carry through to its end the *opus transformationis* so far as the generation of the crowned hermaphrodite, they did not have recourse to women. As far as we can tell, it has been only in recent times that some persons attempting to carry on the hermetic art have not abstained from the "path of Venus" but have interpreted the hermetic operations as referring to that path.

In this respect, we might mention the circles that initiated Gustavo Meyrink in some doctrines that can be found written into his romances in a form that is often rather lively and suggestive. However, some more direct evidence has been provided by the school of Giuliano Kremmerz (the pseudonym of Ciro Formisano), who carried on his activity in Italy near the end of the last century and at the beginning of this within the framework of an organization or "chain" called "Myriam."

The Myriam and the "Fire Magic"

In Christian mystical theology the Virgin Mary, the *theotokos* (Mother of God), is the personification of the church who, as bestower of supernatural life, gave birth to God, the "Christ within us." We find a similar idea in Jewish esoteric doctrine with regard to the Shekhinah, who was also identified with the mystical and effective force of a given initiatic organization. Valli had already observed that in their secret language, the Worshippers of Love spoke of woman as both the "Holy Wisdom" and the organization that was the bearer and administrator of this force. Significantly, in the school of Kremmerz, we find the same idea: every man has his own Myriam or "woman," who is the fluidic essence or living double of his own being. Myriam is also the collective chain or fluidic life force of the organization, invoked as a being or a higher spiritual influence by every participant for his own spiritual and operational integration and for the purpose of enlightenment.[108]

Other references to the path of Venus in Kremmerz's writings seem to be restricted to the lighting of a psychic fire ("fire magic") between a man and a woman in a nonphysical relationship; therefore, the situation would seem similar to the special medieval forms already discussed. In general, Kremmerz said, "Magic, an active state of conquest of the will, belongs wholly to the male, but the male would not be such as he is unless the female lent herself to the male's impulse as a recipient."[109] The female essentially provides the "fluid" to arouse and magnetize the will and bring it, whether integrated or not, to a state of androgyny. But we shall come back to these possibilities or applications later on. Let us overlook, then, the use of woman as a medium guided by man until she becomes his powerful complement in a harmonious and loving relationship "which should exclude every unclean thought."[110] In general, Kremmerz admitted that the practicing magician cannot engage in relations except "where he possesses his fluidic opposite in a woman";[111] thus is developed the necessity of a complement, or special polarity, as a requisite for strong erotic magnetism. This brings us to the saying that he who can distinguish where the soul begins and the flesh ends does not know what love is.[112] Here is how the start of "fire magic" is described: "Love begins to acquire a holy character when it puts the human soul into a state of *mag* or trance. Both the heavy and more subtle matter in man are seized by a state of magnetism so profound that first an intuition and then a feeling begin of a world that is not human but that reaches a human source in the hypersensitivity of a special condition of being."[113] Kremmerz remarked that this exact state is brought about for a few instants in every love, but "the hard thing is to make it last intensely and conclusively"; it is also hard to prevent carnal desire from awakening, which would paralyze it. According to Kremmerz's terminology, it has been *mag* if it has been active (active ecstasy) but trance if it has been passive. The subtle elements in man and woman come into contact magnetically, which makes possible a relationship with forces and influences belonging to the hyperphysical plane.[114]

Let us next go back to a subject we already analyzed. When Kremmerz wrote that "through this door of love" magic truly begins when man, "staying in the most unlikely intensity of the *Pyr*, or magic fire," actually sees in his lover a being proper to the level he has attained ("Diana will come unclothed"). But in union with such a being there begins, together with the magic, the danger of madness.[115] To summarize, Kremmerz formulated three secrets of this art: (1) how to keep the holy fire burning strongly; (2) how to fuel it and make it everlasting; (3) how to unite oneself with the archetypal being using Solomon's seal (a symbol consisting of two overlapping and interlaced triangles, representing the male and female, the active and passive, the Fire and the Waters). This realization might be linked to a writing on the *Porta ermetica*, a Roman monument ornamented with inscriptions and symbols. Kremmerz illustrated this in one of his books: *Rex igne redit et coniugo gaudet occulto* (The king returns with fire and rejoices in his hidden bride).

Further details about "fluidic coitus" and magic love are found in two monographs mainly inspired by Kremmerz and contained in a collection we have already cited.[117] The first states that "it is necessary that eros, the instrument of the work, should be innocent of sexual desire and lust. It must be love in the true sense, something much broader and more subtle, without physical polarization; but its strength will be no less for this reason. It can also be said, 'You must desire the soul, the being of the woman, just as her body can be desired.' " Starting with these platonic conditions, eros propitiates in you the fluidic contact, and in its turn the fluidic state enhances eros. Thus an intensity of dizziness can be brought about which is unimaginable in the normal man and woman. "To love and desire each other in this way, without movement, in a continuous manner, mutually aspiring like vampires, in a state of exaltation that goes on without any fear of possible zones of dizziness. You will feel a sense of real amalgamation; you will feel your companion throughout your whole body, not by contact but in a subtle union that is aware of her at every point and pervades her like an intoxication that takes possession of the blood of your blood. In the end, that takes you to the threshold of a state of ecstasy."

In his other monograph, entitled "The Magic of Unions," the same anonymous writer either refers to unpublished teachings of Kremmerz or is inspired directly by Tantric practices, making use, however, of the symbols of the hermetic-alchemical tradition. In this text[118] the fluidic union without physical contact is considered a preliminary phase or condition. Following that, the union may also develop on the physical plane. "However accustomed you may be to that operation, which is intended only to lead to the magic state by means of an eros held and nourished in the fluidic body, on a second occasion the love and desire without contacts can be made to descend to the depths of sex, that is, of the life force that throbs in generation and is aroused through coitus." In this case it will lead, not to a sudden breakdown of the magic state, but to its strengthening until the "love that slays" is attained. The same condition, however, is indicated in Hindu Tantric, Taoist, and Arabic practices; the peak of the orgasm should be reached but without emitting the seed.

We shall not linger over the other details provided by the author, even though they are of a ritual category. We shall only observe one important point, namely that he distinguishes two phases in the experience, linked to the two systems of Water and Fire, Woman and Man, and Sun and Moon, of which the hermeticists wrote. The author said, "When the two die in unity and the spasm-crisis is resolved in a continuous state, you can call that which is experienced a kind of exalted, cosmic beatitude. . . . But mark well that this state is not the highest state, however irresistibly the urge may then act in you to fix yourself in that state and be mixed in it. If you do this, you will not surpass the cosmic bond, and your path will end where erotic mysticism halts. You must be able to renounce this same beatitude, which is almost that of nirvana, by using the power of the Fire (which other men call the unnatural Fire), if the system of the Waters is truly to end, Woman to be thoroughly conquered, and Matter purified of all its wetness."[119] It is a matter here of a return to the condition of pure activity after the dissolution obtained by the union, through the woman, "with one's own poison"; the process goes on, in correspondence with the level of the Great Mysteries, in that antiecstatic (or, better, superecstatic) sense that we mentioned earlier, when we also cited a passage from the Manduka-Upanishad. Precisely on that basis there would be an essential difference between what the man and woman, in principle, can respectively draw from the experience: "The limit of the participation by the woman, I mean the limit of her attainment when she, being united with you, follows you, is that ecstasy in which the peak of the coitus is crossed and develops. Further than that the woman cannot go, owing to the irrevocable law of her own nature." This agrees with what we understood from the polyvalent symbols and terminology of the Vajrayana (Buddhist Tantrism) and with what can be deduced from the Taoist doctrines when they set up as an essential purpose of their sexual technique the distillation and strengthening of the pure *yang*.

Like Kremmerz, the writer quoted above recommended the use of a special place reserved for the purpose, which only the couple could visit. By "suitable means of the magic of perfumes and consecrating signs," it is "saturated" and becomes "a fateful place in which you will experience almost a change in the woman's personality and will feel, as soon as you enter the whirlwind and rapture of your double operation, both psychic and physical coitus commence."[120] This refers to the climate of the *aropa* or Tantric transubstantiation and to the arrival of "real presences."

Within this genre the two monographs we have quoted are perhaps those in which the secret teachings of sexual magic with initiatic purposes have been expounded with a minimum of veils.

The "Light of Sex" and the "Law of Telema"

We shall now provide two further references. Some writings published by Maria de Naglowska in the period between the two world wars are somewhat spurious. Although personal speculation, rambling literary expressiveness, and a deliberate intention to scandalize the reader through unnecessarily dwelling on Satanism play a role, yet we find traces of themes regarding secret teachings from contacts she made with some Russian Caucasian circles and perhaps also with Hasidic groups. We find here a similar conception of a cyclic development, symbolized by the "cosmic clock" and its course. The first phase is the entry of God into nature, of the "Son" into the process of becoming, and of the male into female. It is the "woman," or Shakti, who predominates in this phase. At the figure six, which corresponds to the lowest point of the clock, that is, the descending arc, "in which woman dominates man and matter imprisons the spirit in the depths of its entrails," we have the limits of the abyss; when we reach this limit, we either die or are reborn to everlasting life. It is the point of the "dangerous passage" or turning point where the great trial is held.[121] After that, themes of sexual magic appear because the trial should also consist in facing the woman in the same spirit as the Tantric principle of "victory over the bad through its transformation into the good."[122] The woman is thought of as the gate through which it is possible to enter into the sphere of death or life. In the fall, sensual pleasure "became the magnet that draws man toward woman, not for the conquest of life (which equals God), but for the conquest of death (which equals Satan), and Eve . . . became the battle field of the struggle between life and death."[123] At the decisive point of this trial, man sees his "bride" again and is invited to immerse himself in her, the female, once more, not in order to enter into the realm of death and becoming, but in order to leave that realm and maintain awareness of his own being instead of dissolving. In this context the woman is presented as the *Ianua Coeli*, or Gateway to Heaven, and as the essential instrument for freedom. From the end of the descending phase (six), the victorious male next finds himself reprojected to the starting point of the cosmic clock's cycle, freed from matter and consecrated King. This is the rite of the "second wedding," which coincides with that of the formation of the Messiah.[124]

We are dealing here not with mere abstract symbols but rather with their arousal within the framework of actual sexual procedures. As regards the technical side of these procedures, once more we find the prohibition against emission of the seed in coitus. Naglowska distinguished two operations, and the first is indeed characterized by this procedure. "He who goes through the trial must remain dry until the end, for it is written, 'Do not let your holy force be crystallized in a deadly liquid.' " Mention is made of "a danger of death [most likely not physical] in the case of failure." She adds that in this first phase "the woman is offered without knowledge for the diabolical operation."[125] Leaving aside the "diabolical," it seems that the end pursued here remains essentially the same as that of Taoism, namely a preliminary "strengthening of the *yang*" inasmuch as the dissolving amalgamation with the woman is linked to a further rite, a successive and separate phase or initiation. In this second operation the man "sacrifices himself and accepts throughout the whole of his being, from top to bottom, the fulminating penetration of the dazzling woman at the sublime moment of holy coitus, and therefore (unlike what happens in the first rite) the woman will remain awake. The man leaves this trial shaken in his reason and is then the sublime madman of the secret doctrines. Then he recovers his balance and becomes a new man."[126] If we are to make sense of this, the sleeping or wide-awake being of the woman in the two successive operations should perhaps be understood not in a literal sense but as referring to whether or not the "naked Diana," the transcendent woman, is aroused in her; and the "being shaken in his reason" might be the same as the "killing of the *manas*" in yoga. Naglowska does not discuss the details of this second rite with the awakened woman. Her premise that in the act of life of the second rite "the vibrations should not give the woman a localized pleasure because pleasure belongs to the man and not to the woman" is both banal and inverted, for according to authentic traditional sources, it is rather the man who should avoid this localization of the feeling, since his very constitution makes him much more prone to it than the woman. It is he who must be careful not to yield to desire for bodily pleasure. Perhaps what is said about "mystical pleasure" is more fitting: "Imagine a caress without any contact, a warmth that has nothing of the flesh about it, a multiple kiss that is not placed on any part."[127] Everything else in the book is confused and set forth within the fantastic picture of the rite of "initiatory hanging" which one must undergo before passing on to the second operation where the woman is awake. In this regard Naglowska wrote, "Only he who has surpassed the rite can usefully be united to an adequately trained woman because, knowing the unspeakable happiness of satanic pleasure, he cannot drown himself in the flesh of a woman, and if he performs the rite of the earth with his wife, he will do so to enrich himself and not to lessen himself."[128] Even though it may not seem so, there is something more here than mere fantasy (quite apart from the inevitable "satanic," which is absolutely out of place here). We might think of an equivalent operation that seems to have been practiced in certain Japanese Zen schools, in which the trauma of a semiasphyxia acts as a means to stretch the limits of conditioned awareness under a given circumstance. If the possession of a principle that in its own way is extranatural (like that which is normally received through initiation) is ensured, the risks of failure of the sexual practice are minimized. Perhaps it is also possible to establish a relationship between the "satanic pleasure" mentioned and the ecstatic pleasure, or *sahaja-sukha*, of Tantrism. This experience hinders the appearance of the normal paroxysmal form of bodily pleasure. But all of this might only be a fanciful description of the rite. B. Anel Kham has indicated that some journalists attended a ceremony in Paris in which some girls intended for use in the "satanic operation" were consecrated, which show the practical application of Naglowska's teachings.[129]

The other source we referred to concerns the Englishman Aleister Crowley, who died in 1947 after a very troubled and adventurous existence. Mystification and an ostentatious Satanism played an even greater part in his behavior than in Naglowska's. (Crowley liked to be called the Great Beast 666.) We have evidence of several people not easily influenced that the man possessed a real force. It is hard to establish to what extent certain results he produced were due to objective procedures or how far those results may have had as their fundamental condition the special and very personal constitution and force of Crowley.

Crowley made a collection of "initiations"; he may have had authentic contacts with a kind of Arabic yogi, Soliman ben Aifha, and with two Hindu exponents of the Tantric Way of the Left Hand, Brima Sen Pratab and Sri Agamya Paramhamsa.[130] Apart from satanic, "heathen," and deliberately scandalizing elements, the so-called Law of the Telema that Crowley espoused was in fact inspired by Tantrism.

Its password was "Love is the Law, love under will." "Love" here meant sexual love essentially, and the aim was to discover one's own true nature through special erotic experiences.[131] A religion of happiness and pleasure was sketched out to which was added a higher idea of death, as a trial and initiation.[132] The "love-death" complex is presented again according to values proper to the path of magical Venus. Crowley also spoke of poisons to be transformed into nourishment;[133] he directed men to seek those things which were poisons for them, even very strong poisons, in order to assimilate them through love, with the aim of destroying the "complexes" (most likely, the conditional qualities) of their own nature.[134] In general, the purpose was to overcome the tension of the Dyad by the marriage of opposites and to integrate one's own nature continuously by means of "new mates" on every plane of being. (This is reminiscent of the hyperphysical unions mentioned by Paracelsus and Kremmerz.)[135] Crowley wrote that we take different and opposed things and compel them to unite in one single thing; participation in this union is ecstatic because the lower element is dissolved in the higher. Every union should be intended to dissolve a more material complex and to create a more sublimated one; and this is the way of love, which rises from ecstasy to ecstasy.[136] Crowley's principle that the greater the polarity, the more savage the force of the magnetism and the quantity of energy freed through coitus, seems to have a specific application in the use of sex, for in the same passage he mentions the negative condition constituted by becoming accustomed to a particular woman.[137]

Crowley indicated both women and drugs as the means to cause openings or breakages of ordinary consciousness and to enter into real or evocatory relationships with supersensual beings. Symonds, Crowley's biographer, wrote, "Sex became for him the means to reach God. It was his vehicle of consecration. . . . He carried out the sexual act not to obtain emotional relief nor for procreative ends, but to start a new current, to renew his force. . . . In his eyes every sexual act was a sacred magical act, a sacrament. A prolonged orgy in honor of the great god Pan. All in due order and proportion, very admirable." "Opus" was the word Crowley used for the sexual act, referring to the Hermetic idea of the "Great Opera," of which he made that act a part. At the peak of this "Opus," or erotic experience, by attaining to the rupture of level, he sometimes found himself face to face with the gods. "Operation prolonged and intense; orgasm multiple . . . the Gods clearly visualized and alive."[138]

The rituals of sexual magic were among the most secret of the Ordo Templi Orientis (OTO) organization of which Crowley was a head. They are described in a manuscript entitled "Agape. Liber C: The Book of the Sangraal," which we have been unable to obtain, so we cannot ascertain whether there was a likeness between the Tantric techniques and Crowley's teachings and experience. The system of Tantric *aropa*, evocation of real supersensual presences, seems however, to have been part of it. In fact, we read, "She knows and loves God in me, not the man; therefore she has conquered the great enemy which hides behind its cloud of toxic gas, illusion" (the illusion of individual identity). In his turn, for Crowley this was a question of understanding what lives behind the mortal and physical appearances of woman and of reaching a great Goddess, strange, perverse, hungry, and implacable. He said that it was to possess this Goddess that he used one woman or another.[139] What he said about every woman having her own particular zone of sensitivity on which it is necessary to concentrate may be technically of value, for, said Crowley, our only duty and pleasure must be to prolong it; we should not pay any attention if the woman asks for mercy, and we must repress any struggling firmly but gently; above all we should remember that, if she is capable of moving a limb afterward for some hours, she will despise us. However, he specified that all brutality must be avoided unless the woman herself, being a vulgar type, should desire it. But even then the brutality should be apparent rather than actual.[140]

It is problematical that, on the one hand, Crowley had children while, on the other hand, he spoke of sex-magic in a homosexual context.[141] Crowley claimed that in fertilizing his female companions he had not acted as an inititate; otherwise there would be an obvious contrast with the system of initiatory coitus, which exclude a procreative outcome. The suspicion arises that Crowley's homosexual sex-magic was not so much a real technique but rather due to an inborn personal disposition, by means of which the orgasm of coitus (as also the effect of drugs) led to openings in consciousness toward the supersensual. Then something similar, an exceptional, personal, psychic predisposition, must be presupposed in his female companions. Even a use of these companions as lucid and powerful mediums, which reminds us of practices found in Cagliostro and Kremmerz, seems to have been considered; indeed, mention is made of women in whom an almost frenzied erotic condition gave way, all of a sudden and without any apparent sign, to a deep calm that was hard to distinguish from a prophetic trance, in which they began to describe their visions.[142]

But the technique most often mentioned was that of excess; through pain or pleasure, sex or intoxication, it was necessary to attain a condition of exhaustion taken to the extreme limit compatible with survival.[143] The magical dagger, used together with all the traditional paraphernalia (signs, invocatory formulas, pentacles, cloaks, and so on), symbolized the readiness to sacrifice all.[144] In the secret ritual of the OTO, called *De arte magica*, we find in article XV a reference to a "death in orgasm," called *mors justi*.[145] The limit of exhaustion or frenzy and intoxication is also indicated as the moment of magical clear-headedness, of powerful trance in man or woman.

The idea that the magic of sex, if it is not to lead to ruin and perdition, presupposes a special strengthening of the will and a practice of asceticism of a suitable kind was acknowledged by Crowley, who said that he had faced everything, even the things most repugnant to his own nature, and had challenged the power of drugs that could have altered the fate of his own life and had a severe effect on his body. He had dominated every habit of his spirit and set himself a code of ethics more strict than any other in the world, although he possessed absolute freedom in respect of every code of conduct.[146] But even though Crowley ended his life at seventy-two with all his faculties intact, yet we hear of others he had contact with, particularly women, who ended in mental institutions or were driven to killing themselves; and this confirms what secret tradition has taught of the dangers of the Left Hand path.

Especially through the use of drugs (but we might say that the same applies to his use of women) Crowley saw, however, the danger of creating addiction. He said that drugs should only be the food of "strong and royal men."[147] But there remains the possibility that such men cannot deprive themselves of that food; even if we use drugs as a means to attain contacts with the supersensual, the bondage of the addict can still occur.[148] The fact that the effects of drugs on Crowley, and perhaps on some of his followers, were most likely the same as those of the "holy potions" of ancient times or of the mixtures used in the experiences of the Sabbat was due not only to the ritual fact and a possible link with some surviving initiatory chain but also to his special personal constitution.

The Presuppositions of Operative Sexual Magic

It remains only to say something about sexual magic in a proper or operative sense, namely the ability to act on other people or on one's surroundings on other bases than physical laws and material or psychological determinisms. Here we shall leave unanswered the question whether such an ability is real or not. We shall only examine the presuppositions that exist in the idea that so many people have acknowledged the reality of that ability when the techniques used are based on sex.

From the metaphysical point of view, if it is true that the mystery of the Three or the reintegration of the single being in the way conditioned by the Dyad tends to be fulfilled through eros, then it requires only one step further to the theory of magical power. What paralyzes man in this regard is his split existentialism. The separation of the sexes is a special method of manifestation of the Dyad principle, which also conditions the division between spirit and nature, ego and nonego. If there exists a metaphysical relationship or coincidence—and we have seen how Scotus Eriugena also recognized it—then there may equally well be a relationship between the experience of transcendence through sex and a nondual state that permits a direct and extranormal action on the nonego, on the outer web of events. Let us recall that in the classical and Platonic version of the myth of the original hermaphrodite, a power such that it struck fear into the gods was attributed to that being before it was split.

That is the position from the metaphysical point of view. From the psychic point of view, the traditions of magic agree that every effective action in extranormal terms has as its premise a state of exaltation, of "mania," of active ecstasy or intoxication that releases the imagination from its physical conditional bonds and brings the ego into contact with Paracelsus' "Light of Nature," the psychic substratum of reality where every image or word formed should acquire an objective power. Now, if eros leads in a natural way to such a state of exaltation, we can understand the move from mystical or initiatory sexual excitement to magical sexual excitement. The ability of eros to produce exceptional power or vitality in the imagination is well known even in the profane sphere, as we said earlier. A "living magical fantasy" is active in all love in a certain way and to a certain degree; and so we should not be surprised that a particular magical technique has employed sex as its means.

Existing documents relating to this subject are scarce. Degraded forms or forms belonging to witchcraft, such as found among primitive peoples, are not of much interest here. Some general references can be found in Hindu Tantrism. Here it is a matter of the *chakra* or chains (literally, wheels) consisting of couples who perform ritual coitus together in a circular formation. In the middle of the circle is the "lord of the wheel" or *chakreshvara* together with his companion, who officiates and directs the collective operation. An adept who has had a perfect initiation is needed to perform this function. Overall, this is a collective and partly orgiastic evocation of the Goddess as the latent force in the group, a force now aroused through the realization of acts and visualization of images by the individual pairs until a fluidic or "psychic" vortex is created and used in the operation. A similar method performed for the benefit of others is used in professional magic rites. Tantric *chakra* have been convened by princes for special profane purposes, such as propitiation of success in war.[149]

We have no details about the sexual procedure followed in such contexts. Therefore, we do not know whether coitus took its natural course here as in promiscuous orgiastic rites, or whether the practice of retention was followed as in initiatory rites. A third possibility is that only the leader of the chain fulfilled the important operations with the woman reserved for him, as was the case in operations of collective magic in general.

Something further about the inner conditions of sexual magic can be inferred from practices of the same type that have gone on even in modern times and our own civilization. In this regard, an indicative document is the book *Magia sexualis* by Paschal Beverly Randolph.[150] Randolph was an enigmatic figure, a writer and occultist of the late nineteenth century. He first joined the Hermetic Brotherhood of Luxor, an initiatory organization with its headquarters in Boston; in about 1870 he set up his own center, which he called the Eulis Brotherhood. The book mentioned above appears to have been written after his death, and based on personal notes of those belonging to the center.

Randolph began by acknowledging that sex is the main and greatest magical force in nature. And when he said that "all force and powers arise from the womanhood of God,"[151] we meet again in him the well-known metaphysical theory of the Shakti. One particular teaching concerns the inverted polarity of the two sexes: man and woman respectively constitute the positive and negative pole on the material and bodily plane, but "on the mental plane, woman is the active and man the negative pole." It was also specified that, if man's sex organ is positive and woman's is negative, the opposite is the case with the "organ of mental manifestations" located in the head.[152] This agrees with De Guaita, but in Randolph's case the teaching was rather distorted and should be related to what we said about the passivity or negative polarization proper to man when he finds himself in a state of strong desire, and about the positive nature of woman where her natural subtle, attractive, mighty, and "nonactive" power is under consideration. Bearing this in mind, in a book already cited[153] the inversion of polarity and the establishment of a positive polarization in man with respect to woman on the spiritual and subtle plane were indicated as an indispensable presupposition for initiatory coitus. To talk of the head as the organ of "mental manifestations," as Randolph did, recalls the jargon of psychology. It is in no way true that man is polarized negatively or woman positively and actively; rather the opposite is true. The inversion and positivization mentioned as regards male negative polarity (a mutation that we have already linked to the symbolism of the inverted coitus) concern deeper layers of being; they are the same in Far Eastern terms as the laying open of the pure *yang*, and it is necessary to arrive at this stage if one is to realize in its occult sense the precept *"Non des mulieri potestatem animae tuae"* (Give not power over your soul to a woman) at the point when her body is being possessed. Although Randolph did not speak of this condition, the qualities that he declared necessary for sexual magic imply it.

The first of such qualities is called *volancie* (exercise of the will) in French and is linked to the ability to control oneself under any circumstances, to "will" in a steadfast and constant way. According to Randolph, "an analogy can be found in the irresistible force of lightning, which breaks and burns but does not tire." "A disciple should develop in himself this elementary force, volancie, which is passive, because it obeys the command of the mind, and is cold because it is free from every passion."[154]

The second quality, which acts as a positive counterpart, is "decretism," the "dictatorial quality or positive power of mankind without which no true good or evil can be done," "the ability to give peremptory orders (beginning with oneself) calmly and confidently without nursing any doubts about the attainment of the desired effect." We have already seen that in Indo-Tibetan Tantrism the male principle is referred to as the *vajra*, a word that also means scepter. To exercise this faculty, "the imagination must be free of every other preoccupation and no emotion should affect the given order."[155]

The third requisite ability is "posism," which consists of attitudes, gestures, or postures of the body that are embodiments, plastic expressions, or signs of a given thought. Apart from the invention of words and certain exaggerations, we are here dealing with what, in general, forms the foundation of ritual and what the yoga doctrine expresses in the *asana* and *mudra*, special postures of body and limbs that possess a symbolic value. They also act as a closure of circuits for some currents of subtle energy in the organism. The premise is that the "posed" gesture is "realized" or lived in its significance, like an incipient assumption of a concrete form of the latter.[156]

This eventually leads to a quality that Randolph named "tiroclerism": the power to evoke and formulate clear, steady images with the inner sight.

We shall not dwell in detail on the magic of scents, sounds, and colors with their astrological correspondences, which Randolph provides without citing his sources. Randolph lists the following aims that can be pursued with sex-magic operations: (1) realization of a project, desire, or precise order; (2) provocation of supersensual visions (as in some of the operations in which Crowley took part); (3) regeneration of vital energy and strengthening of "magnetic power" (which could correspond to one of the purposes of Taoist practices); (4) production of an influence to subject a woman to a man or a man to a woman; (5) liberation of "charges" of psychic and fluidic force to saturate certain objects.

He gives few details about the methods of sexual union to pursue these purposes, and the little information we do find is not at all convincing. We are told that "lust and pleasure should not be the main object."[157] However, it is hard to imagine how in such a context it is possible to seek, beyond pleasure, the "union of souls," insofar as a concrete purpose is pursued in which the woman is used as an instrument. At best, we think there could be a fluidic amalgamation. He speaks of coitus as a "prayer" whose object is clearly formulated and imagined; but if volancie and decretism[158] are activated, the choice of the word "prayer" seems strange to us. Besides this, it would seem decisive in coitus that one should "plunge in" and feel oneself carried on high "at the moment when, with all the forces united, one touches the root of the opposite sex." At this point, the magical act should be introduced. "It is best if the man and woman imagine the same object or desire the same thing, but the prayer of only one of the two is effective just the same, because in the spasm of love it transports the creative power of the other." For the "prayer" to be effective, "the paroxysm of both is necessary. It is also necessary that the woman's orgasm should coincide with the man's emission, for only in this way will the magic be fulfilled."[159] There is explicit mention of the moment "when the man's seed passes into the woman's body and is accepted by her." Even if one guards against the occurrence, at that moment, of "carnal passion," of "bestial instinct," which is almost "suicide for the man,"[160] still, these last instructions are in contrast with most of the genuine esoteric teachings we have referred to earlier. As we have seen, in those teachings, emission during sexual orgasm is deemed an interruption of the sensual possibilities and a hazardous yielding.

To accept as genuine Randolph's instructions, we must assume the possibility that the magic force of the seed, the *virya*, can be separated from its physical substance. After the force has been aroused through the woman's embrace, the insertion of will at the liminal point of orgasm would lead to the separation, to the release and vibration of the magical male force at the level of the preestablished operation; the seed emitted into the woman and held by her flesh would then be only a lifeless substance, devoid of its hyperbiological counterpart. In essence, the power to create would be diverted from the sacred plane of generation (as in ritual assumptions of the procreative conjugal act, which are known to creationist religions, such as Islam) toward a magical plane at the very point when the unhindered, biological, ejaculative determinism occurs. Furthermore, we might think of the extreme dynamic and vitalizing power that the imagination could have at such a moment if a man were to remain aware of himself and able to make use of it. Only thus is Randolph's system of coitus understandable. Moreover, the state of union and simultaneous erotic crisis in the man and woman can perhaps be interpreted in the sense of a creative state rather than on the physical lack of common sexual union. Indeed, we know that such a condition is not required for fecundation; a frigid or raped woman may be impregnated, and biology tells us that the fecundated penetration of the spermatozoon into the ovum can happen mechanically even many hours after the orgasm of the couple, not to mention through artificial insemination.

Randolph outlines some special forms or positions in coitus to suit the specific purposes set by the magical operation; it is most likely here that posism came into play. These remnants of ancient secret traditions surviving to our own day seem to confirm our hypothesis that originally certain coital positions mentioned in profane erotic literature may have had a ritual or even magical significance.

Operations of sexual magic require very special training and almost an internal separation because, on the one hand, there must be a process of dissolution and ecstatic amalgamation with the woman which engages the whole of one's being (this being the condition for attainment of the nondual state or rather the premise for the operation's effectiveness), and on the other hand, a second ego must be present and alert which is occupied with entirely different things and fixed on the image corresponding to the purpose and object of the "magical prayer."

Randolph prescribes a period of seven days' preparation for some purposes, and this period was to be followed by an operative period of forty days, during which the rite was performed every three days.[161] Suitable surroundings had to be prepared. The woman had to sleep in her own room; she was only to be seen when a state of magnetic vibration was aroused in both partners. After each operation, the woman should depart without speaking, which emphasizes her merely instrumental part.

To conclude, Randolph warns against "incubi and succubi, which reflect your vices and hidden desires"; for it is possible to be irrevocably enslaved by them.[162] We found a similar warning in Kremmerz, and we have heard others speak of "tacitly established pacts." The greater danger, however, has no real relationship to "vices and desires"; rather, it concerns the inherent danger when the elementary force of sex is stripped bare and objectified in one or another of its polarizations. Passivity in the participant entails the possibility of obsession and the destruction of his own personality or "soul" in an almost theological sense, for here states of being are entered into or aroused which are much deeper than those experienced when a man "goes mad" about a woman in profane love (or a woman about a man) and goes forth to his ruin or death for her (or him).

Conclusion

Sex is the "greatest magical force in nature"; an impulse acts in it which suggests the mystery of the One, even when almost everything in the relationship between man and woman deteriorates into animal embraces and is exhausted and dispersed in a faded idealizing sentimentality or in the habitual routine of socially acceptable conjugal relations. The metaphysics of sex survives in the very cases where, in looking at wretched mankind and the vulgarity of infinite lovers of infinite races—endless masks and individuations of the Absolute Man seeking the Absolute Woman in a turn of the circle of animal generation—it is hard to overcome a feeling of disgust and revolt and the temptation to accept the biological and physical theory which says that human sexuality springs from the life of instincts and mere animality. However, if any reflection of a transcendence actually experienced unintentionally takes form in ordinary existence, it does so through sex and, in the case of the common man, through sex alone. Not those who busy themselves with speculations, with social or "spiritual" intellectual activities, but only those who raise themselves as high as heroic or ascetic experience, go further into the beyond. But for ordinary mankind it is sex alone which, even if only in the rapture, illusion, or obscure trauma of an instant, leads to some opening through and beyond the conditionalities of merely individual existence. This is the true foundation of the importance that love and sex have and will always have in human life, an importance unmatched by any other impulse.

With those words we can end this investigation. We are well aware of its defects, particularly as regards the phenomenology of normal and "abnormal" profane sexual love, about which only a suitably oriented specialist—a psychiatrist, neurologist, or gynecologist —could have gathered richer material to corroborate many things that we have only been able to mention briefly in these pages. Nevertheless, we believe that the main purpose we set for ourselves has been achieved, that is, to give the sense of the whole, including the metaphysical and hyperphysical dimensions within which is integrated everything normally known as love and sex when their most profound aspect is meant.

To reach such a point we have also had to go forward into two unusual fields, that of liminal experiences that many people will be tempted to exclude from the "sane" and "normal" course of every erotic experience, and that of secret teachings, myths, and traditions of the cults and rites of civilizations far from us in space or time. It is only from this whole that we have been able to gather the elements needed to explain a part by the whole and to draw from the higher the key for understanding the lower. Thus the consideration of those two fields, and especially of the second, has played an important part within the limits of our work, and we have advanced into them without worrying about any impression of strangeness or perhaps even of extravagance and eccentricity which a given type of reader may have sustained from them.

In actual fact, on the subject of that which presents an apparently "abnormal" character, we criticized in the Introduction of this book the mistake of deeming the "normal" to be that which we find in most cases. Instead, we believe to be "normal" in the strictest sense of the word that which is typical, and that has nothing to do with quantity or great frequency of occurrence, because the true norm is generally met with very seldom. In this same sense, a fully healthy and well-shaped man who has all the morphological features of the ideal type is empirically an exceptional apparition, but is not for that reason "abnormal"; instead, he is the very person to give evidence of normality. The same idea is true for aspects of eros, love, and sexuality, which, even when they are thought to be possible, will nowadays seem to most people abnormal and exceptional and therefore such that in practice they should not be taken into account. Besides, in a consideration of a higher category, the criteria may be inverted; the abnormal (the typical) is the normal, while the normal (which we usually find in most cases) is the abnormal.

This consideration is particularly applicable when the universally diffused forms of the sexuality of today are compared with different horizons resulting from the study of other times and other civilizations. Modern man is inclined to think that his own civilization is normal, or rather that the behavior by which this civilization is most characterized is normal. He rarely doubts that every other civilization and every different form that may have existed in the past should be measured at the level of that which is familiar to him. He stays with this queer infatuation, and therefore his idea concerning the idea will be "normal" and the "real" in sex will be distorted and maimed as well. Indeed, as in every sphere of spiritual interest, so too in that of sex and love, almost everything which in our times and in the modern age in general has importance shows a regressive character. To the modern "devilry of sex" which we mentioned in the Introduction there correspond, in general, forms of a sensuality made primitive, or bordering on neurosis and the most banal depravity. The outcome is the level of the sexological, erotic, or crypto-pornographic literature of our times, and innumerable works intended to vulgarize and give guidance in sexual life. Now, the displacement and broadening of outlook, to which we sought to contribute in our other works dealing with other subjects, were the aim of this present investigation in one of its main aspects and specifically with regard to the field of eros and sex. Just as the traditional world and that part of it which has been preserved up to comparatively recent times in non-Western civilizations knew an image of man which, by not being restricted to materialism, "psychology," and physiology, was infinitely more complete than the modern image, so in the world, sex was considered integrally and was studied and aroused in its higher values and capabilities as well. And a real understanding of the forms to which sex is limited today and, in general, of the forms available to the great majority of less differentiated human types, being forms that we may well call the by-products of sex, can be achieved only by recovering the categories, knowledge, and experience of that different world.

These, therefore, are the perspectives that this treatise wishes to open up by simply proposing a broadening of knowledge. Our purpose here was to show that what we are accustomed to seeing and what, almost without exception, are to be found around us so often that they seem to be normal and evident are not the whole story, and that the present sexological theories, especially those influenced by evolutionistic biology or fixed psychoanalytical ideas, do not even touch upon the most important matters. It would already be a great step forward if the mention of the metaphysics of sex no longer seemed to a reader to be eccentric. Moreover, various things we have said could be of service to a more highly qualified and differentiated person in clearing up his own experiences and problems. Concerning the sphere of the sexual *sacrum* and everything that we examined, particularly in the last chapter relating to secret teachings, the benefit will perhaps be the idea that a like category of things has its own possibility, as witnessed in traditions that often go back over several hundred years and are in agreement with each other. Although we have cited instances of prolongations of such traditions down to our own times, almost all of our contemporaries will be unable to do anything more than just note the fact; and perhaps the same is true for the border areas of profane eros itself, on which we have often dwelt. Man now is different, our environment is different, and in practice we can only count on exceptional cases. However, as we said at the beginning when we repeated what we had written on various other occasions and in other contexts about the purpose of making known one or another side of the nonmodern concept of life and of the corresponding behavior, it is quite an achievement just to have an idea of the size of the gap involved so that we can understand where we have arrived today. With regard also to sex, the rediscovery of its primary and deepest meaning and the employment of its highest capabilities depend on the possibility of the reintegration of modern man and on his arising once more and betaking himself beyond the psychic and spiritual lowlands into which he has been led by the mirages of his material civilization, for in this lowlands the meaning of being truly a man or woman is doomed to vanish. Sex will only serve to take him still further downward; furthermore, even apart from what concerns the masses, sex, being reduced to its content of mere sensation, will only be the misleading, obscure, and desperate alleviation of the existential disgust and anguish of him who has stumbled into a blind alley.

Notes

Introduction

1. S. Péladan, *La Science de l'amour*, Paris, 1911, p. 102.

2. C. Mauclair, *La Magie de l'amour*.

3. H. Ellis, *Studies in the Psychology of Sex*, vol. 3, Philadelphia, 1909, p. 7.

4. L. T. Woodward has also rightly brought to light a form of psychological sadism in those women of today who "make a great show of their bodies but apply a symbolic placard bearing the words 'Do not touch.'" Sexual tormentresses of this kind are found everywhere: the girl who wears a minute bikini, the married woman with a provocatively low neckline, the young woman who walks along the street wiggling her hips in very tight pants or in a miniskirt that leaves more than half of her thighs exposed and who wants to be looked at but not touched—all of these types are capable of showing anger.

5. J. Evola, *Rivolto contro il mondo moderno*, Milan, pp.422–423. Comment on J. J. Bachofen, *Le Madri e la virilità olimpica*, Milan, 1949, p. 14 ff. Another sign of the arrival of the Dark Age is that "men become the subjects of women and slaves of pleasure and oppressors of their friends, teachers, and anyone who deserves respect" (*Mahanirvana-tantra*, IV, 52).

Chapter 1: Eros and Sexual Love

1. P. Bourget, *Physiologie de l'amour moderne*, Paris. 1890. As a corollary (ibid.): "The lover who seeks in love something besides love, ranging from interest to esteem, is not a lover."

2. H. T. Moore, *D. H. Lawrence's Letters to Bertrand Russell*, ed. Gotham Book Mart, especially the letter of 8 December 1915.

3. Péladan, *La Science de l'amour* (The Science of Love), p. 210.

4. E. Morselli, *Sessualità umana* (Human Sexuality), Milan, 1944.

5. L. Klages, *Vom kosmogonischen Eros* (Of Eros the World-Begetter).

6. An exception is the case where, at a sacred celebration of sexual

unions in ancient civilizations, the purpose was a desired and conscious pregnancy sometimes linked to symbolic structures and evocatory formulae (in India and the Islamic world, for example). However, even in such cases in the classical world itself a distinction was made not only between unions intended for this purpose and other unions but even between the women to be used for the purpose in question. In fact, the following words have been attributed to Demosthenes in his oration against Neera: "We have hetaerae for lust, concubines for the daily care of our bodies, and wives to bear legitimate children and to guard the home faithfully."

7. V. Solovieff, *Le Sens de l'amour*, Paris, 1946, pp. 7–8, 9, 10–11.
8. A. Joussain, *Les Passions humaines*, Paris, 1928, pp. 171–172. Among other things, sterility has very frequently been found in hypersexual women, even on the most crudely physiological plane; and the analysis of the substance that prevents pregnancy in them during coitus has recently been the basis of one of the varieties of antifecundative seroprophylaxis (cf. A. Cucco, *L'Amplesso e la frode* (Coitus and Deception), Rome, 1958, p. 573 ff.).
9. Solovieff, p. 11.
10. A. Schopenhauer, *Die Welt als Wille und Vorstellung*, II, chap. 4, ed. Cotta, Berlin-Stuttgart, VI, pp. 88–89.
11. Ibid., pp. 90 ff., 96.
12. H. Malraux puts into the mouth of one of his characters the following words: "We always need a poison. This country [China] has opium. Islam has hashish, the West has woman. . . . Love is perhaps the means which the West uses in preference."
13. S. Freud, *Jenseits des Lustprinzips*, Leipzig-Vienna, 1921.
14. P. Piobb, *Venus, la déesse magique de la chair*, Paris, 1909.
15. Ch. S. Féré, *L'Instinct sexuel*, Paris, 1865, p. 6.
16. This takes place particularly in those who do not dream in black and white, as most people do, but dream in color.
17. It has also been verified that in certain animals hormone saturation, which some people believe to be a cause of sexual excitement, is produced only at the moment of coitus. Cf. A. Hesnard, *Manuel de sexologie*, Paris, 1951.
18. L. Pin, *Psicologia dell'amore*, Milan, 1944, p. 145. "Feeling rises at times to such a height that it becomes suffering and indeed has an inhibiting effect on sexual processes."
19. H. Ellis, *Studies in the Psychology of Sex*, III, Philadelphia, 1908, p. 7. Cf. Hesnard, p. 13: "We can say that in its essential aspect in man, that is, in its psychic aspect, sexuality can have a consid-

erable development and can make almost no use at all of the collaboration of the genital system."

20. So it is not just a joke when an American girl is made to say to her partner after coitus, "Do you feel better now, darling?"

21. As a translation of a reflection of the existential fact, the following words, put in the mouth of one of his characters by M. E. Remarque in *Drei Kameraden* (Düsseldorf, 1955, p. 187), can be quoted: "Now for some time I saw that I could mean something to a human being because of the sole fact that I was at his side. When this is said, it seems so simple; but if one thinks about it, one feels that it is an immense thing, limitless: a thing that can destroy you or transform you wholly. It is love and it is love for another person."

22. There are interesting comments in this respect, even as regards certain of the populations in the south of Italy in C. Levi, *Cristo si è fermato a Eboli*, Turin, 1946, p. 93. Thus it is possible to see also the ultimate foundation of the Islamic rule of purdah, the segregation of women.

23. M. Ficino, *Sopra lo amore*, ed. Levasti, VII, 7: "We rightly locate the fever of Love in the blood." Regarding this process, cf. VII, 4–7 and 10, where, however, it is necessary to leave aside the ingenuous concept of images almost materially transported from the glance of one being to another. VII, 11: In common love, understood as being normal love as opposed to platonic love, "the agony of Lovers lasts as long as the stinging [*perturbatio*] induced in the veins by the so-called evil eye." Cf. G. B. Della Porta, *Magia naturalis*, I, XV. Plato (*Phaedrus*, 251a, b) wrote of the "outflow of beauty received through the eyes," which develops and produces a "shiver, which changes into sweating and an unwonted heat." The heat in this case is to be understood in a purely physical sense and forms a part in the previously cited phenomenology of erotic "exaltation." On it is based what Kremmerz called, precisely, "fire magic".

24. G. D'Annunzio, *Il Piacere*, p. 69: "It seemed that a particle of the amorous fascination of that woman entered into him, just as a little of the virtue of a magnet enters into iron. It was truly a magnetic feeling of delight, one of those sharp and profound feelings that people almost always experience only at the beginning of love, which appear to have neither a physical nor a spiritual seat like all other feelings but a seat in a neutral element of our being, an element that I would almost say is intermediate and has an unknown nature, less simple than a soul, more subtle than a form, where passion gathers as if in a receptacle." P. 87: "The man felt her presence flow and mingle with his blood, until his blood

became her life and her blood his life." Perceptions of this kind
are most often more distinct after bodily union but can even be
destroyed if the union is carried out in a primitivistic manner. D.
H. Lawrence, in a letter (ed. by Moore): "When I unite myself to
a woman, the perception through the blood is intense,
supreme. . . . A passage takes place, I do not know exactly of
what, between her blood and mine at the moment of the union.
So even if she withdraws from me, there persists between the
two of us that way of knowing each other through the blood even
if perception through the brain is interrupted."

25. E. Lévi, *La Science des spirits*, Paris, 1865, p. 213.
26. C. Mauclair, *La Magie de l'amour*, pp. 56, 51, 52–53.
27. M. Lolli, *Sulle passioni* (About Passions), Milan, 1856.
28. Stendhal, *De l'amour*, I, 15: "In my view this word expresses the
main phenomenon of the madness which we call love." "I mean
by the word crystallization a certain fever of the imagination
which renders an object unrecognizable in general and which
makes of it a being by itself."
29. It is interesting to note that, without wishing to do so and without analyzing its range, a psychologist was brought to use this
word.
30. Pin, *Psicologia dell'amore*, p. 139; Cf. pp. 121–124, "You should
know that in the moment when I could relax, when your image
might disappear for an instant, I would not love you anymore"
(Ninon de Lenclos in B. Dangennes, *Lettres d'amour*, Paris, p.
55).
31. *Dogme et rituel de l'Haute Magie*, Italian translation, Rome, pp.
58, 84.
32. O. Weininger, *Geschlecht und Charakter*, Vienna, 1918, p. 14 ff.
33. H. Ploss and M. Bartels, *Das Weib in der Natur und Volkerkunde*,
Leipzig, 1897, I, p. 469.
34. Mention has often been made of the examples of Henry III and
Henry IV of France, who are said to have been seized by sudden
and irresistible passions for women whose intimate garments
they had smelled. In the case of Henry III, it was said that his
passion for Mary of Cleves started in this way and survived her
tragic death. Cf. R. von Kraft-Ebing, *Psychopathis Sexualis*,
Stuttgart, p. 25. When that author expressed doubts (p. 18) that
effects of this kind linked to olfactory centers could happen
"with normal individuals," he obviously identified normal individuals as being those having a very limited "subtle" sensitive-
ness. Ploss and Bartels (Vol. I, p. 467 ff.) mention the popular
belief that the smell of the body (we would say, of the being) of a

person can have an intoxicating effect on someone of the opposite sex.

35. Weininger, *Geschlecht und Charakter*, pp. 7–13.
36. Plato, *Symposium*, p. 191d.
37. Ibid.
38. *Metaphysik der Geschlechtsliebe*, p. 102.
39. Weininger, pp. 31–52.
40. A similar idea is the basis of the ancient astrological view that mutual attraction should require that at the birth of a man and woman the sun and moon change places (the former should have the sun in his sign where the latter has the moon; the sun is *yang*, whereas the moon is *yin*).
41. This also seems to be the meaning hidden in the wedding rite, according to which the husband and wife are crowned and imagined to be king and queen.
42. As regards the end-form of modern female by-products: "These ladies without sex who haunt the distinguished quarters of the great cities, full of would-be intellectual ambitions, the major prop of doctors, spiritualists, psychoanalysts and whimsical writers" (L. O'Flaherty).
43. As regards all this, cf. Evola, *Rivolta contro il mondo moderno*, p. 244 ff.
44. In Wilde's play it is necessary to leave on one side the aestheticized trimmings. But both in that play and, even more so, in Richard Strauss's opera, an atmosphere is provided which, apart from its great evocative power, has a very pregnant cosmic and analogical background; the whole is capped by the theme of the *Moon* and *Night*. Furthermore there is Salome's "Dance of the Seven Veils," to which we shall refer again later on.

In the festival of the Mahabarata a ritual copulation of a whore (*pumshchali*) with an ascetic (*brahmacharin*) used to take place regularly on the very spot consecrated for the sacrifice (cf. M. Eliade, *Yoga: immortalité et liberté*, Paris, 1954, pp. 115, 257–258). This can be related to two extreme differentiations of the female and male.
45. For the *samskara* and *vasana*, cf. Evola, *Lo Yoga della potenza*, Rome, 1968, pp. 102–105. Eliade, *Yoga*, pp. 61, 92, 103; 54 ff., 60.
46. Some rites of collective sexual magic are called *choli-marga* on the basis of the name of a kind of vestment worn by the girls employed; by choosing the garment by lot, each man chooses the woman to be used as his partner in the ceremony (references in Eliade, p. 402, and in Evola, *Lo Yoga della potenza*, as regards

the secret Tantric ritual. Cf. also farther on, p. 336 ff. Moreover, reference can be made to the intentional promiscuity practiced at certain seasonal festivals in the Bacchanalia and Saturnalia.

47. There is a certain distant analogy with the Freudian distinction between the "primary psychic process," wherein the charge of the libido is still free and fluctuating, and the "secondary psychic process," wherein the charge is linked to a given representation and is hard to detach therefrom.

48. Schopenhauer, p. 110.

49. Another outcome is the endemic use of divorces and remarriages in quick succession in "monogamous" and more distinctly "modern" civilizations, caused by the displaceability of the eros proper to the more superficial layers of a being. Instead, previous civilizations with an organic nature took greater account of what belongs to the deepest and most individuated layer of the "individual nature" as a normal rule, even setting aside the coercive force of institutions, and thus ensured, instead, a greater degree of stability in the unions of beings of the two sexes, when the system in force was not polygamous, with the various premises to which we refer later on.

50. Cf. Evola, *L'Arco e la clava*, Milan, 1968, chap. 12.

51. E. Crawley, *Mystic Rose*, New York, 1902, p. 318.

Chapter 2: The Metaphysics of Sex

1. *Symposium*, XIV–XV and particularly 189c–190c.

2. Ibid., 191c–d.

3. Ibid., 192c–d.

4. Ibid., 192d–e, Untersteiner-Candia translation.

5. Ibid., 187a.

6. Brihadaranyaka-Upanishad, IV.

7. A. Ricolfi, *Studi sui Fedeli d'Amore*, Milan, 1933, Vol. I, p. 63.

8. Texts in Evola, *Il Mistero del Graal e la tradizione ghibellina dell'Impero*, Rome, 1957, p. 92.

9. W. von Eschenbach, "Parzifal," III, 70–71.

10. Cf. Evola, *Il Mistero del Graal*, pp. 87–88.

11. In that they refer to a personage whom S. Guaita (*Le Serpent de la Genèse—Le Temple de Satan*, Paris, 1916, p. 503) has shown in a sinister light, the following expressions are meaningful for the context mentioned, within the framework of mystic eroticism: "Hear the word of Elijah: If you tremble, you are lost. You must be bold; if you are not, it means that you do not know love. Love

takes in hand, it reverses, it rolls, it breaks. Raise yourselves. Be great in your weakness! Frighten the heavens and hell; you can do it! Yea, pontiffs of Elijah, who are transformed, regenerated, transfigured on the Mount of Carmel, say with Elijah: For us damnation! For us hell! For us Satan!" Moreover, even with a Christian neoplatonist like Marsilio Ficino (*Sopra lo amore*, XI, 19), expressions such as the following are not devoid of a daemonic undertone: "Certainly, we are divided and truncated here; but then, united by Love to our idea, we become whole again; in a way which will appear, we have first loved God in things and then loved things in Him, and we honor things in God, above all so as to free ourselves; *and by loving God we have loved ourselves*." And yet again (XI, 6): "Since in this act [the lover] craves and endeavors to make himself God instead of man." Lastly, as a fortuitous convergence of ideas of a more than profane modern author (H. Barbusse, *L'Enfer*): "Desire full of the unknown, blood in the night, desire like the night, raise their shout of victory. When lovers cling to each other, they each fight for themselves and say, "I love you", they wait, they cry and suffer, and say, "We are happy"; they let each other go, already swooning, and say, "Forever!" It seems that in the depths in which they are immersed, they have stolen the fire of heaven, *like Prometheus*."

12. *Symposium*, 193a.
13. Ibid., 202d–e.
14. *Phaedrus*, 265a.
15. Ibid., 245b.
16. Ibid., 265b.
17. *Sopra lo amore*, VII, 13, 14.
18. Referring to Eros on a universal basis, Plato (*Symposium*, 202e, 203a) said, "Owing to [Eros'] work does divination of every kind go forward, as also does the art of priests charged with carrying out sacrifices and initiation ceremonies, enchantments, and all types of soothsaying and magic."
19. In this respect cf. Evola, *Rivolta contro il mondo moderno*.
20. *Vom kosmogonischen Eros*, p. 63.
21. *Symposium*, 205d–206a.
22. Ibid., 206b.
23. Ibid., 207a.
24. Ibid., 207d–208b.
25. Ibid., 207b–208b.
26. It is significant that, when talking about "temporal eternity" (that within the species), Schopenhauer uses precisely the image of fallen leaves, taken from Homer (*qualis foliarum generatio, talis*

et hominun—as is the generation of leaves, so also is the procreation of men), which J. J. Bachofen (*Das Mutterrecht*, Basel, 1897) rightly put as the basis of the physicomaternal and chthonic concept of ancient Mediterranean civilizations.

27. *Symposium*, 209e.
28. Cf. Mauclair, p. 63: "What is genealogical descent other than projecting into a new being the same desire for the infinite which the new being will feel in his turn when he is grown up?" Moreover, it is only in the best of cases that he will feel it, even dimly, as Plato said (*Phaedrus*, 255d): "He loves and knows not whom he loves; he knows not even what his feelings are; . . . nor is he aware that in a lover he is looking at himself, as if in a looking glass."
29. Kierkegaard, *In vino veritas*, Italian translation, Lanciano, 1910, pp. 52, 53, 55.
30. If E. Carpenter (*Love's Coming-of-Age*, Manchester, 1896, p. 18) is right when he declares that the primary aim of love is to tend toward unity, yet he is only partly correct when he says that creation on a physical plane, that is, procreation, is an effect of the state of intimate union in coitus, the state that arouses the creative power. The possibility that a child can be conceived by a raped woman without her having had any pleasure at all, and also, to take an extreme case, the possibility of artificial insemination show instead that the generative fact can be wholly separate from the state of ecstatic union in coitus. The idea put forward by Carpenter only remains true where there are special applications to sexual magic (cf. chapter 6 of the present work).
31. C. Michelstaedter, *La Persuasione e la retorica*, Florence, 1922, p. 88.
32. R. de Gourmont, *La Physique de l'amour*, Paris, 1912, p. 120, "The sexual inventions of mankind are almost all prior or external to man. There is not one of them of which the model, even perfected, is not provided for him by animals, by the most lowly animals." P. 141: "There is no [human] lust which has not got its type in nature in terms of normality," that is, which does not appear as a way of being, spontaneous and regular, for given species of animals. De Gourmont, of course, uses all the likenesses he compares in a reverse sense; he brings human eros into the general whole of animal eros.
33. To this context can be referred the words of the Koran, LXIV, 14: "Oh ye who believe, verily there is an enemy for thee in your wives and children; take heed of them."
34. *Symposium*, 180d–e.
35. Ibid., 209d–e.
36. Diogenes Laertes, VI, II, 29.

37. *Symposium*, 210a–212a.
38. *Phaedrus*, 248–250.
39. Ibid., 248, 254a.
40. Ibid., 250e.
41. Ibid., 238b–c.
42. *Sopra lo amore*, VII, 15; I, 3.
43. Ibid., I, 3. A curious idea in Ficino (VI, 12), which here follows Plato (cf. *Symposium*, 181c), is the belief that homosexual love for the epheboi or adolescents is closer to love inspired by pure beauty and Aphrodite Urania than the eros aroused by a woman, because in the latter case a person would be excited more strongly by the sexual feeling of the love act; a belief as if homosexual love normally did not have a carnal development, whereas the speech of Alcibiades in the *Symposium* (214 ff.) shows almost too obviously how little "platonic" the Hellenic love for youths in fact was. We return to this question in the appendix to this chapter. Plotinus (*Enn.*, III) instead deems homosexual loves to be shameful and abnormal, like diseases of degenerate persons "which do not arise from the essence of being and are not the outcome of the development thereof."
44. As far as we are aware, the only case is the *nazar ila-l-mord* of certain Arab initiatory circles, which takes up again the theme of the platonic love of the *Phaedrus* based on the beauty embodied in the epheboi and which justifies itself with the following words of the Prophet; "I saw my Lord in the guise of a beardless youth."
45. Plotinus, *Enn*, I, VI, 3; VI, 5.
46. Stendhal (*De l'amour*, XX), after having stated that love-passion is greater than love of beauty, comments that perhaps men who cannot experience love-passion are those who feel most warmly the effect of beauty; at least this is the strongest impression they can sustain from a woman.
47. In a different civilization, even if we wish to consider simple presentiments of transcendence rather than profound realizations able to resolve a crushed and tormented existentiality, it is a fact that such presentiments will be propitiated not so much by the beauty of a woman or ephebos or of some work of art or human institution but rather by the contemplation of that which in nature reflects that transcendence in some way in terms of an elementary state, of an overstepping of boundaries and of an immensity far from human dimensions.
48. G. Bruno, *Degli eroici furori*, Proemio, ed. Universale, pp. 6–7.
49. Ibid., p. 8.
50. Ibid., II, 5.
51. A particular outcome of the theory of love as being "desire of

beauty" is that, as only the eyes can enjoy bodily beauty, every other sense apart from sight should be shut out from eros and be relegated to the sphere of bestial love. Ficino (op. cit., II, 8) writes: "The lust of touching is not a part of love nor a tenderness of loving but is a kind of lewdness and disorder of servile man." If we have acknowledged the essential part played by a look in the magic of sex, yet it is also without doubt the fluidic nourishment which both touching and smelling provide that develops and strengthens the subtle condition of eros.

52. Plotinus, *Enn.* I, v, I.

53. *Symposium*, 203b–c.

54. Ibid., 203c–204a.

55. Desire or thirst, as a metaphysical substratum of finite existence (*tahna* in Buddhism, to be compared with the *concupiscentia originalis* of the Catholic theologians) is, of course, distinct from desire in a specific, sexual sense, which is only a particular manifestation of the former.

56. Plotinus, *Enn.*, III, v, 2.

57. Ibid., III, v, 7.

58. For everything that follows, cf. Evola, *Lo Yoga della potenza*, p. 301 ff.

59. On a profane level, compare the words of H. Bergson, (*L'évolution créatrice*, Paris, 1932, p. 14): "Individuality harbors within itself its own enemy. The need that tries to perpetuate itself in time condemns individuality never to be complete in space."

60. Hesiod, *Theogony*, 521; Op. et dies, 48 ff. The interpretation of Zosimus is interesting (XLIX, 3, Berthelot's text): Hesiod calls the bond with which Prometheus was tied "the outer man." After which he mentioned another bond, Pandora, "whom the Hebrews call Eve." From the viewpoint of an allegory, Prometheus and Epimetheus are one single being, and the disobedience of Epimetheus toward Prometheus was "toward his own spirit, *nous* [mind]."

61. In Clemens Alex., *Strom.* III, 9.63; III 9.64 ff.; III, 13.92. Cf. also the saying put into the mouth of a gnostic initiate: "I recognized and gathered myself on all sides; I did not beget children of the Archon [by procreating] but eradicated the roots and collected [my] members which were spread everywhere; I know who you are because I belong to the region above" (in G.R.S. Mead, *Fragments of a Faith Forgotten*, London, 1900, Ital. translation, p. 437).

62. Plotinus, *Enn.*, III, v, I.

63. Cf. *Symposium*, 181c, 191c, 192a; *Phaedrus*, 151c, 253b, 265c,

240a, etc. speak almost solely about love roused by ephebot.

64. Some psychoanalysts would like to explain homosexuality in terms of a regression on the psychological level, as a regression in the bisexuality which would be proper to a baby (while bisexuality is considered to be detected in ontogenesis) or else in terms of the reemergence of a complex due to the fact that eros in the baby was "fixed" on the father (or on the mother in the case of lesbianism). As in many other cases, psychoanalysis explains nothing here but merely replaces one problem with another, for even if we accept its caricature of a concept of the erotic life of a child, it still does not explain how on earth such a fixation can be produced.

65. Cf. Evola, *L'Arco e la clava*, Milan, 1868, chap. 3.

Chapter 3: Phenomena of Transcendency in Profane Love

1. Cf. Kerenyi, *Tochter der Sonne*, Zurich, 1944, p. 166.
2. Krafft-Ebing, *Psychopathia sexualis*, p. 2.
3. *Symposium*, 179a–b.
4. In a chivalrous romance Lancelot says to Guinevere; "Alone, I would not have had the courage to undertake any chivalrous action nor to attempt things that all the others have renounced through lack of strength." But Guinevere herself points out that everything he did for this love, to possess her, made him lose the right to fulfill the other adventures of the Holy Grail, in honor of which the Round Table was instituted (Delécluze, *Roland ou de la chevalrie*, Paris 1845, p. 245).
5. *Symposium*, 183a–b.
6. Ibid., 183b.
7. *De arte amandi*, I, 635–636.
8. *Metaphysik der Geschlechtsliebe*, pp. 85–88, 109, 112.
9. Bourget, *Physiologie de l'amour moderne*.
10. Thus it is accurate to say: "Bad luck to the man who, in the first moments of an amorous relationship, does not believe that the relationship should be everlasting! Bad luck to him who, when in the arms of a lover whom he has had for the first time only a while before, retains a dismal foreboding and foresees that he may leave her" (B. C. de Rebecque in B. Péret, *Anthologie de l'amour sublime*, Paris, 1956, pp. 158–159).
11. On the basis of what has been just said, it would be possible to arrive at a union of the opposed theories of Freud and Adler, one of them having as its center the *libido sexualis* and the other the

impulse to have worth, for eros itself embodies an impulse toward self-confirmation, the urge toward individual reintegration. If the ultimate root of the latter is an "idea of power and of
likeness to God" which acts in the unconscious (Adler, *Praxis
und Theorie der Individualpsychologie*, Munich, 1924, p.53), we
have found the same meaning for eros in the myth of the
hermaphrodite.

12. Cf. O. Helby Othman, *El Kitab des lois secrètes de l'amour*, Paris, 1906, p. 261.
13. *Vita nuova*, II, 4.
14. Trans. by Ruckert, in Klages, p. 68.
15. A. Marro, La Pubertà, Turin, pp. 203–204, 106.
16. A. Mairet, *La Folie de la puberté*, in Marro, p.122.
17. For this phenomenology, as seen from the profane point of view, that is, "positivistic" psychiatric, cf. Marro, *La pubertà*, pp. 103, 106 ff., 159, 118–119, 121.
18. Marro, p. 159.
19. In Lawrence, for the man there was a look (from the woman) of expectation, and a little tongue of fire wriggled suddenly at his kidneys, at the root of his back.
20. Cf. Evola, *Lo Yoga della potenza*, and Avalon, *The Serpent Power*, London. 1925.
21. Cf. Marro, p. 206.
22. Cf. W. James, *The Varieties of Religious Experience*.
23. Ibid.
24. *De l'amour*, II, 59.
25. Krafft-Ebing, *Psychopathia sexualis*, p. 7.
26. M. Eliade, *Le Chamanisme et les techniques archaiques de l'extase*.
27. Ibid.
28. Cf. H. Schurtz, *Altersklassen und Männerbunde*, Berlin, 1902, passim but especially pp. 99–108; H. Webster, *Primitive secret societies*.
29. As a corresponding fact in the case of women, we shall mention hereinafter the custom of ritual isolation of girls during the period of puberty and, later, during menstruation, so that the magic womanly force of which they become the bearers is circumscribed.
30. For documentation there is a wide choice, ranging from the Brihadaranyaka-Upanishad, IV, i, 7 ("The heart is the essential part of beings, who all have in their heart their foundation"), to Zeno *Armin*. II, phr. 837–839 ("The main part of the soul resides in the heart"), and from the same Scholasticism (Ugo di San Vittore, *Vis vitalis est in corde*), to Agrippa (*De occulta philosophia*, III, 37).

31. Cf. Brihadaranyaka-Upanishad, II, i, 16–17; cf. Agrippa, III, 37.

32. *Vita nuova*, II, 4.

33. Cf. Plutarch, *Lycirgus*, 23. We have chosen the case of Sparta because the modesty factor could not come into the question; in fact, girls at Sparta used to display themselves naked on many occasions in ordinary life, and men were accustomed to seeing them in that state.

34. In Chinese tradition the name *p'o* is given to the elementary energy of life; unconsciousness with a feminine nature was called *yin*, being related to the dark side of the moon, which is only apprehended when the lunar crescent is shining.

35. We refer especially to the last verses of the first hymn: "On the altar of night, on the soft resting place, the enfolding robe falls, and the sweet holocaust is lit up like pure fire by the ardent embrace and burns. My body is consumed with the fire of the spirit so that the night of the nuptials mingles more intimately with you and lasts forever."

36. Cf. Brihadaranyaka-Upanishad, IV, IV, 1–2, and Katha-Upanishad, II, VI, 15–16.

37. "Suddenly, I don't know how, while I was turning to look at the empty road, on the windows of the dark houses, a burning desire for Pat [the woman] struck me, like a blow which caught me hard. It was so terrible that I thought I was dying" (E. M. Remarque). Cf. the words of the Persian poet Khusrev: "Her image came to me in the night, and the fright almost killed me."

38. *Inni spirituali*, XV.

39. Klages, *Vom kosmogonischen Eros*, p. 199.

40. *In vino veritas*, p. 76 ff.

41. *Inni spirituali*, VII.

42. Klages, p. 95 ff. Cf. Bruno, *Eroici furori*, I, iii, 9: "Heroic love is a torment because it does not enjoy the present, as brutal love does, but belongs to the future and the absent."

43. In ancient Rome cases of madness are attested due to love potions; it is even said that such potions ended the lives of Lucullus and Lucretius. In fact, in some cases the awakening of the force of eros in its elementary state by a true potion can have effects corresponding to hebephrenia, or mental derangement during puberty, which we mentioned earlier; the action of the potion is too sudden and violent, and therefore a break in continuity with the previous state of the normal psyche takes place, especially when the superego is opposed to the development of the passion.

44. Bruno, *Eroici furori*, I, ii, 10.

45. It is well known that *Tristan and Isolde* was a product of the sublimation of Wagner's strong but frustrated passion for Matilda of Wesendonk. The following expressions in one of his letters to her are of interest: "The devil! He passes from one heart to the other. . . . We no longer belong to ourselves! Devil, devil becomes a god!" (Letter no. 54 of the summer of 1858, ed. Golther, Berlin, 1904).

46. According to Freud, the vital instinct in the organism would fight against the tendency of organic matter to return to the preliving inorganic state from which it sprang. On the one hand, there would be the virtually everlasting germinal plasma, whereas, on the other hand, there would be everything that produces the deterioration and death of the organism. To correspond to this there would be the instinct of sex opposed to the instinct of death. It is necessary to reject the attempt, undertaken by Wilhelm Reich in particular, to deduce the urge to destruction from the repression of the urge to pleasure. Among other things, that ignores one of the most interesting dimensions in the experience of sex.

47. Mauclair, *Magie de l'amour*, p. 145. Cf. p. 24: "Nothing is more like physical love than death. Whether it be physical or moral, love is the positive image of death. The spasm is a momentary incursion into the realm of death, it is a sample that nature grants to the being who is alive. Coitus consists of two people hurling themselves into death but with the ability to come back to life and to remember." In actual fact, in the vast majority of men and women such a memory is, instead, relative, just as their consciousness of the state momentarily reached is confused and peripheral.

48. Novalis, *Werke*, ed. Heilbron, vol. II. p. 650 ff.

49. Cf. *Metafisica del dolore e della malattia*, in *Introduzione alla magia* (edited by the Gruppo di Ur), Rome, 1956, vol. II, p. 204 ff.

50. Cf. W. B. Seabrook. *Adventure in Arabia*. New York, 1935, p. 283.

51. These significant words may be cited: "There was the struggle, the conquest, the mutual surrender, the affirmation and the furious denial, the keen sensation of self and the full dissolution of the ego, the elimination of personalization and the reduction to one being alone, all of this at only one time and at the same moment." I. M. Daniel (N. Arzhak), *Qui parla Mosca*, Italian trans., Milan, 1966.

52. In the *Kamasutra of Vatsayana*, apart from a detailed examination of the technique of biting, the use of the nails and other

painful practices in lovemaking (II, iv–v; cf. VII; for this, cf. also *Ananga Ranga*, XI, 3, 4), there is an interesting reference to a possible, objective, erotogenic-magnetic effect caused by the sight of the corresponding marks remaining on the body.

53. *Oeuvres posthumes*, p. 107.

54. *Rev. nat.* IV, 1081. Cf. D'Annunzio (*Forse che si forse che no*): "Filled with the same delirium that stirs lovers harsh with carnal hate on the shaken bed when desire and destruction, sensual pleasure and torment are one single fever."

55. *Untergang des Abendlandes*, Munich, 1923, vol. II, p. 198.

56. Quoted by Hesnard, p. 233 n. D'Annunzio (*Il Piacere*): "He would have liked to entwine her and draw her within himself, to suck her and drink her and possess her in some superhuman way."

57. *Canti spirituali*, VII: "The divine symbol of the Supper is an enigma for earthly senses, but he who has once drawn the breath of life from an ardent beloved mouth and whose holy zeal has melted the heart in waves of shivering and whose eye is opened will eat of his own body and drink of his own blood forever."

58. These words of a poet, for instance, are expressive: "My feelings for you are a cry. . . . Desire has cleft me, the kiss has taken blood from me. . . . I am wounded, burnt, hungry for new torments. . . . I am wounded; kiss me, burn me, be my firebrand" (André Ady in Peret, p. 341).

59. In "Prodomus Galaleatus" of the *Christliche Mystik*.

60. We may suppose a similar purpose in the sexual unions practiced in certain ancient temples when virgins and even women in general believed they were copulating with a god. It is known that in the reign of Tiberius in Rome the profanation and abuse of practices of this kind led to the closing of the temple of Isis by the Senate because of the scandal caused by the patrician Mundus, who corrupted the priests and in this way enjoyed the unwilling matron Paulina.

61. An ancient ritual manuscript belonging to a Scottish witch, which was shown to us by Professor G. B. Gardner, director of the Museum for Witchcraft on the Isle of Man, contemplates precisely the practice of whipping a woman in the context of sexual initiation. Gardner was wondering whether this context might be linked to certain Orphic initiation scenes in the frescoes of the Pompeian Villa of the Mysteries; as is known, among them is one of a young woman being beaten. This seems rather questionable because those scenes are essentially symbolic. However, in principle we do not exclude the ambivalence of many symbols or their capacity to have meaning on a merely

spiritual plane as well as on a real plane.

62. Krafft-Ebing, *Psychopathia sexualis*, p. 18.

63. Regarding this world of mystic sensualism, cf. the rather daring expressions of E. Lévi (*Il Grande Arcano*, Italian trans., Rome, 1954, pp. 77–78): "Maria Alacoque and Messalina suffered the same tortures, both of them exalted desires greater than nature and impossible to satisfy. Between the two women there was the difference that, if Messalina had been able to foresee what Maria Alacoque had to experience, she would have been envious of her." "Erotic passion, detached from its lawful object and exalted by an insensate desire to do violence to the infinite in some way, like the madness of the Marquis de Sade, has a thirst for tortures and blood"; sackcloth, penitence, self-mortification, "attacks of hysteria and priapism, which make us believe in the direct action of the devil." "Delirium of the nuns, the foresaking of the Heavenly Bridegroom, resistances of the succubus crowned with stars, disdain for the Virgin queen of the angels." Lévi concluded, "The lips which have drunk of this deadly cup will remain changed and trembling; the hearts, once burnt with this delirium, will thereafter find the true springs of love insipid." These are, however, strangely limited views for a writer such as Lévi, who professes to be an esoteric but here speaks of "true springs of love" and, further on, of the "exaltation beyond nature." In fact, the truest and deepest springs of eros, even though in deviated forms of manifestation, are precisely those which do produce such "deliria."

64. Krafft-Ebing, *Psychopathia sexualis*, p. 9.

65. Trans. Ruckert (in Klages, p. 68). In a work by Goethe there is interesting evidence for the sensation that was caused by the waltz when it first appeared; for in it could be seen a rather worldly reflection of the techniques of the ancient *vertiginatores*. Besides the whirling movement of such a dance, the protagonist shows such a capability of intoxication and inner possession of the woman as to make unbearable the thought that his lover could dance the waltz with other men. Cf. Byron's reaction to the waltz, which is, however, rather moralistic.

66. Piobb, *Venus*, p. 80.

67. Brihadaranyaka-Upanishad, IV, iii, 21.

68. Ellis, *Studies*, V, p. 161.

69. *Framm.*, pp. 101–102.

70. "I feel you are mine to my lowest depths, just as my soul is mingled with my body" (D'Annunzio, *Il Fuoco*). Werther in Goethe's novel says, to indicate the effect of woman on him: "It is as if my soul permeated all my nerves."

71. Apart from the specific context above, a reference in the *Kama-sutra*, II, I, states that in the exalted levels of passion during coitus, woman "ends by no longer being aware of her own body" and "then in the end experiences a desire to cease the coitus."

72. In the meantime we should remember the application of this visual symbol to sexual union when the woman plays the active part by standing astride upon the man, who lies stationary, "and she twists herself with a searching up-and-down spiral." Cf. further on, the Tantric *viparita-maithuna*.

73. The scholastic classifications of Hindu erotic treatises cite three types of women who faint during coitus, a fourth type who lose their senses at its beginning, and yet another type who "in the grand passion almost dissolve in the body of their lover" in such a way that they can almost no longer say "who he is, who she is, or what is the sensual pleasure in love" (texts in R. Schmidt, *Indische Erotik*, Berlin, 1910, pp. 191–193).

74. *In vino veritas*, p. 52.

75. Ploss-Bartels, *Das Weib*, I, p. 359.

76. Schopenhauer, *Metaphysik der Geschlechtsliebe*, pp. 119, 128, 129.

77. It may be observed that here, from yet another aspect, the inner difference between the sexual and the nutritive function is evident. If these functions were equally "biological" and "natural," then eating would be as shameful as copulating.

78. Cf., e.g., E. Westermarch, *History of Human Marriage*, London, New York, 1891, chaps. 4–6.

79. M. Eliade, *Traité d'histoire des religions*, Paris, 1949, pp. 168, 173.

80. Ibid., p. 299.

81. Ibid., p. 307.

82. Ibid., pp. 175–176n.

83. *Degli heroici furori*, intr. 22–23.

84. *Oeuvres posthumes*, p. 78.

85. Regarding all this, cf. E. Dühren, *Der Marquis de Sade und seine Zeit*, Jena, 1901.

86. De Sade, *Juliette, ou les prospérités du vice*, ed. 1797, II, pp. 314–350. There "exists a God who has created everything I see, but for the purpose of evil; he is only glad with evil, and evil is his essence. . . . It is in evil that he has created the world; it is through evil that he upholds it; it is for evil that he perpetuates it; creation has to exist by being impregnated with evil. I can see everlasting and universal evil in the world. . . . The author of the universe is the wickedest, the most ferocious, and the most dreadful of all beings. He will exist, therefore, after all the crea-

tures that populate this world, and it is to him that they will all return." Cited by M. Praz, *La Carne, la morte e il diavolo nella letteratura romantica*, Milan-Rome, 1930.

87. De Sade, *Justine, ou les malheurs de la vertu*, I, 95–96.

88. De Sade spoke of a "going astray on the path of virtue" and concluded that "as virtue is a way contrary to the system of the world, all who follow it can be sure to undergo dreadful torments for the trouble they will have in returning to the bosom of evil, which is the author and regenerator of everything we see" (*Juliette*, II, 345–346).

89. *Juliette*, II, 117.

90. Ibid., II, 63.

91. *Justine*, IV, 40–41.

92. Praz, p. 104.

93. Marshal Gilles de Rais, a nonintellectual kind of sadist, was the actual perpetrator of unheard-of atrocities and perversions and had already fought under Joan of Arc. Apart from the fact that he appeared to be a sort of victim of obsessions, even he died in a state of perfect contrition. Oscar Wilde, a defender of perversity, repented in prison for everything to which this condition in him really amounted, namely homosexuality with strong aesthetizing characteristics, whereas we see his hero, Dorian Grey, acting continually with the knowledge that he was doing evil and therefore close to knowing its opposite, good, in spite of everything.

94. Regarding the Way of the Left Hand, cf. Evola, *Lo Yoga della potenza*, Rome, 1968.

95. This is the counterpart of what was said by de Sade, *Justine*, II, p. 249: "If destruction is one of its [nature's] laws, he who destroys, therefore, obeys them."

96. About all this, see Bhagavad-Gita, IX.

97. Ed. Heilborn, vol. II, pp. 230, 650, 586, 502 ff., 514.

98. F. Schlegel, *Kritische Schriften*, ed. Rasch, Munich, 1956, p. 101.

99. This view corresponds to the theory of Plotinus of the *pró-odes* (advance) and the *èpistrophē* (turning around), and the second of these phases, in turn, can be compared to what the Stoics called *èkpurōsis* (conflagration) and the early Christian writers the *àpokatástasis pantós* (a breaking away from everything). The meanings here in these latter concepts, however are materialized in the form of happenings that will take place at the end of time.

100. This can be compared with a saying of Valentino Gnostico (in Mead, p. 224): "Since the beginning you were immortal and sons of Life, Life like that which the Aeons enjoy. And yet you

would like to divide death among you, to squander it and give it away, so that death may die in you and for your hands; for inasmuch as you dissolve the world and are not dissolved yourselves, you are the lords of all creation and all destruction." For some references to the "left" in the kabbalistic tradition, cf. Agrippa (*De occulta philosophia*, III, 40), who recalled how the Kabbalists distinguished between two aspects of divinity; one of these was called phachad (fear), left hand and sword of the Lord, and corresponded to the awful sign that is impressed on man, which subjects all creatures to him; whereas the other aspect was called *hased*, clemency or right hand, the principle of love.

101. About all this, see J. Woodroffe, *Shakti and Shakta*, London-Madras, 1929, p. 147-ff.

102. Ibid., p. 153.

103. Cf. N. Tsakni, *La Russie sectaire*, Paris, 1888, chap. 4, pp. 63–73; K. Grass, *Die russischen Sekten*, Leipzig, 1907–1909. As an analogy, we can cite the rites of certain dervish groups among the Mavlavi and the Izawi, where songs that usually have the intoxication of love and of wine as their theme excite them to dance; but it is necessary to refrain from any movement for as long as possible; only when the urge becomes impossible to withstand do the participants, who are sitting in a circle, get to their feet and start dancing, spinning around by themselves or taking part in circular dances. Then, unconsciously or at a sign from the sheikh, they start invocations on the basis of given formulas (*dhikr*); Y. Millet, "De l'usage technique de l'audition musicale" in *Etudes traditionnelles*, December 1955, pp. 353–354.

104. Tsakni, pp. 72–73.

105. R. Fulop-Miller, *Le Diable sacré*, Paris, 1929, p. 45. From this work we have also drawn the notes that follow.

106. Ibid., p. 202; cf. also pp. 31–33.

107. We allude to the treatise *Contra advers. legis*, I, 26–28, where Augustine wonders why God allows girls to be raped during wars or disorders. Apart from the unfathomable nature of heavenly designs and a hint of possible compensation in the afterlife for sufferings on earth (supposing that the rape of a girl amounts only to suffering), he wonders whether the girls in question had not sinned by their pride in showing their virtue. In Augustine's eyes the virtues acquired only by the innate power of the individual such as those of "heathens," without the help of divine grace, would be "splendid vices." The Lutheran *pecca fortiter* (sin manfully) prescribes that we should not resist sin but should abandon ourselves to it wholly, in the hope of obtaining the divine saving grace by our own humiliation and by the

confession of our own powerlessness.
108. Fulop-Miller, pp. 268–269.

Chapter 4: Gods and Goddesses, Men and Women

1. Cf. C. G. Jung, *Die Beziehungen zwischen dem Ich und dem Unbewussten*, Zurich-Leipzig, 1928, chap. 4. For a deeper critique of Jung's ideas, cf. *Introduzione alla magia*, undertaken by the Gruppo di Ur, Rome, 1956, III, p. 411 ff.
2. According to the views of Jung's school, "when the boundary between the limited personality of the individual and the archetypes ceases to exist," only a "delirium" can take place, "a psychopathic catastrophic state of obsession" (cf. L. von Franz, *Aurora consurgens*, Zurich, 1975, pp. 175, 219). Nothing is more significant for the horizons of that school.
3. Aristotle, *De gen. anim.*, I, ii, 716a; I, xx, 729a. Cf. also II, i, 732a; II, iv, 738b.
4. *Timaeus*, 50 b–d.
5. Cf. Plotinus, *Enneadi*, III, vii, 4; III, vii, 10; III, VIII, I; I, i, 8; III, ii, 2; V, vii, 12.
6. *Ta Chiuan*, I, sec. 4.
7. Ibid., sec. 5.
8. *Shi-kua*, I, comm.
9. Cf. J. Woodroffe, *Creation as Explained in the Tantra*, Calcutta, p. 9.
10. Cf. E. Pander, *Das Pantheon des Tschangtscha Hutuku*, Berlin, 1890.
11. Cf. Evola, *Lo Yoga della potenza*.
12. In Woodroffe, loc. cit.
13. Cf. Woodroffe, *Shakti and Shakta*, chaps. 14–19.
14. A. and E. Avalon, *Hymns to the Goddess*, London, 1913, pp. 46–47.
15. Plutarch in *De Is. et Os.*, 56, says that Penia "is the raw material which in itself is privation but is filled with good [synonymous here with being] and always tends toward it and is able to participate in it."
16. Zohar, I, 207b; III, 7a.
17. Ibid., I, 288b.
18. F. Cumont, *Les mystères de Mithra*, Brussels, 1913, p. 96 ff.
19. In Origene, *In Johan*, II, 12. Cf. Hieronymus, *In Math.*, II, vii, 7, where the same expression occurs and it is recalled that *ruah*, or spirit, is feminine in Hebrew.

20. Cf. G. Glotz, *La Civilisation égéenne*, Italian trans., Turin, 1954, pp. 282, 290. He writes of the goddess-dove or goddess of the dove, the dove being either a symbol of the goddess or identified with her. "Emanation of the goddess, the dove is the spirit which sanctifies all beings and objects on which it settles, and divine possession works through it."

21. Homer, *Odyssey*, XII, 63.

22. Cf. G. R. S. Mead, *Fragments of a Faith Forgotten*, pp. 247–248.

23. Ibid., pp. 129–130.

24. Cf. A. Mosso, *Le Origini della civiltà mediterranea*, Milan, 1909, pp. 90 ff., 100.

25. Cf. J. Przyluski, *La Grande Déesse*, Paris, 1950, pp. 26–27, 48, 50, 127, 156–157; U. Pestalozza, *La Religione mediterranea*, Milan, 1951; G. Contenau, *La Déesse nue babylonienne*, Paris, 1914.

26. Ploss-Bartels, *Das Weib*, I, pp. 137–138. As will be remembered, the symbol of the inverted triangle is at the same time the sign of the Waters, of Shakti, and of desire.

27. Cf. J. J. Bachofen, *Le Madri e la virilità olimpica*, p. 82 ff.

28. Cf. F. Altheim, *Der unbesiegte Gott*, Hamburg, 1957, p. 31.

29. Cf. Pestalozza, *Religione mediterranea*, pp. 450, 408.

30. Cf. K. Kerenyi, *Le Figlie del Sole*, Turin, 1949, pp. 110–111.

31. Tacitus, *Annals*, IV, 53.

32. Cf. A. and E. Avalon, *Hymns to the Goddess*, London, 1913, pp. 41, 127.

33. Cf. E. Wallis Budge, *The Gods of the Egyptians*, London, 1904, pp. 213–216; Apuleius, *Met.*, XII, 5. It is necessary just to note that the Virgin of the Christians, who is a figure that plays objectively a very small part in the New Testament, having become the "Queen of the Skies," is an example of this same essential principle.

34. From the name Innini-Ishtar of the goddess came that of the sacred prostitutes, themselves called "Virgins," of which we shall speak; however, this name is also used for the common prostitutes, *ishtaritu*; both types of prostitutes took their name from the goddess because it was thought that in some way they reflected or embodied her nature. Cf. S. Langdon. *Tammuz and Ishtar*, Oxford, 1914, pp. 75–76, 80–82.

35. L. R. Farnell, *The Cult of the Greek States*, Oxford, 1896, pp. 413, 442, 449; R. Briffault, *The Mothers*, New York, 1927, pp. 169–170. A similar meaning belongs also to the word *kumari*, which in India can mean not only "virgin" but also "young woman" or "girl" (as with the German *Jungfrau*) without the question of anatomical virginity being necessarily involved.

36. Thus Plutarch said about Isis, "As Isis is the female principle in nature, the principle that can receive all genesis, for which reason Plato called her the 'foster-mother,' 'she who receives all,' the 'multitude,' 'she of the ten thousand names,' because she is transformed by Logos and receives all forms and all ideas." Therefore Isis-Nut was called in an ancient hymn "the unknown one," the "deeply hidden," "she who is difficult to reach" and "the great divinity never defeated" and was begged to show herself naked and to "free herself of her clothes." Cf. Wallis Budge, *The Gods of the Egyptians*, vol. I, p. 459.

37. In W. King, *Seven Tables of Creation*, London, 1902, p. 223.

38. *La Grande Déesse*, p. 28.

39. King and in general W. H. Roscher, *Die Grundbedeutung der Aphrodite und Athena*, Leipzig, 1883, p. 76 ff.

40. Cf. Avalon, *Hymns to the Goddess*, pp. 70–71, 76, 115, 117.

41. It is evident that the theological attributes of the Virgin Mary in Christianity are an absurdity if we examine the part which the mother of Jesus played in the Gospels; such attributes can be understood only by considering the transfer to her of those which were already proper to the pre-Christian Great Goddess. Even some attributes in the canonical litanies, such as "inviolate mother" and "mighty virgin," have a Durga hue no less than those of "closed garden" and "sealed fountain." Amazonian features are not lacking, in ancient invocations, alongside other features; thus, for instance, in the hymn sung standing up which was attributed to Saint Germanus, the Patriarch of Constantinople, we find that the "inviolate bride" is also called "begetter of unspeakable light, mistress who surpasses all teaching, enlightener of the spirit of believers, entrance to the gate of paradise, radiant knowledge of grace, light which brightens the soul, lightning which frightens the foe, living image of the Waters of baptism, thou who washest away the stain of sin, thou who givest victories, thou who scatterest the foe, salvation of my body," etc. Cf. P. Regamey, *Les Plus Beaux Textes sur la Vierge Marie*, Italian trans., Rome, 1952, pp. 95–105.

42. Cf. F. Cumont, *Les religions orientales dans le paganisme romain*; Przyluski, pp. 29, 30.

43. *Enneadi*, I, vi, 7.

44. Cf. Evola, *Yoga della potenza*.

45. Cf. A. J. Pernety, *Dictionnaire mytho-hermetique*, Paris, 1758, p. 266. In passing, we should mention the magical side of ritual nakedness. It is when the elementary "naked" state, separated from form, of the principle which is embodied and which corre-

sponds to its true nature is renewed that it shows its superphysical power. Whence comes the advice to be naked in carrying out given operations, as an analogical-ritual counterpart.

46. Cf. Przyluski, p. 139; *Mahanirvana-tantra*, X, 110. It is of interest that among the Incas the queen took her name, Mama luca, from that of a substance causing intoxication, namely cola, which had a divine origin according to tradition (cf. L. Lewin).
47. Cf. Avalon, *Hymns to the Goddess*, pp. 26–28, 58–59.
48. Cf. Glotz, *Civilisation égéenne*, pp. 290–291.
49. About what follows, cf. Bachofen, *Das Mutterrecht*, pp. 76, 109, 111–112.
50. Aeschylus, *Eumenides*, 658–666.
51. This is echoed to some extent in the biblical myth according to which Eve was taken from Adam and formed with a part of him, and also in the idea that only man was made in the image of God. Cf. E. Lévi, *Dogme et rituel de l'haute magie*, Italian trans., Rome, 1949. "Woman comes out from man as nature comes out from God; thus Christ raised himself to the sky and took up with him the Virgin Mother."
52. This metaphysical situation is reflected in nature in the fact that the lower we go in the biological scale, the more female societies prevail and the female is predominant over man.
53. *Corpus Hermeticum*, I, 15.
54. Cf. G. G. Cholem, *Les Grands Courants de la mystique juive*, Paris, 1950, pp. 247, 293; M. D. Langer, *Die Erotik in der Kabbala*, Prague, 1923, p. 116.
55. Mead, *Fragments of a Faith Forgotten*, pp. 307, 309.
56. In ibid., pp. 281–282.
57. *Philosophumena*, V, i, 6–7, 8.
58. Pernety, *Dict. mytho-hermet.*, pp. 408, 522.
59. *Corpus hermeticum* (Pimandro), I, 9–15.
60. Langer, *Erotik in der Kabbala*, p. 111; cf. also S. Peladan, *La Science de l'amour*, Paris, 1911, chap. 2.
61. *More Nevokim*, II, 30.
62. Leo the Hebrew, *Dialoghi d'amore*, ed. Caramella, Bari, 1929, p. 417 ff.
63. *De divisionibus naturae*, II, 6; II, 9; II, 12.
64. Ibid., II, 4; II, 8.
65. Ibid., II, 12, 14.
66. Ibid., II, 6. We should also observe the idea in Scotus Eriugena that from the division of the sexes should arise the fact of earthly and corruptible nature and of the separation of the earthly from the heavenly (II, 9; II, 12). F. von Baader in *Gesamm. Werke*,

III, p. 303, said that if Adam had fixed in himself the nature of a hermaphrodite and had not destroyed it by yielding to temptation, "he would have also dominated the cosmic spirit within himself and outside himself and would have become the actual lord and sovereign of the world outside according to his destination."

67. About the story of the Hermetic Rebis, cf. *Introduzione alla magia*, p. 312 ff.

68. Cf. Scholem, p. 51.

69. Cf. G. A. Wallis Budge, *The Book of the Dead*, London, 1895.

70. Cf. S. Radhakrishnan, *The Hindu View of Life*, London–New York, 1927, pp. 112, 122. In relation to the meanings that emerged in the ancient Mediterranean world from the contrast of opposed myths, Bachofen wrote, "Woman brings death, man overcomes it through the spirit," not with phallic but with spiritual manhood (*Das Mutterrecht*, p. 191).

71. In *Der Engel vom westlichen Fenster*, Italian trans., Milan, 1949, p. 344 ff.

72. Although within a medley of rather profane situations, D. H. Lawrence described this context quite well when he wrote of an ardent being, like a bacchante, who flees through the woods in search of Iacchus, the luminous phallus that has no independent person behind itself but is only the pure god-slave of woman; a man, an individual who had to be stopped from interfering, said Lawrence; for he was only a slave of the temple, the bearer and guardian of the luminous phallus which belonged to her; thus in the wave of her rebirth, the ancient vehement passion burned for some time in her, and the man was reduced to a worthless instrument, a mere bearer of the phallus, destined to be torn to pieces after fulfillment of his duty. G. R. Taylor was partly right when he wrote that, however unpleasant the idea may be, the sexual act provides an analogous symbolism because the end of the sexual orgasm is equivalent to a miniature death and in a certain sense woman always performs castration of the male. See Taylor, *Sex in History*, p. 263.

73. In M. Eliade, *Le chamanisme et les techniques archaiques de l'extase*, Paris, 1951, pp. 86, 87.

74. Cf. Evola, *La Tradizione ermetica*, Bari, 1948, 19.

75. About all this, cf. Pestalozza, *La Religione mediterranea*, p. 71 ff.; see p. 51, where it is recounted that in some texts of the Pyramids a similar situation is linked to Isis herself, since the goddess is described as copulating with her brother and associate (the theme of the symbolism of incest, not with the mother this

time, but with the sister, is based on the bipartite division of the Dyad, the male and female considered as brother and sister, both "children" of the primordial One), who lies on his back as if dead but still ithyphallic; the goddess descends on him like a female hawk, says the text, so as to spread herself over him and take his seed. Cf. T. Hopfner, *Plutarch über Isis und Osiris*, Prague, 1940, I, p. 81.

76. Cf. G. Tucci, *Il Libro tibetano del morto* (Tibetan Book of the Dead). Milan, 1949, pp. 25, 71–72, 74.

77. Tantric representations also exist with Shiva lying down, like a dead body, while Shakti, made of flame, dances on his body; to this stillness of Shiva we must give the same meaning as earlier. As the "dance of Shiva" is a very well known image, it is appropriate to note that the symbolism it obeys concerns the god Shiva as conceived synthetically or as he who combines in himself both detached stillness and movement.

78. In Hippolytus, *Philos*, VI, 17.

79. In D. Mereshkowski, *Les Mystères de l'Orient*, Paris, 1927, p. 163.

80. An interesting detail is that the segregation is interrupted in some cases at night.

81. For all that, cf. Frazer, *The Golden Bough*, Italian trans., Turin, 1950, I, chap. 20, 3; II, chap. 60, 3, 4, especially pp. 318–319.

82. E. Harding, *Les Mystères de la femme*, Paris, 1953, p. 65.

83. Black Elk, *The Sacred Pipe*, Norman, 1953, p. 116.

84. For all that, see Ploss-Bartels, *Das Weib*, I, pp. 324 ff., 327, 335, 351, 338, 339; H. Ellis, *Studies in the Psychology of Sex*, I, Philadelphia, 1905, p. 208 ff.; Harding, p. 66 ff.

85. Ploss-Bartels, p. 349.

86. H. von Wlislocki, *Aus dem inneren Leben der Zigeuner*, Berlin, 1892.

87. In passing we should observe in this respect that a serious research worker such as Ellis (op. cit., I, pp. 213, 215–216) mentions certain phenomena having a "metapsychic" character which are attributed to the presence of girls during their menstrual period and which in some non-European countries, such as Annam, for example, are deemed quite normal (in this respect Ellis cites the monograph of Dr. D. L. Laurent, "De quelques phénomènes mécaniques produits au moment de la menstruation" in *Annales de sciences psychiques*, September-October, 1893), but which have taken place in Europe as well. Furthermore, Ellis gives the evidence of girls who said that they felt something like "an electric charge" during the critical

period. Not among ordinary people, but in certain circles where sexual magic is practiced consciously, the menses is sometimes used as an ingredient.

88. *Nat. Hist.*, VII, 13; XXVIII, 12.
89. Ploss-Bartels, I, pp. 350–352.
90. Philo Alex., *De off. mundi*, 165.
91. Weininger, *Geschlecht und Charakter*, Vienna, 1918, pp. 388, 404–406, 398–399.
92. M. Alessandrini, *Cecco d'Ascoli*, Rome, 1955, pp. 169–170. J. Sprenger goes further; in the *Malleus maleficarum* (I, 6) he derives *foemina* from *fe* and *minus*, *"quia semper minorem habet et servat fidem"* (because she always has and keeps less faith).
93. H. Ellis, *Man and Woman*, Italian trans., ed. Sandron, Milan, pp. 354–357, 381–382. What a Danish author said about the female smile is meaningful: "In the smile our greater virtues *but also our great inner emptiness* are reflected." She added that a "history of the smile has still not been written"; only a woman could write it, but she never would do it "because of solidarity with other women"; cited by F. O. Brachfeld, *Los Complejos de inferioridad de la mujer.*
94. Cf. P. J. Moebius, *Über den physiol. Schwachsinn des Weibes*, Italian trans., p. 12: "Just as the animals have always acted from time immemorial in the same way, so the human race would have remained in its original state if women alone had existed."
95. Weininger, part II, pp. 183 ff., 191, 239–240.
96. Ibid., p. 191.
97. *Jataka*, LXI; *Anguttara-nikaya*, II, 48.
98. Weininger, *Geschlecht und Charakter*, pp. 113, 115, 116.
99. Cf. Ellis, III, p. 199: "That [sexual] emotion which, one is tempted to say, oft unmans the man, makes the woman for the first time truly herself."
100. We may recall here the verses of Baudelaire in a presentiment of the Durga archetype:

And in this strange and symbolic nature
When the inviolate angel mingles with
the ancient Sphynx . . .
The cold majesty of the sterile woman . . .
Shines for ever . . .

101. Weininger, X, especially pp. 280 ff., 287, 304, 310–311; "physical life and physical death, both united in such a mysterious way in coitus, are divided between woman as mother and woman as prostitute." By insisting on speaking of "prostitute," Weininger notes the significant nature of the fact that "prostitution is something that appears only among human beings" and is extraneous

to all animal species. This fact is related to the Shiva potentiality of the pure type of lover. A treatise assigned to Alberto Magno (*De secretis mulierum*), when describing the kind of woman who loves coitus, refers to her characteristics as a scantiness or irregularity of menses, a scarcity of milk when she becomes a mother, and also a tendency toward cruelty; the latter is a point to which we shall return.

102. Weininger, p. 307.

103. Ibid., p. 402.

104. From the subtle point of view it is not a question of material seed but of its immaterial counterpart. Paracelsus (*Opus Paramirum*, III, ii, 5) wrote, "In the womb was placed a force of attraction, which is like a magnet, and this draws in the seed." He distinguishes the seed from sperm: "The womb separates the sperm from the seed and rejects the sperm but keeps the seed." On this basis Paracelsus also dealt with the transbiological conditional qualities of fecundation. For the distinction mentioned just now, see Cosmopolita, *Novum lumen chemicum*, Paris, 1669, p. 37: "sperm can be seen but seed is, therefore, something invisible and is almost like a living soul which is not to be found in dead things."

105. Thus in the ancient East the saying was valid that "the sensuality of woman is eight times greater than that of man," while in the ancient West there are expressions such as that of Ovid (*Ars amandi*, I, 443–444), "*Libido foeminae acrior est nostra, plusque furoris habet*" (The lust of woman is keener than ours and contains more frenzy).

106. Here it is a matter of an abnormal control over the *constrictor cunni* (the muscle that constricts the vagina) and also of certain smooth fibers of the female organ, which enable this automatic sucking movement to be intensified. In certain cases the development of this capability is a part of the erotic teaching of women; among some peoples a reason for the disqualification of a girl is that she is not very skillful (for all of this, cf. Hesnard, *Manuel de sexologie*, pp. 94–95; Ellis, *Studies*, V, pp. 159–165; Ploss-Bartels, *Das Weib*, I, pp. 399, 408). In women employed in Tantric sexual magic, a training of this kind seems to be brought up to a high level in the *Hathayogapradipika*, III, 42–43, 87–89; for the practice called *yoni-mudra* there is presupposed to be such a power of voluntary contraction of the *yoni* as to hinder the emission of the male seed by strangling the *lingam*. In the field of ethnology we find in Ploss-Bartels, I, p. 408, some cases of women able to reexpel the sperm after having received it.

107. Lombroso-Ferrero, *La Donna delinquente, la prostituta e la donna normale*, Turin, 1915, pp. 55–59, 79. In the field of pathology, for the prevalent appearance of "spasmodic outbreaks of savage and destructive violence" in women, cf. Krafft-Ebing, *Psychopathia sexualis*, p. 361.

108. M. Praz, *La Carne, la morte e il diavolo nella letteratura romantica*, pp. 233–234.

109. Cf. also in *Forse che sì forse che no*. "Whereas in the man desire was that irrevocable choice, her desire was without circumscription, without limit or time, like the evil of being and the melancholy of the earth." "He discovered between her eyelashes a look that was more remote than a human look and that seemed to be expressed by the dreadfulness of an instinct older than the stars."

110. P. Viazzi, *Psicologia dei sessi*, Milan, 1903, p. 72.

111. E. Harding, *Les Mystères de la femm*, Paris, 1953, pp. 125–126.

112. E. Erkes, *Credenze religiose della Cina antica*, Rome, 1958, pp. 10–13.

113. Cf. *Una Notte a Bucarest* in *Roma*, 9, II, 1951. "The muffled basic rhythm [of the music] quickened, and then a violin changed to a tune which ran along high notes; and the more spasmodic the accompanying rhythm became, the more the tune was brought up to limits which seemed final but which were suddenly broken and surpassed by new and unexpected themes, as in a last walk on a tightrope or on a razor's edge. Again there was the cry, 'Baskie!' Then, lastly, a girl came forward, did some dance steps, hindered by her long clothes, took one look around and then threw off her clothes and underwear until her brown body was wholly naked. The music went on following her, and now it was as if a whirlwind had found its center in that naked girl. Sudden movements of that body, which in the end stopped motionless with arms raised except for a kind of shivering motion and for the play of an expression of elementary sexuality mingled with something ambiguously intangible. Only that shiver and the play of the features and shining of her half-shut eyes accompanied and enhanced the devilry of the gypsy music until there was an unbearable tension which seemed to call for and require an elementary deed, absolute violence: a killing rather than the violence of possession of the flesh."

114. *In vino veritas*, p. 25.

115. Cf. Ovid, *De arte amandi*, I, 658: "*Pugnando vici se tamen illa volet*" (I won by fighting whenever she allowed me).

116. The *Kamasutra*, I, ii, counts among the types of women whom one should not enjoy, "those women who openly express their desire for sexual intercourse."

117. Ellis (*Studies*, III, Philadelphia, 1908, p. 47) said quite rightly that the seeming reluctance of woman should be understood not as inhibiting sexual activity in the male or in herself but as increasing it in both of them. Passivity, therefore, is not real but apparent, and this remains true both in our species and in the lower animals. Ellis also said that an intense energy is hidden behind that passivity, a preoccupation wholly concentrated on the end to be attained. It is not necessary to note that the inhibition of which he wrote has nothing to do with the neurotic inhibition, studied by psychoanalysts, through which sexuality is rejected hysterically; it is, instead, an inner and normal moment of integral female sexuality.

118. Marro, *La Pubertà*, p. 453.

119. Cf. Lao-tze, *Tao Te Ching*. Taking up again the ideas of Aristotle, Scotus Eriugena, *Divis. Naturae*, I, 62, said that "he who loves or desires endures; he who is loved is active."

120. The American saying that a man chases a woman until she catches him is not just a joke. Concerning a certain male violence, Viazzi (p. 148) was not wrong in using the image of a man who stormed a penitentiary and overcame all the resistance of the guards only so that he could be shut inside.

121. Giamblico, *De vita pythag.*, XI: "They ought to consider [women] victors when they allow themselves to be beaten by men."

122. Cf. Harding, p. 45: "The attitude of disdain adopted by many men toward women bears witness to their unconscious attempt to dominate a situation which they feel to be to their own disadvantage." In this same context it is possible to accept various things said by Adler about the neurotic character of many affected male demonstrations of superiority toward woman.

123. *Les Mystères de la femme*, p. 46.

124. Cf. Evola, *L'Arco e la clava*, II.

125. Evola, *Rivolta contro il mondo moderno*, part I, 21.

126. Cf. Meunier, *L'Amour maternel chez les animaux*, Paris, 1877.

127. Cf. Klages, *Vom kosmogonischen Eros*, p. 18: "The almost impersonal mother love of one woman resembles that of another woman to the point of confusion. . . . Since every instinct has something of the soul in it, mother love has a depth of soul but in no way a depth of spirit and does not belong to the animal mother in a different way than it does to the human mother.

128. As interesting evidence of this disposition, we may cite the words written by Mlle. de Lespinasse to De Guilbert: "That 'Ego' of which Fénelon speaks is an illusion; I feel positively that I am not Ego. I am you, and to be you I need to make no sacrifice. Your sentiments, your thoughts, my friend, they are the Ego

which is dear to me and intimate to me; all the rest is foreign to me" (In B. Dangennes, pp. 152–153). The Sita of Hindu epic poetry says that for a well-born woman the path to follow is not parents, children, or friends, "nor even one's own soul," but one's own husband.

129. S. Bonifacio said that Nordic women absolutely did not want to survive their husbands and that with "unheard-of fury" they had themselves burnt with them; the sagas contained the same theme in the figures of Nama and Brunhilda. Among the Letts, Goths, and Heruli, the women of men who had died in battle often killed themselves. Cf. also E. Westermarck, *History of Human Marriage*, pp. 125–126.

130. The modern world knows of women who wish to be emancipated materially and socially from man but not of men who feel they want to be emancipated inwardly and spiritually from woman. The ambience created by the "rule by women" in contemporary Western civilization and, to the greatest extent, in America is demonstrated in D. H. Lawrence's *Aaron's Rod*, in which it is written that the most profound belief professed by the white races is the fundamental importance of woman in life, as the bearer and source of life; almost all men, Lawrence said, accept this principle; at the very moment when they impose their selfish rights of male masters, they accept tacitly the fact of the superiority of woman as the bearer of life; they believe tacitly in the cult of that which is feminine; they agree in admitting that woman is everything that is productive, beautiful, passionate, and essentially noble in the world; and in all their reactions against this belief, in detesting their women, going with prostitutes, taking alcohol, and in other ways rebelling against this great ignominious dogma of the holy superiority of woman, they are doing nothing other than continuously desecrating the god of their true faith; in desecrating woman they still worship her, even though negatively; the spirit of manhood has vanished from the world; the men of today will never be able to join together to fight the good fight, because, as soon as a woman appears with her children, she will find an army of sheep ready to defend her and put down the rebellion.

Chapter 5: Sacred Ceremonics and Evocations

1. Propertius, *Carm.*, IV, II, 33; Lattantius, *Div. Inst.*, I, 20, 36 (in Pestalozza, pp. 387, 407). Cf. also A. De Marchi, *Il Culto*

privato in Roma antica, Milan, 1896.

2. Cf. S. Radhakrishnan, *The Hindu View of Life*, London–New York, 1927, p. 84.

3. F. De Coulanges, *La Cité antique*, Paris, 1900, pp. 107, 166.

4. I, viii; I, 9; J. Woodroffe, *Shakti and Shakta*, Madras-London, 1929, pp. 96–97.

5. *Brihadaranyaka-Upanishad*, IV, iv, 3.

6. *Chandogya-Upanishad*, II, xii, 1–2.

7. *Brihadaranyaka-Upanishad*, VI, iv, 20–22; a similar shortened formula is in *Atharva-Veda*, XIV, ii, 71.

8. Cf. Kerenyi, *Figlie del Sole*, p. 134.

9. It is interesting that in some Latin languages, for instance, Italian and French, the female sexual organ is commonly called "nature," in the same way that *prakriti* in front of *purusha* represents "nature."

10. P. B. Randolph, *Magia sexualis*, Paris, 1952, p. 28.

11. C. De Saint-Martin, *Le Ministère de l'homme-esprit*, Paris, 1802, p. 27.

12. *Yashna*, 53, 7.

13. Haleby Othman, *Les lois secrètes de l'amour*, Paris, 1906. The evocation of Brahma at the moment of ejaculation of the seed, together with the formula cited earlier, can be found, for example, in the *Mahanirvana-tantra*, IX, 112–116.

14. Ibn Arabi, *La Sagesse des Prophètes*, (The Wisdom of the Prophets), trans. T. Burckhardt, Paris, 1955, pp. 187–189.

15. Cf. Scholem, *Mystique juive*, p. 251.

16. M. Granet, *La Pensée chinoise*, Paris, 1950, pp. 293–295.

17. To make sexual intercourse a part of "original sin" has no basis in the texts; Genesis 2:24 speaks of the two, Adam and Eve, becoming one single flesh even before the sin and at the time when they were still not ashamed of going naked. Moreover, Roman Catholicism, as opposed to Protestantism, has declared that man's subjection to sexuality is not the cause of original sin but only one of its consequences.

18. In Moreno, *Antologia della mistica arabo-persiana*, Bari, 1951, p. 232.

19. Cf. H. Delacroix, *Essai sur le mysticisme spéculatif en Allemagne au XIV ème siècle*, Paris, 1900, pp. 60–63, 65, 91, 122.

20. From De Potter, *Vie de Scipione de Ricci, évêque de Pistoie et Prato*, Brussels, 1895, I, pp. 460, 418, 420, 428 (in Woodroffe, pp. 597–598).

21. Herodotus, I, 99; Strabo, XI, 532.

22. S. Langdon, *Tammuz and Ishtar*, Oxford, 1914, pp. 80–82.

23. Concerning such young women, who were skilled in these

various arts as well as having beauty and other attractions, the text says, "In a society ruled by men they had the right to a position of honor. . . . They were always respected by the king and honored by the learned, and they enjoyed universal repute."

24. Glotz, *La civilisation égéenne*, pp. 308, 312.

25. Eliade, *Traité d'histoire des religions*, p. 305.

27. Because of their explicit character, it is valid to cite these words addressed to the women in the puberty rites of the Sioux: "You are the tree of life" (Black Elk, *The Sacred Pipe*, p. 123).

28. Evola, *Il Mistero del Graal*, 6.

29. *Opus paramirum*, II, v, 3.

30. *Le Temple de Satan*, Paris, 1916, p. 222.

31. We should not exclude the possibility that some maniacal forms of masturbation have a hyperphysical background of magical union based on the unconscious evocation of an erotic phantasm vitalized by the imagination, which then assumes the part of an incubus or succubus. Those cases are meaningful in which the "excitement and satisfaction are produced only by the influence of the image, provoked almost automatically at first but then reproduced ever more readily until it becomes automatic and even obsessive" (Hesnard, *Manuel de sexologie*, p. 268). No less meaningful are the cases wherein such orgasms can take place an unlikely number of times a day (ibid., pp. 266–267); this leads us to a possible emergence of the "nongenerated" and "continuous pleasure" dealt with in Tantrism.

32. *Psychopathia sexualis*, p. 15 ff.

33. *Studies in the Psychology of Sex*, v, V, pp. 86–87 et seq.

34. V. Solovieff, *Le Sens de l'amour*, pp. 86–87 et seq.

35. G. Bruno *Eroici furori*, II, iii, 62, described this process: "The eyes apprehend the species and propose them to the heart (to the deep consciousness, by arousing the latent image); the heart longs for them and its longing presents them to the eyes (making them perceive behind the appearances the archetype or entity in the beloved being). . . . Thus in the first place the perception moves the affection, and then the affection moves the perception."

36. E. Carpenter, *The Art of Creation*, pp. 137, 186.

37. C. Meiners, *Geschichte des weiblichen Geschlechtes*, Hanover, 1899, p. 58; cf. also P. La Croix, *Moeurs, usages et coutumes au moyen-age et à l'époque de la Renaissance*, Paris, 1873. If we are to judge by the poems and romances of the time, it seems that whenever any knight found an unprotected young woman, his first thought was to rape her. Gawain, who was often cited as the epitome of nobility, violated Gran de Lis notwithstanding the

cries of the young girl when she refused to lie with him (Traill-Mann, cit. by F. Saba-Sarti, *Sesso e mito*, Milan, 1960, p. 233).

38. Cf. C. Fauriel, *Histoire de la poésie provençale*, Paris, 1846. The *asag*, the final trial undergone by the knight (namely to pass an entire night naked with the lady without giving in to temptation), was meant to fuel desire to paroxysm and not as a penance of chastity. It is singularly like the Tantric preparation for magical coitus.

39. G. Garimet, *Histoire de la magie en France*, Paris, 1818, p. 292.

40. L. Valli, *Il Linguaggio segreto di Dante e dei Fedeli d'Amore*, Rome, 1928, pp. 205–206.

41. Cf. R. Schmidt, *Indische Erotik*, pp. 30–31. To a certain extent the same is the case with Hafiz.

42. Above all in *Il Mistero del Graal*, 25 and 26, and *Lo Yoga della potenza*, appendix II.

43. *Le Rime*, ed. Rivalta, Bologna, 1902, p. 156.

44. *Vita nuova*, II, 19; cf. I, 12,; XI, 13.

45. Ibid., III, 1–6.

46. Drinking song in Manget, *Biblioth. chemica curiosa*, I, 417, and Dorn in *Theatrum chemicum*, p. 578.

47. In Valli, pp. 185, 186; the references in what follows have been taken from that book, Dante, and also from A. Ricolfi, *Studi sui Fedeli d'Amore*, I., Milan, 1933; II, Milan, 1941; *Rapimento e iniziazione nei Fedeli d'Amore*, extracted from *Rivista di sintesi letteraria*, 1935, no. 4.

48. *Vita nuova*, XV, 4.

49. Ibid., XIV, 8, 14. It is interesting that Dante gives a warning here that such experiences are not understandable to one who is not "a Worshipper of Love of the same grade"; this is a clear reference to the existence of various levels of initiation.

50. Ibid., IV, 3; V, 1.

51. Although his interpretations are only symbolic and intellectual, Bruno also mentions this in *Eroici furori* (II, i, 47; I, iv, 19): "This death of lovers, which starts from supreme love, is called by the followers of the Kabbala the *mors osculi* or death by the kiss; this same death is everlasting life, which man can have at his disposition at this time and in effect forever." Cf. Ibn Farid (in Moreno, p. 215): "When my eyes saw the beauty of those features, I said farewell to life even before love was born." The presence of the expression "murderous eyes" in slang is not without interest. In the literature of the Spanish "golden cycle" the expression "eyes that cast love and death" is often found.

52. The Hindu equivalent of "potential intellect" is *buddhi*; furthermore, the Hindu Great Goddess is also thought of as she

who dwells in all beings under the form of *buddhi*, she whose nature it is to enlighten (*djotanashila*). Cf. A. and E. Avalon, *Hymns to the Goddess*, p. 130.

53. *Convivio*, IV, 16; XII, 4.

54. Cf. Ricolfi, *Rapimento e iniziazione*, p. 358.

55. *Reggimento e costumi delle donne*, p. v.

56. Valli, p. 247, where the illustration is given; F. Da Barberino, *Documenti d'amore*, ed. Egidi, Rome, 1905–1924, III, p. 407 ff.

57. *Vita nuova*, II, 4.

58. *Convivio*, III, 2, 8.

59. In Ricolfi, *Studi sui Fedeli d'Amore*, I, p. 63.

60. Dante: "This woman who spiritually was made into one thing together with my soul" (*Convivio*, II, 2); abandonment by the woman was called the departure of his "salvation" (*Vita nuova*, XXXII, 6).

61. In Alessandrini, *Cecco d'Ascoli*, Rome, 1955, p. 195.

62. *Vita nuova*, II, 1; III, 1; XII, 9; VI, 2; XXIII, 1.

63. Ibid., XXIX, 3.

64. Dorn ("Clavis philosophiae chemisticae" in *Theatrum chemicum*, I, pp. 214–215), when referring also to the Tritemium, said that the One reexpels the Binary (the Two), which in connection with matter has led to separation from it; and the Ternary (the Three) will be brought back to the simplicity of the One—an ascent well known to those in whose mind is the Ternary; who reject the Binary (the Two) and are raised by assumption of the Ternary to the simplicity of unity.

65. Valli, pp. 94–99; Perez, *La Beatrice svelata*, Palermo, 1898.

66. Valli, p. 100.

67. We should note that the same relationship is often met in Sufism; divinity is considered as a woman, the "fiancée" or "beloved one," instead of as "the heavenly bridegroom" of the soul. Thus, for example, in Attar, in Ibn Farid, in Rumi and others.

68. Cf. J. De Nynauld, *De la lycanthropie, transformation et extase des sorciers*, Paris, 1615: *Les ruses et tromperies du diable descouvertes, sur ce qu'il pretend avoir envers les corps et les ames des sorciers, ensemble la composition de leurs onguens* (The ruses and tricks of the devil uncovered, about that which he claims to have toward the bodies and souls of sorcerers, including the composition of their ointments), Paris, 1611 (in De Guaita, II, pp. 172–174). These are the works containing the most information about the magical ointments.

69. It is said of the Tibetan ascetic Milarepa that he had the power of

projecting his subtle body so that he went to preside, as a master of yoga, over meetings of invisible beings in holy places; this is a part of a general practice called *phowa* (cf. *Vie de Milarepa*, trans. by the lama Kazi Dawa Sampud, French ed., Paris, 1955, p. 68).

70. Cf. M. Murray, *The God of the Witches*, Sampon Low, 1933.
71. Cf. G. Rattray Taylor, *Sex in History*, Italian trans., Milan, 1957, pp. 117 ff., 298.
72. For some views about the birth of Satanism in general, cf. Evola, *Eros e magia*, Milan, 1969.
73. De Guaita, *Le Temple de Satan*, I, p. 154 ff. The bibliography of the texts used by him for what follows is on pp. 156–157.
74. Cf. R. Taylor, pp. 298–299.
75. Among primitive peoples, traditions are also found about powers transmitted to some women on the basis of their unions with nonhuman entities. Cf., for example, B. Malinowski, *The Sexual Life of Savages*, London, 1929, p. 40. We may also recall the magical power assigned to the orgies of cults; linked to this is the fact that, when the Romans conquered Sicily in the third century B.C., they consecrated two temples to Venus of Erix, who was the object of such rites.
76. Collum in *Eranos Jahrbücher*, 1938, p. 257 ff. (in Przyluski, p. 167).
77. *Nat. Hist.*, V, 1.
78. P. De Lanere, *Tableau de l'inconstance des mauvais anges et démons*, Paris, 1613, p. 119 ff.
79. The main evidence given by Christian authors and mystics who have dealt with the theory of the hermaphrodite has been gathered together in E. Benz, *Der Mythus des Urmenschen*, Munich, 1955. From that book we shall take the quotations in what follows.
80. Cf. Benz, pp. 50–65.
81. *Dialoghi d'amore*, p. 432 ff.
82. J. J. Wirz, *Zeugnisse und Eröffnungen des Geistes*, Barmen, 1863, I, pp. 215–216 (Benz, 240–241).
83. Cf. Benz, p. 73 ff.
84. J. G. Gichtel, *Theosophia practica*, Leyden, 1722, III, 2–4; VI, 29–31.
85. Cf. Benz, pp. 200–202. Hahn wrote (p. 202): "If Adam had always possessed his wife, the Tree of Life, spiritually and magically, the fruit of life would have been born in him and of him."
86. Cf. Benz, pp. 126, 127, 129.
87. Boehme, *Von den drei Prinzipien des göttlichen Wesens*, XIII, 40.
88. Cf. Benz, p. 242.

89. F. von Baader, *Gesamm. Werke*, III, p. 306.
90. Regarding this doctrine of Gichtel, cf. *Introduz. alla magia*, II, p. 16 ff.
91. *Theosophia practica*, V, 31.
92. *Gesamm. Werke*, II, p. 315.
93. Ibid., III, p. 306.
94. Ibid., p. 309.
95. Ibid., p. 308.
96. Ibid., VII, p. 236.
97. Ibid., III, pp. 301–302.
98. As the only suggestion that could possibly be used in practice, we might perhaps indicate Boehme's identification of the male with the "fire" principle and of the female with the "light" principle, namely the idea that "the hue of fire covets that of light in the flesh," so as to give an ignition of light and an illumination (liberation) of fire as the sense of a magical, "hermaphroditic" love or coitus. In effect, "the hue made by Venus and Mars, the union of fire and light (the one related to man and the other to woman), is considered "the shortest and quickest way" and the essence of the transmutative process of human nature. Cf. also C. A. Muses, *Illumination on J. Boehme*, New York, 1951, pp. 149–150.
99. N. Berdyaev, *Der Sinn des Schaffens*, Tübingen, 1927, pp. 211–213 (Benz, pp. 219–292).

Chapter 6: Sex in the Realm of Initiations and Magic

1. Hippolytus, *Philos*, V, i, II.
2. O. Wirth, *Le Tarot des imagiers du moyen-age*, Paris, 1927, p. 169.
3. *La Practique de la méditation*, Paris, 1950, pp. 276–277, 100, 278.
4. Ibid., p. 278.
5. Ibid.
6. See W. Y. Evans-Wentz, *Tibetan Yoga and Secret Doctrines*, London, 1935.
7. In what follows we shall summarize the more lengthy details set out in *Lo Yoga della potenza*. The texts which we shall cite here are, in general, only those not already indicated in that book. The saying quoted now in our text is exactly like the following hermetic passage: "Our Adam was a hermaphrodite although he appeared in male guise, for he always carried Eve or his woman

around with him, hidden in his body" (a lyric in Manget, *Bibl. chemica curiosa*, I, p.417).

8. We find in Tantric texts the expression that the kundalini personified "takes pleasure in a lover." It is also mentioned in Hindu treatises on profane erotics. In an enchantment procedure intended to put a woman into a man's power, the lover is told, among other things, to evoke the kundalini mentally in the breast, on the forehead, and in the "dwelling of the god of love" (in the vulva) of the woman he desires. Cf. R. Schmidt, *Indische Erotik*, Berlin, 1910, pp. 676, 677.

9. In a text it is said of the kundalini, "Unite yourself then in the lotus of a thousand petals with your husband after having purified the whole path of the family of the powers, the earth in its fundamental base, the fire in its proper seat, the air in the heart, the ether in the wheel of purity, and the intellect in the wheel of command," all these seats being arranged along the axial line. G. Tucci, *Teoria e pratica dei mandala*, Rome, 1949, p. 136.

10. *Hathayogapradipika*, III, 107; cf. Dhyana-Bindu-Upanishad, 43–47. The center where it dwells controls at one and the same time "the attachments and [ascetic] detachment of the living."

11. A principle of the school of the Natha Siddha is "He who does not know the secret of this inversion process cannot obtain everlasting life." D. Das Gupta, *Obscure Religious Cults*, Calcutta, 1946, p. 266.

12. Avalon, *Hymns to the Goddess*, p. 35.

13. *Hathayogapradipika*, III, 109.

14. *La Tradizione ermetica*, Bari, 1949.

15. The German and Italian translations of this work have a foreword, written by the psychoanalyst C. G. Jung, which distorts their meaning completely. A full analysis of this work can be found in *Introduzione alla magia* (undertaken by the Gruppo di Ur), Rome, 1956, II, p. 422 ff. Cf. also E. Rouselle, *Seelische Führung im lebenden Taoismus*, Eranos-Jahrbücher, 1943.

16. P. 151, Italian trans.

17. *Berakhoth*, 57b, in M. D. G. Langer, *Die Erotik in der Kabbala*, Prague, 1923, p. 30.

18. On this passage from the Zohar, cf. Langer, p. 23.

19. Cf. Langer, pp. 30–44.

20. Furthermore, it seems that Kabbalism knew of practices like those of Hindu yoga, based on mystical and hyperphysical physiology; it was believed that in the human body are the *sephiroth* or metaphysical principles studied by the Kabbala and arranged like a tree with three columns; and as in yoga there are two lateral

streams to be united so as to make the resulting force flow along the axial direction, so here, too, the union is considered of the *sephiroth* corresponding to the male and female principles, the Father and Mother, the Bridegroom and the Bride, the Right and the Left in the middle line which comprises the *sephiroth* called *Kether* (crown), *Tiphereth* (beauty), *Jesod* (basis), and *Malkuth* (kingdom).

21. *Orat. IV contra Julian*, I, 115. Cf. Pesialozza, *Religione mediterranea*, pp. 217 ff., 271, 300–301, 306.
22. Hippolytus, *Philos.*, V, i, 8.
23. Cf. *Mahanirvana-tantra*, IV, 80; VIII, 203; *Kalivilasa-tantra*, V, 13 ff.
24. Woodroffe, *Shakti and Shakta*, pp. 591, 619.
25. H. Delacroix, *Essai sur le mysticisme spéculatif en Allemagne au XIV ème siècle*, Paris, 1900, pp. 119–120, 121; cf. also pp. 72–73: "It is understood that these two opposed forms of moral life, the orgy and renunciation, both have a religious significance; they are intended to glorify God, the one of them by reproducing the exuberance of his creative power. . . . the other by sacrificing everything that is not he, following the motion with which he turns back on himself toward the source of his energy."
26. *Prapanchasara-tantra*, VII, 103–111; L. De La Vallé Poussin, *Bouddhisme: études et matériaux*, Paris, 1898, p. 138.
27. Cf. S. Das Gupta, *Obscure Religious Cults*, Calcutta, 1946, pp. XXXVII, 155–156.
28. For more details and references to texts about what follows, see chap. 7 of part 2 of Evola, *Lo Yoga della potenza*.
29. M. Eliade, *Le Yoga: liberté et immortalité*, Paris, 1954, p. 262.
30. Das Gupta, pp. V, 156.
31. De La Vallé Poussin, *Bouddhisme*, pp. 131–132.
32. Das Gupta, p. 162.
33. Cf. Eliade, *Yoga*, p. 262.
34. Das Gupta, p. 144. Mulk Raj Anand, *Kama-kala*, Geneva, Paris, 1958.
35. For the same reason, in the popular cult Shiva is considered generally as the god and patron of all those who lead a life opposed to the common one, and therefore not only of ascetics, but also of vagabonds, traveling dancers, and even outlaws.
36. Eliade, p. 265.
37. Das Gupta, p. 163.
38. Expression of R. A. Schwaller de Lubicz, *Adam l'homme rouge*, Paris, 1927, p. 242.
39. In *Introduzione alla Magia*, II, p. 374.
40. *Hathayogapradipika*, III, 85, 87–90.

41. Cf. G. Tucci, *Tibetan Painted Scrolls*, Rome, 1949, I, 242.
42. Eliade, p. 255.
43. A "death in love" is actually spoken of, and it is said, "Only he who knows it lives truly through death in love." Cf. Das Gupta, p. 160.
44. H. von Glasenapp *Buddhistische Mysterien*, Stuttgart, 1940, p. 56.
45. Thus, in translating this passage of Kanha (*Doha-kosha*, 19), "He who has immobilized the king of his spirit by the identity of enjoyment [*samarasa*] in the state of the Inborn [*sahaja*] becomes a wizard at once; he does not fear old age and death" (in Eliade, p. 268).
45a. It is said that this pleasure is "not generated" in the transcendent and continuous state and is proved in certain experiments with the next world; cf. Tucci, *Il Libro tibetano del morto* (The Tibetan Book of the Dead), Milan, 1949, pp. 130, 210. It is possible that it occurs at random in some abnormal temperaments where an unbroken repetition of the liminal phenomenon of the sexual orgasm takes place either during one incident of coitus or during one and the same day; the Kinsey reports cite cases of an unbelievable number of times a day, above all in women, since the separation of the psychic and emotional condition from the strictest physiological conditional qualities is easier in woman. When the ordinary, physical level of awareness persists in such cases, the matter is a question of pathology, which as we said, would richly instruct if it were studied from adequate esoteric reference points.
46. *Hathayogapradipika*, III, 92–101.
47. Cf. Tucci, *Tibetan Painted Scrolls*, I, p. 242.
48. When talking of unions, a common name for the woman is *surya*, the word for sun put into the feminine. This takes us back to the somewhat positive aspect of energy itself, to its "splendor" aspect. In this same context we may remember that in ancient Hellas the fascinating and "bewitching" types of women, such as Circe and Medea, were also considered to be Heliads or offspring of the Sun. Cf. K. Kerényi, *Le Figlie del Sole*, Turin, 1949. Some sensations described by poets could be cited as similar on a much more conditioned plane; for instance, in her presence he always experienced "the feeling of being enfolded in an inflamed atmosphere, a quivering aura," and he therefore recalled how, as a baby, "when crossing a deserted terrain one evening, he felt himself enveloped suddenly by will-o'-the-wisps and let out a cry" (D'Annunzio); through the effect of the woman's breath, beyond the senses the soul finds a sharp and savage perfume, like

burning dew dissolving in the bosom of a frozen shoot (Shelley). A. Léger: "O woman and fever made into woman! Lips which have tasted you taste not death."

49. Cf. Eliade, *Yoga*, p. 261.
50. *Scritti scelti*, Milan, 1943, p. 139.
51. In Das Gupta, p. 167.
52. Ibid., p. 163.
53. Ibid., pp. 145–146.
54. "An Introduction to the Study of the Post-Chaitanya Sahajiya Cult," pp. 77, 78 in Eliade.
55. De La Vallé Poussin, *Bouddhisme*, p. 144.
56. *Manduka-Upanishad*, II, 45 (comm.).
57. Das Gupta, p. XXXVIII.
58. Some similarities are also indicated in the field of hyperbiological physiology, in terms analogous to those of Taoism, in respect of the two principles conceived, on the one hand, as "enlightenment" or *prajna* and, on the other hand, as operating force or *upaya*; the first is located in the lower part of the body near the solar plexus (more or less where Taoism locates the "space of force"), while the other is in the head. Here, too, the practice has the purpose of making the goddess ascend from the lower pole to the Lord in the area of the brain (cf. Das Gupta, p. xxxviii). In the Tibetan iconography of the *yabyum*, the mother or *yum* and the male or *yab* whom she embraces correspond to the *prajna* and *upaya* which unite and make the enlightenment-thought ascend (cf. Tucci, I, p. 244).
59. Cf. Das Gupta, p. 180.
60. Cf. Tucci, I, p. 242.
61. G. Mayrink, *L'Angelo della finestra d'occidente*, Milan, 1949, pp. 467, 470.
62. Das Gupta, p. 108.
63. H. Maspéro, "Les Procédés de 'nourir l'esprit vital' dans la religion täoiste ancienne," *Journal Asiatique* 229, April-June and July-September 1937.
64. R. H. van Gulik, *Erotic Colour Prints of the Ming Period with an Essay on Chinese Sex Life*, Tokyo 1951, and also *Sexual Life in Ancient China*, Leiden, 1961.
65. Maspéro, p. 199. It seems that the two realizations have been sometimes linked together in the sense that "after having lived for a long time" we pass into the dwelling of the "Sovereign on high," who is, however, confused with the Great Principle (*T'ai-chi*) and therefore with transcendence and everlasting life in a proper sense. There are statements on these same lines in Chuang-tze as well.

66. Ibid., pp. 208, 213–214, 234, 245–246, 394–395.

67. Ibid., pp. 380–381.

68. Ibid., p. 386. It is also said that "they are few who can practice this art, thus I dare not make it known" (in van Gulik, p. 41).

69. Maspéro, pp. 409–410.

70. Ibid., pp. 295–296. But this opinion is also found in ancient general treatises on the art of the alcove, and it is even written that "he who knows not this art and lies with only one or two women will die soon" (cf. van Gulik, pp. 17, 42).

71. Maspéro, p. 384.

72. Ibid., p. 396.

73. Cf. van Gulik, p. 11.

74. Cf. A. David-Neel, *Magie d'amour et magie noire*, Paris, 1938, pp. 104–105.

75. Brihadaranyaka-Upanishad, IV, iv, 10.

76. Ibid., IV, iv, 4.

77. This procedure had already been often recommended in general treatises on sex except where procreation was deliberately intended; however, the woman must always be brought to orgasm ("even so far as to make her cry out," it is said in the *Tung-houan-tzu*, VII; cf. van Gulik, pp. 8, 20, 33, etc.). Van Gulik claims that the Taoists had given to the technique a "cruel" twist such as to make the art of the alcove be called the "perverted doctrine" or *hsien-chiao* and not seldom to cause the death of their unhappy victims, from whom it was wished to extract the "primordial female" (*yuan-p'iu*, pp. 11, 12). But we should believe that in this matter van Gulik based himself on the unfriendly gossip of hostile or profane circles.

78. Maspéro, p. 384.

79. Ibid., p. 385.

80. Ibid., p. 384. In general erotic treatises, too, we find a connection between the symbolic numbers (odd and even) of the *yang* and *yin* and the number of movements to be carried out inside the woman; thus it is prescribed that groups of four (or eight) movements are to be made, followed by a strong, deep movement ($4 + 1 = 5$; $8 + 1 = 9$), odd *yang* numbers; the man should stop when the woman has an orgasm and cries out, and should then begin again (cf. van Gulik, pp. 43, 55).

81. Maspéro, p. 386. Perhaps we can link to that the general formula of livening the *yang* force in the whole body, to be kept integral in its own fluid; this is also thought of as a coagulation or fixing process. Cf. C. Puini, *Taoismo*, Lanciano, 1922, pp. 117–118.

82. Ibid., pp. 397, 400.

83. Ibid., p. 386.
84. Ibid., p. 385. Cf. p. 218, where he talks of the capability of the inward view, *ni-che* or *nei-kuan*, owing to which one can see the inside of one's own body so as to be able to guide the operations. The texts do not regard this as an extraordinary faculty.
85. Here is the text itself: "May the Great Essence of the Highest Majestic One coagulate the humors and make the Transcendent One as hard as a bone! May the six breaths of the Great-Real-one-having-no-one-higher coil themselves inside! May the Mysterious Ancient One of the higher Being make the Essence come back to reintegrate the [center of the] brain! Make it so that I may unite [the *yin* and the *yang* by joining myself to a woman] and that the embryo be fused and the Jewel conserved!" (Maspéro, p. 386).
86. In this case the conscious participation of the woman and also her knowledge of the procedure are evident; this is the opposite of what we have seen recommended in other texts (according to which the woman should not know the secret operation carried out with her).
87. Maspéro, p. 386.
88. Ibid.
89. Ibid., pp. 404–405.
90. Ibid., p. 405.
91. Ibid., p. 409.
92. *Introduzione alla magia*, III, pp. 365–374 ("Esperienze fra gli Arabi").
93. Ibid., p. 371.
94. Ibid., p. 372.
95. Ibid., p. 371.
96. Ibid., p. 372.
97. Ibid., p. 371.
98. Ibn Arabi, *La Sagesse des Prophètes*, pp. 186–187.
99. *La Tradizione ermetica*, p. 149.
100. B. Valentinus, *Practica, cum duodecim clavibus et appendice, de Magno Lapide antiquorum Sapientium*, Frankfurt, 1618.
101. Reconstruction of the hieroglyphic figure in O. Wirth, *Le Tarot des imagiers du moyen-age*, Paris, 1927, p. 174 ff.
102. E.g., Zosimus, in M. Berthelot, *Collection des anciens alchimistes grecques*, Paris, 1887, III, p. 147.
103. *Introitus apertus ad occlusum regis palatium*, I.
104. In Berthelot, p. 8.
105. A suggestive reference to the woman's action is given in the mention of the "Hermetic slaying of her husband which, according to the *Turba philosophorum*, the woman commits

during the *coniunctio* [union] with the 'arms hidden in her body,' and which in other texts is called the 'struggle of the female,'" M. von Franz, *Aurora consurgens*, p. 233. Furthermore, similar expressions compel us to think of the concrete sexual plane as well.

106. See my book cited earlier, especially the second part. As an example, we give here just a few typical expressions in Hermetic texts. "First the woman gains the upper hand over the man and dominates him so as to change him to her own nature; she does not leave him until she has become pregnant. Then the male regains his force and the upper hand in his turn; he dominates her and makes her similar to him." "The Mercury of the philosopher is a dissolving water. . . . The King dies and comes back to life because the same Water kills and revives. The [Hermetic] philosophers have also given the name of Life and Resurrection to the color white." "When this Water has made the perfect solution of the unalterable, it is called the Fountain of Life, Nature, naked and free Diana." "Prometheus represents their Sulfur animated by heavenly Fire," etc. (A. J. Pernety, *Dictionnaire mythohermétique*, Paris, 1758, pp. 220, 237, 467, 407.)

107. Cf. the figures reproduced in Jung, *Psychologie und Alchemie*, Zürich, 1944, figs. 167, 226, 258.

108. See *Fascicoli della Myriam*. A passage in one invocation is "May the prodigy be great—may Myriam appear—may the destiny of triumph be one thousand times faster than lightning, one hundred and more times faster than Light!"

109. *Opera omnia*, ed. L'Universale di Roma, Rome, 1951, I, pp. 351–352.

110. Ibid., I, p. 190 ff.

111. Ibid., I, p. 146.

112. Ibid., II, p. 327.

113. Ibid., II, p. 326.

114. Ibid., II, p. 327.

115. Ibid., p. 329.

116. Ibid., p. 332.

117. *Introduzione alla Magia*, I, p. 248 ff.

118. Ibid., II, pp. 363–368.

119. Ibid., pp. 371–372.

120. Ibid., p. 376.

121. M. De Naglowska, "Le rite sacré de l'amour magique", Paris, 1932, pp. 16–18.

122. M. De Naglowska, "Le mystère de la pendaison"—Initiation satanique selon la doctrine du troisième terme de la Trinité, Paris, 1934, pp. 11–12; thus it is also said, "The overflowing of

all the passions represents nothing other than the first clumsy step of regenerated evil."

123. M. de Naglowska, *La Lumière du sexe: rituel d'initiation satanique*, Paris, 1932, pp. 56–57.

124. Ibid., pp. 56–57; *Le Rite sacré de l'amour magique*, pp. 17–18.

125. *La Lumière du sexe*, pp. 112–113.

126. Ibid., pp. 136–137.

127. *Le Rite sacré*, p. 42.

128. Ibid., p. 132.

129. *Théorie et Practique de la magie sexuelle*, Paris.

130. Cf. J. Symonds, *The Great Beast: The Life of Aleister Crowley*, London, 1952, p. 118.

131. Ibid., p. 167. The formula of the oath of the disciple was "I [name], in the presence of the Beast 666, consecrate myself solemnly to the Great Opus, which is to discover my true will and to realize it. Love is the law, love under will."

132. Ibid., p. 126.

133. Ibid., p. 237.

134. In the extracts of the unpublished *Liber Aleph, the Book of Wisdom or Folly*, published in *Introduzione alla magia*, III, pp. 442 ff., 450.

135. Ibid., pp. 447, 449.

136. Ibid., pp. 447, 448.

137. Ibid., p. 450.

138. Symonds, p. 135.

139. Ibid., p. 148.

140. Ibid., p. 131.

141. In his *Esoteric Record*, Crowley said that the technique can be either heterosexual or homosexual; the use of the woman would be much more dangerous for the wizard; he also mentioned the period of pregnancy. But no further explanation was given there (cf. Symonds, *The Magic of A. Crowley*, London, 1958, p. 113). About homosexual love, we can only think of the possibilities offered by an occasional form of intoxication which can arise in abnormal types without having a specific connection with the metaphysics of sex since it lacks the premise of bisexual polarity (cf. what we said about homosexuality in the appendix to chapter 2).

142. Ibid., p. 110; *The Magic of A. Crowley*, p. 147 ff.

143. *The Magic of A. Crowley*, pp. 48, 130–131.

144. Ibid., p. 205.

145. Ibid., p. 131. We might perhaps link to what R. A. Schwaller de Lubicz said in a book about mystical eroticism, concerning the "system of excess." "Out of the need for the infinite which exists

in man it should be necessary to make the sense of excess." "Provided that it is absolute, every excess leads to mysticism." The properly called sexual orgasm "is an excess of erotic tension . . . the most natural excess, imposed by nature. Now, every excess, whatever it may be, leads to this awareness [of the infinite], even if it should happen that its outcome is death. The outcome is secondary. The essential is that which happens in the consciousness of a being who knows that excess can bring about death. If his deed is the outcome of a logical decision deliberately taken it is therefore a fully conscious deed carried out after mature reflection on his own desire for ecstasy. . . . even if death were to follow the deed, it would not be morally blameworthy. For in such a case he would wish not for death but for the highest exaltation, in which he hopes to find the annihilation of himself, of his selfishness, and of his sexually fascinated being." *Adam l'homme rouge*, Paris, 1927, pp. 170 ff., 184. Schwaller de Lubicz also observed that in man there is not a superiority but an inferiority, a kind of "impotence of his capacity for coitus," which does not reach death in coitus, as some animals do.

146. *The Great Beast*, p. 170.

147. Ibid., pp. 181, 186, 228.

148. Cf. De Guaita, *Le Temple de Satan*, I, p. 354; he said that with the common use of drugs certain compressive bonds of man's hyperphysical nature are loosened which usually and for most people are a guarantee of their good health. Man enters into a relationship with things he did not know existed. De Guaita added, "In short, a tacit pact has been made." He also rightly observed (pp. 369–370) that in some cases drugs of this kind restore to the individual "the unspeakable power of showering outside himself without any effort everything of which he bears the image within himself. It seems that the word 'creator' which belonged to him before sin has been restored to him."

149. Cf. Woodroffe, *Shakti and Shakta*, p. 583.

150. *Magia sexualis*, Paris, 1952. The book has been translated into Italian (Rome, 1969, Edizioni Mediterranee).

151. Ibid., pp. 81–82.

152. Ibid., pp. 23–24.

153. *Introduzione alla magia*, II, pp. 373–374.

154. *Magia sexualis*, p. 33 ff.

155. Ibid., pp. 39, 40, 59.

156. Ibid., pp. 41–49.

157. Ibid., p. 77.

158. Ibid., p. 88. "By means of decretism, volancie, and posism, ac-

centuate desire at the moment of ejaculation and think hard
about the thing desired before, during, and after the act."

159. Ibid., pp. 76–78, 81. A Hindu parallel may perhaps be indicated
in the *Tantrasara* (translation Gnoli, Turin, 1960, pp. 280–281),
where there is talk of the union of the *vira* with his companion in
coitus "being substantiated by each other as they are, they co-
operate reciprocally in the awakening of the power of Shiva, of
the first motion of energy until the creative emission."

160. Ibid., p. 80.

161. Ibid., pp. 86–89.

162. Ibid., p. 210. Here, however, there is reference mainly to the
practices with the "magical mirror."

Index

cf Mx "the anatomy of man is a key to the anatomy
of the ape"